# SHORT-TERM
# PARENT-INFANT
# PSYCHOTHERAPY

# SHORT-TERM PARENT-INFANT PSYCHOTHERAPY

Paul V. Trad

BasicBooks
*A Division of* HarperCollins*Publishers*

*Designed by Ellen Levine*

93 94 95 96 ❖/HC 9 8 7 6 5 4 3 2 1

Library of Congress Cataloging-in-Publication Data
Trad, Paul V.
 Short-term parent-infant psychotherapy / Paul V. Trad.
     p.   cm.
  Includes bibliographical references and index.
  ISBN 0–465–08215–7
  1. Infant psychiatry.   2. Family psychotherapy.   3. Mother and infant.   4. Brief psychotherapy.    I. Title.
RJ502.5.T75   1993
618.92′89156—dc20                                                          92–56179
                                                                              CIP

# Contents

# *Preface*

I AM ESPECIALLY EXCITED by the challenge offered by *Short-Term Parent-Infant Psychotherapy*. In contrast to some of my previous work, I have attempted to set forth primarily a pragmatic point of view. My hope is that the dynamic combination of previewing techniques and short-term psychotherapy can be broadly disseminated to all health care professionals involved in the treatment of families with young children. Much like the convert who becomes a zealot, I am firmly convinced—based on my own clinical experience with patients—that these two strategies provide parents and infants the best chance of a successful and productive therapeutic outcome.

One reason for my staunch advocacy of early intervention in these cases is that—as noted throughout the text—psychopathologic responses are being encountered in increasingly younger populations. Moreover, the modern family confronts an ever-growing barrage of stresses, from divorce, to poverty, to social violence, to drug abuse, to homelessness, to AIDS. In this critical situation, mental health care professionals are in desperate need of a technique that can be expeditiously applied, such as the short-term approach. Equally important, however, is the need for a strategy that engenders hope for the future and a mastery orientation. Such optimism may be found in the techniques of developmental previewing.

As with all the books I have been involved with, this one was written during a time of significant change in my life. It is these periods of transition that make me more appreciative of the constants in my life. Among these constants are New York Hospital–Westchester Division, my professional home for the past ten years; my extended and extensive family; and my friends and faithful supporters: Richard H. White, Wendy J. Luftig, and Mary J. Raine.

To a better world for the children who will inherit it from us.

I would like to dedicate this book to my parents, Jorge and Blanche, for their unflagging support and their continuous encouragement.

Paul V. Trad, M.D.
New York
December 1993

# Introduction

THE RELATIONSHIP between mother and infant is a rich and psychologically complex one that leaves an indelible imprint on the newborn
child and burgeoning adult-to-be. In recent years, researchers have focused increased attention on this relationship, as evidenced by a wealth of
literature for health care professionals outlining the dimensions of mother-
infant adaptation as well as dysfunction. This material has frequently described techniques of psychotherapeutic interventions for such dyads. Often,
however, case material illustrating in detail specific diagnostic and intervention strategies has been lacking.

*Short-Term Parent-Infant Psychotherapy* attempts to provide health care
professionals—including family therapists, child psychiatrists and psycholo-
gists, infant development specialists, social workers, pediatricians, nurses,
and other professionals who deal with parents and infants—with practical
models for evaluating and treating new mothers, new fathers, and their infants.

*Short-Term Parent-Infant Psychotherapy* highlights five key goals that health
care professionals who work with infants and parents confront in their daily
practices:

1.  Presentation of effective techniques for assessing interpersonal strengths
    and weaknesses of both infants and caregivers.
2.  Identification of key interpersonal issues that may compromise develop-
    mental outcome.
3.  Review of the models of brief psychotherapeutic intervention for dyads.
4.  Application of previewing to the short-term approach to organize and
    direct the therapeutic intervention.
5.  Review of criteria for predicting conflict in the imminent future.

This book also clarifies the diverse factors that influence the infant's development as a unique personality as well as a member of a family that displays adaptive functioning. Many researchers agree that analyzing an individual in terms of both typical human traits and unique traits requires an understanding of normative developmental trends and of individual variations. This perspective necessitates that factors indigenous to the individual and factors pertaining to the environment both be weighed. With regard to dyadic psychotherapy specifically, it means that infants and young children should be viewed as actively determining the scope of their interactions with others. Each child is dramatically affected by the relationship with the caregiver and uses this relationship to fashion an individual personality as well as to advance developmentally.

As a result, *Short-Term Parent-Infant Psychotherapy* proposes a comprehensive theory that may be used for intervention with mother-infant dyads. This model incorporates nature and nurture factors in a dynamic manner. In particular, the model seeks to account for differences in the infant's emotional responses to the environment and to the primary caregiver; moreover, this model strives to ascertain the subjective realities of both mother and infant. In this regard, the methods by which each dyadic member represents, inculcates, implements, and reacts to the environment become pertinent. By delving into the subjective perceptions of the dyadic members, the therapist may come to understand how mother and infant generate expectations about their environment. In addition, the therapist may formulate a view of how each dyadic member exhibits typical interpersonal behavior or dysfunctional behavior in the presence of an adverse environment. Examining individual factors with this level of probity enables the therapist to identify and even predict specific deviations in either the environment or constitutional endowment of the infant and parent.

*Short-Term Parent-Infant Psychotherapy* relies on the developmental phenomenon of *previewing* for assessing adaptive and maladaptive behavior within mother-infant dyads. As a developmental phenomenon, previewing refers to the process by which the caregiver envisions imminent maturational skills and translates these skills into interpersonal exchanges designed to introduce the infant to the upcoming skill and to rehearse how the relationship will change as a result of this skill. For example, a mother correctly interpreting her infant's physical development and cues may predict that walking is an upcoming milestone, and she will preview this experience by helping her infant rehearse walking, supporting him or her through the motions of a few steps, and thereafter easing the transition back to the infant's already mastered developmental level. Because it is based on a normally occurring phenomenon, previewing is a valuable diagnostic and intervention strategy that helps therapists predict and avert upcoming conflict. The use of previewing by caregivers, and the use of previewing as an intervention strategy during psychotherapy, is a consistent theme of this book.

Previewing enables the therapist to assess the adequacy of the infant's constitutional endowment and familial environment. Moreover, previewing helps to predict how more advanced developmental skills will evoke different responses in the mother. Ascertaining the level of adaptive or maladaptive manifestations permits the therapist to modulate these behaviors before they become entrenched in interpersonal patterns. This modification involves altering the mother's representation of future behavior, thereby enhancing validation of a healthy dyadic relationship. In this manner, brief psychotherapy offers strategies for enhancing the infant's optimal functioning in a relatively short period of time.

## Organization of the Book

Although a marital unit consisting of a husband and wife may technically be viewed as a "family," it is only with the birth of a child that our notion of a family as a viable social and psychological reality seems fulfilled. Indeed, the word *family* implies a complex series of relationships among individuals within a designated group and among all those group members as an entity. Over the past two decades, parent-infant psychotherapy has gained widespread popularity. One reason for the prevalence of this form of treatment is that many of the psychological obstacles patients experience appear to stem from the behavior patterns of their own families of origin. The strong influence this form of therapy can have on promoting an individual's use of optimal interpersonal behaviors makes it especially appropriate for altering maladaptive patterns within the family. In addition, recent evidence suggests that brief dynamic psychotherapy, which is limited in duration and intensive in technique, may be beneficial for eradicating dysfunctional behavior patterns within mother-infant dyads. The integration of preview strategies into the model of short-term therapy for dyads is, therefore, also discussed in detail.

The introductory chapters serve to acquaint readers with some of the concepts and theories advocated in the book. In particular, readers are exposed to the previewing process designed to promote adaptive development between mothers and their infants and learn how this process may be used psychotherapeutically with dysfunctional dyads. Moreover, readers are also informed about how brief dynamic psychology, a comprehensive treatment of limited duration, may be combined with previewing techniques to work as an effective therapy in cases of mother-infant discord.

Chapter 1 discusses the phenomenon of previewing, the process by which adaptive caregivers seek to introduce their infants to imminent developmental change. Previewing consists of the mother's representation and enactment of new maturational capacities with the infant in a supportive atmosphere. Among the repercussions of previewing are reinforcement of the intimate mother-infant relationship, promotion of mastery and self-regulatory capacities in the infant, and instilling the perception that seemingly uncontrollable developmental challenges may be overcome. Because it fosters this type of adaptive rapport, the clinical application of previewing strategies is also highly beneficial in treating dysfunctional dyads. This chapter highlights the application of previewing techniques for treating and predicting conflict.

Directly addressing how conflict may insinuate itself into the relationship, chapter 2 offers a forthright explanation of the origins of dyadic dysfunction. The chapter begins by describing some typical examples of how the mother-infant relationship can become distorted as the channels of communication go awry. Specifically discussed are the transference of unresolved conflict from the mother's past, the mother's failure to reconcile the "imaginary infant," and maternal fears triggered by the infant's growing autonomy. In addition, some circumstances known to cause dyadic distress are also examined. These include postpartum depression, marital distress, and abuse and neglect.

Chapter 3 is devoted to a highly popular and efficient mode of treatment, short-term psychotherapy. The chapter first explores various aspects of the short-term approach, including selection criteria, strategies, and factors influencing treatment outcome. Subsequently, the discussion focuses on how previewing techniques may be integrated with the short-term model to create a viable treatment for parents and their infants. The chapter offers explicit guidance relating to how previewing may be used to establish a therapeutic alliance, foster an empathic treatment atmosphere, and assist during resolution and prediction of conflict.

Five case studies using brief psychotherapy are described in part II on a moment-by-moment basis. Each session includes discussion of the infant's developmental status, the caregiver's response to imminent developmental changes, the caregiver's perceptions of her own past history and psychological profile, and how intervention was used to generate a more adaptive interaction between caregiver and infant. The discussion of these cases demonstrates the evolving nature of the dyadic relationship. At the same time, *Short-Term Parent-Infant Psychotherapy* charts the effect of therapeutic intervention on the dyadic relationship, disclosing the application of treatment strategies during specific circumstances.

Chapter 4 discusses the emergence and resolution of distorted prenatal fantasies. A pregnant woman in treatment with a diagnosed borderline personality disorder copes with ambivalence concerning her pregnancy and the child she carries. This case is notable for its exploration of the patient's vivid dream imagery as examples of the fantasies that may be used to analyze and even predict conflict before it surfaces within the dyad.

Chaper 5 discusses the effects of postpartum depression on the early mother-infant relationship. This case examines the debilitating effect an episode of postpartum depression can have on the attachment bond being established between mother and infant. In the context of a compelling case history, the reader is exposed to the most effective methods for diagnosing and treating this condition in order that adaptive developmental patterns may be asserted.

Chapter 6 discusses how the advent of a new skill causes crisis in the mother-infant relationship. A highly adaptive mother without a previous history of psychopathology experiences a profound state of depression at the prospect of separation precipitated by her infant's incipient weaning behavior. This case demonstrates how developmental changes can unexpectedly awaken latent conflict, even in a case in which the mother's behavior with the infant has been exemplary.

Chapter 7 discusses the compounding of the dyadic failure by marital distress. Parents in a profoundly dysfunctional marriage deflect their psychopathology by creating a disability for their healthy infant and focusing their attention on the fantasy child they have created. This chapter probes the dynamic of "scapegoating," a common strategy whereby the weakest family member becomes a magnet for the dysfunctional patterns of the other family members. Only severance of the dysfunctional patterns being displaced onto the "problem child" will return the family to adaptation. Short-term strategies for achieving this goal are demonstrated.

Chapter 8 discusses the recurrence of conflict during the first 2 years of life. A primiparous mother with a history of disordered personality structure, compounded with episodic self-destructive behavior, endeavors to manage fear aroused by the attachment with her infant. Three suicidal episodes that were triggered by specific developmental changes are analyzed in detail. This chapter portrays how the principles of brief psychotherapy may alleviate dysfunctional patterns and reestablish equilibrium.

In sum, *Short-Term Parent-Infant Psychotherapy* provides both treatment techniques and lucid examples of how a clinician may implement protocols of brief psychotherapy for intervening with parents and infants. The book offers health care professionals new insights for understanding dysfunction in parent-infant dyads and for alleviating maladaptive patterns.

# PART I

## EVOLVING
## A THEORY OF SHORT-TERM
## PARENT-INFANT
## PSYCHOTHERAPY

# CHAPTER 1

## Previewing: A Key Developmental Phenomenon and a Therapeutic Strategy

DYADIC THERAPY involving a caregiver and infant has become increasingly popular in recent years. Therapists have heralded the benefits of such early intervention, and, in some cases, treatment may be recommended as early as during the pregnancy period. In addition, early therapeutic intervention has been shown to be effective in helping new parents to adjust to a newborn with a handicapping condition or a difficult temperament.

Despite the demonstrated efficacy of early intervention, conventional therapy continues to focus on problematic situations that have already surfaced, with alleviation of the presenting problem considered the goal of treatment. A more productive approach, however, might involve predicting potential conflict areas before they hinder the prospective dyadic rapport. Predictions of this type might then be used to instruct parents in techniques for averting potential episodes of conflict and for enhancing adaptive parental rapport with the infant.

### The Importance of a Supportive Environment in Early Infancy

To what extent do adaptive techniques actually exist? The answer may reside in a consideration of the dyadic relationship as an integral part of the developmental process. For the infant, the first 2 years of life are a remarkable period. The infant struggles to attain control over physiological processes, to learn to communicate through language, and to formulate a coherent sense of individuality. Consolidating these changes, the caregiver's emotional and psychological support is necessary to help the infant to master this rich roster of maturational changes. But if the caregiver is not available to lend support to the infant's efforts, what then? Spitz and Wolf (1946), key investigators of early-life psychopathology, observed that institutionalized infants not exposed to a consistent, nurturing caregiver lapsed into a state of emotional apathy. Characteristically, such infants exhibited a physical syndrome referred to as "anaclitic depression." They had shriveled bodies and affect and displayed no signs of the robust physical control exhibited by infants of comparable age who had been ministered to by adaptive caregivers. More compelling than their physical characteristics, however, was their psychological status. Their muted expressions, lack of curiosity, and general apathy to virtually any external stimulation suggested extreme emotional withdrawal. Although Spitz and Wolf found that these infants were physiologically capable of displaying age-appropriate motor skills, their overall recorded developmental capacity seriously lagged behind that of their counterparts.

The possibility of an infant developing the clinical syndrome described by Spitz and Wolf (1946) underscores the critical role of the caregiver in early infant development. Correspondingly, research underscores the probability that, without a nurturing caregiving figure, the infant's maturational achievements may become seriously and permanently impaired. Moreover, is it possible to articulate specifically the assertive developmental achievements such caregiver nurturance fosters in the familial infant? The answer is resoundingly affirmative. Researchers have, for example, identified the types of communication forged between caregiver and infant. Instead of relying solely on words, the caregiver intuitively builds this communication network by using a spectrum of specific interpersonal response patterns. These intuitive responses are triggered by the unconscious interpretation of the infant's cues. Intuitive behaviors are much more than merely innate reflexes occurring in the absence of external stimuli. However, the latency of these behaviors usually is from 200 to 600 milliseconds, meaning that their rate of occurrence lies somewhere between that of simple reflexes and rational decisions (Papousek & Papousek, 1987; Papousek, Papousek, & Haekel, 1987).

THE ROLE OF CONTINGENT AND DISCREPANT EXPERIENCES

Interpreting the infant's cues, the caregiver responds by creating a challenging environment that both encourages and assists the infant in reaching the next developmental hurdle. Techniques for doing this include the caregiver's exposing the infant to various *contingent* and *discrepant* experiences. *Contingency* here refers to cause-effect relationships (Watson, 1972), and studies have found contingency learning to be a positive experience (Sullivan & Lewis, 1990). More than a 3-second delay between stimulus and response, however, may terminate the infant's vibrant awareness of a contingency (Miller, 1990). Indeed, when the infant recognizes a contingency relationship, a remarkable ability has been gained: He or she begins to understand that the world is governed by rules that can be both repeated and tested. As a result, the infant comes to view the world as predictable and, gradually, controllable. Social experiences, then, become molded partly as a result of the contingencies experienced by the infant during interactions with a caregiver. Indeed, when contingent stimulation with appropriate social responses are provided, positive interpersonal outcomes have been observed (Kohler, Strain, Maretsky, & DeCesare, 1990; McConnell, Sisson, Cort, & Strain, 1991).

Another skill that exposes the infant to the predictability of his or her environment is *discrepancy* awareness. In this regard, a discrepancy refers to a notable difference in perception. As expounded by McCall and McGee (1977), infants are attracted to stimuli moderately different from those with which they are familiar. At the same time, however, because infants are not particularly interested in, or fascinated by, stimuli either dramatically different from or remarkably similar to those to which they have already been exposed, they thus learn best when offered only moderately discrepant stimuli. Just as the communication system mentioned hinges on the mother's attentive skills, the caregiver is the primary source of the infant's exposure to contingency and discrepancy relationships. The world incidentally bolsters the rationale underlying such programs as Head Start and similar enrichment protocols. If the environment from which an infant extrapolates predictability is lavishly enhanced—by intensely colored spinning mobiles over a crib or by multisyllabic and polyglot caregiver's crooning in rapt response to every infant cue—the discrepant awareness ante is considerably increased, making the high-exposure infant that much more receptive to more advanced, moderate-stimuli refinements. Conversely, an environment poor in caregiver attentions of the sorts described will necessarily tend to yield low-tolerance infants with smaller attention spans, more inhibited imaginations, and a proclivity to withdrawn affect. In the long run, consistent incremental advances from infancy onward create a disparate age cohort that has sociologists at a loss for explanations beyond raw genetic endowments. Parents exhausted from overwork or away from the baby's immediate vicinity for other reasons tend to impoverish the infant, accidentally lowering the discrepant awareness threshold of the child, whether he or she comes from a wealthy home or not. Neglected children thus fulfill the expectation of poor performance.

THE ROLE OF PREVIEWING

In addition to involving the infant in these experiences, the caregiver also serves as the infant's guide, acquainting him or her with changes that will take place in the imminent future. Just as was the case with provoking contingent and discrepant challenges, this prognosticating role is another crucial building block to the infant's optimal development. If the caregiver is able to predict how imminent skills will change the course of the relationship with her infant in the future, she can prepare the infant for the onset of these intra- and interpersonal changes; this relational duality helps the infant to experience seemingly uncontrollable events in an adaptive fashion (Trad, 1990) and to integrate them into his or her emotional topography. Recent investigations of dyadic interactions have shown that adaptive caregivers not only engage in these predictions but also communicate the nature of the upcoming skill to the infant (Becker, 1987; Heinicke, 1990). This process of presenting interpersonal outcomes has been referred to as *previewing* (Trad, 1989). As we will see, previewing may also be adapted to the context of caregiver-infant psychotherapy, to prepare both dyad members for upcoming changes in the infant's development that will have an impact on their relationship. The upcoming discussion explains the previewing process and describes how it may be integrated into psychotherapeutic protocols to enhance the dyadic exchange.

## The Previewing Process

Each parent-infant relationship is unique, incorporating the distinctive constitutional endowments of the parent and of the infant and the shape of their interaction. Forging this relationship adaptively is, to a large degree, dependent on the caregiver's motivation for interpersonal exchange. The prevalent view is that parents begin to harbor distinct representations about their infants as early as the pregnancy period (Ammaniti et al., 1992; Raphael-Leff, 1986). For most women, pregnancy and prospective motherhood represent a dramatic new frontier in their lives. During pregnancy they speculate about how their imminent motherhood will affect their relationship with their husbands, other family members, and their careers. Significantly, mothers-to-be soon begin speculating rather specifically about the baby growing within them. These representations may involve imagining what the baby will look like, envisioning his or her personality, and anticipating a variety of actual episodes of interaction with the infant. Not to be outdone, prospective fathers are also surprisingly prone to these speculative hypotheticalizations (Clinton, 1987). In particular, new fathers-to-be may weigh and ponder whether they are ready to assume the responsibilities associated with fatherhood and how their relationship with their wives will change after the birth. They speculate on the various ways in which they may have to alter their recreational patterns to accommodate "their boy" or how to handle sports and leisure activities with "their girl." Male parents, more than female parents, tend to speculate more on the career path of the infant, especially if there is a family business for the child to participate in.

Once the infant is born, the parents confront the challenges rapidly posed by the advent of a new baby. Not only must they become familiar with the real infant, but also they must somehow reconcile the projected infant they imagined during the 9-month-long pregnancy with the real-life infant in their laps. Adaptive parents are generally able to negotiate the transition from the envisioned baby to the real child without much difficulty. Such parents observe their infants minutely, eagerly attending to the new creature who has entered their lives.

## GOALS

Previewing is a potent process that introduces the infant to maturational coherence. During this period, mothers begin previewing upcoming developmental events for their infants in a dynamic fashion. Infants will be confronting a series of the most monumental challenges during the first 2 years of life, challenges that implicate both the external world and the changes within their own body. In fact, never again will a person have to face the enormous challenges every infant confronts and largely overcomes during these first 2 years of life. Those affecting the infant's body begin immediately after birth and are governed, to a large degree, by genetic endowment. For example, the infant depends on the caregiver to fulfill physiological needs, including nutrition, warmth, and safety, and to provide dry clothing and cleanliness. Lacking a sensitive and nurturing caregiver, the infant would be hard-pressed to make sense of the seemingly unfathomable, often uncomfortable forces that emanate from his or her own body. Gradually the infant begins to internalize interactions with the external world and perceptions of bodily transformations. Here, internalization refers to a process by which the information perceived is assimilated so that it becomes an integral part of the infant's representational landscape. During the first few months of life, assertion of control over the body's biological imperatives commands vast attention and is of paramount significance. The adaptive caregiver assists the infant in coordinating the diversity of early developmental changes. Previewing facilitates this process by helping the infant to reconcile internal and external perceptions and by fostering continuity between past, current, and imminent developmental achievement.

## STEPS IN THE PREVIEWING PROCESS

To grasp the previewing process fully, we must outline the specific components of this activity in which the experiences of the newborn infant and of all future infant-caregiver interactions with the world become increasingly self-validating. The previewing process has essentially three components. The first is the caregiver's capacity to formulate *representations* of imminent developmental change. *Representation* refers to a reflective state during which perceptions of past, current, or future interaction become accessible through imaging (Trad, 1990), that is, comprehensive images that are endowed with meaning. Previewing involves not only the caregiver's awareness of the infant's current status but also a sense of imminent maturational attainments in the context of past experiences. The pregnant woman who has an imaginary conversation with her unborn baby is engaging in a representational experience, as is the new mother listening to the baby's babbling and envisioning the infant eventually mastering the complexities of language. One glaring difference between these two is that until the end of the first trimester, the pregnant woman must rely exclusively on her imagination and spirit to generate a representation of the not-yet-born infant; after that, the new mother may devise representations based on concrete visceral feelings and observations of her infant's behaviors. During both stages, however, women are engaging in representations—rehearsals—that allow them to construct scenarios of future interpersonal exchange.

The second component of previewing involves the caregiver as *auxiliary partner* who helps the infant to master new developmental skills. When playing this role, the caregiver observes each gesture exhibited by the infant and then considers the environmental circumstances that have evoked these signs. The auxiliary partner asks how the infant's behaviors have emerged thus far and will continue to change from the way they were before the new behavior appeared. Most new mothers possess an intuitive reflexivity to their infant's maturational rhythms.

The caregiver thus contrasts intuitive knowledge of infant development with in situ observations of the infant's *precursory behaviors*, manifestations indicating that the infant is beginning to demonstrate a developmental change. Once a particular precursory behavior is identified, the parent devises specific interpersonal exchanges to supportively introduce the infant to the probable visceral content of the seemingly uncontrollable changes. During these episodes, the caregiver conveys to the infant not only that she will be available to guide precursory developmental skills, but also that she will provide a safe haven within which the infant can practice and thus gradually learn how to predict their future relationship. Such an episode fosters developmental continuity and emotional sharing for the infant. Examples of previewing behaviors are extraordinarily diverse and wide-ranging, because an adaptive mother will preview virtually every new skill in her infant.

The third and final component of previewing involves *parental empathy* to the infant's moods. *Empathy* is defined as a "vicarious affective response" that is "more appropriate to someone else's situation than to one's own" (Hoffman, 1982a, p. 281). An individual who possesses an optimal level of empathy actually endures the distress of others and spontaneously displays comfort and affection to those who are suffering. The use of empathy imbues interpersonal relationships with a dynamic sense of intimacy and emotional fulfillment. Studies reveal that empathic individuals tend to enjoy rewarding interactions with others (Zahn-Waxler & Radke-Yarrow, 1990). The mother's sensitivity detects when the infant has become overly tired with the previewing exercise and wishes to remain at the level of achievement mastered prior to the previewing exercise. When fulfilling this role, the parent's attunement to the infant's manifestations assumes a preeminent position; this sensitivity enables the caregiver to view the world from the infant's perspective. As a result, the mother quickly senses when the infant is in a playful and inquisitive mood, unresistant to being exposed to new developmental skills. At such times, the caregiver will wisely initiate a previewing episode with the infant. But the mother's keen "sensitivity antennae" are also used to monitor the infant's mood throughout the previewing episode. At these times, the mother gradually ends the previewing experience, easing the infant's transition to a more subdued state. A related skill, known as *affect attunement* (Stern, 1985), further generates an atmosphere of positive emotion during mother-infant interactions; this refers to the emotional sensitivity the mother uses to access the infant's most profound emotional state and to respond appropriately to it.

Previewing exerts a powerful effect on the dyadic team, offering either member an innovative perspective on the future of the relationship. Given the dramatic effect of the process on the dyadic relationship, it is reasonable to investigate how the mother formulates representations about herself and the infant and comes to predict the interpersonal responses each will exhibit in the imminent future. That is to say, how does the infant's progressive development enhance his or her ability to respond to the caregiver's previewing behaviors, thereby enabling the infant to make predictions about his or her own body and social interactions?

## Predicting and Sharing Interpersonal Outcome

The mother's ability either to facilitate or to undermine the infant's development has long captivated the imagination of researchers. Most theorists agree that most mothers intuitively nurture their infants' new developmental skills. Wood, Bruner, and Ross (1976) used the term *scaffolding* to explain, for example, the behaviors adaptive mothers use to compensate for deficiencies in the infant's skill. By contrast, Vygotsky (1978) proposed that a *zone of proximal development* exists that enables competent parents to combine their supportive behaviors with the challenges of the environment to help the infant to achieve skills just ahead of the current level of infant mastery. According to Vygotsky, the caregiver intuitively predicts the next level of developmental competence the infant will reach. With support and encouragement, he or she then guides the infant's development in an adaptive direction toward achieving these new skills. Kaye (1982) has used the term *apprenticeship* to describe the interaction between caregiver and infant. For Kaye, the parents are partners in the relationship with the infant and help the infant to achieve knowledge by delicately balancing or compensating for the infant's lack of mastery while motivating the infant to strive beyond his or her current developmental achievement. The parent-partner accomplishes this compensation by establishing a specific goal, sharing this goal with the infant, breaking the interaction down into substeps, and monitoring the infant's behaviors to achieve these goals. As a result, the infant's performance becomes a joint endeavor by mother or father and infant for the purpose of complementing the infant's developmental skills.

## EXPECTATIONS AND ACHIEVEMENTS

Numerous other researchers have shown a connection between maternal expectation and the infant's developmental competence (Heckhausen, 1987), which in general reflects adult expectation of child performance. Numerous pedagogical studies attest to the correlation of high teacher expectation—warranted or otherwise—and pupil performance; the converse, unfortunately, has also been repeatedly demonstrated. Such interlocking theoretical models, therefore, are continually reaffirmed. Data from these studies suggest that such interpersonal processes as previewing contribute to the infant's adaptation in the face of developmental change. Many of these studies have shown a direct correlation between maternal expectation and behavior and developmental outcome. The interplay of these variables is reinforced by *previewing*, which posits that new caregivers initially represent imminent developmental change and subsequently transform their representations into interpersonal behaviors to be rehearsed with the infant. The very proactive dynamic of expectation, furthermore, works as a template for the parent. The parent intuitively plots a developmental goal irrespective of the particular infant's capabilities, then develops that mental script playing it to its logical denouement. As a result, adaptive mothers not only encourage their infants to anticipate upcoming developmental attainments, but, significantly, they also expose their infants to a sphere of safety within which the infant can share the interpersonal meaning of the change.

INTUITION

Researchers have used microanalytic techniques to evaluate interactions between new mothers and their infants (Koester, Papousek, & Papousek, 1989; Papousek & Papousek, 1987). These assessments have revealed moment-to-moment dyadic interactions imperceptible to the naked eye. Among these interpersonal behaviors are visual and vocal cuing, appropriate holding behavior, adequate stimulation cues, and competent feeding behavior. The work of Hopkins and Westra (1990), for example, shows that such maternal behaviors as stroking and handling directly influence the infant's maturational achievement. Researchers have found that early parental encouragement results in increased sophistication of a toddler's linguistic abilities, as well as in advancements in play behavior. Therapeutic behaviors that encourage the infant's development predict a wide range of skills, including play competence (Belsky, Goode, & Most, 1980), language (Tamis-Lemonda & Bornstein, 1990), vocabulary capacity (Bornstein, 1985), and cognitive competence (Yarrow, Morgan, Jennings, Harmon, & Gaiter, 1982). The consistent care and stimulation the mother provides the infant are also of great significance, because they reaffirm the nature of the mother's sensitivity to the infant's moods. Combined, these behaviors constitute the repertoire of intuitive skills manifested by adaptive mothers. Maladaptive mothers, by contrast, generally fail to display these behaviors or display them with minimal success. Thus, intuitive manifestations—by parent or child—are a palpable indication of the dyad's level of adaptation. Intuitive skills are used by caregivers as the building blocks of a previewing experience.

Substantial evidence indicates that this repertoire of behaviors fosters adaptive developmental skills in the infant and encourages the blossoming of a strong emotional rapport between caregiver and infant. The previewing process, in particular, seems to encourage this dual, positive effect. As a result, one may ask whether the previewing techniques prevalent among adaptive dyads might not be introduced therapeutically in cases in which conflict has stifled normal developmental trends. In such situations, previewing may well serve to instill adaptive and normative interpersonal skills when other modalities have failed.

## Implementing Previewing within the Dyad

As noted, the previewing process appears to promote adaptive development and interpersonal rapport with the caregiver. The process encompasses the mother's representations of upcoming developmental changes, the enactment of these representations through specific interactional exercises, and the considerable sensitivity necessary to help the infant to make the transition between episodes. Several researchers—including Benoit, Zeanah, and Barton (1989); Bretherton (1987); George and Solomon (1989); and Main, Kaplan, and Cassidy (1985)—have discussed how internal representations are generated. In this regard, we must ask how internal representations are transformed by the mother into interactional patterns to be enacted with the infant.

Representations used by the mother are a composite of experiences embodying not only previous and contemporaneous interactions but also predictions about upcoming interactions.

Some researchers have suggested that representations are organized hierarchically, with the general representations superseding the more specific ones. Interactions between mother and infant are initially encoded by both dyadic members as episodic memories (Stern, 1989). The mother will be adept at forming episodic memories; she will generally group these memories together to form *prototype memories*. According to Stern, the prototype is then extrapolated to encompass similar interactive sequences, such as feeding, walking, or talking. The next level is that of a *scenario*, which incorporates diverse interactive sequences. Eventually, sequences are integrated into a unified whole that has been referred to as an *internal working model*, a concept originally described by Bowlby (1969). The internal working model encodes not only content but also the emotions experienced and the meaning associated with these experiences. Internal working models help to regulate the interpersonal behavior enacted within the dyad. Observations of mothers during previewing episodes validate the notion that development of an internal working model is a continuous process, during which both individuals experiment with numerous responses in a continual effort to improve the response to the other dyadic member.

Successful interactive moments should help the infant to modulate knowledge about both the external world and internal bodily perceptions (Nelson & Gruendel, 1981). Causal sequences within the dyadic interaction facilitate the integration of related experiences. For example, when mothers are questioned, they provide sensitive descriptions of their interpersonal experiences with their infants, that is, they show a proclivity for sharing specific goals with them. As their interaction progresses, however, each dyadic member continues to evaluate the mood of the other before engaging in any further purposeful action requiring mutual collaboration. The phrase "goal-corrected partnership" (Bowlby, 1969) is particularly appropriate in this context and refers to the way each dyadic member continually enhances communication insofar as possible in order to enhance rapport with the other dyadic member.

Conversely, maladaptive mothers may well view themselves as being ineffective in perceiving or interpreting their infant's cues, because they consider themselves unable to empathize with their infant's perspective. Such caregivers typically ignore or distort their own (often true) perceptions of relevant cues concerning their child's capabilities. For example, they may fail to recognize or may underestimate potential threats to the child, may discount the child's distress, or may believe that their support is unnecessary, even in the presence of the child's precursory displays of new skills. As a result, the child may end up in a distress-provoking, or even physically dangerous, situation. Zeanah, Benoit, and Barton (1986) used various dimensional measures to explore these maternal interactive qualities. *Richness of perception* refers to the detail in the parents' descriptions of the infant as an individual with a unique personality. *Openness to change* refers to the parents' ability to internalize new information about the infant, whereas *flexibility* concerns the mother's emotional receptivity to infant developmental change. *Intensity of involvement* reflects maternal preoccupation with the infant. The *coherence* of the maternal narrative reflects an overall organization that characterizes the mother's representations of the infant; coherence in this regard focuses on the lucidity of the mother's ideas about the infant and her relationship to the infant. *Maternal sensitivity* involves the mother's ability to empathize an awareness of the infant's emotional experience. For example, sensitivity involves whether the mother perceives the infant as experiencing the full spectrum of emotions, whether, in other words, the mother views her infant as a full individual with a range of unique needs.

Studies using these criteria suggest that some mothers formulate distorted impressions of their infants. In such cases, the mother may be preoccupied with other concerns not necessarily related to caregiving or confused by the infant and insensitive to him or her as an individual. The representations formulated during the previewing process provide an excellent opportunity to explore these criteria, because previewing depends on causal connections while incorporating plots, characters, and actions derived from the interactive sequences between mother and infant over time. That is, by exposing her infant to previewing exercises, the mother promotes the infant's experimentation with causal connections, predicts temporal sequences, and establishes her reliability.

Exploring how these mental representations evolve provides us with a more profound knowledge of how the mother pictures the dyadic relationship and then guides it in the direction of either adaptation or psychopathology. As an example, when parents exhibit dysfunctional responses during general supervision or parenting of the infant—such as in cases of abuse or neglect—this dysfunction often emanates from experiences deep within their own negative pasts (Fraiberg, 1982a,b). By examining the parents' representations of future interpersonal outcomes, it is often possible to predict whether they will interact in a flexible or rigid fashion, whether they will replicate dysfunctional patterns from their pasts, or display spontaneous patterns that reflect the new developmental skills the infant is experiencing. To be sure, maladaptive parents tend to resist change by adhering rigidly to inflexible patterns that were set independently of the current dyadic relationship. Adaptive mothers, on the other hand, tend to formulate flexible internal representations that enable them to better generate interpersonal behaviors that reflect the baby's needs and that elicit positive emotion and the motivation to continue the interaction. Exploring the nature of the caregiver's previewing abilities, then, largely enables the therapist to diagnose the caregiver's capacity to respond free of inhibiting conflict.

## The Infant's Response to the Previewing Process

As the caregiver sporadically introduces the infant to future developmental attainment through specific previewing exercises, the infant correspondingly contributes to the previewing process. To understand the previewing process from the infant's perspective, it is essential to examine the infant's emerging representational skills. As indicated, numerous maturational events occur during the first 2 years of life. The most significant of these events are the acquisition of such representational skills as language; the ability to predict; and promotion of the infant's emerging self-regulation. For example, the ability to self-regulate, as evidenced by ability to delay gratification, has been associated with later cognitive and academic competence and with the capacity to cope with frustration and stress (Shoda, Mischel, & Peake, 1990). Understanding the process by which self-regulatory capacities coalesce provides insight into how the infant coordinates perceptions of the external world and then formulates a subjective view of his or her own position in it. Soon after birth, infants emerge from the cocoon of neonatal status and begin to exhibit a variety of increasingly sophisticated skills, such as discrepancy awareness (McCall & McGee, 1977), contingency awareness (DeCasper & Carstens, 1981; Watson, 1977), and expectancy awareness (Fagen & Ohr, 1985). Although infants have not yet begun to introduce purpose and intention into their actions, they seem to be motivated to elicit new interactions from the parent. These skills help them to master the challenges of the external world, to exert control over bodily changes, and to forge an adaptive relationship with the caregiver. From these abilities, researchers have inferred that infants begin to represent the world at an extraordinarily young age—even within the first few weeks of life. Representations of images and relationships ultimately facilitate the infants' discernment of contingencies and foster development of predictions and expectancies about their bodily changes and the external world. To explain the how and why of these events, the infant relies on two very important endowments, *amodal perception* and *categorization*.

## AMODAL PERCEPTION

Amodal perception refers to the ability to transfer information perceived through one sensory modality—such as sight—to another sensory modality—such as smell (Meltzoff & Moore, 1977). Sensory information refers to discernments of visual, auditory, tactile, olfactory, and taste information. Infants possess the ability to translate between their own sensory perceptions. For instance, in experiments by Dodd (1979) and Walker (1982), infants of 5 and 6 months of age were able to match the sight of a parent's face with the sound of that parent's voice during speech presentations. Similarly, the same investigators found that if infants were given objects when blindfolded, after the blindfolds were removed, they were subsequently readily able to identify the objects they had held. They had not previously smelled, seen, tasted, or heard these objects, just felt them, yet they were sensitive to touch and other proprioceptive cues despite their lack of previous exposure. This skill thus enables the infant to synthesize the varied panorama of external events into a coherent composite of external reality. The spontaneous integration of stimuli across and between the senses permits infants to compare themselves with objects and thus to begin to understand their placement in, and relationship to, the greater world.

Werner (1948) has posited that emotions serve as a common denominator for converting sensations from one sensory modality to another. Facility with this skill helps to explain how infants can coordinate perceptual information that enables them to conclude that what is seen, heard, tasted, smelled, or touched may actually originate from a single entity. When a mother engages in "motherese," for example, she is not merely previewing conversation for the infant, she is also incorporating diverse perceptual communications into her concomitant behaviors; thus, the auditory quality associated with the mother's speech will be coordinated in the infant's cosmogony with the rhythmic stroking of the infant's cheek, as well as with exaggerated facial expressions that attract and maintain the infant's visual attention. The speech, too, will stand out, in that it will feature an exaggerated series of sounds and even crooning or singsong elements geared to rhythmic absorption. As soon as the infant responds positively, the mother will repeat these behaviors to elicit yet a further response.

## CATEGORIZATION

Categorization refers to the process by which perceptually distinct stimuli sharing certain qualities are grouped together (Medin, 1983). It is one of the earliest innate capacities, as apparently, from perhaps as early as 3 months of age, infants categorize experience (Hayne, Rovee-Collier, & Perris, 1987; Resnick & Kagan, 1983). Each new experience the infant encounters, then, either reinforces or modifies a previous category, with objects and experiences being categorized based on either their outstanding perceptual or conceptual features. In one study, Kestenbaum and Nelson (1990) tested the ability of 7-month-old infants to categorize faces portraying various emotional expressions. Their findings suggested that the infants preferred to categorize the faces on the basis of perceptual (i.e., the emotion being expressed) features that reinforce the immediacy of the infant's sensory aspects of experience. Given this finding, it is important to expose the infant to as much sensory stimulation from various modalities as possible to provide an interactional arena from which to promote cognitive and categorizing skills.

## INFANT MODES OF COMMUNICATION

During the first few months of the infant's life, previewing behavior of the mother and father significantly advances the infant's capacities for amodal perception and categorization. By examining how categorization and amodal perception provide the infant with a sufficient skill for progressively internalizing the vicissitudes of external reality, we may begin to fashion a substantive theory of how previewing significantly influences the infant's developmental course. These observations reinforce the notion that infants experience the world in the form of perceptual unity and subsequently form representations of these perceptions to predict future outcomes. Allowing the infant from its earliest days to act on representations will encapsulate the perceptual qualities of the experience (Meltzoff, 1981, 1988). When engaging in previewing exercises, mothers rely on the infant's mood to facilitate the transition from one state to another. This mode of nurturance, in which the content of the message and the means used to communicate the message overlap, is referred to as the *analogic-behavioral* mode (Watzlawick, Beavin, & Jackson, 1967). Indeed, one sign of the caregiver's previewing skill is the capacity to assist the infant in making the transition from states of quiescence to states of activity.

When the mother engages in previewing behavior with her infant, she is not merely conveying a message about current activity, but she is also orienting the infant toward the interpersonal implications of imminent developmental achievement. For example, when the mother previews crawling, she communicates to her infant, "This is what the sensation of crawling will feel like someday, when you develop sufficient skill to crawl on your own," while she simultaneously conveys, "This is how our relationship will be modified when you are able to crawl by yourself." These messages are symbolic in nature in the sense that the simulated crawling behavior serves as a *paradigm* for the infant's future as he or she successfully negotiates this developmental milestone. The communication of symbolic messages occurs through the *digital* mode of communication, during which the medium used to represent the message differs from the message itself. The most sophisticated type of digital communication is language. When language is used, objects and concepts may be signified by arbitrary symbols. This is not to suggest that previewing exercises resemble digital communication in the same fashion that words do. Nonetheless, previewing provides the dyad with an effective and unifying form of communication, because it combines both digital and analogic communication. This combination brings to mind the amodal perception experiments discussed above, in which infants could identify objects not previously seen, smelled, or heard. This communication occurs because previewing is a flexible type of communication that exposes the infant to the visceral experience of analogic communication while it simultaneously conveys a symbolic or digital component.

Exposure to these two powerful modes of communication during previewing exercises further encourages and abets the infant in reconciling perceptions emanating from both internal and external sources. Furthermore, because much of this communication involves the mother's messages about the infant's current and future developmental status, infants receive immediate and ongoing assistance in their efforts at predicting the future.

As they progress developmentally and master more sophisticated skills, infants begin to recognize a difference in their perspective from that of others, in particular, from that of the mother. This realization, which occurs between 7 and 9 months of age, is boosted by the infant's concomitant awareness that internal subjective experiences can be shared with others. Stern (1989) posits that at approximately this time a shared framework of meaning characterizes the infant's experience with the mother. The subjective experiences the infant seeks to share with the mother do not require translation into digital communication.

As the infant becomes more aware that others possess subjective experiences separate from his or her own, a quality Trevarthen (1980, 1985) has labeled *intersubjectivity*, the mother's attempts at regulating the infant's subjective experience attain further eminence. The mother's repeated previewing initiatives provide the infant with iterated opportunities to test perceptions of reality, as well as with encouragement to proceed with the developmental tasks at hand. These endeavors motivate and promote greater intimacy between mother and infant.

The culminating event in infant self-regulation has taken place by the end of the second year of life, when spoken language emerges full-fledged; at this time, infants can themselves represent events and objects through the use of symbols. Moreover, they can now envision how reality ought to be, or how they want it to be, rather than how it actually is. In other words, infants can engage in autonomous predictions without the mother's initiating or prompting. This observation probably suggests that as the infants' representational abilities become more sophisticated, quite likely they use previewing experiences for representing more complex expectations.

## Conclusion

This chapter has introduced the concept of previewing, a unique phenomenon that occurs within the dyadic relationship. Previewing allows the caregiver to acquaint the infant gradually with imminent developmental change and with the implications such change will have for transforming the relationship between mother and infant.

The previewing process is based on three primary components. First, the caregiver represents the infant's current and prospective developmental status. Second, the caregiver translates these representations into previewing exercises that are then enacted with the infant, during which the infant is supportively introduced to a specific developmental milestone. The caregiver will here use various intuitive behaviors such as visual and vocal cuing, as well as physical support of the body, to simulate and demonstrate the behaviors characteristic of the upcoming milestone. Third, the caregiver empathizes with the infant's moods to curtail the previewing activity when disinterest or fatigue prompts cessation and returns the infant to his or her earlier developmental status.

To engage in adaptive previewing, the caregiver should learn to pay attention to her own representations of infant development, while recognizing, however, that the infant also possesses a particular perspective on events. As development proceeds, the infant gradually separates from others, particularly from the mother. The mother's sensitivity to the infant's development enables her to devise time- and age-appropriate previewing episodes, as the infant begins to differentiate a clearer sense of self. The caregiver's previewing behaviors during the first 2 years of life are especially crucial, because the infant is striving to forge an adaptive relationship with the mother. In this respect, the mother guides the course of imminent development, while profoundly assisting the infant in asserting autonomy. This chapter has described the dynamics affecting the maturational process the typical infant undergoes during this period. Only when a parent is sensitive to the implications of these events can he or she help the infant to achieve an appropriate balance between reliance on the parent's goal-oriented ministrations in forming a partnership in order to assert autonomy and self-actualization.

We examined various "deprivation scenarios" in which the infant was denied previewing experiences. In these situations, the infant experiences developmental events as being arbitrary, and thus his or her ensuing relationship with the caregiver will likely reflect insecurity, highlighting the infant's risk for onset of subsequent psychopathology. When such cases occur, short-term treatment—using supervised previewing as a form of intervention—may help to bypass and eliminate the emotional conflict. By introducing previewing into the relationship, the therapist offers the parent an invaluable skill for enhancing parental perceptions of developmental trends and for asserting a dynamic and ongoing role in fostering the infant's optimal development.

# CHAPTER 2

## Conflict in the Parent-Infant Relationship: Paradigms and Paradoxes

THE CHANGING PROFILE of the American family is reflected in the variety of parents who seek counseling. Single-parent families and working mothers are becoming increasingly commonplace. Within this already substantial category of caregivers, one also finds large numbers of adolescent mothers seeking advice on caregiving skills. Moreover, the problems that have seeped into the infrastructure of the family have become more elaborate in recent years and are no longer affected by a "conspiracy of silence." Wife beating, child abuse, incest, alcoholism, and a patient's HIV status—once subjects scarcely mentioned and then only in hushed tones—are now encountered frequently during clinical assessment and boldly discussed almost without regard to their "difficult" content.

These family issues are challenging for several reasons. First, they are often difficult to diagnose, despite the decline of what might once have been termed "silent suffering." In addition to psychological trauma, these problems promote delusive, deceptive, and collusive modes of interaction that necessarily sever the bonds of intimacy between parents and child. Finally, the families of today are called upon to overcome a host of virulent suprafamilial social ills that may erode even the strongest and most resilient kinship relationships. Included among these blights are pandemic chemical and substance abuse, inner-city violence, random crime, poverty, and a generalized disintegration of social support. There is a growing awareness of what some call "sympathy erosion," a problem laid at the door of media overexposure to global coverage of "too much misery." The end product of these is often a marked upswing in blunted affect.

Experience with these varied populations and the perplexing issues they face have taught me a significant lesson: Human interaction—particularly the complex collaboration between mother and infant—is remarkably intricate and resilient. By understanding the dyadic interaction, we can not only draw inferences about the functioning of an entire family unit but also custom-design a treatment protocol to serve all family members.

Recent studies indicate that early intervention efforts in families experiencing distress have beneficial and enduring results. Armed with this knowledge, treatment protocols now frequently focus on parent-infant dyads. Regarding the parent-infant relationship as a fundamental building block of the family structure, therapists have sought to reinvigorate this bond and, in so doing, to revitalize all the relationships within the family. In fact, researchers have become more sensitive to the varieties of relationship disturbance originating within the mother-infant dyad that eventually reverberate within the entire family structure (Fiese & Sameroff, 1989). Responding to this contrast, clinicians have focused on identifying optimal interactions between partners in mother-infant dyads in order to replicate such fertile sequences within the larger family. Thus, intervention done with parent-infant dyads has become increasingly popular in the past few years (Fraiberg, 1980; Palacio-Espasa & Cramer, 1989). Such interventions result in symptom relief while they enhance the relational bond between mother and infant, often within a bare few therapeutic sessions (Shapiro & Shapiro, 1982; Smith, Glass, & Miller, 1980). As an extension of this thinking, the likelihood of rapid realignment of adaptive interaction within the dyad is greatly enhanced when psychotherapeutic intervention is asserted promptly (Cramer & Stern, 1988).

## Advantages of Short-Term Psychotherapy

As mentioned in chapter 1, one strategy especially advantageous in the treatment of parent-infant dyads is *short-term psychotherapy*. Although the specifics of short-term psychotherapy are discussed in chapter 3, it is useful to emphasize here some of the features that make this model so effective with parent-infant dyads. As a preliminary matter, short-term psychotherapy refers to a treatment of brief duration—ranging from 6 weeks to 4 months—that focuses on resolving a single specific problem. During the short-term modality, the treatment goal is to rapidly establish an alliance that will allow the therapist to question the patient's resistances and defensive style. Beyond this, patients are assigned specific tasks relating to their child's developmental profile that should be completed as treatment progresses.

Short-term psychotherapy is appropriate in treating parent-infant dyads confronting conflict for a variety of reasons. First, infants are especially vulnerable to maladaptive handling and responses emanating from their caregivers—even brief exposure to abuse or other dysfunctional nurturance patterns can distort infant perceptions of developmental progress at a time when it is of paramount importance for the infant to establish interpersonal contact with and trust in the primary caregiver. A method of intervention that promotes rapid change is therefore crucial in these cases.

Second, as a matter of logistics, research in the area of psychotherapy reveals a high level of patient attrition after just a few sessions. In America this attrition is not confined to the precincts of psychotherapeutic treatment. Patient compliance with regard to routine medical matters, pharmaceutical regimens, and other compliance-related protocols is so routinely poor that the "revolving-door syndrome" has become a popular entity even outside psychotherapeutic circles. The syndrome, it is well to remember, would not exist if patients followed the treatment regimen to its decreed terminus. Instead, as evidenced throughout the medical literature, unless particular patients are "highly motivated" for some exogenous reason, they are frequently apt to stop whatever regimen has been advocated as soon as the preliminary management of symptoms is achieved. As the underlying conditions are rarely controlled in the minimal time span budgeted by the "impatient patients" in this unusually speed-driven culture, the patient is usually back for further treatment within a brief time after cessation of protocols. The culprit in the issue of therapeutic session attrition can be generalized across fields and disciplines; it is our particular mind-set in the United States. Thus, a treatment format designed to effect enduring change in a relatively brief period is strongly advised.

Third, many of the techniques of short-term therapy are compatible with the developmental pace that characterizes adaptive parent-infant exchange. Just as the parent-infant dyad proceeds at a relatively quick pace—and cannot for obvious reasons stop the ongoing interaction between dyadic teammates—the short-term modality echoes the real-time home regimen and is almost a one-on-one guidance system for sidetracked parents. Finally, the short-term approach strives to provide patients with usable methods for predicting and overcoming potential future conflict. Such methods are of special benefit for parent-infant psychotherapy in light of the rapidity with which developmental changes occur.

Therapists treating parent-infant dyads should recognize that conflict generally stems from a variety of conditions confronting families. Pregnancy may, for example, ironically awaken long-buried conflicts deriving from the expectant mother's own childhood. Other issues can arise after the birth. Some women have difficulty reconciling the fantasized baby who dominated their imagination during the pregnancy with the live baby who has been born. In other cases, postpartum depression takes hold of the new mother, preventing her from quickly establishing an adaptive relationship with her infant. Marital distress and lack of social support are other factors that may precipitate or presage a disturbed (dysfunctional) interaction between mother and infant. Moreover, the therapist should be alert to signs of child abuse or neglect, to determine whether the infant will need to be independently assisted or separated from his or her parents. Although the causes of dysfunction within the dyad may be diverse, therapists should also be sensitive to a consistent principle—the paradox of development affects these families. In effect, the entire developmental process embodies this paradox. The paradox may be described as follows: The infant's acquisition of new skills results in both greater intimacy with the caregiver and, simultaneously, greater autonomy from the caregiver. If the parent adjusts adaptively to this paradox, development is likely to proceed in a healthy fashion; however, if the parent cannot accept the duality of the process, it is highly likely that conflict will interfere with the dyadic relationship.

## Defining Dysfunction in Parent-Infant Dyads: The Origins of Psychopathology

### THEORETICAL MODELS

The psychopathology that can insinuate itself into the parent-infant dyad may stem from a variety of sources. Indeed, most of the major psychoanalytic theories have discussed the origins of psychological conflict and disorganized behavior. For example, Freud views psychopathology as a struggle between three primary structures—the id (the domain of dreams and the unconscious), the ego (the domain of personality), and the superego (the domain of the conscience) (Freud, 1910, 1926). For the father of psychoanalysis, conflict is due to a disequilibrium among these three "structures" of the mind. Certain wishes arising during early infant development are not accommodated within the mind's constructs, and these wishes begin to compete for dominance. In essence, Freud considers conflict an intrapsychic phenomenon. Although the events of the parent's infancy might influence the nature of the current dyadic conflict, it nonetheless remains an internal parental dialectic. To resolve conflict, extensive working-through during psychoanalysis is necessary (Freud, 1937).

### Object-Relations Theory

The object-relations theorists view conflict differently; they attribute psychopathology to the parent's erratic representational skills. During infancy, the mind generates mental representations of external objects and of the self (Beres & Joseph, 1970) that encompass emotions, attitudes, and cognitive beliefs based on experiences and perceptions. In this regard, psychopathology represents a definitive turning inward as a means of avoiding interpersonal relations (Fairbairn, 1940). This aversion to life necessarily also causes the individual to retreat from the world of social interaction (Guntrip, 1961). For adaptive development to occur, the infant must experience a rich and mutually rewarding relationship with the caregiver. If, by contrast, the relationship with the caregiver is emotionally depriving, the infant will most likely formulate a representation of the relationship with the caregiver that incorporates these negative qualities, along with the tendency eventually to attribute their negatives to the self and to other mental representations (Hartmann, 1950). For the object-relations theorists, conflict is resolved when the internal discrepancies in the relationship between the self and the object are eliminated. Old images must thus be replaced with new representations in order to resolve interpersonal conflict. This substitution can occur during psychotherapy, as the interactions with the therapist gradually displace internalized representations.

## Interpersonal Theory

Theorists from the interpersonal school of psychiatry propose a slightly different view of the origins of psychopathology. For the interpersonalists, an infant's disordered relationship with the caregiver heightens the infant's anxiety, while diminishing his or her sense of security (Sullivan, 1953). Psychopathology then emerges as a reaction between the individual and the environment, with the environment extending to the significant persons in the child's life. Indeed, Sullivan noted that "a personality can never be isolated from the complex of interpersonal relations in which the person lives and has his being" (Sullivan, 1940, p. 10). In effect, this means that conflict derives from the infant's first significant relationship, that with the caregiver. As Sullivan explains, the infant's sense of emerging security functions as an antidote for the countervailing helplessness that can be engendered by early parental rejection (Sullivan, 1940, 1953). According to Sullivan, the infant can sense the difference between the anxiety associated with bad maternal experiences and the security associated with good maternal experiences. For Sullivan, the caregiver's empathic ministrations cause the child to become either less or more anxious. Theorists from the interpersonal school posit that conflict may be resolved later in life during psychotherapy, because the therapeutic relationship gradually supersedes and stands in for the individual's early life experience of deprivation.

## Theory of Self

For the self theorists, such as Kohut (1978), conflict arises because of a failure to fulfill the infant's needs. If the gap between the infant's needs and the parental response is too substantial, the infant loses the perception of feeling good and fails to regulate internal states. A decade and more ago, in formulating a theory of self, Kohut noted that conflict originates in an external discrepancy between the infant's needs and the parental response. A mother or father who fails to provide the infant with an adequate caregiver response promotes a defect in the sense of self. To overcome such actual or posited deficiencies, Kohut recommends that the therapist take an empathic approach during psychotherapy.

## Previewing

In contrast to these other models, previewing—the prospective approach—posits that psychological conflict stems from the inability to predict the interpersonal consequences deriving from developmental change. We argue that conflict is a manifestation of the fact that the infant is unable to predict or rehearse the interpersonal changes that imminent skills should evoke in the dyadic relationship. The inability to predict may arise from two sources. First, manifest or latent psychological conflict in the parent may cause him or her to hold the infant back, preventing the infant from evolving adequate predictive skills. Second, the parent may (unconsciously or otherwise) accelerate the pace of the developmental processes, causing the infant to exhibit certain skills precociously. Under the previewing model, then, conflict is the failure to sustain a sense of continuity in the relationship toward developmental change; as a consequence, self-regulating behaviors do not permit the infant to coordinate both subjective perceptions and interpersonal manifestations. The individual cannot assert continuity among past, present, and future perceptions. As a result, developmental change is experienced as random, arbitrary, and thus uncontrollable. Resolving conflict under the prospective model means that the patient will learn how (or be "taught") to assert continuity and coherence, to negotiate developmental transitions with relative ease, while developing mastery over seemingly uncontrollable developmental events.

Among parent-infant dyads with harmonious relationships, the tendency of the dyadic members to predict each other's interactions is apparent. In one case, Sandy, the mother of a 6-month-old, was acutely sensitive to her son's feelings (inferred from his behaviors and facial expressions) and attuned to her own feelings. She used these perceptions as she previewed changes in crawling behavior for her son. Sandy told the therapist that "sometimes he seems both excited and frustrated at the same time. I know he wants to crawl. I can predict it, and he's just getting the hang of it now. Watch." She then demonstrated by gently moving his feet to simulate crawling gestures, smiling as he slowly progressed forward. After helping him practice for a few minutes, she became sensitive to his fatigue and quiet signs of distress. She stroked his head, scooped him into her lap, and comforted him with soothing words, "Aw, sweetheart, that was a *lot* for you!" (with mother and infant here establishing and maintaining eye contact). This mother's attentive ministrations suggested that she possessed a keen perception of developmental rhythms, which enabled her continuously to monitor and predict her infant's status as well as her response to infant development. Moreover, the infant appeared to perceive that his mother was quickly sensitive to his moods, suggesting that the dyad shared a healthy, even robust, rapport. These mothers often attend caregiver-infant support groups to enhance their knowledge of infant development.

In the cases discussed in part II, one of the more striking characteristics of the caregivers is their inability to exhibit virtually any persistent intuitive behaviors during interaction with their infants. A bottle may be thrust into the infant's mouth, for example, when he or she cries. This cannot help but startle the infant, who learns it is dangerous to express itself orally. The caregiver's gestures when holding the infant may be rigid and mechanical, as if she were holding an inanimate object rather than a human being. Looking at this from the infant's perspective, the sense would be one of being held as if one didn't very much count beyond one's literal volume in space. Moreover, the mothers described rarely look at their infants directly or engage in noticeable visual cuing episodes. In turn, lack of parental intuitive skill is then reflected in the typically subdued and lethargic demeanor of the infants. It is as if the infants have given up trying to entice their mothers into participating in a meaningful interaction. Absence of these intuitive behaviors contributes to both the diagnosis and treatment direction of the dyadic intervention. That is, a key aspect of the treatment is to guide the caregiver along in developing intuitive skills. As the parent's facility in this area is enhanced, so too is the ability to relate to the infant in an adaptive fashion. The mother's new, attentive ministrations become instrumental in encouraging the infant to emerge gradually from a state of emotional stupor and nonresponsivity. The issue of trust for the infant comes to the fore as he or she learns to rely on the parent's sensitivity to his or her needs.

## Short-Term Psychotherapy

These cases exemplify why short-term psychotherapy is of great benefit during intervention with mother-infant or parent-infant dyads. The application of the short-term psychotherapy model to mother-infant dyads was first proposed by Fraiberg (1980). The technique emphasizes symptom relief and amelioration of dysfunctional relationships, often within a few sessions. A major goal of this form of treatment is to overcome a specific problem, subsequently evaluated by objective change in the patient's demeanor (infant *or* parent). These changes should be enduring and measurable and should predict future adaptive outcomes (Cramer et al., 1990; Trad, 1992b). The essence of short-term psychotherapy for mothers and infants is to define spheres of disruptive conflict that interfere with the dyad's smooth adaptive functioning. Thus, at the outset of treatment, a symptomatic sequence of interaction should be noted and analyzed. Subsequently, by successively modifying the caregiver's spectrum of representations and behaviors, a marked improvement in functioning should be detected (Buckley et al., 1984; Cramer et al., 1990).

## PARENTAL FACTORS

Whereas the multiple causes of conflict in a parent-infant dyad are not usually easy to demarcate, the affect surrounding such conflict is generally more apparent. Specifically, the mother-infant interaction will be noticeably disrupted, interfering with the caregiver's ability to preview and rehearse future developmental change with the infant in an adaptive fashion.

## *The Pregnancy Experience*

The parent-infant relationship begins during pregnancy. Throughout pregnancy, the mother-to-be undergoes radical physiological changes (Caplan, 1979; Pines, 1972). Investigations have demonstrated that both expectant parents experience a vivid fantasy life with regard to the unborn child while awaiting the infant's birth. Indeed, these fantasies are so richly embellished in detail and specific in content that they may be categorized based on trimester of the pregnancy. Exploration of the parents' perceptions of their relationship with their unborn infant has permitted researchers to be able to detect and identify the potential for maladaptation as early as early pregnancy.

During the first trimester of pregnancy, the woman's body is subject to dramatic physiological transformation, changes in some respects reminiscent of the physical alterations associated with puberty. As a result, during this time the woman may experience either dreams or daytime reveries that approximate a revival of the emotions common during adolescence. Very often, the expectant mother may seem self-absorbed in her own subjective experience. She has seemingly become totally entranced by the changes occurring to her body.

By the second trimester, a significant shift will be noted in the content of the parents' fantasies, particularly, investigators have noted, in the woman's thoughts. At this time, the growing evidence of the birth becomes inescapable to the woman, as well as the infant-to-be's extended family. Fetal movements make the woman aware of the presence of the infant within her. Over and above these physiological markers, modern technology (in the form of ultrasound, amniocentesis, and chromosome examinations) makes the reality of the infant even more palpable. As the infant's presence becomes even more evident, a change in the prospective parents' subjective experience transpires. Parents now focus on the role they will shortly assume. Mental representations in which the expectant parents symbolically acclimate and psychologically adjust to their imminent role as caregivers now become dominant.

As the third trimester begins, yet another change may be observed. Now the expectant mother begins to negotiate the inevitable physical separation that will occur with the birth. The imminence of this separation may at the same time precipitate some frightening thoughts. It is not unusual for mothers-to-be at this time, for example, to fantasize about giving birth to a handicapped child or of dying in childbirth. This is perhaps less fantasy than reality-gauging: Since multiple-handicap children are born yearly, and the still only partially understood mechanisms of chemically mutagenic and teratogenic factors are rife, it is not untoward to have an eye on potential complications of birth or defects in the child-to-be.

Whereas these thoughts may indicate that the pregnancy is proceeding adaptively, other fantasies may suggest the presence of psychological conflict. These negative concerns may also presage a potentially dysfunctional relationship between caregiver and infant. For example, in the case discussed in chapter 4, a pregnant woman related a series of dreams dominated by images of mutilation and violence. The dreams occurred early in the pregnancy, at a time when one might have expected the woman to be celebrating the changes in her body and looking forward to the birth with eager anticipation. These distorted conceptualizations deviating so dramatically from the fantasies one might expect with a psychologically healthy mother enabled the therapist to diagnose the potential for abuse of the unborn infant and to initiate a treatment protocol designed to avert any similar episodes in the future.

In another case, a 35-year-old, first-time expectant mother in her seventh month of pregnancy consulted a therapist because of "disturbing dreams." The patient told the therapist that she had become increasingly nervous as her delivery date approached. She reported several dreams in which she remembered her intense "loneliness" as a child; when her parents had moved to a new state, she and her sister had had no friends. Shortly thereafter, her mother had died of cancer. In effect, she had not fully mourned these earlier losses in her life; in the case under discussion, they were now materially interfering with her ability to begin representing her infant.

Conflict that interferes with the dyadic relationship may be traced to an even more remote source than the ideations of pregnancy itself. At any given point, conflict from the mother's past may interfere with her predictions of the infant's imminent development. Under normal circumstances, mother and infant will forge an adaptive relationship; the infant will likely achieve most maturational milestones on schedule and appear to be more or less in optimal condition developmentally. At some point during the pregnancy or thereafter, however, the mother may experience a vague dissatisfaction that prevents her from representing the infant's developmental status. Even when this sense of discontent is not obvious, diffuse negative feelings may work to hinder the future dyadic interaction. With the passage of time, the mother's dissatisfaction if left unresolved gains momentum. The "unfullfill-ing relationship" with the infant causes her to ignore the infant's intentional communications and to rely increasingly on her own (distorted) expecta-tions. By replacing the infant's expectations with her own, the mother im-pedes her ability to relate to the infant in an objective fashion. Out of touch, literally and proverbially, with her infant, she no longer strives to harmonize her emotions and behaviors with those of the infant. Rather, her impaired impressions are imposed on the infant, effectively blocking her perception of the infant's objective status from her consciousness. In one case, a teenaged mother was monitored both during pregnancy and after the birth. Although the mother seemed to be adjusting well to her new status, she often had dif-ficulty representing the imminent skills the infant would ordinarily exhibit. When the infant was 6 weeks old, the young mother unexpectedly offered this vivid and disturbing portrait of the upcoming dyadic relationship. "She's being real bad, refusing to listen as I tell her how to walk . . . I want her to listen to me. When she's older, I think I'll have to beat her if she's this bad." Asked what had provoked this outburst, the young mother declared, "She hits me with her fists and doesn't listen to me, so I just put her in her crib and let her stay there." Extensive psychotherapy was needed in this case to help the mother understand how she had allowed her own conflict to obliterate her objective view of the infant.

Strong prenatal fantasies can also lead to conflict. A climax of sorts is reached once the baby is born. At that time, the new parents must reconcile their vision of the imagined infant who dominated the trimester fantasies during the pregnancy with the real baby who has entered the world. Reconciliation can be a complicated process, and some new mothers must endure a period of "mourning the fantasied baby" before they can psycho-logically embrace the real one. On occasion, this process actually disrupts the parent's psychological equilibrium. Unable to relinquish her vision of the "constructed" infant, she approaches her relationship with the real baby ten-uously, carrying an unrealistic load of psychological baggage. The tempo-rary incapacity to view the infant objectively undermines the mother's em-pathy for the infant's current needs. As time passes and the mother's failure to accept the actual infant objectively persists, family confusion ensues. This situation is potentially damaging for the infant who receives no stable con-sensual validation of developmental progress. Lacking maternal guidance, the infant endures an unpredictable existence devoid of interpersonal responsive mutuality. At the core of the problem is a dyadic relationship that has already begun to wither before it has gotten off the ground. Parents and infants alike are unable to coordinate their subjective representations with objective information: Maladaptive interpersonal responses routinely surface in this atmosphere as conflict (between the depressed parent's inability to give versus the infant's thirst for mutuality) intrudes on the dyadic relationship.

The previewing process is invariably affected by changes experienced by the parent. Most adaptive parents automatically devise previewing experiences when they sense that the infant is ready to assert new developmental skills or tasks. When conflict emerges, however, the parent stonily tends to ignore the infant's signs of readiness. Instead, the parent interacts with the infant as if he or she were an object to be molded to the personal parental whims. Adaptive developmental trends are thwarted as the parent perverts the relationship with the infant to perpetuate conflict stemming from earlier unresolved, traumatic losses in her own life. If this pattern persists, the infant may exhibit several responses. Initially, the infant may seek to escape from the mother using the only means at his or her disposal. This may involve a retreat by the infant to a state of hungry, inchoate withdrawal in which self-regulatory capacities are at risk (Barr, 1990). From the infant's point of view, the goal is to escape from a nonresponsive environment in which developmental progress is at best ignored and at worst purposefully stifled. At some point the infant may even find it so difficult to pursue maturational advancement that a condition of helplessness becomes preeminent. This resignation is marked by the infant's further withdrawal from participation in the receding world of interpersonal events.

The infant's disposition and sense of motivation are modulated by innate temperamental proclivities and attachment patterns. With regard to temperament, most researchers agree that the concept refers to an individual's general disposition or behavioral style (Thomas & Chess, 1984). Whereas the individual's personality may change during the course of life, temperamental proclivities tend to be consistent from an early age (Goldsmith & Campos, 1982). Nine distinct dimensions of temperament have been identified, including activity level, rhythmicity, approach or withdrawal, adaptability, threshold of responsiveness, intensity of reaction, quality of mood, distractibility, and attention span or persistence. These dimensions tend to cluster into three identifiable temperamental groups or typologies: difficult, easy, and slow to warm up (Thomas, Chess, & Birch, 1968, 1970).

The environment shapes the infant's innate disposition that, in turn, exerts influence on the environment. This interplay of nature versus nurture appears to be in accordance with Henderson's (1982) notions of "goodness of fit" and "poorness of fit." "Goodness of fit" refers to the infant's sense of consonance with the environment, whereas "poorness of fit" has been associated with infant nonresponsivity to the environment. For example, the infant's temperament may either facilitate or hinder his or her ability to perceive and respond to contingencies. If temperamental proclivities undermine the ability to experience developmental phenomena optimally, infant apathy may ensue.

Another scenario is also possible. The infant may mature precociously to avoid the emotional distress caused by interacting with the mother. If this occurs, it is likely that the infant's enthusiasm for experiencing imminent milestones and for exploring the mysteries indigenous to developmental change will be severely compromised at best. In both these scenarios, psychotherapeutic intervention is warranted. The conflict being experienced by the mother will need to be resolved before adaptive patterns can reasonably be reintroduced into the dyadic relationship. During this period, previewing exercises encourage the mother to regain enthusiasm for interaction with the infant. In one case, for example, previewing exercises helped the mother to recognize that her infant was on the verge of crawling. She was subsequently able to devise an exercise to introduce the infant to the sensations of full-fledged crawling. By successfully previewing this skill with the infant, and by reaping the full reciprocal enthusiasm of her attuned infant, the mother regained her exuberance for predicting imminent developmental change.

Depressive symptomatology may also emerge because of the infant's attachment behaviors. Attachment refers to the balance between behaviors that lead the infant away from the mother and toward exploration and behaviors that draw infant and mother together to promote the nurturance of the infant's skills (Ainsworth & Bell, 1979; Bowlby, 1982). A stable pattern of attachment behavior is generally documented to emerge by the age of 9 to 12 months and may be measured by Ainsworth's strange situation (Ainsworth & Wittig, 1969). Secure attachment to the caregiver has been related to self-esteem, the ability to explore the environment, independence, and a sustained capacity to withstand fear and lack of expected response ("failure") (Arend, Gove, & Sroufe, 1979).

Numerous factors can undermine the attachment relationship between mother and infant. For example, separation from the caregiver has been found to precipitate a dramatic emotional response in the infant, as well as physiological disturbances (Kalin & Carnes, 1984; Spitz & Wolf, 1946). Difficulties in the attachment process may be most evident among children with depressed parents. Gaensbauer et al. (1984) reported aberrant attachment patterns among the toddlers of depressed parents, while Radke-Yarrow, Cummings, Kuczynski, and Chapman (1985) found that more than twice as many children of parents with major depression exhibited an insecure attachment than children with normal parents. Atypical patterns of attachment can surface early in life and have been encountered among the infants of the postpartum depressed (Kennerly & Gath, 1985; Zaslow, Pederson, Cain, Suwalsky, & Kramer, 1985).

## Dysphoria During the Postpartum Period

Postpartum depression is one of the conditions that may exert substantial and potentially irrevocable damage on the early relationship between infant and caregiver. Recent investigations suggest that a majority of women worldwide experience some form of negative emotional episode in the period immediately following the birth. These episodes may endure for a few days or may linger for several months. Typical symptoms include an acute affective lability: Extreme happiness may surface at one moment, for example, but almost immediately thereafter, the woman may plummet precipitously into the depths of gloom and despair. Other women report a pervasive sense of apathy. They display minimal interest in or curiosity about the infant and appear to lack energy for performing the most basic nurturing tasks. In one case, a 24-year-old mother requested counseling with her 3-day-old son. Most striking was the mother's physiological apathy toward the infant. She did not try to establish eye contact with her son, engage him in vocalizations, or hold him in a supportive fashion. Absence of these intuitive behaviors frequently signifies the presence of postpartum depression. The therapist is here called upon to diagnose serious postpartum disorder. Infants of mothers who have suffered an episode of postpartum depression have thus been observed to be more insecurely attached to their mothers, more likely to exhibit mild behavior problems, and to perform more poorly on object-concept tasks at 18 months—even though the mother recovered from her depression as early as 3 months after the birth (Murray, 1991).

Therapists should possess a clear-cut understanding of three issues relevant to the treatment of postpartum depression. First, the therapist needs to become proficient at diagnosing the condition. Key symptoms, such as intermittent weepiness, dramatic mood fluctuations, pervasive apathy, or psychotic thinking, need to be identified rapidly and differentiated from the normal emotional vicissitudes that occur following a regular birth. Of crucial importance is the ability to diagnose whether the mother's depression is interfering with the infant's adaptation and quickly to ascertain the magnitude of this interference. Other diagnostic indicators of postpartum depression include a range of negative presences: the absence of intuitive phenomena—such as reciprocity, mutuality, empathy, and affect attunement—typically manifested by adaptive caregivers. The therapist should also determine whether or not there are signs of an incipient emotional bond that may be detected within the dyad. Does the infant establish eye contact with the mother? Does the mother demonstrate appropriate intuitive behavior, such as cradling the infant in her arms or vocally cuing the infant? Each of these behaviors reveals the quality of the bonding that exists between the pair. Interviewing the caregiver, in addition to observing unmediated interaction between mother and child, can also provide the therapist with important insight about the presence of postpartum depression.

In addition, the infant develops both primary and secondary thought processes during early development. How do primary and secondary mental processes interact? As categorization emerges (Bornstein, 1985), the infant begins to organize sensory information. During the transition from representation to the enactment that takes place through a previewing exercise, images are formed, events are organized, and object representations are constructed in relation to the needs they satisfy. External experience promotes further categorization. As a result, the emergence of a reality orientation eases the transition from primary (emotional/perceptual) processing to secondary (cognitive) processing. It is likely that emotional experiences first internalized by the primary process are later recategorized and relegated hierarchically to the secondary process. Conversely, perceptual information derived from reality that was first processed by the secondary process may be reorganized into primary process categories.

Examples of this transition are as follows: Josh's mother told us how she had discovered that he was aware of discrepancies in everyday life. "This morning I came out of the bathroom with a towel around my head, and he burst into tears; I realized that I looked totally different to him with the towel—and that it was as though a stranger were coming at him."

Peter and his family had taken a trip to California when he was just 1 year old. They left the family dog—to whom he was very attached—at a neighbor's. "Poor Peter was inconsolable; he kept saying, 'Kay, Kay' (his name is Clay), and crying. I brought over another dog for him to pet, but he cried louder, and said over and over, 'Not Kay, no Kay.'"

Jeanne described her 7-week-old daughter's growing awareness that her fussing sounds, when she was hungry, would bring her mother to feed her. "We're communicating more now. I notice that after she starts fussing, because she's hungry, there's a little delay. She cries 4 seconds later than she used to. It's as though she's learned that I will come, that she can wait longer, knowing I'll come and feed her."

Gradual development of the self is posited to emerge from the reciprocity and balance between primary and secondary process. Achieving this fine balance is most likely facilitated by the caregiver's previewing behaviors. Previewing enables the infant to validate categorization, to explore perceptual material, and to experiment with symbolic representations of imminent skill safely. Indeed, previewing significantly assists the infant in evolving a coherent biographical script, a meaningful "story" with sequence, plot, and action (Schank & Abelson, 1977). If the caregiver fails to engage in previewing because of depression, for example, the infant may have difficulty distinguishing different kinds of perceptual stimuli. Perceptions of the world are then likely to become either highly literal or overly symbolic. Both extremes frustrate optimal adaptive development.

Whenever postpartum depression is present, the therapist's duty is to devise strategies for addressing the infant's needs while the mother is undergoing treatment. Clearly, the mother's presence alone may not in this circumstance ensure that the infant receives adequate care: During these early weeks of life, the infant requires an alert and attuned caregiver to nurture the newborn's basic physiological needs, and postpartum depression strips the mother of her alertness and attunement to others' needs, even her own. As the weeks progress, the infant also needs a sensitive caregiver capable of providing adequate stimulation and of responding sufficiently to subtle developmental changes. If the mother is incapable of performing these tasks, the therapist would be well-advised to recommend a surrogate until the mother's depressive mood abates. Psychotherapeutic interventions in cases of postpartum depression should enable the mother to become more attuned to the effect of her moods on the infant. Moreover, therapists should assess whether the use of concomitant medication is indicated.

Short-term psychotherapy may be especially beneficial in cases of postpartum depression because the strategies are designed to speed the rapid abatement of symptoms and to guide the sufferer toward resumption of normal functioning. This form of treatment results in behavioral changes that may be noted after the first few sessions. Indeed, half of all patients receiving short-term psychotherapy show improvement by the eighth session (MacKenzie, 1988). Some studies have reported effectiveness with short-term strategies after only seven sessions (Bentovim & Kinston, 1978; Kinston & Bentovim, 1990; Orlinsky & Howard, 1986; Proskauer, 1971; Shapiro & Shapiro, 1982; Smith et al., 1980), findings that highlight and endorse the expediency of this model.

The following vignette describes how dysfunctional responses may emerge when the mother fails to reconcile the thought-about baby with the real one. Steve and Martha, first-time expectant parents in their early 20s, had joined a support group during Martha's pregnancy. The expectant mother had no males left on her side of the family, and two of Steve's brothers had been killed in a car accident. Because of these earlier losses, Martha told the group that the couple was secretly hoping for a boy, although she noted that a healthy girl would also be welcome. The couple asked that the gender of the child not be divulged during the various pregnancy assessments they undertook. In spite of Martha's declaration that she would be "as happy" with a little girl as with a little boy, the group members pointed out that she repeatedly spoke about the infant using a male pronoun. "He moved an awful lot last night and kept me up late," she would say. The group also found it curious that the couple had only selected male names. "We'll get around to choosing girls' names soon," the mother said. "We just haven't had the chance." When Martha gave birth to a girl, she spoke of her extreme sense of disappointment. She told the group that she felt as if the baby boy she had previously envisioned had been "taken away" from her and "a stranger" substituted in his place. While still in the hospital after the birth, she occasionally joked with the nurse by saying, "I thought I had a boy. Why are you giving me a girl?" (while gazing away from the baby's face).

The couple was referred for parent-infant psychotherapy in light of their inability to exhibit adaptive interactional patterns with the infant. Over a period of 4 weeks using a regimen of short-term psychotherapy, Martha recovered. She was finally able to fully acknowledge and relinquish her relationship with the gestational thought infant. Moreover, she then began addressing the little girl's developmental changes in an adaptive fashion. Thus the mother was able to relinquish her own unconsummated need (the *desire* to have a son) and replace it with the objective realities of the situation (her infant's status as a girl).

## The Paradox of Normal Development

Another illustration of how psychopathology may interrupt the rhythms of a healthy dyadic relationship involves adaptive caregivers. Paradoxically, such mothers may develop a conflict precisely because they are so sensitive to the developmental trends of their infants. In these cases, the mother engages in previewing exercises designed to practice prospective developmental skills with the infant. These mothers, as opposed to many maladaptive parents, find the caregiving experience highly rewarding. Adaptive mothers welcome the opportunity to become involved in the infant's development and find the tasks of daily caregiving to be enormously rewarding. Shortly after giving birth, they establish an intimate form of mother-infant bond that enables them to interact and attach meaning to the infant's intentional communications. Until well into the first year of life, the infant depends almost entirely on the parents to fulfill all basic physiological needs. As the intimacy between the members of the dyad deepens, however, parents may also arrive at some sobering conclusions about the outcome of the developmental process. They gradually realize that the more they encourage the infant's efforts, paradoxically, the greater the infant's tendency to assert autonomy. The process of achieving full autonomy is, of course, a quite lengthy one.

At a certain point, however, the infant's efforts to assert autonomy may be interpreted as a threat. Sometimes the emerging autonomy may emerge in the form of a skill that has symbolic implications for the caregiver. Regardless of the developmental skill that triggers the parent's awareness, however, the fact remains that the caregiver is suddenly sensitized to the implications developmental progress has for the dyadic relationship. Upon being questioned, such mothers note that they are now acutely sensitive to the changes of imminent development. In particular, they are concerned that the intimacy they previously enjoyed with the infant may be altered and even disrupted. A key word here is *may*. Suddenly, a mother who was highly adept at predicting outcomes becomes confused, her new anxiety attributable to the uncertainty she now associates with the infant's growth. Will the previous closeness she enjoyed with the infant diminish because of developmental changes or will she be able somehow to preserve the intimacy, despite the infant's burgeoning autonomy?

As a result of these realizations, the mother's attitude toward the infant undergoes a dramatic transformation. In some cases, the mother attempts to rein in development, as if freezing the infant figuratively will serve to stem the tide of maturational progress. In other cases, the mother paradoxically pushes the infant ahead developmentally in order to urge precocious development. This response, attributable to her fears that an alteration in the relationship with the infant will soon sever the intimacy of the dyad, makes her precipitously thrust the infant beyond her orbit of control to elude the slow anguish of separation. Finally, in those cases where the caregiver may be cognizant of her reaction to the infant's burgeoning development, she may then compound the conflict by experiencing guilt about her sabotaging the advancement of her own child. This form of guilt may quickly progress to full-fledged depression. Both these attitudes are psychologically detrimental, since they foist the parent's preconceived notions onto the child rather than allowing the child to assert skills at the child's own pace. It is vital to affirm, in other words, that each child is an individual with unique needs and that special strategies for interacting with each infant are necessary (Landry & Chapieski, 1989; Stern & Karraker, 1989). Paradoxically, often the most sensitive caregivers experience great trauma both at expected as well as unexpected vicissitudes of development. Treatment here focuses on encouraging the mother to reexamine her relationship with the infant. In the therapeutic setting, these caregivers may be helped to recognize that, although infant development results in some autonomy and separation, maturational skills also concomitantly promote more sophisticated forms of communication that probably foster greater intimacy. Inappropriate responsivity to the infant's cues is not limited to mothers, of course; measurements of changes in first-time fathers interacting with their newborn infants show that a similar proportion of paternal figures is also sensitive to the infant's responses during interactions with the child (Jones & Thomas, 1989).

Among the maturational attainments that may be particularly significant signals of a diminishing or, at least, altering intimacy in the dyad are weaning, walking, and—especially—the advent of language. Chapter 6 discusses the case of a mother with a 9-month-old daughter who lapsed into a major depressive episode when her infant exhibited weaning behavior and turned away from the breast. The incident was especially painful for the mother who had previously experienced an extraordinary sensitivity to her daughter's needs. In particular, breast-feeding her daughter had been a time of great emotional satisfaction for the mother, fostering an intimacy she had come to cherish. This mother had also begun to prepare for weaning, commenting that she knew how important it was for her child to be allowed the independence of the bottle. Nevertheless, despite her preparedness, the mother's depression was precipitated when the infant unexpectedly weaned herself by intentionally turning away from the breast. The mother's grief at this event was so acute that short-term psychotherapy was strongly advised. Shortly after entering treatment, the mother remembered a series of events from her own childhood that involved episodes of loss. Gradually, the mother realized that she feared losing the intimacy she had established with her daughter as a consequence of the weaning behavior, and that the real pain she experienced was unrelated to her new infant but recalled unresolved childhood trauma that had been reignited by current circumstance.

Analyzing how conflict may develop in a mother-infant dyad requires sensitivity to the paradox of the developmental process. This paradox may be summarized as: mother and infant grow together in order to grow apart. The close dyadic relationship that fosters adaptive interaction also enables the infant to gain sufficient autonomy to move toward independent functioning. A therapeutic strategy that can be applied for interpreting and handling this paradox is previewing. When used adaptively, previewing helps both parent and infant appreciate that for optimal growth a delicate balance must be maintained between intimacy and autonomy. On one level, the intimacy of the dyad is a gratifying interpersonal experience; if the mother clings to this intimacy by reining in the infant's proclivities for advancement, however, the interaction may grow distorted. If efforts to preclude the infant from further natural progress are perpetuated, autonomous functioning may eventually be thwarted, and the infant's desire to explore and rehearse upcoming developmental skills will be stunted. In contrast, if the mother is overly challenged by the implications of autonomy, she may seek to unwontedly accelerate the infant's progress, thereby depriving him or her of the needed supportive intimacy of the dyadic relationship.

## Abuse and/or Neglect

Another situation that may seriously threaten the dyadic rapport involves abusive or neglectful behavior by a caregiver. As researchers have become more sophisticated in detecting these impaired responses, they also have become more adept at recognizing subtle variations on these conditions

(Harper, 1991; Lanktree, Briere, & Zaidi, 1991). For example, examining family structure is helpful for diagnosing abuse, since families in which abuse occurs tend to be less organized than nonabusive families (Cappell & Heiner, 1990; Long & Jackson, 1991). Emotional neglect is sometimes more difficult to detect (Trad, 1987). Therapists should here be alert to affective surliness or apathy by the infant. Equally significant is the child's inability to articulate appropriate emotions in the context of particular situations or an incapacity to display a broad spectrum of emotions in a flexible fashion. Such children often fail to establish eye contact and engage in minimal vocalizations. Infants not exposed to a stimulating environment may exhibit signs of withdrawal by turning away listlessly when stimulation is offered, as if their desire for interaction with the world has atrophied or been severely blunted. Infants subjected to emotional neglect may also display problematic feeding patterns that result from a deprivation of emotional attention (Chatoor, 1989). Important clues to distant eating disorders often appear here at this "deprivation nexus." Certainly, a well-supported, warmly attended child will not as readily develop a distorted body image or eating disorder as a neglected or emotionally mishandled child.

A home environment typified by deprivation lacks the life-affirming qualities necessary to promote an infant's optimal development. As a result, the infant is precluded from experiencing maturational events and environmental challenges as opportunities to assert new skills and consolidating the intimacy with the caregiver. Instead, interaction becomes a barren experience from which the infant attempts to escape either by retreat into a domain of anomic nonresponsivity or by the frantic gestures of precocious manifestations. Most poignant of all, the caregiver's role as the figure who invigorates the infant's world perspective declines.

A wide variety of other factors may also contribute to dysfunction in the dyad. Some of these factors inherent in the parent's psychological status include parental psychopathology, marital discord, and the parental inability to acknowledge the child's burgeoning autonomy (Crittenden, 1985a,b; Jenkins & Smith, 1991; Stern & Karraker, 1990). Among factors that may precipitate dysfunction in the dyad and are inherent to the child's constitution are prematurity, physical illness, the need for hospitalization, and the presence of handicapping conditions. A related consideration that implicates both infant and caregiver involves the infant's unique self-regulatory capacities (Barr, 1990). Episodes of excessive fussiness exhibited by a colicky infant, for example, may strain the dyadic relationship. Or a mother with a "slow-to-warm" temperament may resent the "difficult" disposition exhibited by her infant and manifest her resentment in the form of neglect or abuse. Each of these factors may provoke similar forms of deprivation in the early life relationship between caregiver and infant.

## Marital Discord

Marital distress is among the conditions that may exert debilitating effects on the infant's early development. Statistics in this area are startling, reflecting a dramatic transformation in the configuration of the nuclear family over the past few decades. Single-parent households are becoming increasingly prevalent, and, in the majority of these cases, the parent with custody is the mother. Conflict over child rearing in split marriages or unions has been associated with physical and verbal abuse as the parents struggle over the children in a fierce, ongoing psychological tug of war (Edelson, Eisikovits, Guttmann, & Sela, 1991). Marital discord may also surface if disparities exist between the legal agreement and mother's expectations of the father's support and his actual support (Nicolson, 1990). Where no such conflict exists, often the father has simply abandoned any financial and emotional support of the family. Prior to separation, children tend to exhibit a full spectrum of behavioral problems, and postdivorce family relationships often require emotional adjustment (Tschann, Johnston, Kline, & Wallerstein, 1990). Researchers have also found evidence indicating that ongoing conflict, rather than divorce itself, triggers behavioral and emotional problems in children (Sharpley & Webber, 1989). Moreover, the sense of loss that accompanies divorce may further exacerbate behavior problems, guilt, and anxiety (Healy, Malley, & Stewart, 1990).

Although the prevalence of divorce has led therapists to devise strategies for coping with this type of family crisis, it should be stressed that family breakups have a devastating emotional impact on the child that may linger for years. Although salvaging the family unit and resolving marital distress remain the foremost goals of treatment, the therapist should not lose sight of the fact that the psychological and physical welfare of the children remain of the utmost concern. In addition, marital distress is frequently disguised within the family. That is, families often present for treatment because a particular child in the family is "causing problems." Frequently, the child has become the "scapegoat" for all the painful emotional issues that family members have difficulty confronting directly. Using one child as a scapegoat is a convenient strategy that allows parents to avoid dealing with their own problems. In effect, the scapegoated child comes to embody all of the difficulties confronting the family.

In one case, parents in their 20s sought counseling because of the tantrums of their 2-year-old son. Apparently, the tantrums had increased when the mother became pregnant with her second child. Sessions with the entire family revealed that the 2-year-old son was often ignored by his mother. In effect, the marriage was failing, and the mother had become pregnant in a desperate effort to hold the family together. The 2-year-old became a repository for the hostility both parents had for each other but were unwilling or unable to express overtly. In essence, the child became their scapegoat.

To diagnose problems such as marital discord, the therapist needs to acquire a longitudinal perspective on the life cycle of the particular family. Some theorists recommend that the therapist assess emotional communication within the family for at least three generations (McGoldrick & Carter, 1982). Constructing a family tree that focuses on the psychological patterns that have characterized past generations is recommended. Moreover, the therapist should evaluate both horizontal and vertical patterns of interaction between and among family members. Vertical interaction refers to patterns transmitted between generations. In contrast, concerns arising within one generation of the family unit—such as the birth of a new child, the death of a parent, or the departure of an adolescent for college—are issues that lie along a family's horizontal life span.

One method for grasping the key issues influencing a particular family is to focus on transitional periods between different stages of familial development (Fincham, Beach, & Bradbury, 1989). During these transitional periods, family members tend to reevaluate their identities and reformulate their roles in the family order. The underlying motives for the behavior of family members become accentuated and exaggerated during times of transition, since the family's future is called into question. Families that lack strategies for adaptive coping will more likely exhibit dysfunction during these periods than at others. In fact, it is common for individuals to seek psychotherapeutic assistance, particularly during these periods.

One of the seminal transition periods in the life span of a family occurs with the birth of an infant. If a mother with a new infant enters treatment, it is probable that she or another member of her immediate family is experiencing the transition to parenthood as a form of developmental crisis. As mentioned, in these cases, the therapist should begin the assessment by obtaining a full psychological history of at least three generations of the family. Emotional material, including descriptions of the relationships between siblings, temperamental dispositions, and distinctive personality traits of family members, should be reviewed. Analyzing how each set of parents (great-grandparents, grandparents, parents) has negotiated various transitional periods during their life cycles and examining their ability to cope with successive infant births are also important.

As will be seen in chapter 7, these strategies help family members to acknowledge and handle the source of the conflict.

## Lack of Social Support

Of infant populations most susceptible to depressive phenomena, the offspring of depressive parents carry the highest risk (Trad, 1986). Aside from a possible genetic predisposition to affective disorder, these infants experience a nurturing environment—or, rather, an antinurturing environment—that plays a seminal role in the onset of depressive symptomatology during infancy and early childhood. If the primary caregiver is depressed, this symptomatology will almost inevitably filter into and become a key component of the dyadic interaction (Fogel, Diamond, Langhorst, & Demos, 1982). Eventually, the infant cannot help but transfer the parent's hopeless, or defeated, perspective not only to interactions with the caregiver but also to others in the environment. If all the infant has experienced in its formative years is suffused in attitudinal defeat, the universe of affective referents is defined in this matrix, ensuring the continuance of this mode until such time as the child or adult experiences psychotherapeutic intervention of perhaps a radical order to undo the negative affect.

Exacerbating this situation is a probable lack of real social support—the combination of resources that the community, social networks, and confiding partners offer in terms of perceived and actual support to individuals and families. The degree to which the individual has access to these resources represents the person's level of social support (Lin, 1986). Dolgoff and Feldstein (1984) adopt a similar definition, observing that social support also encompasses the available nonprofit societal facilities that are engineered specifically to alleviate distress or ameliorate crisis situations. When therapy functions as a social support, it is acting, first, outside of its rightful province, and second, as a reflection of the paucity of available proper and standard societal supports. Because the level of social support has been tied to the emotional status of the dyad, therapists should assess this factor in families that present for treatment and ensure that families lacking adequate social support receive these services.

The foregoing discussion strongly suggests that previewing contributes to adaptive growth within the dyad. In most instances, this is the case as mother and infant successfully negotiate new developmental challenges. The process of maturation is highly complex, however, and occasionally the mother-infant rapport may go astray, culminating in conflict.

To understand how conflicted perceptions and behavior patterns become entrenched in the mother-infant relationship, it is important to grasp the fundamental *temporal paradox* inherent in developmental change. The acquisition of language, for example, may lead to outcomes that appear to be contradictory and conflictual for the parent. On one level, the infant will be motivated to consolidate intimacy with the mother by using verbal skills, yet speech also liberates the infant to communicate with others besides the mother. As a result, acquiring this developmental skill may lead to both greater intimacy and simultaneously greater independence, specifically from the mother. If these "paradoxical" results do not collide, the dyadic rapport will survive intact and, indeed, even be enhanced. If, however, the infant or mother cannot arrive at an accommodation of competing outcomes, conflict may ensue.

## THE EMERGENCE OF CONFLICT

At any given point, clinical experience has demonstrated that the inability to engage in adaptive previewing is often one sign of conflict. A defect may surface at any point in the previewing process—during the representation, the formulation of an enactment exercise, or the termination of the previewing episode. Moreover, although conflict may originate with either mother or infant, it may then become indigenous to the dyadic interaction. With conflict suffusing the relationship, the mother may be unable to represent upcoming maturational change in the infant; she then becomes emotionally unavailable to engage in enactment episodes or may lack the sensitivity necessary to help the infant to negotiate the transition to different developmental states. Determining whether the infant is the source of conflict may be more problematic since the infant cannot yet fully express himself or herself. Careful scrutiny is then needed to determine whether the infant possesses a difficult temperament or other negative characteristic that obstructs adaptive interaction. Interactional conflict may be diagnosed based on careful observations of dyadic exchange between mother and infant. The lack of laggardliness or impedance intuitive behaviors suggests the presence of conflict.

Conflict in the dyad naturally results in distorted communication between mother and infant. With the passage of time, the infant internalizes the sense that he or she cannot depend on the mother as a secure base from which to master change and formulate notions of reality. These feelings undermine the infant's capacity to predict a positive outcome. Instead, the infant experiences sensations of uncontrollability, negative affect, and diminished self-esteem (Fagen & Ohr, 1985; Trad, 1986). Infants may, however, perceive themselves as being responsible for negative outcomes; they may furthermore feel helpless to achieve positive outcomes (Gunnar, 1990). Gradually, these perceptions of helplessness and lack of control are incorporated into the infant's sense of self (Trad, 1987). The infant's global experience of negative affective states may thwart motivation to seek prosocial interactions (Spitz & Wolf, 1946). In sum, a diminished capacity to self-regulate promotes a vicious cycle of self-defeat, greatly damaging the infant's ability to predict an adaptive future and a corrected picture of his or her place in the external world.

## THE SOURCE OF CONFLICT

How can a process that stems from such positive impulses culminate in this stagnation? The answer may lie in the paradoxes inherent in developmental change. Specifically, as noted, all developmental change has the potential of upsetting the delicate equilibrium that exists in the mother-infant relationship. Developmental advance tends both to enhance dyadic intimacy and to promote autonomy, to foster proximity-seeking while encouraging exploration. Unless the mother understands that these seemingly paradoxical tendencies call for nurturance, she may thwart the infant's adaptive development. In some instances, the mother may come to believe that developmental advance is benefiting the infant by conferring advanced autonomy but is depriving her of expected closeness and intimacy with her infant. Based on this distorted perception, she may attempt either to undermine further maturational progress or to push the infant precociously away from her, speeding the process of distancing she fears is inevitable.

Developmental achievement also embodies a temporal paradox. In order to help the infant to negotiate new skills, the mother will use only her own memories of the past to assist the infant to master present capacities and formulate predictions concerning the future. Yet, however fluid the mother's mental flow among the memories and predictions of the past may be, present and future behavior may paradoxically trigger conflict. Conflict often intrudes when the mother interjects unresolved conflict from the past (her own or both her's and the infant's) into a representation of the future. During previewing episodes, mother and infant contrast predicted and real outcomes, helping the dyad to select an appropriate course of action. If a negative representation is forcibly interjected from the mother's past, however, some of the infant's options for the future will automatically be foreclosed. Development is a cumulative process, and, therefore, past skill is needed to progress to future capacities. Paradoxically, if conflict has marred the acquisition of skill, the past ironically becomes an impediment to smooth developmental advance. Advance of course is still possible, but it is impaired and snagged by the child's efforts to overcome the roadblocks presented by nonoptimal representation.

These descriptions of the paradox of development suggest that the introduction of conflict into the dyadic exchange is often the fault of the mother. However, the infant may also be the agent of conflict. The infant, it will be remembered, possesses a broad spectrum of skills, such as amodal perception and categorization, used to enlarge the scope of his or her interactions that heighten awareness of the external world. Paradoxically, however, these capacities may also heighten the infant's sensitivity to distress as well as to harmony during dyadic interaction. The lack of harmony may occasion infant uncertainty and lead to either retreat from interaction or to aggressive forward movement to preclude further interaction with the "distressing" mother.

Finally, the previewing process itself may be paradoxical. The first time a new skill is practiced by mother and infant, the dyadic interaction is fresh and spontaneous. If previewing episodes are then repeated in a rote fashion, however, without accommodating incremental growth and maturation in the infant and variations in the environment, rigidity enters the dyadic interaction, and the infant may eventually practice the new developmental skill with a decreased potential for successful adaptation.

## EXAMPLES OF CONFLICT

The following three examples clarify how the paradox of development may disrupt the mother-infant dyadic interaction. The first case describes a flaw in the mother's tendency both to represent adaptive future outcomes for the infant and to design previewing enactments to facilitate the optimal infant development. As noted, representation of the infant begins during pregnancy and intensifies during the second trimester as perceptions of the infant's body assume greater importance. From their experience and reactions to fetal movement, expectant mothers begin to construct an entire picture of the infant. Thus is the imaginary child born. The expectant mother's relationship with the imagined infant reaches a climax at the time of delivery, when the mother must reconcile the image of her thought baby—a conglomeration of somatic impressions and her wishes—with the real baby who has been born. Reconciliation is an intricate process that may involve even mourning the loss of the fantasized baby. Sometimes new mothers are overwhelmed by this process. And in some cases, the mother may have difficulty reconciling discrepancies between the ideated baby and the real one.

An illustration involves a mother whose conflict from her own past significantly interfered with her ability to make objective predictions concerning her infant's future. Over time, the mother continued to overlook the infant's communications and relied increasingly on her own distorted expectations. Gradually, these expectations smothered the expectations she had of the infant. The mother no longer made the effort to harmonize her representations with those of the infant. Slowly, she imposed her distorted view on the infant, effectively obliterating the infant's objective status from her awareness. She also began to undermine the previewing process by devising enactments for upcoming skills well before the infant was ready to assert them. By ignoring the infant's cries and subtler protests, the mother transformed the infant into an object to mold to her whims. In most such cases, as one expects, the infant achieved the great majority of developmental milestones on schedule and was developmentally on target. Nevertheless, a long-buried conflict from the mother's childhood can be awakened when the infant begins to express or master a particular skill, such as walking. This new conflict will unexpectedly prevent the mother from accurately representing the infant's developmental status. This portrait characterizes how development may be thwarted and how the mother may use a current relationship (with her infant) to perpetuate or resolve conflict deriving from an earlier loss (in her own life) (Polan et al., 1991; Sturm & Drotar, 1991). Assuming that this pattern continues, the infant may be expected to exhibit some typical responses. First, the infant may seek to escape from the mother by retreating to a state of withdrawal, embarking on a path of self-delusion in which objective reality is fairly well obliterated from consciousness. Alternatively, the infant may be forced to develop *precociously* to cope with the demands of the failed relationship and merely to keep pace with the unmodulated mother's schedule of previewing and devising enactments. As an outcome of this problematic interaction, the infant's zest for predicting the future and enthusiastically exploring the mastery and mysteries of developmental change will be dampened and, with time, may entirely sour.

Ironically, the third common example of the paradox of development concerns the adaptive mother. Many such mothers report that the caregiving experience is highly rewarding. They display a keen attunement to the infant's cues; after the birth, they establish a complex communication system with the infant. As intimacy becomes more profound, however, the mother may reach some unwanted conclusions about the developmental process. She will realize that the more she encourages the infant's efforts, the greater the infant's assertion of autonomy. By the end of the first year of life, the infant will display diverse signs of autonomy, including rudimentary talking and walking. For some mothers, these skills become looming threats toward termination of the intimacy the dyad once enjoyed. One developmental event that may be especially symbolic of the end of dyadic intimacy is weaning, as discussed in the case study examined in chapter 6. This case captures the paradoxical nature of the developmental process and may be summarized as follows: Mother and infant grow together in order to grow apart. The emotional intimacy typical of unexceptional adaptive interaction promotes the necessary self-esteem that fuels the infant's autonomous functioning. Used adaptively, previewing helps both mother and infant to learn to appreciate that a delicate balance must be maintained between intimacy and autonomy. On the one hand, the dyad's intimacy results in an enormously pleasurable experience. But if the mother clings to the intimacy by reining in the infant's aborning developmental skills, the interaction may become distorted. If efforts to hold back the infant continue, the infant's autonomy may eventually be thwarted, and the infant's drive to predict the future stifled. On the other hand, should the mother become too excited with infant development, she may also deprive the infant of the intimacy needed for establishing an adaptive sense of self. Both attitudes embody the paradox of development.

THE CONSEQUENCES OF CONFLICT

In something of a vicious cycle, if the caregiver fails to provide the infant with sufficient support and modulated stimulation in the course of previewing, the infant may be unable to regulate the intra- and interpersonal experiences that developmental changes may precipitate in its relationship with the caregiver. Such experience of uncontrollability (chaotic environment) and fractionated support can lead to somatic, emotional, cognitive, and motivational deficits that severely hinder further adaptive interaction. The emergence of any or many of these deficits propels the infant in desperation to master maladaptive interactions. Rather than overcoming deficits, the infant may internalize these deficits into his or her sense of self. These deficits then stand a fair chance of becoming enshrined as permanent aspects of the self. In turn, this situation may then lead to abuse and neglect, maternal postpartum depression, and marital distress. Conversely, if the mother's previewing behaviors provide the infant with adequate means of predicting and coordinating new skills, however, potential developmental interference or conflict may be avoided; indeed, the infant will acquire a sense of competence and control over its own developmental destiny, as well as the confidence to master maturational challenge. To create an optimal relationship with the infant, therefore, the therapist should encourage caregivers in adaptive previewing with their infants.

Inadequate or faulty previewing may occur for a variety of reasons ranging from maternal depression to caregiver abuse and neglect to infant illness or a handicapping condition. Failure to experience previewing episodes in a consistent fashion before the infant is capable of representing symbolic thought may contribute to psychopathology or its analogs. Similarly, if an implied threat is communicated to the infant by the caregiver as a consequence of her own feelings of inadequacy from historical causes, the child may absorb the insecurity, tainting his or her future efforts at mastery. This kind of negative previewing may also force the child to exhibit stressful precocious behaviors during the relationship with the caregiver by manifesting maturational skills without being in any way prepared for their implications. Furthermore, lacking exposure to adaptive previewing, the infant naturally fails to attribute interpersonal significance to the particular achievement and entertains any attainment in confusing isolation. Without a clear recognition of his or her own achievements and ability to interact with others, the infant will have difficulty establishing a coherent relationship with other people and with the external world.

THE IMPORTANCE OF PSYCHOTHERAPY

But whereas missing or insufficient previewing can expose the infant to future psychopathology, *short-term* psychotherapy based on previewing may deter, prevent, or even overcome this outcome. One reason why previewing is so effective as an intervention technique is that it focuses attention on imminent events. The prospective approach of previewing alerts the therapist to the possible emergence of potential conflict in the mother even before any conflict is subjected to defensive operations and becomes entrenched within the dyadic relationship. Previewing focuses on the mother's perceptions of the future and permits the therapist to secure insight about the meaning these perceptions will eventually have on the prospective dyadic relationship. As a therapeutic strategy for preventing psychopathology, previewing enables the parent both to become attuned to her own perspective and the infant's and to integrate adaptive, growth-enhancing behaviors into her interaction with the infant. These gains argue persuasively for timely psychotherapeutic intervention well before the birth of the child, so as to prepare the ground for the substantial work ahead in previewing and to work out any unconscious conflict possibly obstructing the mother's full access to her empathic processes.

Previewing highlights the infant's role in the developmental journey. As a consequence, caregivers in treatment come to recognize that the infant is not merely an amalgam of parental expectations and delusional wishes but also is a unique creature capable of autonomously influencing the direction of representations and interactions. As such, the infant can, in ways, predict and refine future interactions, just as the mother can engage in behavior that indicates genuine mastery and self-regulation, thus validating clinical data that suggest infants are equipped with a broad spectrum of innate skills that assist them in navigating through the challenges posed by the world.

## Conclusion

As discussed, mental health professionals are becoming increasingly sensitive to the benefits of early intervention in mother-infant dyads. Indeed, early short-term intervention—especially during the infancy years—has been demonstrated to have remarkable effects, as well as to be a necessary step in light of the risk of early onset of psychopathological symptoms. The relationship between mother and infant—so fragile and, at the same time, so vital for the infant's future development—is responsive to a wide variety of intervention techniques designed to enhance rapport between the dyadic members. Moreover, certain specific conditions, such as maternal postpartum depression, marital discord affecting the family, familial abuse or neglect, and parental failure to acknowledge or encourage developmental change, tend to render the dyad susceptible to a psychopathological response. In addition, lack of adequate social support may exacerbate any of these situations, and other factors inherent to the infant, such as temperament and attachment behaviors, may interfere with functioning and warrant intervention. The most common situations that appear to promote a negative developmental response are childhood illness and hospitalization, such as keeping a newborn in a preemie ward, a handicapping condition, or a difficult infant temperament that is not fully understood or easily coped with by the parents.

Consequent to each of these situations, lack of intervention may result in a substantial impairment in the child's development. This impairment may be manifested by maladaptive behavior between mother and infant. Therapeutic observations of such a dyad will reveal the breakdown or absence of an attuned reciprocal exchange or of previewing episodes designed to introduce the infant to a new skill. The infant may instead seem apathetic, phlegmatic, lacking an appetite for developmental growth and exposure to new experience or, on the contrary, may exhibit precocious development indicative of a fruitless attempt to extricate himself or herself from the unfulfilling and demoralizing environment provided by the caregiver.

Caution is urged. This portrait of the dyad should not be based solely on an interview with the caregiver. Therapists need to immerse themselves in the dyadic interaction, observing discrete episodes of exchange between caregiver and infant, then analyzing these episodes on a moment-by-moment basis. Numerous aspects of this interaction should be evaluated, including the prevailing emotional tone, the presence of intuitive behaviors, secure attachment patterns, and overall enthusiasm at the infant's newly manifest developmental skills. Based on an assessment derived from a dyadic interview and observations, the therapist can formulate a preliminary diagnosis and begin administering strategies of short-term psychotherapy to enhance the rapport between parent and child and to foster adaptive development.

# CHAPTER 3

---

## *Working Through Developmental Conflict by Using Short-Term Psychotherapy*

---

S HORT-TERM PSYCHOTHERAPY has recently become a popular treatment protocol for achieving dramatic transformations in behavior within a relatively short time (Trad, 1991). Because, as the name implies, short-term techniques are designed to elicit adaptive behavior patterns fairly quickly, they may be especially appropriate for cases of parent-infant psychotherapy, in which adjustment to developmental change necessitates a rapid acclimation to new conditions.

The short-term model differs from the traditional approach in several respects. For example, traditional psychotherapy, with no time paradigm in the overall goal profile, posits that treatment could last for an indeterminate, often lengthy, period with no endpoint predetermined or, indeed, predictable. Under this format, the therapist acts as a neutral observer, while the patient is committed to divulging the minutiae of life's events, diligently working through resistance in order to explore avenues of conflict. The short-term process, by distinct contrast, is a pragmatic endeavor with the specific goal of effecting perceptible change or modification in interpersonal patterns. To expedite this process, the patient is encouraged to pursue conflict resolution actively, while the therapist is expected to function as a full-fledged treatment participant. Moreover, short-term treatment is undertaken only after rigorous criteria are used for patient selection. In particular, short-term treatment is specifically advised for highly motivated patients with a circumscribed emotional problem or conflict. This patient profile contrasts sharply with the description of patients in long-term treatment, who tend to present with more diffuse symptoms, usually coupled with a failure to acknowledge their own contribution to the problem. The most vivid difference between the short-term and the long-term formats remains, however, the assertive nature of the strategies used to overcome conflict. Advocates of the short-term approach recommend such assertive techniques as anxiety-provoking strategies (Sifneos, 1972), the active challenging of the patient's resistance (Davanloo, 1986, 1989; Mann, 1973), and task development and implementation (Reid, 1990; Wolberg, Aronson, & Wolberg, 1976). In current parlance, these methods would be called proactive as opposed to the more passive strategies of the conventional approach.

Although it may be different in technique, the short-term approach resembles traditional formats in its presupposition that conflict is rooted in early developmental crises the patient has experienced. In this regard, developmental conflict often emerges as an issue of control or domination within the family (Gustafson & Dichter, 1983). In fact, the brief duration of the short-term treatment actively fosters the process of therapeutic alliance and separation that replicates the experience of separation-individuation experienced by the infant during the early years of life (Mann, 1973, 1986). Short-term techniques thus trigger memories of the patient's formative development and often evoke a reenactment of behavioral patterns indicative of conflict that in itself is a prime healing component of treatment.

Because the intensity of short-term techniques tends to catalyze the patient's memories of early developmental trauma, previewing techniques appear especially compatible with the customized format. Several aspects of the previewing process may actually chart the course of short-term treatment. The previewing process that emerges from the reciprocal dynamic and intimate alliance between parent and infant builds up—as a consequence of this bond of affection—the confidence needed by the infant to predict upcoming developmental trends. Predictions of prospective growth and milestone developmental events are then enacted with the parent. During these episodes the infant becomes gradually acclimated to the visceral complex associated with the imminent change. Thus, when the new skill is consolidated, the previous previewing rehearsals are reinforced, and accord with the parent is affirmed. Repeated successful previewing episodes bolster the infant's emerging sense of self, promoting the idea that developmental change—regardless of its complexity—may be mastered with the aid of a supportive partner. In effect, the process of the short-term model mirrors the sequence of these aforementioned events. The therapist rapidly seeks to establish an alliance with the patient. Using this alliance, the therapist rigorously challenges the patient to confront and overcome conflict by predicting future adaptive behavior patterns (Trad, 1992b) that are rehearsed in order to motivate the patient to overcome defenses and expose the conflict. Once the conflict is revealed, the therapist works toward supporting the patient's efforts to complete transition to an adaptive state.

The following discussion focuses on the benefits of marrying previewing strategies with the principles of short-term therapy for the treatment of parents and their infants.

## Characteristics of Short-Term Psychotherapy

Short-term psychotherapy has several unique features. First, treatment is limited to a brief period, generally 2 to 6 months, during which attention is focused on a circumscribed problem identified by the patient (Butcher & Koss, 1978). The limited duration of the treatment necessitates intensive screening criteria to select those patients suited for this form of therapy and to screen out inappropriate candidates. The self-identification symptomatic of the short-term candidate sets both an easier and a more difficult task for the therapist. Under conventional protocols, in lengthy therapeutic settings the therapist must establish what the problem is, where its parameters and probable direction of resolution lie, and what terminus to establish. Short-term patients-to-be have a preset agenda, making them in one sense simpler and more attractive to treat than analysands who may be stumbling about in the psychotherapeutic dark. It is attractive to treat patients who can identify and face their particular problem, in contrast to patients unable to articulate a specific issue. Careful screening therefore removes subjective judgments from the problematic questions of whom to choose and why not accept all, no matter the prognosis. Because of the stringent time limits of the treatment, assertive intervention strategies are warranted. Moreover, as a consequence of the parameter of shortened time, the therapist's role assumes an added dimension in the briefer format: An active participant from the establishment of the alliance onward, the therapist swiftly and supportively motivates the patient to explore significant areas of conflict, to challenge assertively ingrained patterns, and to engage in new ameliorative behaviors. Finally, the variety of modalities employed by the therapist within a brief span mandates a more active approach for handling the patient's emerging reactions.

Another valuable aspect of the short-term model is that its very brevity is another way to handle almost transference-free therapy. The patient is in and out of treatment so swiftly it is unlikely he or she will have time to develop a strong transference with the therapist, no matter how conflicted the childhood or how troubled the relationship with parents may have been.

RIGOROUS SELECTION CRITERIA

Proponents of the short-term approach have advised that precise patient-selection criteria be used so that conflict resolution may be achieved within the limited time parameters of the treatment (Worchel, 1990). The selection process begins with a patient capable of articulating a specific problem that usually stems from earlier interpersonal experience. Thus, by definition, patients most suitable for this treatment format tend to suffer from a circumscribed conflict that originated at a particular developmental point.

To deal effectively with this stated conflict, the short-term approach solicits patients with a concomitantly strong motivation for the requisite change in interpersonal patterns and sufficient ego adaptation—the ability and expressed desire to be actively involved with the therapeutic process (Alexander & French, 1946). The capacity to articulate a circumscribed complaint, to express emotions appropriately while interacting with the therapist, and to have a clear-cut memory of at least one meaningful childhood relationship are additional criteria in selecting short-term patients (Sifneos, 1972).

For the past 14 years, other investigators, including Malan, Mann, Godlman, Davanloo, and Gustafson and Dichter, have been offering parallel selection criteria. Malan (1979, 1986) provided a checklist for screening applicants for short-term therapy. His patients had to have psychological insight into what motivated their behavior; had to recognize the interpersonal origins of presenting problems; had to manifest a willingness to accept interpretation; and had to be able to withstand the anxiety that would possibly be generated by such interpretation. For both Mann (1973) and Mann and Godlman (1982), patients had to have the capacity to muster sufficient determination to confront their own resistance. In Davanloo's (1984) opinion, selection criteria must be based on an assessment of ego functioning, an appraisal of the patient's ability to express emotions, and the quality of the patient's interpersonal relationships. When one reviews the criteria of the spectrum of researchers, it seems that parent-infant dyads would seem to be especially suitable for the short-term format. Specifically, parents and infants are undergoing a relentless process of development, necessitating that their relationship continually adjust to new maturational changes in one of their members. Since the parents are in the throes of constant development transition, each must learn to identify rapidly the direction their relationship is taking, then to assert expeditiously the change within the context of that relationship. The circumscribed nature of short-term treatment, coupled with its assertive techniques, strongly suggests that this form of therapy—in contemporary parlance, "therapy lite"—may indeed be efficacious with dyads.

The short-term approach is usually contraindicated, however, for certain types of psychological disorder. People with borderline personalities, for example, are inappropriate short-term patients, since the complex defensive strategies of these patients—for example, splitting, primitive idealization—often mandate lengthy periods of working through. Similarly, patients with separation anxiety, psychotic regression, or suicidal tendencies may also be unsuitable candidates, since they often require extensive contact with the therapist to effect useful conflict resolution (Gustafson & Dichter, 1983). Although this does not exhaust the possibilities, diligent application of the agreed-upon criteria can generally filter out the inappropriate candidate and locate the apt one.

## THE THERAPIST'S ROLE

To assist the patient in withstanding confrontational techniques, the therapist designs strategies to elicit anxiety-laden material. The therapist, it must be understood, provides a dual function: At one time he or she must offer a bulwark against too much defense onslaught; at the same time, a considerable attempt must be made, consistently but steadily, against the patient's defense mechanisms. The intensive nature of this approach necessitates that a durable empathic alliance exist with the patient from the treatment's onset even more than in conventional treatment modes (Sifneos, 1972). Transference reactions are subject to being interpreted from the immediacy of the present, since the therapeutic time frame restricts the range of stimuli provided for the patient, and a special effort is made to relate these transferential reactions to the patient's relationship with his or her parents (Malan, 1986; Rosenberg, 1988) or affiliated others.

The therapeutic alliance in short-term therapy should be continually reinforced. In Davanloo's (1989) view, therapists must be sensitive to their causing a collision between the transference resistance and a desired goal, since the heightening of resistance will generate tension in the therapeutic alliance. To defuse this tension, the therapist would be well advised to emphasize repeatedly the central issue of transference in general as well as in particular and to focus on the patient's inherent experience of suffering, drawing on a reservoir of empathy to support the patient while disengaging from transferential involvements (Mann, 1973; Mann & Godlman, 1982). Delicately accomplishing this requires substantial skill.

In regard to the therapist's role, short-term treatment would appear to accord well with the lineaments of the parent-infant relationship, in which the parent displays empathy for the infant while persuasively guiding the infant toward new developmental achievement. The therapist echoes this behavior for the parents, encouraging growth and developmental perspective in their guiding task of parenting. The parallel we are drawing, it should be understood, is to the manifest interaction, not the *content* of the interaction. In other words, the therapist is trying to replicate the mood and ambience of the parent's interaction with the infant to elicit continually more content, more interactive dynamics, more inner feelings for the dyadic pair. The interplay of parental sensitivity and the forceful instruction on seizing opportunities to introduce the infant to upcoming challenges typifies adaptive rapport. When some sorts of conflict disrupt the dyadic rapport, however, this collaboration is lacking. Short-term treatment, using approaches that parallel the patterns of adaptation prevalent during developmental transition, may facilitate the resolution of conflict. In effect, the therapist mimics the role of an adaptive caregiver and supportively directs the patient to achieve practical conflict-resolution goals.

TECHNIQUE

The short-term model is unique in its forceful dual challenging of patient resistance and implementation of strategies designed to promote intrapsychic realignment while dramatically altering behavior (Davanloo, 1984). In this regard, short-term treatment may be divided into two phases: During the preinterpretive phase, the therapist identifies, clarifies, and interprets the patient's resistance; later, in the interpretive phase, the therapist assists the patient in working through the previously determined conflict. Subsequently, the therapist explores the patient's impulsive threshold, thereby promoting a paradoxical intensification of the resistance. Shortly, transference feelings begin to collide with the resistance. As the patient experiences anger and directs it toward the therapist, unconscious material is "unlocked" or released, setting the stage for the analysis of conflict (Davanloo, 1978).

From this description, it becomes apparent that short-term techniques can evoke intense emotions. The risk in these cases is often that an emotion not previously expressed will rise to the surface in the form of destructive acting-out behavior. In order to avoid this outcome, another short-term technique, known as plan-of-action (p.o.a.) implementation, may be used (Wolberg et al., 1976). Essentially, this p.o.a. implementation requires the parent/patient to complete certain concrete assignments at each session. Focusing on the circumscribed problem that motivated the patient to enter into treatment, patient and therapist collaborate on a strategy for asserting goal-oriented outcomes. The therapist works conscientiously with the patient to design various alternative tracks in order to negotiate conflict-laden episodes likely to occur in succeeding sessions.

Some therapeutic goals will be extraordinarily precise, whereas others may be more flexible. The important point is that the patient understand goals, predict outcomes, and accept and be committed to the execution of the plan. The element of prediction is especially pertinent in this regard because patient and therapist will both evaluate the patient's skill in generating an adaptive outcome. As with endeavors in the arts, the likelihood of successful completion of a task is enhanced when rehearsals or practice sessions are instituted. In effect, the patient is helped to represent possible or prospective obstacles during execution of the task and to enliven them dramatically in order to practice overcoming them successfully. Nonprofessional terminology for this gained a lively phrase in the 1970s: psychodrama.

Task implementation is a technique especially congenial to parent-infant psychotherapy. The parent-infant relationship—particularly during the first 2 years of life, prior to the infant's mastery of speech—is based on the enactment and practice of behaviors. Thus, a strategy such as task implementation, which relies on experimentation with various behavioral alternatives, should be a familiar mode of interaction to the new parent.

Because it is time limited, short-term psychotherapy encourages the patient to assess his or her own progress. Progress, in this instance, involves not merely freedom from symptoms—the ridding of patient restraints from historic conflict—but also correct patient insight into the causes of the conflict. In addition, it is recommended that the patient become aware of the range of situations that may predict and thus help to overcome future similar conflicts. The suggestion here is that short-term therapy results in an internal restructuring whereby old patterns of interaction are relinquished in favor of patterns that enable the patient to deal more adaptively with future challenges. In this sense, the strategies of short-term psychotherapy also are compatible with dyadic treatment. One sign that parent and infant share an adaptive rapport is the parent's capacity to adapt to more advanced developmental skills (with the infant's reciprocal cooperation) while relinquishing older, less adaptive modes of interpersonal exchange. This form of realignment meshes especially well with the maturational change experienced by parent and infant in the act of mellifluous dyadic interchange.

## The Outcome of Short-Term Therapy: Influential Factors

As short-term therapy has gained credibility, investigators have highlighted those therapist and patient variables influencing the outcome of the treatment. Rogers (1957) and Luborsky, Barber, and Crits-Christoph (1990), among others, have determined that a supportive neutral-to-positive relationship between therapist and patient is mandatory for constructive personality change. Indeed, numerous variables appear predictive of treatment outcome (Strupp, Hadley, & Gomes-Schwartz, 1977). These variables may be divided into patient variables, therapist variables, and variables characteristic of the treatment itself.

### TREATMENT VARIABLES

### *Patient Variables*

Among the patient variables positively correlated with change are adequacy of personality functioning, motivation, intelligence, and education. According to Kernberg et al. (1972), patients' ego strength has been correlated positively with overall treatment success. Some recent studies have also correlated the patient's initial presentation with treatment outcome. Piper, Azim, McCallum, and Joyce (1990), for example, determined that patients with high ratings on object-relations scales attained greater improvement than patients with low ratings. Frank, Gliedman, Imber, Nash, and Stone (1957) reported that the patient's perseveration, ostensibly indicative of a willingness to change, influences continuation in treatment. Following a similar logic, Steinmetz, Lewinsohn, and Antonuccio (1983) found that patients who expected to be less depressed after completing therapy unsurprisingly demonstrated the most substantial level of improvement. This outcome is echoed widely in postoperative results, when optimistic expectations are voiced by patients, and in the popular press, when patients spontaneously "bounce back" after several setbacks that would fell the less supported.

Additional patient variables that have been linked to a positive outcome include the level of the patient's involvement (Gomes-Schwartz, 1978), plus the patient's subjective perception that he or she is being helped through treatment (Garfield, 1986). Age has been a more inconclusive factor to evaluate. Luborsky, Auerbach, Chandler, Cohen, and Bachrach (1971) found that of 11 studies examining age in relation to therapeutic outcome, 4 determined that younger patients had greater success than older patients, 5 found no significant differences based on age, and 2 concluded that older patients did better than younger ones. In another study, Sargeant, Bruce, Florio, and Weissman (1990) determined that female patients older than 30 who had completed treatment retained more recalcitrant levels of depression than did female patients under 30. Such results should be viewed with great caution, as they are quite likely to be disparate in terms of definitions, hidden research biases that play a still unacknowledged role, and bias resulting from comparing unequivalent cases. The reasons for this are many, some beyond the scope of this presentation. But among the factors that can be posited are the decided disdain often visited on older female patients when they present for treatment of many varieties of dysfunction. Another reason for more deeply rooted depression is the general view that women exaggerate their incipient complaints—or indeed have no basis for their complaints at all. A third problem confronting older females in society is that they become in general "invisible" as medical patients, unless they are unusually assertive or socially important and thus reflect the esteem society has for males.

## Therapist Variables

Beside patient variables, therapist variables have been found to exert a measurable influence on treatment outcomes. Among the therapist-related variables determined to be most significantly associated with treatment improvement are experience, general level of empathy, and the rapport established between therapist and patient (Luborsky et al., 1971). Therapists with greater levels of experience showed more tolerance for their patients' anger, rated angry patients more favorably, and displayed more self-confidence and less discomfort with angry patients than did less experienced therapists (Haccoun & Lavigueur, 1979). Therapist age is another factor studied for its effect on treatment outcome. Some studies have suggested that a congruity in age between therapist and patient may contribute to the more rapid formation of an alliance (Luborsky, 1984).

## Therapist-Patient Variables

Variables inherent to the therapeutic process may also presage a more successful outcome with short-term treatment. One predominant factor that emerges from the short-term studies concerns the alliance between therapist and patient. This alliance will need to be especially durable if progress is to occur, since patient and therapist must rapidly develop a psychological intimacy and therapeutic alliance that are capable of withstanding rigorous assault to the patient's defenses. This onslaught provoked by the brief duration of treatment protocols might, under other circumstances, undermine the foundation of the therapeutic rapport. Without either rapport or basic trust, developmental growth or change is unlikely. Symptom remission is another variable used to assess the success of a short-term treatment (Horowitz, Marmar, Weiss, Kaltreider, & Wilner, 1986).

During the course regimen, that is, several weeks after the start of the therapy, short-term psychotherapy must also evaluate whether the patient has achieved enduring intrapsychic change. It would be unwise to assume any change to be long term. According to Maxim and Hunt (1990), for short-term treatment to be deemed successful, a significant alteration in the patient's interpersonal relationships and expectations needs to have taken place. For Crits-Christoph (1992), the quality of the patient's object relations at termination of treatment indicates the level of intrapsychic change. Those with more functional relationships, in other words, are likely to enjoy a better outcome. Another view holds that the patient's perceptions of supportive relationships prior to treatment are correlated with posttreatment ratings of their level of functioning, symptoms, and social adjustment. Marzialli (1987) studied the patient's attachment relationships, social integration, opportunity for nurturance (parent for child), and alliance with the therapist; the study showed that the patient's satisfaction was a significant gauge of the ability of short-term therapy to modify intrapsychic structure and behavior.

Others have focused on the bond between therapist and patient as a key indicator of the success of the short-term approach. For Ursano and Hales (1986), Piper, Azim, Joyce, and McCallum (1991), and Piper, Azim, Joyce, McCallum, et al. (1991), the fortitude of the therapeutic alliance in withstanding the rigors of the unbridled short-term techniques is the most reliable predictor of the longevity potential of the treatment, acknowledging its debt to the application of such aggressive strategies as the no-holds-barred challenging of the patient's resistance. Interestingly, even during the initial session, the endurance of the alliance may be evaluated as the therapist discovers and assesses those interpersonal elements that reveal the patient's suitability for the short-term format. Along these lines, Malan (1975, 1976, 1980) has noted that factors such as a patient's resistance, need for working through, and potential for transference and dependence should be carefully noted to weigh the patient's suitability for treatment, as well as to predict its ultimate success.

PREVIEWING

Despite the proliferation of selection guidelines proposed by these investigators, accurate prediction of successful outcomes with short-term therapy remains at best uncertain. The brief period of time available to the patient to establish an alliance with the therapist and gain insight into unconscious processes may be woefully insufficient for effecting enduring structural change. It is in this regard that the application of previewing to short-term psychotherapy may offer significant solutions. When previewing occurs between infant and caregiver, its goal is to introduce the infant to imminent developmental changes likely to appear and consolidate in the future. As the previewing process evolves, the caregiver directs the infant's physical efforts while simultaneously infusing the relationship with a maximally supportive, empathic atmosphere. Incorporating these insistent, careful ministrations, the infant gradually acquires a sense of developmental autonomy. Positing the investiture of a mastery orientation in the infant, previewing then enables the infant to become adept at welcoming and predicting upcoming change.

*Observing the Patient*

Researchers have recently determined, for example, that people can detect the personality traits of others based on brief observations of their behavior (Babad, Bernieri, & Rosenthal, 1987, 1991) and that predictions about personality were deemed correct even when individuals are presented with only brief (2-minute) depictions of the target individual's behavior (Estes, 1938). These perceptions appear to be almost instantaneous and bypass rational thinking. We simply flash onto states or modes of feeling in others and are sometimes unaware of our insight. Furthermore, extending the accuracy potential, judgments about others made from 30 seconds of observation are apparently as accurate as judgments derived from 5 minutes of exposure (Ambady & Rosenthal, 1992). From these observations, individuals are able to characterize another's personality traits as well as affective states. For example, Rosenthal, Hall, DiMatteo, Rogers, and Archer (1979) found that individuals identified emotions correctly after being exposed to only 375 milliseconds of nonverbal behavior.

Expressive behavior, then, continually conveys information through almost imperceptible nonverbal cues that appear to be unintended and nonconscious. Not only does the individual convey information nonconsciously, but also the observer processes this information automatically, beyond the level of conscious awareness (Chaikan, Sigler, & Derlega, 1974; Christensen & Rosenthal, 1982; Harris & Rosenthal, 1985). Attributions are then made during interpersonal exchange (Bargh, 1988). It follows that people form intuitive judgments about others based on this kind of limited information (Schneider, Hastorf, & Ellsworth, 1979); we make judgments about people with whom we interact, as well as about those whom we "just" observe.

Several processes appear to be operating when the individual identifies traits and affect and uses the perceptions to predict future behavior. First, data are supplied through subtle expressive behaviors. Next, this information is neatly categorized into personality traits that are then used to predict future behavior. Despite the highly significant implications of predictive abilities, few attempts have been made to explain how they influence our perceptions of the self or evolve during the life span. By exploring these issues, it may be possible to differentiate genuine predictions from mere expectations of future outcomes and thereby to enhance the accuracy of our predictions.

Previewing is a form of managed interaction that is predicated entirely on predictions (physiological, somatic) of future outcomes. During previewing exercises, the caregiver mentally predicts and then rehearses with the infant imminent developmental changes. In addition, sequelae of predicting "coming achievements" during previewing are diverse: When caregivers predict future outcomes, they rely on nonverbal cues (Argyle, Alkema, & Gilmour, 1971). Indeed, as indicated above, nonverbal information has many times the weight of verbal reportage for determining the accuracy of emotional perceptions (Mehrabian, 1972); in point of fact, it is 13 times as potent a data bearer as merely verbal information. Dispositions or mood states are inferred more readily from nonverbal than from verbal behavior, since the nonverbal requires less cognitive processing and is therefore less influenced by peripheral cognitive activities. Moreover, nonverbal behavior, processed despite peripheral cognitive activity, is therefore understood without conscious processing (Gilbert & Krull, 1988). Thus, clearly, an alert parent can glean substantial input without having to hear a verbal report from the infant. Processing this input, the parent can and should react in keeping with the child's mood and telling behavior.

Observations of behavior are obviously not the only source of traits attributed to a target individual. The manner by which observed behavior is categorized is influenced by the individual's ability first to remember and then to access the emotional information. Researchers have determined what governs to some degree the selection and interpretation of social information (Higgins & King, 1981; Wyer & Srull, 1981). It appears that people sustain mental representations of interpersonal information by using networks of traits that they then assign to others (Rosenberg & Jones, 1972), which allows them to do pattern recognition. This has resonant implications for the dyad.

How does the capacity to detect cues about others in order to predict their behavior relate to previewing? In partial answer, the first step involved in previewing is representation; in the context of the parent-infant dyad, the caregiver uses spontaneous perceptions of the infant to help represent future interpersonal outcomes for the infant. From the time of the infant's birth onward, the parent has fastidiously observed the infant's expressive cues. Using them, the parent predicts the infant's affective state (mood). This information contributes to forming a specific representation of the interpersonal implications precipitated by the developmental change (indicated by the "interpersonal outcome").

Observation begins with the parent's steady scrutiny of the infant's facial expressions. The parent may study the infant's eyes or attempt to engage in visual cuing, and thus determine whether the infant is visually tracking. The face will be carefully observed to identify the specific emotion or emotions being expressed. Researchers have confirmed that within the first few days of life, infants exhibit a repertoire of primary emotional displays that they manifest during interaction (Field, Woodson, Greenberg, & Cohen, 1982). Eight primary emotions, each with its corresponding facial demeanor, have been identified: happiness, interest, fear, sadness, soberness, distress, anger, and disgust (Izard, 1978).

Observations of the dyadic interaction are important for several reasons. First, although the caregiver will in all likelihood use language to convey her perceptions and subjective states to the therapist, the infant—at least during the first 2 years of life, before language skills are acquired—cannot. In addition, even during the years of toddlerhood, children are not as adept as adults at using words to describe their inner perceptions in situ. Consequently, the therapist must rely on a number of creative methods of accessing different levels of the dyad's experience. One of the most effective ones, as discussed earlier, is through the observation of external indications such as facial expressions (Kopp, 1990). Thus, carefully observing the infant's behavior either alone or, more significantly, during sequences of interaction with the caregiver becomes the prime route for achieving insight into the infant's perspective.

Second, observation of mother-infant interaction reveals the level of developmental progress and the degree to which the mother is effectively promoting developmental changes. Since one of the therapist's goals is to assess and treat the dyad's ability to integrate developmental change, observations of the dyadic interaction during various times become essential.

Third, communicative gestures offer the therapist a profound encapsulation of the inner perceptual workings of both infant and caregiver. From an evaluation of these behaviors, the therapist can detect how the landscape of inner emotion contributes to the individual's behavior (in this case, the adult parent's with the infant) in establishing a relationship with others. Careful observation of dyadic interaction, then, should not signify a substitute for the verbal disclosures of the caregiver. Nor do behavioral observations serve merely to supplement the material the caregiver has provided the therapist through verbal narrative. Rather, by observing the dyadic relationship over time, the therapist can witness the transformations of development and how these various incremental changes have an impact on both caregiver and infant.

Perhaps because they have been trained for the most part to rely on verbal interactions almost to the exclusion of visual observation, many therapists are reluctant to use observation for acquiring insight into the dyadic interaction. Other clinicians are uncertain about what phenomena they should be observing; as a consequence, they avoid or ignore careful scrutiny of the behavioral displays of their patients. This problem may be handily rectified if the therapist is offered some straightforward guidance about the kinds of manifestation that should be noted.

Essentially, five aspects of the interaction may be observed. First, the therapist should carefully study the *facial expressions* of both participants in the interaction in order to detect emotion; it should be remembered that, even from a very early age, infants are capable of exhibiting a full range of emotional expressions. Therefore, the therapist can expect to see evidence of flexible and diverse emotional displays. *Gestures* are a second feature to which the therapist should be alert. Many caregivers and infants design an effective means of communication through body movements. Third, the therapist should be alert to signs of *intuitive behavior* by the caregiver—specifically, does the caregiver exhibit visual and vocal cuing, hold the infant properly, and provide sufficient stimulation? A fourth feature evident during adaptive interaction is *rhythmicity* or *affect attunement*. This quality refers to the capacity of caregiver and infant to match the soothing gestures of each other, so that the interaction has a flowing quality. Finally, therapists should be alert to signs of *previewing* on the part of the parent. That is, does the caregiver appear to be sensitive and responsive to the infant's imminent developmental progress? By becoming adept at recognizing all of these qualities, the therapist begins first to develop a clearer picture of the typical imprint of interaction characterizing a particular dyad and then to home in on the important skills that may still be lacking. Subsequently, this information may be used to infuse the dyad with more adaptive skills and to encourage the caregiver to attempt further application of previewing.

How do both observations—of subtle cues and emotional expression—contribute to the use of previewing during short-term dyadic treatment? It should be remembered that one unique factor of this process is the presence of the infant; during a session the therapist is able to observe how both care-giver and infant conduct interpersonal patterns. Moreover, this same obser-vational vantage point enables the therapist to witness how dyadic members adapt to some of the myriad developmental changes that they will experi-ence throughout their interactional lives. Does the caregiver embrace the in-terpersonal consequences of change, integrating the infant's new skills into the parental repertoire of interactional behaviors while previewing further imminent skill, or does the caregiver fail—intentionally or otherwise—to ac-knowledge these changes during interactions with the infant? Observation and other interviewing strategies play a pivotal role in the diagnosis of these abilities. It is incumbent on therapists to use the session to become familiar with methods of observation and to hone their skills especially in this area.

It is important that the therapist always observe and analyze the compo-nents in each sequence of dyadic interaction in addition to inquiring about the caregiver's interpretations of his or her own behaviors. During this pre-liminary observation, the therapist's goal is to establish whether the parent is attuned to the infant's mood and bodily gestures. Subsequently, the thera-pist might ask the parent to share subjective speculations of the skills the in-fant might manifest in the near future. The therapist would carefully analyze the parent's representation to determine whether objective parental observa-tions are employed to predict final outcomes of the infant's precursory mani-festations. If the parent's predictions are deemed inaccurate, strategies of the short-term method should be applied in order to discern the presence of po-tential conflict.

## Using Metaphor

Another therapeutic tool that may be of assistance during short-term ther-apy with parent-infant dyads involves the use of metaphor. Previewing functions as a metaphor in that it provides the therapist with an innovative means of addressing interpersonal issues within the dyad; it functions as a shared language that promotes intersubjectivity and helps the patient deal with conflict in a nonthreatening manner that may circumvent defensive op-erations. In other words, the previewing process may be regarded as a metaphor by which the caregiver and infant exchange "messages" about how the future will affect their relationship.

Metaphor, in general, is also a powerful means of communication within the therapeutic environment (Erikson, 1966/1980). In effect, the therapist's introduction of metaphor into the treatment setting activates the parent/patient's unconscious thought processes. Old behavioral patterns are inter-rupted and dislodged by the introduction of the paradigm's new meaning. In turn, this new meaning naturally precipitates new behaviors.

Therapists treating parents and their infants with the short-term model

may apply paradigms during previewing enactments to represent and analyze contemporaneous interaction. Specifically, after the parent has engaged
in therapist-observed interaction with the infant, the therapist would begin a
discussion of the infant's developmental achievements using a metaphorical
cast. As an example of how metaphor (paradigm) is compatible with discussion and enactments of infant growth, a mother of a 3-month-old son was
asked to describe for the therapist the developmental milestones her son
would soon exhibit. Pausing briefly to absorb the question, the mother told
the therapist that she imagined her infant would soon be "walking all over
[her]." Although simple observation revealed that although the infant had
been exhibiting kicking gestures indicative of crawling, the mother did not
predict crawling as the next milestone. Rather, she had skipped to walking
behavior. Furthermore, rather than assist or encourage the infant's movements, she instead restrained the infant's legs and almost forced him to sit
quietly in her lap. The therapist observed this mother's reluctance to assist
her infant in his development and commented, "Crawling is slower than
walking and tends not to be as 'all over' the place." A possible interpretation
of this is that crawling—not being an activity that would threaten autonomy
for most people—was an activity she could countenance, whereas walking
"previewed" for the mother her fear of abandonment and loss of dyadic intimacy. So she had jumped to the irrational, unlikely outcome. Although the
prior maternal statement has a literal meaning, the mother's metaphor might
also trigger unconscious associations within the caregiver about issues of autonomy and the image of being "walked all over." Because the mother may
fear that the infant's achievement of autonomy will threaten the current intimacy of their relationship, she may unconsciously wish to prevent the infant
from attaining certain milestones, such as crawling, that facilitate autonomy.
By exploring the issue of separation on a literal level through a discussion of
crawling behaviors following a previewing enactment, the therapist may
well be able to help this mother express and clarify her genuine feelings regarding the meaning of the infant's changes. That is, how does this mother
really feel about separation and its implications for future interpersonal exchange? Moreover, the therapist will need to be especially alert to the enactment behaviors the parent engages in after the metaphor has been introduced. These behaviors will signify the parent's subjective response to the
therapist's introduction of previewing activity.

In addition, previewing enactments may signify a way of communicating
information about events so that such events are imbued with interpersonal
meaning. That is, previewing is not simply a technique that enables the parent to respond to the precursory behaviors the infant is exhibiting; rather, it
is a way of sharing emotions and achievements with the infant and of conveying to him or her that the dyadic relationship will evolve in complexity
as the infant continues to develop. Therapists using the short-term approach

with parent-infant dyads can monitor the dyad's progress by combining the observation of behaviors and parental subjective response through the use of applied metaphors.

## Priming

In a variety of ways, the therapeutic use of previewing resembles a process that has been referred to as priming. As defined by Ratcliff and McKoon (1978), priming is the "facilitation of the response to one test item by a preceding item" (p. 403). Priming as defined is applicable to the short-term therapeutic context; specifically, therapists should develop the ability to predict behavior and to use these predictions both diagnostically and therapeutically during psychotherapy (Richardson-Klavehn & Bjork, 1988). The use of priming can have a variety of effects on a patient. For example, when certain stimuli are primed, the patient makes decisions more quickly on a later presentation of the same stimuli. Clearly, priming also heightens the patient's ability to recognize a variety of stimuli (Ratcliff & McKoon, 1981), and it also enhances the ability to understand later interpretations of stimuli (Eich, 1984). The phenomenon is seen in learning of all sorts: Prior learning, prior reading, and prior preparation invariably speed up the absorption of similar and extended material based on allied principles. Other results of priming include greater accessibility to certain concepts, the ability to influence preferences, enhanced problem-solving skills, faster attitude formation, and even associative social behaviors (Nisbett & Wilson, 1977). One of the important effects of priming, however, is its ability to influence subsequent behavior and perception. In the context of short-term psychotherapy, this means that a therapist can have the patient visualize aspects of intended change as a method of reinforcing the probability—and expectation—that the change will occur. The same principle of visualization—based on priming—is much in evidence in general today as a method of overcoming deficits of various eugenic sorts. Visualization is credited for overcoming fear of failure or its adverse, for achieving success. Priming oneself for the notion of besting illness or disability is by the same token fast gaining credibility and adherents in every walk of life, spreading out from behaviorists and sociobiologists. When extended, the concept leads to so-called asseverations, mantralike self-primings that help extinguish defeatist behaviors and attitudes.

For these reasons, priming and previewing are related processes. Previewing is, in effect, a comprehensive mode of priming used by adaptive parents to prepare the infant for imminent developmental changes. During previewing exercises, the caregiver acquaints the infant with the perception of developmental change, an exercise analogous to the priming of stimuli. Later, when the skill actually consolidates, its influence is reinforced, just as a stimulus that has been primed for assumes exaggerated importance because it is recognized when it appears later. Thus, previewing not only familiarizes the parent and infant with particular skills but does so in a manner that emphasizes, on an unconscious level, fundamental modes of interaction.

The priming influence of previewing has special relevance for the short-term model of psychotherapy. Essentially, priming reinforces selected stimuli. This form of reinforcement is crucial in the short-term model, since time is brief and the therapist will need to establish an alliance and convince the patient rapidly that support will be maintained and bolstered even during rigorous challenging of defenses. If certain events are primed during early treatment, they become landmarks or touchstones to which the patient may continuously return for reassurance of the therapist's support. Moreover, patients will correspondingly prime therapists, a phenomenon that may be especially strong in the short-term model. Such priming occurs when the patient spontaneously introduces certain themes or refers to certain events in a manner unrelated to previous discussions. That is, should the therapist become puzzled at a particular reference provided by the patient that does not follow from a previous inquiry or that seems incongruous with earlier narrative, the therapist should recognize that the patient may be unconsciously priming. The therapist will then need to analyze the precise content of the patient's message; does such priming involve a message about predicted outcomes? If the patient predicts a negative outcome, for example, the therapist will need to evaluate its source and determine how to redirect this impression correctly. Subsequently, the therapist may reconfigure and prime the patient with a cue concerning a more positive outcome.

Previewing is also beneficial in the short-term context because of the unique role of time in this form of therapy. Short-term psychotherapy is, after all, designed to promote rapid change. As a consequence, to make progress in the face of threatened defenses, patients need to feel secure about making transitions from the present moment, the "here and now," to the future, the "there and then," which may be accomplished by helping the patient to generate new experiences. The therapist would therefore buoy patient confidence while guiding the patient during transition to the next experience (Polster, 1990). One way of achieving this goal is through previewing exercises, which, with their condensed sequentiality, story line, and logical conclusion, generate a sense of inevitable outcome. The patient becomes convinced that experiences are successive and cumulative. As previewing experiences are iterated, the primed patient becomes successively attuned to differences between random events and deliberate acts, selecting the latter, because the model patient in short-term therapy is already primed to change.

Not only is the temporal element pivotal in short-term psychotherapy, but also the patient will need to negotiate an orientation for the future. Howard, Nance, and Myers (1987) speak of "client readiness" with this form of treatment, alluding to the eagerness of such patients for change. Moreover, it will be important for the parent to terminate the treatment in possession of a wide variety of adaptive strategies that may be relied upon in the future with the infant. As Budman et al. (1988) point out, if one can hazard an ideal time to terminate long-term (traditional) therapy, for short-term therapy, this is clearly contraindicated; there is no such thing as ideal termination in the short-term context. One study determined that, even among analyzed patients, more than 60% returned for additional treatment (Hartlaub, Martin, & Rhine, 1986). Thus, it is crucial that the parent exit treatment with strategies for adapting to future change and for predicting potential conflict. Previewing techniques are ideal for accomplishing this goal because they teach patients how to predict imminent difficulties, to represent outcomes, to experiment with alternative courses of action, and, finally, to adopt a particular strategy that will be instrumental in the achievement of their goals. As a consequence, previewing is particularly suited to the short-term format and to a model that incorporates care for parents and infants who are caught in the throes of continual developmental change.

## Previewing and Short-Term Psychotherapy

The brief, defined duration of the short-term model is ideally suited for previewing. Since therapeutic time is limited, patient and therapist will concentrate on achieving specific outcomes. Patient readiness for change (as evidenced by a variety of indices, including their own self-description of conflict or problem to solve during the therapy; their overall discipline, which helped select them as opposed to others who did not fit the criteria; and the general compliance manifested by early establishment of therapist-patient rapport) will be used to institute a plan of action (Howard et al., 1987). The tight sequences and coherent story line of previewing also focus the patient on making transitions to a more adaptive state. Moreover, the steps necessary to achieve a particular outcome will need to be spelled out explicitly.

The first step involves establishing a firm alliance between therapist and patient. Next, aggressive therapeutic modalities will be required to reveal the patient's conflict expeditiously. Third, the patient will need to acquire a viable strategy for overcoming conflict. A sense of mastery regarding the future is another desired outcome. Finally, the patient should be able to terminate treatment conversant with techniques for averting and resolving future conflict. As discussed below, with its emphasis on imminent developmental achievement in a positive interpersonal milieu, previewing is highly pertinent to attaining these outcomes for parent-infant dyads in treatment.

## USING PREVIEWING TO ESTABLISH A THERAPEUTIC ALLIANCE

Infants undergo a remarkable developmental transformation during the first 2 years of life. One of the more noteworthy events of this maturational era is the attainment of autonomy and self-regulatory abilities. Such autonomy would, however, be traumatic for the infant if not for the parent's attentive and empathic ministrations during each step of infant progress. As the infant experiences autonomy, the infant's sense of self becomes increasingly sturdy and differentiated (Stern, 1985). At the same time, the sense of self gleaned from feedback at points along the way paradoxically also causes him or her to experience the fear of separation (Maheler, Pine, & Bergman, 1975). These changes promote the transition from a state of separation to one of attachment (Bowlby, 1969). All of these developmental theories raise the same question: Does the infant seek intimacy with or autonomy from the caregiver? With time, it becomes apparent that both developments are concurrent. The dramatic maturational changes of infancy necessitate—indeed, are predicated on—the infant's reliance on the parent. Despite the parent's support, episodes of developmental change when new skills are rapidly and dramatically emerging may inculcate the perception of helplessness in the infant (McCall, 1979; Trad, 1986). This sensation is disarming for the infant who strives to assert internal control. The empathic caregiver facilitates this process (Emde, 1983; Hoffman, 1982b; Sander, 1983) and will be especially attentive in ministrations to help the infant overcome the feeling of uncontrollability associated with developmental transition. Flowing from the parent's empathic interactions, the infant evolves a coherent personality with an intact sense of past, present, and future. The emotionally supportive ambience generated by the parent thus enables the infant to establish the perception of continuity while making the transition from one maturational skill to the next. During previewing, the therapist strives to emulate the role of the adaptive caregiver. The therapist attempts, in particular, to acquaint the patient with upcoming themes. The therapist can use previewing to reinforce notions of coherence and outcome. By doing so, the patient gains the confidence to move flexibly from present to future and from future to past perceptions.

## USING PREVIEWING TO PROMOTE EMPATHY

Perhaps the factor most instrumental in promoting the infant's acclimation to developmental transition is empathy. For infants deprived of this, it is likely that developmental transitions will become episodes of conflict dur-

ing which the infant will become overwhelmed by sensations of uncontrollability, which may eventually mushroom into somatic, socioemotional, cognitive, or motivational deficits indicative of helplessness (Seligman, 1972).
With time, these deficits may displace adaptive functioning, causing maladaptive responses whenever the individual is confronted with a psychological challenge. This description of the genesis of psychopathology highlights
the vital role played by the empathic caregiver in the infant's early life.

In analogous fashion, therapists practicing short-term psychotherapy
with parent-infant dyads are advised to adopt a similar empathic approach
in order to promote an optimal outcome. To understand the parents'
responses to the infant best, as well as probable receptivity to future developments, the therapist must remain keenly attuned to the parent's need to
relive and reexperience painful episodes from his or her own early development. The therapist can help the parent sustain this flexible journey through
the creation of a strong working alliance and by priming the parent for a
likely positive outcome.

Second, the therapist must convey to the parent that the infant's autonomy is desirable. Just as the empathic parent conveys the notion that someday the infant will exercise skills independently, so, too, must the therapist
in short-term therapy convey and reiterate to the parent that she can achieve
and sustain an adaptive relationship with the infant despite the infant's
gains toward autonomy. In effect, the therapist uses empathy as a conduit,
through which the parent receives the message of effectiveness and mastery
orientation. As the parent's sense of esteem rises, this message is gradually
transmitted to the infant. In a like manner, the parent also learns how to
prime the infant for adaptive future outcomes.

## USING PREVIEWING AS A VEHICLE FOR EVOKING CONFLICT

As we have indicated throughout these pages, in the short-term format,
time is of the essence. As a result, the therapist expeditiously needs to provide the parent with techniques for rapidly identifying both the nature and
source of conflict with the infant. Since previewing begins with representation, the parent must consciously represent a skill the infant is likely to exhibit in the near future. To formulate this representation, the parent relies on
precursory behaviors manifested by the infant.

During psychotherapy, the therapist focuses on the parent's representations. In this regard, the therapist needs to orient the parent to the interpersonal implications of whatever representations have been made to the infant.
This encompasses asking questions to help the parent explore these representations in greater detail. Two outcomes are likely to emerge from this
course of action: First, the parent will delve more deeply into personal memories; second, as the parent's enthusiasm grows, the therapist will encourage

further predictions of outcomes of all scenarios represented. The key here is to urge the parent to free-associate. Typically, the more intense the nature of the patient's predictions, the greater the likelihood that material relating to earlier developmental experience will be evoked and loosed.

A variation on this outcome occurs when previewing is applied during short-term psychotherapy with a parent-infant dyad. The parent in treatment will be asked to predict a significant developmental event that the infant will likely experience in the near future. Once that prospective skill has been articulated, the parent—assisted by the therapist—will predict several of the interpersonal repercussions to be evoked following the advent of the new skill. The more alternatives the parent is able to explore, the better. For example, if the parent predicts that the infant will soon be crawling, the questions to ask are how this skill will change the parent's current relationship with the infant, how the infant's newfound independence will feel to the parent, and how the infant will likely perceive of this heightened capacity of mobility? Throughout the sessions, the therapist must remain alert to the parent's expressive cues. Encouraging the parent to view the situation from a variety of different perspectives is another way to heighten the parent's perceptions. The therapist would also do well to help the parent to explore the diverse emotions awakened in the parent's encoded emotional representations by the onset of the child's crawling. Moreover, the therapist might encourage the parent to pretend that the infant is now capable of crawling and to describe how this outcome will alter the dyadic rapport. These representations allow the parent to explore probable responses to the advent of new infant developmental milestones while in the supportive presence of the therapist.

The element of prediction should be reemphasized here. Helping the parent understand that developmental events occasion diverse repercussions—and that these may be rehearsed in advance to determine which are most effective—should lend enormous confidence to the parent. In contrast to other psychotherapeutic techniques, previewing focuses on the future and on the continually evolving relationship with the infant to mold adaptive interpersonal behaviors available after treatment has terminated.

The orientation toward the future inherent in previewing also enhances the effect of short-term therapy, especially for dyads. In essence, the prospective approach enables the parent to negotiate the transition to a more carefully adaptive emotional state, focusing the parent's attention away from grief over separation and toward the most likely outcomes, as well as on the rapid, optimal resolution of conflict. As Polster (1990) has noted, helping the patient manage these transitions smoothly is a key responsibility of the therapist, who guides the parent in predicting the outcomes of interpersonal behaviors with the infant. Whereas the parent's relationship with the infant will necessarily evolve during treatment, a helpful sense of continuity is maintained. This continuity is evident in the bond between parent and therapist and, by analogy and example, in the bond between parent and infant. Because of the continuity offered by the therapist's support, the parent's transition from possible states of overt conflict and disquiet to one of adaptive functioning is less stressful for both members of the dyad.

To ease this transition for parents, therapists should strive to elicit a full spectrum of positive emotions and, further, to encourage parents to infuse the dyadic interaction with this emotionality. This positive emotional ambience will result if the therapist emulates the empathy of adaptive caregivers engaged in previewing exercises with their infants. Via empathic emulation, the therapist offers an immediate model that the parent can comfortably mimic during interactions with the infant. Encouraging the parent to engage in previewing enactments in the supportive therapeutic setting enables him or her to more easily become attuned to the previewing process. The parent now gains the confidence to predict a developmental change the infant will soon experience, to anticipate when the infant will be receptive to a previewing enactment, to guide the infant in the interpersonal experience of the new skill, and, finally, to ease the infant back to previous comfort levels—already attained developmental strata—once the previewing exercise has been experienced for the length of time available to the infant's attention span.

In recent years short-term psychotherapy, once the foundling of the psychotherapeutic family, has made impressive strides. Researchers have specifically reported on the efficacy of brief dynamic treatment (Davanloo, 1980; Luborsky, 1984; Mann, 1973). The short-term approach has been lauded for measurable symptom remission, amelioration in patient functioning, and the enhancement of interpersonal skills. Yet two key issues remain unaddressed. First, is it possible to determine the endurance of symptom abatement when short-term techniques are used? Second, does short-term treatment result in intrapsychic as well as interpersonal change? Thus, although Horowitz et al. (1986) determined that short-term patients improved in assertiveness, interpersonal skills, self-concept, and symptom abatement, it was unclear whether and to what extent these changes were long-lasting and whether they heralded modifications of intrapsychic perception.

Previewing addresses both issues and thus may predict the outcome of a particular short-term treatment. In effect, previewing helps to assess whether remission of symptoms indicates genuine intrapsychic change or is of a more superficial nature. To achieve this, the therapist must engage in four levels of evaluation. The first level is to assess the ease with which the patient establishes an alliance with the therapist, a skill indicative of general interpersonal competence, and, next, to explore the patient's receptivity to the therapist's suggestions. For example, does the patient view the therapist's interventions without hostility or resentment? Does the patient communicate priming cues? On the plus side, is the patient receptive to the therapist's suggestions? Such inquiries help the therapist target the degree to which the patient is amenable to using the therapist for predicting outcomes.

The second level requires that the therapist ask the patient to make some self-predictions—some about the infant and some about the future course of their dyadic relationship. This inquiry examines the patient's skill in anticipating future outcomes without predicting conflict. As described earlier, the parent's narrative should be explored. As a result of continuously questioning and probing, the therapist should generate a serviceable impression of the parent's skill in representing imminent outcomes, especially those relating directly to the infant's developmental skills. The therapist should also ask, using the extracted narrative content of the parent, whether the infant's future is being envisioned in an optimistic fashion. What is the parent's self-portrait in terms of interaction with the infant? Is the parent an active participant in the infant's growth; does he or she coax forth new maturational skills? Is the parent perhaps a reluctant observer? These inquiries permit the therapist a glimpse or two into how the parent represents the parental role in the relationship with the infant.

The third level to be evaluated concerns the parent's ability to represent the person who previously generated the former conflict. This means that parents in short-term psychotherapy will need to represent a conflicted figure from their own past in an adaptive fashion, as well as to generate positive predictions about this person. In most instances, they will need to retraverse problematic events of childhood and resolve the inevitable conflicts arising from these incidents. During these forays into the past, the therapist provides support and encouragement.

Patients who have successfully completed a course of short-term psychotherapy also manifest a fourth level of intrapsychic change. At this level, parents demonstrate enthusiasm and curiosity about the world of others. When the previewing process is applied to short-term treatment, they effectively move into deeper concentric circles to encompass increasingly complex segments of the external world. During the early phases of therapy, patients use the therapist as a source from which to derive predictions. As the treatment progresses, patients gain confidence in their own abilities, so that the self becomes a focal point of attention. With further progress, they generate predictions about the person with whom conflict was previously experienced. During the last stage, a level of psychological maturity is attained, enabling the patients to engage freely in predictions about others in their psychological environment, such as mates, relatives, friends, and acquaintances. Following the intervention, these individuals are now viewed more favorably. For parents in short-term psychotherapy, it is likely that during the second and fourth stages predictions concerning the infant will bubble up in a prolific fashion. That is, as the parents gain confidence, they will look to the infant as a source from which to predict events. During this period, the parents will explore their own perceptions concerning the infant. After conflict has been worked through, they—in the presence of the therapist—will be likely to return to the infant at the conclusion of treatment. This is the phase during which predictions about others in the patients' life assume preeminence. As an affiliated other for the parents, the infant becomes one of the individuals about whom they make abundant predictions.

Additional strategies for appraising whether the interpersonal change has affected the parent on an intrapsychic level are as follows. First, the therapist must explore the resiliency of the therapeutic alliance. Does the parent discuss the dyadic relationship with the therapist in an open and timely fashion? Is the positive adult-adult rapport exhibited with the therapist transferred to the infant during interaction? One advantage of dyadic therapy is that the therapist has an unparalleled opportunity to observe directly the interpersonal exchange between parent and infant. Next, the therapist can explore the parent's capacity for making adaptive predictions about the self and can ask that the parent make some predictions of this nature, a request that should be reiterated as it pertains to the infant. In those instances when the parent manifests a deficit, impeding free-flowing predictive abilities, the therapist should return the parent to perceptions in the "here and now." The therapist's key task in this event is to move the patient forward. The existence of a block preventing further predictions suggests the presence of a conflict that has not been dealt with or has not yet risen to consciousness. To probe the conflict further, the therapist should encourage the parent to elaborate on the perceptions experienced immediately prior to the advent of the block. By returning the patient to the "here and now" in this fashion, a significant portion of perceptual information is likely to surface. This material may clarify for the therapist the impressions that the patient had been experiencing before the defensive operations began to disguise content from consciousness. By analyzing and tracking these clues, the insightful therapist can eventually detect the nature of the conflict.

Dyadic therapy has an added advantage over other forms of therapy because the infant will be present, enabling the therapist to assess patterns of interpersonal exchange between parent and infant on an ongoing basis. One of the most significant roles the therapist can play in this context is that of an observer. During each phase of treatment, the therapist monitors changes experienced in the interaction with the parent and watches to determine whether the parent then transfers these changes to the domain of interaction with the infant. In fact, this mirroring effect may be a particularly useful strategy for evaluating the efficacy of treatment with regard to intrapsychic change. Change manifested during interaction with the therapist, but *not* exhibited during interaction with the infant, may safely be deemed relatively short-lived. When the changes exhibited with the therapist are later employed with the infant, however, it is probable that a realignment in the parent's intrapsychic structure has occurred.

The therapist should also investigate the parent's ability to make adaptive predictions about a person with whom known conflict has previously been experienced. The therapist might here encourage the patient to disclose dream material; material concerning the infant is even more helpful. In one dramatic case, the mother of a 3-year-old son, who had just given birth to her second child, a daughter, reported the following dream the night before she was scheduled to take the new baby home from the hospital: "As we left the hospital, I had the baby cradled in my arms. Everything was fine. We got in the car, and my husband began driving us home. Suddenly, things started to look a little dark. We noticed all the lights in the city were going out. As we entered the tunnel, everything went black. I felt for the baby, but she didn't seem real in the darkness." This dream, which occurred early in the treatment, revealed that the mother harbored some still-unresolved conflict concerning birth or her infant's birth. Moreover, the therapist should also "test" the patient's facility for interacting more adaptively with others by suggesting that the parent enact previewing exercises. Watching the parent enact predictions with the infant yields further insight about the scope of change and about whether therapeutic changes have penetrated to an intrapsychic level.

## Conclusion

Although a relatively recent advent, short-term psychotherapy is an effective treatment protocol for parents and infants experiencing conflict. Moreover, previewing is particularly compatible with the strategies used during short-term treatment. Over the past few decades, short-term methods have attained widespread popularity. This form of treatment is of limited duration—generally lasting for 2 to 6 months—which is announced at the outset of the treatment. A rigorous patient-selection process is applied, and the techniques employed tend to be highly aggressive, even confrontational, with regard to challenging the patient's resistance. In addition, the therapist in the short-term format adopts a highly interventive stance to further the aggressive therapeutic modalities.

Previewing techniques are compatible with the short-term approach. First, previewing strategies promote an empathic atmosphere that fuels the therapeutic alliance. A high level of empathy—from both therapist and parent—is essential for short-term treatment, because the therapeutic alliance will be strenuously tested during application of the rigorous techniques designed to confront conflict. Previewing also alerts the therapist to the patient's priming cues. With its focus on imminent events, previewing fosters the evocation of conflict. Moreover, previewing fosters the therapist's observation skills and promotes the use of metaphors, giving the caregiver opportunities to explore unconscious conflict in a symbolic fashion. Consequently, conflicted material may thus be prevented from entering the patient's prospective representations. Finally, previewing offers parents strategies for approaching potential conflict with an attitude of competence. Therapists can monitor the extent of intrapsychic change by observing the enactment of previous previewing episodes during the course of therapy between parent and infant.

# PART II

APPLICATION OF SHORT-TERM
THEORY TO CLINICAL CASES

# CHAPTER 4

## Tiffany: The Emergence and Resolution of Distorted Prenatal Fantasies

LTHOUGH MOST of the physical changes that accompany pregnancy may be readily observed, concomitant psychological changes may not be as apparent. Nor are these psychological changes always overtly present in the pregnant woman's consciousness. Rather, emotional responses to pregnancy in general and the physical alterations it precipitates may only be manifest in the form of dreams or fantasies. Such dreams and fantasies may be colored by anxiety, fear, depression (Chehrazi, 1986; Chessick, 1988; Freud, 1931; Sherwen, 1981) and, in particular, fears and conflicts regarding developmental change (Bardwick, 1971; Trad, 1990). These mental representations constitute the woman's symbolizations of and feelings about her unborn child and their future relationship. Whereas mental characterizations of this nature are not uncommon during pregnancy, at times they may provoke distorted or maladaptive behaviors. They may also herald potential conflict in the dyadic relationship after the infant's birth. The therapist can explore these fantasies and their meaning with the pregnant woman in an attempt to stave off future conflict and promote adaptive representations and patterns of interaction.

The physical changes experienced by a woman during pregnancy affect her emotional transition into motherhood (Benedek, 1959a,b). For example, pregnant women may initially perceive the fetus as a foreign object, but eventually they recognize that the infant is a separate and autonomous being (Pines, 1972, 1982).

Representations of the infant may also underscore a sense of incomplete differentiation in which the boundaries between self and other are blurred (Blos, 1980; Lester & Notman, 1988). Even the sensation of the infant moving inside her may threaten the pregnant woman's sense of fusion with the infant. Moreover, thoughts about the infant's impending birth and separation from the mother may trigger feelings of loss and abandonment. By addressing these fantasies, the therapist may help to alter the woman's representations, which, in turn, may have a positive impact on the nature of her relationship with the child who will eventually be born.

Women with a previous history of psychiatric disorder may be particularly prone to harboring feelings of anger and hostility toward the unborn infant. These feelings may be magnified during pregnancy if psychiatric medication is discontinued in order to avoid the adverse effects it may have on the developing fetus. If medication is reestablished after the birth, the woman should not breast-feed, because, although the dosages may be small, all major psychotropic drugs—including antidepressants, antipsychotics, and antianxiety agents—have been shown to enter breast milk following maternal ingestion (Buist, Norman, & Dennerstein, 1990). In addition, the woman should understand how the side effects of her medication or her failure to take it may effect her interaction with the infant. Interventions that address these issues may be particularly important for women with distorted prenatal fantasies signaling potential for conflict. Exploring such feelings during the pregnancy may prevent the pregnant woman from engaging in behaviors that may potentially harm her unborn infant.

In cases in which the woman's prenatal fantasies indicate that she is at risk to engage in potentially harmful behavior during her pregnancy, the therapist should alert her to the potential hazards of such behavior and attempt to discern the underlying motivation for the wish to hurt the unborn infant. One potentially harmful behavior during pregnancy is the consumption of alcohol. Although many women recognize the dangers of exposing the infant to alcohol prenatally, a woman's subconscious desire to harm the unborn baby may fuel her desire to continue this habit. The therapist should first alert the woman to the potentially detrimental effects of alcohol. Whereas children born with fetal alcohol syndrome or fetal alcohol effects sustain major handicaps into adolescence and adulthood, even moderate exposure to alcohol can create problems that can be measured the day after birth and may continue into adulthood (Streissguth, Sampson, & Barr, 1989). These effects include fine and gross motor problems; psychosocial problems; intellectual decrements; organizational, problem-solving, and learning difficulties; as well as memory and attention problems.

Next, the therapist should explore the expectant mother's motivation for wanting to engage in behaviors that are potentially dangerous to the infant. She may be attempting to punish the infant for the feelings of loss and abandonment that the infant's development will precipitate. Or she may be attempting to exert control over the infant who seems to be controlling her by dictating what she may ingest and what activities she may or may not engage in. By helping the woman cope with these feelings in an adaptive manner through altering her representation of the infant, the therapist may motivate the caregiver to engage in positive behaviors during the pregnancy and adaptive interactions following the birth.

Although mothers may not engage in potentially harmful behaviors during the pregnancy itself, distorted prenatal fantasies may predict pathological behavior following the birth. For example, an expectant mother who represents the infant as "abandoning" or "controlling" her may engage in maladaptive patterns of interaction with her infant. She may form an enmeshed relationship with the infant in order to prevent him or her from abandoning her. Again, the therapist's interventions should address the pregnant woman's representations in order to help her to form more realistic and adaptive representations of the infant's development and to understand the implications of developmental change for their relationship. In this way, the therapist's interventions should stave off potential maladaptive outcomes once the infant is born.

This chapter describes the therapist's application of previewing to address the distorted prenatal fantasies of an expectant mother with a history of schizoaffective disorder. Prior to the birth she had been taking mild dosages of neuroleptic medication but had discontinued the medication once she learned she was pregnant. She was interviewed by the therapist throughout her pregnancy and following the birth. Her prenatal fantasies illustrated her inability to envision an adaptive future relationship with the infant. The images in her dreams vividly depicted her representational deficits and her ambivalence about her pregnancy and underscored her inability to make any predictions about the birth itself or her infant after the birth. Moreover, the woman was unable to represent how her illness would have an impact on her relationship with her baby. Previewing enabled the therapist to predict this woman's potential to harm her child both before and after the birth. Previewing also helped the woman to resolve the conflict manifested in her prenatal fantasies, and it enabled her to engage in adaptive patterns of interaction with her infant following the birth.

## Patient Identification

The patient, Tiffany R., a 23-year-old expectant mother, although referred by her original therapist, initially came to see me of her own accord. Her presenting complaint, according to the first therapist, was her ambivalence about her prospective pregnancy. Beyond this, the patient was uncertain as to whether she should bear the gestation to term or, instead, terminate it. She suspected the reason for her ambivalence could be found in her acute past history of psychosis.

Tiffany R. presented as an engaging individual whose affect ranged from an extreme of friendliness verging on excessive chattiness to a defensiveness that bordered on the combative. Indeed, during our first session, her manner was so forthcoming as to immediately suggest inappropriate attachment behavior and potential distortion of reality perceptions. The patient's apparent rapid bonding with the therapist and her indiscriminate disclosure of intimate details of her life indicated an underdeveloped sense of interpersonal boundaries. In sharp contrast to her vivid demeanor and easy revelations, the patient's tone became artificially nonchalant when the subject of her pregnancy was raised.

The patient's casual dismissal of the subject, as if this one topic did not at all interest her, revealed a fundamental narcissism underlying her overly casual demeanor. I had the impression that conversing about the upcoming birth prevented her from exploring the more enjoyable or important topic, herself, and, therefore, was not deemed worthy of her—or my—time. The patient was neatly groomed and wore bright clothing that definitely called attention to herself. Yet, she would gaze directly at the therapist only sporadically; more often, she avoided eye contact. Although she was only 2 months pregnant at the time of the first interview, her body language indicated that she was very conscious of her enlarging abdomen. For example, she alternately leaned back as if to display her pregnancy, patting and stroking her abdomen, then slumped over as if to hide it. Both actions appeared to be unconscious aspects of the same ambivalent process.

## DESCRIPTION OF MALADAPTIVE BEHAVIOR

Tiffany R. was being treated for borderline personality disorder. During the second month of her pregnancy, she had been referred to the mother-infant psychotherapy service by her regular therapist, who requested an evaluation of Tiffany's overall perceptions of her pregnancy. From this evaluation, it became evident that Tiffany was reluctant to discuss the expected baby, although she would readily discuss the effects of pregnancy on her life. During our initial session, in fact, she refused to discuss the pregnancy except occasionally to mention that the baby might be "deformed, mutilated, or stillborn." Tiffany also complained of unsettling dreams, although she chose not to disclose these during her first appointment. Moreover, throughout this initial session, Tiffany referred to "the" baby, as opposed to a more personalized, responsible, maternal-directed "my baby" or, in the objective case, "her baby." At this point in the therapeutic process, such detachment reflects the patient's uncertainty, an ambivalence that I will be following closely and noting in all future encounters.

## FAMILY HISTORY

Tiffany was the third of six children from a midwestern family. Her father worked as a museum custodian, whereas her mother was an executive secretary at a real estate company. Tiffany's mother—despite having to rear six children—had worked throughout Tiffany's childhood. According to the patient, she had been singled out by both parents—particularly her father—as the child "most likely to succeed."

Her mother had always considered Tiffany to be a cooperative child who helped out at home, got good grades, and was interested in art. Although she portrayed herself as popular, Tiffany remembered having few close friends and had always, she reported, maintained a "sense of herself" and a need for privacy. This need apparently became so pronounced as to be obsessive when Tiffany entered her teen years. Her mother had told her daughter's first therapist that she believed Tiffany had used painting to "let things out," adding that it was only after Tiffany began college that her art involvement stopped, coinciding with the deterioration of her mental condition. Tiffany's college career was not exceptional; both her parents and her siblings had also attended college, so one could not ascribe a particular focus on her higher education as unusual enough to have prompted her psychiatric episodes or her deteriorated mental status. When asked to speak about her interest in art, Tiffany dismissed it: "There's no point to painting when you have to get ahead."

Tiffany reported that she had experienced "odd spells" from the onset of adolescence; in her senior year of high school, she suffered her first psychotic break. The episode was characterized by a nonstop pattern of speech, compulsive behavior, uncharacteristically sloppy dress, a decreased need for food and sleep, and hypergregarious behavior with strangers—specifically approaching and talking to them incessantly. Her hospitalization had lasted several months, following which she was released to recuperate with her family. In recalling this episode, Tiffany was vivid, even slightly humorous, demonstrating considerable insight into her condition. At approximately that period a young man, Frank, the son of friends of Tiffany's parents, was living with the family. Frank had always been romantically interested in Tiffany, and 6 months after her return from the hospital, the two became engaged.

Following hospitalization, Tiffany's behavior stabilized. Maintained on a mild dose of neuroleptic medication, she attended both group and individual psychotherapy. During this time, as she and Frank began to plan their wedding, Tiffany also started to talk about going back to school again, "now that she was well." At about this time she became preoccupied with the idea of becoming pregnant. Monitoring her menstrual cycle meticulously, she experienced symptoms of "morning sickness" for several days prior to the onset of menstruation. Each month when she began to menstruate, she experienced disappointment that she was not pregnant. Eventually, these disappointments became minidepressive episodes, with Tiffany berating herself for being unable to give Frank "what he wanted." Her attitude at this time, though highly unrealistic, prompted an inevitable fatalism from Tiffany. Frank reported that Tiffany had talked almost nonstop about having a baby and that she was bitterly despairing each time her anticipation of pregnancy was dashed. As time went on, Tiffany's disappointment increased. Not long afterward, the maladaptive behavior characterizing her first psychotic break returned. Almost a year after her first hospitalization, she was rehospitalized. This time her stay was shorter; she was released after a psychiatrist pronounced her "fully recovered" only 2 weeks later. Following this hospitalization, Tiffany abandoned plans to return to college and became immersed in planning her nuptials.

Comments Tiffany made during her first therapy session suggested that she viewed marriage and motherhood as an alternative to finishing college—an alternative that would be acceptable to everyone, including her parents and Frank. She was, in this respect, willfully deluding herself about the priority of becoming pregnant as a value over the alternative—and more obvious—choice of becoming precipitously pregnant. After they were married, Tiffany and Frank, a police officer, moved to an apartment in close proximity to Tiffany's family. Tiffany claimed this was as important to Frank as it was to her, as his family was in Vermont, and he "missed the family atmosphere."

Tiffany worked part-time at a clerical job until she became pregnant. Although the patient's subjective perception was that the pregnancy "took a long time to happen," in fact it was not a long time, and the patient's near-desperation to become impregnated provides yet another clue to the disorder in her mind (as well as illustrating her proclivity to see real events in a distorted time frame). Although family members privately expressed reservations about the pregnancy to Tiffany's therapist, they were generally united in their support. Still, Tiffany was aware of this family tension, saying, "sometimes I think they don't want me to have this baby." At one point her thoughts became slightly disordered: "They are plotting against me." Then she would immediately correct herself: "No, the baby's okay, nobody's gonna do anything to this baby."

## MENTAL HEALTH STATUS EXAMINATION

An intelligent and energetic woman, Tiffany initially gave no indication of delusional thinking. When discussing her history, however, she exaggerated, became easily distracted, and returned repeatedly to certain subjects, as if dissatisfied with specific events in her past. Despite this pattern, Tiffany displayed both insight and humor about her condition. Denying suicidal thoughts, she nevertheless expressed some fear of the hazards she would confront at labor. Several times during the initial meeting, for example, she asked whether the therapist thought she would have a difficult delivery.

When the therapist asked her to elaborate, Tiffany said definitely, "I keep telling myself the delivery is going to be okay, but sometimes I'm so scared. I start thinking the baby will be born deformed like in a horror movie."

Tiffany was always in motion: Her hands fluttered, her feet tapped against the chair, or her eyes darted around the room as she glimpsed her reflection in the room's glass surfaces. Accentuated by an assertively cheerful tone, her demeanor appeared to be artificial, even insufferable at times. Initially, I felt the impact of my therapeutic intervention gloss off the impenetrable barrier of busyness she had created. She seemed to accept all input superficially and without any deeper intellectual or emotional resonance. In short, there was a quality of "faking" to Tiffany's responses that I distinctly felt. In a sense, Tiffany was pretending to maternality.

In my first session with Tiffany, direct inquiry failed to yield demonstrable results. When asked to discuss an issue, she would frequently digress and be hard put to return to the topic. However, when permitted some control over the course of the discussion, Tiffany could be highly cooperative and often enthusiastic. When immersed in recounting the earlier delusional episodes of her life, Tiffany had become obsessed with marriage, pregnancy, and child rearing; ironically, now that she actually *was* pregnant, Tiffany appeared interested in every topic but her developing child. When pressed, she raised a number of technical questions about the pregnancy, but these centered largely on the effects that pregnancy, delivery, and child rearing would have on her. Would she get much bigger physically? Would delivery be very painful? Would she like breast-feeding her infant? Although such considerations indicated awareness of some of the basic challenges facing her in becoming a mother, Tiffany seemed unable to formulate her own responses or to make informed presumptions about her developing baby. Nor did she possess a realistic perception of the responsibilities of motherhood, despite all of her previous involvement and absorption in the ideation of pregnancy.

When she was finally coaxed into discussing the impending birth, one of Tiffany's most frequently voiced concerns was that the baby would somehow be "deformed or sickly" or would "inherit [her] disorder." After some sessions, it became evident to me that the only way Tiffany could visualize her expected infant was as a deformed or mutilated creature, someone not entirely whole. This obsessional thinking would become a predictor of future adaptation. It is noteworthy that although the patient exhibited unusual objectivity in being able to describe her deformity of thought as "a little crazy," this ideation is a current that runs through her entire therapeutic tenure, until she has modified much of her thinking and previewing (quite late in these sessions). Even then, her concerns were primarily for her own self, her projected burden of having to care for a damaged child, and her fear that her family would be disappointed in her, ultimately rejecting her for creating "a monster." Although she knew this train of thought to be delusional, and she could laugh, she would add soberly that "sometimes [these fears] seem very real to [her]."

## Therapy

### SESSION 1

When I entered the room for our first session, the patient's posture suggested that she was suspicious of me. I certainly sensed that she was on guard as I introduced myself and took a seat facing her. Tiffany was a tall, somewhat heavyset young woman in her second month of pregnancy. Her bright yellow dress and matching childlike hair ribbon seemed flamboyant and at odds with her sullen demeanor. Within a few moments, when her nervousness at being interviewed by a new therapist had abated, she appeared to relax and become affable and gregarious—at times excessively so.

I began the session with a brief review of Tiffany's psychiatric history. She immediately became agitated at my comments, fidgeting and swinging her legs, responding to questions with "I can't think right now," or "I don't understand what you want to know." Sensing that direct questions would only elicit repeated resistance, I adopted a more flexible approach and allowed Tiffany to assume control of the early portion of the session. An open-ended inquiry about why Tiffany had come for an evaluation evoked an animated response. Expressing deep hostility toward her regular therapist, she noted in particular her feeling that this therapist, a woman, had "problems dealing with her own femininity." After several minutes of criticism, Tiffany stopped abruptly, eyed me suspiciously, and said, "I don't know why I'm telling you all this stuff about her. You're just going to tell her everything I said." When I reassured Tiffany that any statements she made during a session would be held in strict confidence, she became calmer, leaning back in her chair and nodding.

The patient's high level of volubility struck me as being "overdetermined." Because prior psychotherapeutic experiences had resulted in what the patient herself deemed "failure," perhaps her continuous chatter to no particular end was a symptom of overcompensating. Indeed, her fear of childbirth or gestation could be seen as another index of Tiffany's pattern of "failure," at least in her conscious awareness.

Tiffany then commented a series of free associations that were both desultory and disconnected, alluding to several "nervous breaks" during adolescence. During these "breaks," she told the therapist, she had been able to "control other people's thoughts." I asked her to elucidate. "I could control what my father was thinking, for example. I always knew just what he was going to say to me, and I could make him say those things just by thinking them. Whenever that happened, I knew I was controlling his thoughts. I know this sounds strange, but it's true." The issue of control emerged several times during this first session: The patient's insistence that she had had the ability to "control" her father's thoughts is just one example of her conflicting preoccupation with both her ability and her inadequacy to exercise power over external individuals and events.

By this point, Tiffany had relaxed her guard considerably. She sat back comfortably, rubbing her abdomen slowly with one hand, smiling as she made a point. She also focused directly on me; there was a sense that she was performing for me, as if she were on stage. When I explained that as part of the therapy we could discuss her dreams, she interrupted eagerly and asked if I would like to hear one. She dreamt all the time, she said, and could remember all of her dreams, although she would only recount three of them at this juncture. These three dreams were "special" and had occurred since she had learned of her pregnancy. She described her first dream:

> I was trying to get my wedding band off, but it wouldn't come off because I had suddenly gotten fat. I finally removed it and put it on the dresser with my earrings. The next day, when my fingers weren't so fat, I went back to find it, but it wasn't there. Frank told me that I had dropped it on the floor under the bed, but I said "No, I put it on the dresser." But he made me look, and there was my ring on the floor, just the way he said.

"That's a very interesting dream," I said. "What do you think it means?"

"I always lose things," Tiffany said nonchalantly. Then she furrowed her brow, looking serious. "But I think this is a very spiritual dream, you know?" Before I could ask her to elaborate, Tiffany began describing the second dream:

> I was in bed, but I got up to go to the closet to get a hanger. When I got it, I twisted it all up, then put it on the floor under the bed. I don't know why. I just felt that I had to put the hanger there. It was like a compulsion.

Questioned about the dream, Tiffany admitted that the hanger could symbolize "the way some women get rid of babies they don't want," although she added, "I don't think you're right because you don't know me well enough yet to make an interpretation," deftly avoiding acknowledging that the abortion imagery might be related to her own feelings. In the third dream Tiffany related, she was sitting in her backyard, looking up into the sky:

> Suddenly, I saw my dog up in the sky. He died when I was 18. But he was all broken up in the dream. His liver was in one place and his eye was somewhere else, and his leg was attached to his ear. As I was staring upward at his apparition, I smelled something burning, like dried leaves, or like I hadn't turned the stove off and dinner was burning.

Asked to interpret, Tiffany smiled mysteriously. Then she said she thought she understood what it meant but couldn't say just yet. "You're not my therapist yet," she explained. "Besides, you wouldn't understand, since you don't know enough about me. This is a very spiritual dream." She added that she was a very unusual person and that "it would take a long time to know [her]."

Clearly the imagery of Tiffany's dreams with regard to her pregnancy was disturbing: dismemberment, deformity, even death figured unmistakably and prominently. Tiffany's comments also suggested she felt that these dire outcomes could be the result of her own carelessness, as with the burning dinner in the dog dream. The abortion imagery of the hanger dream and the images of loss in the ring dream are strong and disturbing. Other salient issues in connection to this dream include the abdication of responsibility for actually getting pregnant; the disingenuousness vis-à-vis what sex and marriage obviously lead to; her clear noncommitment to Frank and her prospective child; the impending loss of her body image as a sexual and desirable woman (in particular, to her husband); all these, together, added up to an enormous sense of loss of control and powerlessness. Although the significance of these dreams and their imagistic freight is undeniable, at this time in the process, the analysand was presumably unaware of their symbolic import. However, as later sessions and material disclosed, the patient was quite aware, in fact, of the significance of her dream imagery and made frequent reference to these and subsequent dreams. The language with which she described her awareness of the physical changes in her body became increasingly menacing and violent:

> I can't eat so much any more because of the taste in my mouth that the baby gives me, like I've been sucking on a penny or something. It's a horrible taste, like the baby doesn't like the food I like, so he makes it all taste really bad. What else? Well, I can't sleep on my side or my stomach any more because I know I'll crush the baby. The doctor says I don't have to worry about that yet, but I don't think he's right. I know I could kill the baby if I slept on my stomach. So I sleep on my back because of the baby, and the baby makes me snore like an old dog growling or something. I woke up the other night, and I couldn't figure out what the awful noise was. I thought it was my husband growling at me. But it was me snoring. I sound just like my old dog.

Tiffany became pensive, adding that she could no longer urinate or defecate while sitting on the toilet. "I have to go to the bathroom a lot now, and I have to stand up when I do it. I feel like a dog in the street." She looked sideways at me after this comment, trying to gauge my reaction to this disclosure. Tiffany clearly attributes the negative aspects of her pregnancy to her fetus, endowing it with a supranormal control over her physical reality and psychological perceptions that are clearly frightening to her. "I can't figure you out," she said to me. "You look curious, and I like that, but I don't think you've asked me the right questions yet." A critical tone edged her words.

"Could you give me some suggestions about the questions you would like me to ask?" I said.

As if on cue, Tiffany opened her purse and brought out a list she had apparently prepared, neatly typed on a sheet of crisp pink notepaper. She told me that before her other therapy sessions she always thought about what she wanted to say that day, preparing an "agenda" for the session; moreover, after each session she gave the therapist a "grade." She clearly felt that she needed a highly structured forum within which to state her fears and to exert some sense of empowerment or control over both therapist and therapeutic relationship. "I have a long list of questions," she admitted, her manner somewhat chiding, as if she were scolding me for failing at being a therapist. This seemed to be another example of her attempts to assume control over the session. I encouraged her to read the list aloud so we could both take a stab at questions:

First off, how will I feel the first time the baby moves? Will it scare me? Will the baby be healthy? Will the baby be accepted, even though I have a disease? What if it has my disease, or it's sick or deformed or something? Will I be scared when I have to deliver? What if the baby is born dead? How will I feel? Will it be a boy or a girl? Will I feel different if it's a boy? Will I like breast-feeding? How will I feel about sex after the baby is born?

Tiffany read this list off in a rapid-fire fashion. When she finished, she stared challengingly at me. "Well, are you going to answer my questions?" she asked at last.

I replied that they were all excellent questions and that I thought we could find answers to each of them if we worked together. On a pragmatic level, she likely realized that her inquiries could not be addressed in one session, and thus she consented to return again. "There are some other questions you may want to think about, too," I added, "such as how you feel about the future; what you think the baby will be like; how you think you will get along with the baby. It seems a lot of your questions involve your feelings about the baby in the future."

Tiffany burst in with, "What about me? How am I going to feel? You seem more concerned about the baby than about me. And I don't think you know the answers to my questions." Before I could respond, she added, "You can't know what's going on inside of me. My other therapist thinks she knows, too, but she doesn't either."

Throughout the interview I was struck by how little Tiffany focused on the baby she was expecting and by her simplistic views of pregnancy. Her questions concerned her own reactions and feelings about the pregnancy, and when I tried to evoke predictions about the baby, she became quite angry, accusing me of taking the baby's "side" rather than hers. Her response again seemed childish and narcissistic. From Tiffany's reaction to my questions, as well as from the list of questions she had brought with her, I hypothesized that this expectant mother lacked the ability to envision her baby or to formulate any imagery concerning her prospective life after the birth of her child.

"Perhaps you can tell me more about what you think is going on inside of you, and then we will be able to clarify what it means. That's what I meant by working together," I said calmly. Tiffany nodded and said that would be all right with her. The session concluded soon afterward; she agreed to return again in 2 weeks. I left the session feeling slightly overwhelmed by Tiffany's powerful and combative presence. Her demeanor, sullen and withdrawn at the outset of the session, had rapidly evolved to a more demanding and expansive one, and her attitude had become at once amiable and challenging toward me.

Preliminary evaluation indicates that this patient's perceptions of reality are distorted, as evidenced by her odd responses to pregnancy; that she suffers from narcissistic tendencies, as evidenced by her compulsion to turn all conversations back to herself; and that she manifests a difficulty with attachment behavior, as evidenced by her disjointed verbose disclosures and simultaneous wariness. Tiffany's ability to preview or rehearse upcoming events seems largely limited to negative, almost calamitous, outcomes, outcomes that explain—perhaps even justify—her underlying agenda to lose or abandon her baby. Using previewing as a diagnostic to predict the outcome of her pregnancy and the kind of relationship that will later characterize the mother-infant interaction, one can see that it appears that without intervention, there is a good to better chance of termination now as well as a strong risk that the patient will have difficulty handling motherhood should the pregnancy run to term.

## SESSION 2

For our second session, Tiffany wore a short, bright pink dress and lacy white stockings. Since she had mentioned twice during the previous session how distressed she was by the loss of her figure as her pregnancy progressed, I wondered whether the dress was an attempt to camouflage or emphasize her pregnancy. Here was another example of her unconsciously battling the inevitable: her enlarging body. Coupled with this was also a desire to thwart the realization that as her body grew, it diminished (in her eyes) in sexuality, at least insofar as her love, Frank, was concerned.

Although Tiffany fidgeted nervously during the session, her jitteriness and disconnected comments were far fewer than they had been at our first meeting. At the outset, I asked Tiffany if her pregnancy had been planned.

"Planned and worked for!" she replied. Initially, she noted, she and her husband had been unable to conceive despite repeated efforts. In describing their efforts to conceive, Tiffany was vehement in defending her husband; she "knew her failure to conceive" initially could not be laid at his door, because he was healthy, a "real stud in bed—and [he] took vitamins."

Returning to an issue I had raised at our first session, I asked Tiffany: "Have you envisioned what the baby will be like?" Tiffany looked at me blankly. "Did you, for example, think about whether you would have a baby boy or a baby girl?" I persisted.

Looking annoyed, she responded, "A girl, I guess. Well, when I think about it, I'd be very scared to have a boy! But I'm scared to have a girl, too!"

Hearing ambivalence, I smiled: "Do you think you could state a preference?"

"Girl," Tiffany said, more definitely this time. "A boy scares me more. I think boys go through life afflicted, you know? Girls get through life more easily. They know how to cope with people and stuff. Boys have to do things the hard way all the time. It's as if they have a special burden," she added, with a meditative quality to her voice. "I'm not sure I understand," I said to elicit more information.

"Well, I think men are very defensive, which is what I guess I would be if I had genitals hanging out where anyone could hurt them," Tiffany said, looking at me brazenly, then giggling with embarrassment. "Women are much more secure because no one can come and hurt them down there since their sex organs are inside," she explained with gusto. "So men are more vulnerable and they don't like it; it makes them suspicious, and they can behave dangerously. You understand? But you're a man, so maybe you don't see it this way."

"Tell me more," I urged.

"It's like trust. Men don't have much trust, which is why when they die their spirits go into trees or dogs or something like that. When women die, their spirits pass into other people." Her comment reminded me of her dream in which the imagery of a disembodied dog was preeminent. Dismemberment, symbolic of a fragmented sense of self, still appeared to be a prevalent concern with the patient. The content of this second session suggested that the gender of the infant was problematic for Tiffany. In explaining these ideas, Tiffany next invoked a genetic theory she had devised for understanding how the emotions of one generation might be transmitted to later generations. "I really think our emotional problems are passed down to us through the genes." Tiffany carefully monitored my reaction as she spoke. "I think maybe my baby will be sensitive to my sickness because of the genes I am giving it." Now in her third month, Tiffany seems to regard her fetus very much as an object, with a potential for manifesting its inheritance—particularly her "sickness." At this point, as is evident in the factual and historic quality of her statements, Tiffany's views were becoming gradually more objectified.

"Can you explain how the baby will be sensitive?" I asked.

"I don't know. I'll get back to that in a minute," Tiffany said, abruptly changing topics, seemingly resentful at my interruption. "You mentioned last time that we could work with dreams. Do you want to hear some of my dreams?" Tiffany had been slumped back in her chair with her arms crossed over her abdomen. Now she leaned forward with a provocative look, as if inviting me to share something special, perhaps titillating. She began to relate a dream that involved her best girlfriend, who had recently had a baby:

> I had my baby, too, and my girlfriend and I were going to start breast-feeding. She started, and I began to follow her, but my baby wouldn't suck. I guess I didn't have any milk in my breasts. So I panicked and got very paranoid because I wasn't prepared. I didn't have any bottles or formula. So I improvised something. There was also a point in the dream when she and I were together . . . you know? We were having sex together. Actually, the sex part came first, then the part where we were breast-feeding.

"I wonder if you could clarify whether the baby couldn't suck or whether the baby tried but did not succeed," I said.

Tiffany then contradicted her earlier statement: "I don't know why, but he just pushed me away." Perhaps this episode of rejection by a boy baby previews Tiffany's fear that her infant, sensing his mother's need for nurturance, will reject her attempts to nurture him. It is clearly important to Tiffany that the baby respond to her in an empathic fashion—perhaps she believes that a female infant will be more likely to do so than a male infant. In some respects, such issues involve Tiffany's capacity to form an attachment to another. Her dialogue with me increasingly reflected the essential dichotomy of her desires. Hence she declared, "I knew I had milk. And this got me really scared because I knew the baby was very hungry."

"What made you think he was hungry?" I asked.

"I just knew I hadn't fed the baby in a long time," she leaned back, seemingly enjoying the details she was providing.

"You think he gave up trying to get milk from you?" I persisted.

"I don't know. But I was upset because I had to think fast and feed the baby, or else he would starve." Tiffany could not posit any other interpretation as to why the infant in the dream had rejected her nurturing. The most she could proffer was to repeat her husband's joke—his reaction when she had told the dream to him: "You must have an ugly breast," she said, giggling.

Thus, we may safely say her primary focus remained on herself, although she was beginning to speculate about the impact the baby would have on her life. The dream she related about breast-feeding indicated the beginnings of concern for her infant as a separate individual with unique needs; it suggested that Tiffany was beginning to move away from fantasies that involved destroying the fetus and move into the arena of nurturance. The dream also indicated that Tiffany was experimenting with the power that she, as primary caregiver, would have over the daily needs of her child. Her ability to consider and speculate about these events in the form of a dream was a positive sign that she was beginning to regulate her feelings about the pregnancy and the baby adaptively.

However, there were also signs that Tiffany still harbored negative feelings about her child. The breast-feeding dream, rich in nurturance imagery, suggests that Tiffany not only was troubled about her potential inability to nurture another (her infant) but also feared that she required nurturance from others—in this case, the friend with whom she engaged in sex and from whom she obtained formula to feed the baby because her own breasts were putatively dry. It is interesting to note, particularly in light of Tiffany's ambivalence about the baby, that since a lesbian relationship is one that would not be expected to produce a pregnancy, such a relationship would obviate the need for Tiffany to become a nurturer. This dream, then, like Tiffany herself, projected contradictory images. One might consider some of the imagery to be positive in that Tiffany conceptualized herself as a mother, a mother whose primary task is to feed her baby. On the other hand, the fact that this biological mother then lacked milk (a prime requisite for this role) to feed the baby is problematic. Whereas a certain component of the dream might be considered deviant, much more of its latent meaning had to do, I believe, with the yearning to be nurtured and fed, supported and reinforced, all of which might well originate from the nurturative attention of an older female (such as a sister), particularly in recognition of Tiffany's statements about male nurturing inadequacy.

"After relating your dream today, what feelings do you have?" I asked.

"I'm scared that I couldn't think of anything else to feed the baby." Tiffany shrugged and avoided making eye contact. She looked down as if ashamed of herself, but I sensed that she was not really upset so much as she was actually more interested in my reaction. For several minutes she silently and critically observed her reflection in the window. Finally she commented that she speculated about whether her child would look like herself or her husband.

"Would you want your baby to look like you?" I asked. Tiffany shrugged.

"Ummm. . . . It's just, you never know what genes a kid is going to get. Maybe the baby will be very different from me."

"Would you want the baby to be different from you?" I asked.

Tiffany considered my question. "I'd like the baby not to have my sickness," she said, almost wistfully. Then, with a smile, "It would be nice if the baby had Frank's hair." With all her sophistication and awareness, Tiffany repeatedly referred to her "sickness"; she was in fact being euphemistic deliberately, since, as was evident throughout, she had acquired a compendium of sophisticated terminology and could display remarkable insight. So her choice to invoke the simple term "sickness" repeatedly indicated a decided dependency on the therapist. Tiffany had proclaimed herself "sick." He can make her "well."

Tiffany remained calmer throughout this session than she had during the first one. This is possibly because the sessions allowed her to explore distressing perceptions fraught with anticipatory anxiety. I realized I must remain on guard, however, lest Tiffany use the sessions to indulge in her narcissistic tendencies and exert control. Her increasingly calm affect might also suggest her growing trust. In contrast to our first session, Tiffany monitored my reactions to some of her more shocking or problematic revelations much less intensely. Generally, Tiffany finds other people's opinions of her very important—when the session was formally over and we were leaving, she commented that I had not, so far, asked her how it felt to be a person with a psychiatric disorder in a society where such disorders were viewed with disapproval. This comment suggested that I might disapprove of her. When I asked her how that situation made her feel, she said with a touch of bitterness that people who had such thoughts "weren't very smart" and that she felt sorry for them. Still, considering her earlier comment that she hoped her baby would not "inherit her sickness," it appears Tiffany had begun to reflect on society's disapproval of her disease, not only as it currently affected her but also as it might have an impact on her child. These observations will be explored further in future sessions.

## SESSION 3

The first thing I noticed as the session began was a marked difference in the patient's mood, which appeared confrontational, if not actually combative. Tiffany's facial expression suggested that she was surly and hostile. She stated that she had almost not come because she was convinced that "the baby didn't like the room" in which we met.

"Do you think the baby knows which room we meet in?" I asked.

"She's psychic!" Tiffany said archly, leaning toward me with a flirtatious gesture. By attributing psychic powers to her baby, Tiffany is "creating" a baby strong enough to take care of its own needs as well as its mother's in case something should happen to her. Perhaps Tiffany is reasoning that the psychic baby will know how to take care of its mother and will know not to expect nurturance from her. This might be an example of "magical thinking," a throwback to her thinking of prepregnancy days, but it indicates vulnerability and a lurking predisposition to psychotic thinking.

She reported that she had had a dream about her former therapist the night before. "Doctor Bennett [who is Jewish] and I met with Hitler, and he beat her up!" She laughed derisively. Once again her anger emerges; the more Tiffany perceives herself as not receiving support and nurturance, the more her rage erupts in bizarre and violent imagery. Ostensibly Bennett, her previous therapist, is being targeted here by "Hitler," but in essence, the thinly disguised target of the patient's wrath is undoubtedly her current therapist, myself.

I asked Tiffany to comment on the meaning of her dream.

"I don't know. I guess I'm angry with her. She's leaving for another job. It doesn't really matter though because I never thought she was very good." Tiffany leaned toward me again and said threateningly that I had "better not leave, too." The threat implicit in the dream with Hitler is made explicit here in her sentences. She warns the therapist not to disappoint her and not to step out of line. Mostly, she is furious at the potential for his abandoning her, too, the way others have in her past, either in actuality or symbolically. Suddenly, with an instantaneous change of facial expression, Tiffany demanded that I "never, ever" leave her. "I hope you'll be a good doctor to me," she said, pulling the hem of her skirt over one knee. "I'll have the baby soon, and I'll need a good doctor to help me take care of her." Thus, we see a distinct defensive style of Tiffany emerging; it is to get the therapist to fulfill her needs through seduction and a variety of ancillary behaviors. Tiffany's oscillation between seduction and hostility is quite pronounced. Given a response to her flirtatiousness, the hostility can be expected to abate. When the seductiveness is shown to be unavailing, her hostility reemerges. The patient then added in a supplicating tone that the baby did not want me to leave. Her manner seemed designed to enlist me so that I would not "disappear" or "betray" her, as her other therapist was doing.

For the remainder of the session, Tiffany continued to attribute her feelings and observations to the baby, as if the two were one fused person. She stopped occasionally to close her eyes and "commune" with the baby so she could report the baby's thoughts or feelings on a given subject. "I use my psychic powers," she explained when I asked her how she was obtaining information from the baby. Tiffany then began to interrogate me about our discussions at the last session, saying the baby needed to be sure that I was paying attention and would be a good doctor for *them*.

Tiffany's ambivalent irrationality and latent volatility continued to permeate the session. She launched into an account of a complex dream in which God takes her baby away because she has "been such a bad mother." It worried and annoyed her, she said, that the baby was "controlling her thoughts so much." When I commented that Tiffany had once told me she could control her father's thoughts, she agreed enthusiastically and said she was happy I remembered. "The younger generation can control the older one's thoughts." That would all stop, however, when her baby was born and christened, according to Tiffany. "The Holy Spirit will fill the baby up, and it will stop all that controlling and just be a good baby. But until then, it's like we are one person with one mind."

The events of this session stood in startling contrast to our prior meeting. Her ambivalence about her infant, manifested in the dream about God taking the baby, and her remarks about how the child was controlling her mind, were striking. These comments suggested an abiding underlying hostility for the infant as well as an inability to differentiate her personality from the infant's.

Despite Tiffany's extreme volatility, I sensed that she was experiencing vulnerability and an ongoing concern for her baby and their aborning relationship. Her dream that the deity would remove the baby might well be symbolic for expressing a forbidden wish: "How do I shed this responsibility?" Again, the baby's removal cannot be presented, even symbolically, as her fault. Anyone else is to blame for the loss of her baby. Rather than face her fear of failure at motherhood head on, she skirts this abyss with "excuses" that leave the matter entirely out of her hands. At the same time, the dream content indicates that Tiffany herself is afraid that when her disorder is active she may not be able to function adequately as a mother. In the session, she asked repeatedly for reassurance that she would be a good parent and that things would be all right. The temptation to regress into her disorder, to ensure that she would be cared for, was evident in Tiffany's flirtatious, disordered, and volatile state. These elements translated into the certainty that her status in the coming weeks needed to be carefully monitored.

## SESSION 4

In contrast to our previous session, Tiffany's manner today was energetic but not volatile, disordered, or provocative. She was neatly dressed, her hair carefully arranged, and she looked businesslike and eager to proceed.

At the outset, I asked Tiffany how her pregnancy was progressing. With a mixture of wonder and annoyance, she stated that she believed her baby had begun to kick. I asked when she had first experienced the sensation and how it had felt. She responded matter of factly. "The baby started kicking about a week ago. At first I thought I had gas. Then I thought something was wrong with me, but when I described it to my girlfriend, she told me he was just kicking."

This pronoun is telling. As she had earlier made clear that a female child is preferred, the sudden assumption of the male pronoun "he" is puzzling until one thinks that perhaps it is another stratagem to disavow alliance with the infant. If she dislikes the fetus, a he, then she won't feel the pain of failing with a desired baby, a she.

"What does the kicking feel like?" I pursued.

"It's like a tingling nudge. Sometimes it's a hard nudge, too."

I asked why she thought the baby was kicking, whether she thought the kicks were deliberate or were a form of communication or were perhaps just random. After several minutes, however, she admitted that sometimes she imagined the baby kicked because he was trying to communicate with her. Consistently during this discussion she referred to the fetus as male.

"He's just lying in there, and he says to himself, I'm gonna kick Mommy because there's nothing else to do." She giggled. This locution shows a thought process not unlike that of most normal pregnant women. She does not manifest a bizarre or untoward sensibility in every regard (to pregnancy), a sign I found encouraging.

"Is this the way you imagined you would feel before you became pregnant?" I asked.

Tiffany shook her head vehemently. "I didn't imagine anything about what it would feel like to be pregnant. I just couldn't imagine the future. We had to work very hard to become pregnant. I took pills to make me ovulate, and I monitored my cycle. But I wish I had had a few years to prepare myself for this before I got pregnant, because sometimes when I think about being a mother, it's scary." This statement implies that she is finally beginning to apprehend the significance of the upcoming birth and the need to find strength for adaptive motherhood in the future. In other words, Tiffany is now able to preview that characterological strength will eventually be available to her. My goal remains, then, to increase her confidence so that she can easily access this strength.

"When you were trying to get pregnant, did you envision what it would be like to be a mother?" I asked.

Tiffany remained silent for a long moment, mulling over her thoughts. "I was prepared in a kind of fantasy way," she said at last. "I just didn't think about all the real things that I wouldn't like. It makes me feel very stressed, which isn't good for the baby, is it?"

"What are the changes you don't like?" I asked.

"All the changes—like losing my shape, so I'm not as attractive, and what's happened to my skin; it's dry in some places, but I've got acne, too, and my skin is all blotchy. I can't even think of what having this baby will be like. If I feel this tired and ugly now, what will I feel like after the baby is born?" She begins to show a marked shift from self-absorbed comments and narcissistic reflections to questions that can be answered by a trusted confidant and advisor.

"Knowing now what you would have to deal with, the weight gain and the physical changes in your body—how would you prepare for pregnancy if you had to do it all over again?" I asked.

Tiffany shook her head and examined her reflection in the window. "I would drink a lot beforehand. I really miss that. I think after the baby is born it will be hard for me not to become an alcoholic because I'm going to drink so much to catch up," she giggled as she spoke.

"In what way would becoming an alcoholic make your role as a mother different?" I asked.

> Someone gave me a bottle of cream liqueur for my birthday, after I found out I was pregnant. I haven't had any, but sometimes I just want a little of it. I really get tempted to make a fancy drink with that liqueur and ice cream in the blender and just get really drunk. I want it so bad I can taste it sometimes. I feel like the baby is teasing me to be an alcoholic each time I go into the pantry and see that bottle. I'm not drinking now because I'm pregnant, but it's a sacrifice. Every time I don't have a drink I think about it: I like to fantasize about it. I feel as if my mind is preparing me for a whole different way of looking at that liqueur. I even thought of asking my husband to bring the bottle to the hospital so I could have a drink right after the baby is born. Sometimes I even think I'll take a drink just to spite the baby!

She looked at me searchingly, to gauge my response to these comments. This series of admissions that, although she's desperate for the liqueur, she will not taste it, is a growing indication of her new determination to be a good mother. Though it would be easy to cheat—and drink—and to justify it by saying selfish things about her "need" to indulge, Tiffany is able to refrain.

"Do you think you could take care of your newborn baby and drink at the same time?" I asked.

Tiffany considered my question thoughtfully. "The baby may get a little drunk if I'm breast-feeding him."

"If he became drunk, would this make it easier for you to interact with him?"

"No, it wouldn't. But maybe I won't have enough milk, or if I do, he just won't want my milk anyway." She seemed to grow sad suddenly. It is interesting that Tiffany now refers almost exclusively to the infant as a male baby and has again raised the possibility that this boy-fetus would reject her nurturing behavior. Whereas she is beginning to address her fears, she is also concomitantly less defensive, more to the point than she had been prior to this. Her answers have a more thoughtful aspect. She is exploring her responses rather than reflectively bouncing them off the therapist's supposed expectations.

"Would he reject your milk like in the dream you related two sessions ago?" I then asked. It took Tiffany a moment to recall what she had related during that session. "Oh, yes. Maybe the baby knew I was having fantasies about drinking, and that's why I had that dream. The baby in my dream fantasy wanted to keep me from having what I want."

"That's one way of looking at it," I said. "Another way of looking at this issue is to understand why you feel the baby is exerting this kind of control over you. It's as if you were setting up a relationship with the baby already, giving him or her a great deal of control over your actions now and after the birth," I noted. I purposely include the two gender choices here despite Tiffany's seeming focus only on the masculine.

Tiffany shrugged off the control issue, explaining that she sometimes thought drinking her liqueur was the only thing that would clear her mouth of the "terrible brassy taste" she had been experiencing since becoming pregnant. I then asked her what she thought would happen to the baby if she had a drink. "Liquor might destroy its mind a little bit," she conceded. As the dialogue reveals, Tiffany demonstrates steady improvement in her willingness to view the infant as a distinct entity and to consider its needs. Moreover, she is beginning to differentiate her needs from the infant's. Her capacity to extrapolate the baby's mind-set seems to have awakened Tiffany's unmasked urge to attribute responsibility for some of the desired fantasies and behaviors to the fetus. The baby has "made" her yearn for a drink and "makes" her food taste bad. Despite this comment, Tiffany added that if she were offered a sip of her liqueur she might break down and have a little, since "thinking about it all the time must be worse than just doing it! The thought of having a drink sometimes controls my mind."

"In the past you also thought that your father controlled your mind," I commented. "It seems to me that you attribute this power to individuals who play a meaningful role in your life. Perhaps that is why you think the baby can control your thoughts." This flip-flop is a product of new relationships reactivating past conflicts. Interventions involve a vicious cycle of who will control whom, though the irony (and the index of illness, of course) is that all conflicts stem from one person alone: Tiffany, with no input at all from her father, her child, or her husband.

Yet Tiffany reacted to this with resistance: "I know that's probably not true. It's just the way the baby makes me feel sometimes." By "making" Tiffany drink and by "making" her dependent, the baby would then be setting her up as the object of nurturance. In some respects, such thought processes suggest an underlying hostility toward the infant. Tiffany crossed her legs, then her arms, a deliberate "keep off" gesture, and changed the subject, wondering aloud if her baby would be afraid of the dark as she was.

"Do you think it would make any difference if the baby were alone or with you when he was in the dark?" I asked.

"I think he would feel very scared if he stayed alone," Tiffany responded reflectively.

"Why are you afraid of the dark?"

"In the light you can't think about all those deep, scary things that you can think of so easily in the dark. In the light you don't see things you shouldn't see. But at night I have scary thoughts, like someone is controlling my mind. Maybe if I could hear the baby's heartbeat I wouldn't be afraid of the dark, either." Significantly, this "scary thought" theme is a constant throughout the therapeutic process with me. Tiffany consistently imputes the genesis of scary thoughts to external beings, events, forces. It is never *her* response or *her* responsibility.

Tiffany's previewing skills, at least with regard to her pregnancy, have been poor during these first four sessions. She is either unable to ideate the baby's behavior and her own response to motherhood realistically, or her depictions of the baby are implausible and tinged with hostility or projection. My reviewing her past predictions with her in sessions in light of her current status is a useful exercise that may eventually enable her to gain additional insight into her situation. Despite her evident evolving insight, she seems to want and need me to guide her. She senses she is not yet at a point where she can formulate accurate predictions (about the baby) on her own. Tiffany's statement that she had not imagined anything about this pregnancy accurately suggests that she may be starting to understand the value of previewing and predictive fantasy. In fact, it is an encouraging signal that she can state that she wished she had had "a couple of years" more to prepare for the birth. She generalizes here that all women experience to some degree the fears she experiences. And in truth, the intrapolation is valid here, a legitimate thought that means she is thinking not about her closed self but of the larger issues of how the life she bears is fragile and reactive to life's traumas and various insults.

## SESSION 5

Tiffany appeared in good spirits today. After an initial inquiry about her physical health and her latest obstetrical checkup, I asked Tiffany to discuss the ways, if any, in which being pregnant has changed her emotional life. She immediately responded by saying that being pregnant has made her "paranoid." She added, "I don't mean paranoid in the sick way, though." When asked to elaborate on her notion of "paranoid," she readily volunteered:

> I'm paranoid about everything. You know, I think women in general are paranoid about life. Women are able to sort out the whole picture of life, whereas men only see particular details. When women are little girls they prepare themselves to be women and to have babies growing inside their bodies when they grow up. When you actually become pregnant, though, you start having these fears, getting paranoid about all the things that are and can happen inside your body.

"What kinds of changes can take place within you?"

"Carrying a baby inside causes you to think about so many things. . . ."

You begin predicting all the things that can happen. Like death, loss, grief, and unhappiness. So many things can happen to the baby . . . stillbirth, death . . . and all of it takes place inside your body."

"Do you feel you lost control over something in your life when you became pregnant?"

"Yes. It's as if I have no control about anything now. And that makes me go numb, like the baby is the one who is alive, and I'm dead. Not that many people can relate to these fears."

"Do you feel your family understands these feelings?"

"Yes, but not all the time."

"That must feel very lonely."

Although Tiffany mentions her husband frequently, she does not indicate how he accommodates her wish to be nurtured. He does not, however, permit her to "regress" but requires that she behave as an adult and take over the nurturing role. "I can understand that carrying the baby makes you think of the possibility of loss and of the grief that accompanies such loss. It may be a surprise to you to know, however, that many pregnant women share the same fears and concerns."

"Even those who don't have my sickness?" Tiffany sounded incredulous.

Yes. These concerns are universal. Pregnant women are often afraid of the kinds of losses you are talking about. It's important to be aware of these fears—and to contrast these concerns with other more positive feelings triggered by the pregnancy. One way to do this is to learn how to predict upcoming changes and to prepare for them. I have labeled this skill "previewing." By using this skill many of these troubling issues may be anticipated and handled more adaptively. For example, are these losses the only things the baby makes you think of? Do you have any pleasurable feelings associated with the baby or with the experience of pregnancy?

Tiffany frowned briefly. "I think I do, but the positive feelings are sometimes not as clear as the negative feelings. For me it's easier to be cautious about paranoid feelings." For her, she meant, it is easier to experience paranoid feelings. The very fact that she phrased the sentence in this backward-leaning, somehow paradoxical way might be an indication of her confusion and the continuation—even well into the therapeutic process—of condensing a raft of unconsciously irreconcilable opposites. That is, "cautious about paranoid feelings" in a less agitated person would usually be expressed as "I feel more at ease with paranoia than with positive feelings," or some variation thereof. "Do you think that by feeling 'paranoid' about your pregnancy you're better able to exert control and master the changes that the pregnancy is going to cause?"

Tiffany smiled. "Yes."

"Can you explain why that is?"

Tiffany commented that one characteristic of her emotional illness was a tendency to feel "too good" when she became sick. At these times, she would spend money, talk nonstop, and sleep very little. "I get a little nervous about having happy feelings because they may be a sign that my sickness is coming back." Of course, the illness was under control now, she hastened to add. She had had a flare-up of hypomanic behavior toward the beginning of her pregnancy, she told me. At that time, she had given gifts and money to her family and friends but had experienced no symptoms since. Although it was clear from Tiffany's tone that she feared such episodes, there was also an undercurrent of suppressed excitement as she discussed her hypomanic episode. It had evidently energized her with an empowering charge she ordinarily lacked. Though she would not ordinarily be characterized as listless, Tiffany did vary in her energy and dynamism. In this instance, discussion of her hypomanic episode seemed to evoke a sort of "flashback" excitement. I asked if she felt that her pregnancy had had something to do with the recurrence of this behavior. Tiffany nodded, but she added that other things could stir up a recurrence of her sickness as well:

> For me, talking about the past is very bad. I become sick again when I have to talk about the times I was sick in the past. Right now I'm much better; I feel I can control myself and my thoughts. Still, it's frightening when I think I could get sick again. I lose all control when I'm sick. After a brief pause she continued. Another thing that frightens me is that I'll wind up a homeless person or in an institution because of my disease. I won't have any money or home. That's what happens to a lot of people like me. Sometimes I walk past a homeless person on the street and think that's what will happen to me.

Tiffany looked somber when she said this. Then brightening, she offered to discuss some recent dreams:

> Two days ago, and then last night, I dreamed about the baby. In my dream I heard a baby crying, so I woke my husband and asked him if he heard the crying. At first he said no, and then he told me that it wasn't a baby crying, it was him. But I knew it wasn't him. When I woke up, it seemed so real that I felt my baby was crying, and I began thinking, how could I hear the baby cry when he's still inside of me?

I am convinced that the previewing of a baby crying is a positive sign. This imagery suggests that she is beginning to predict, on some appropriately intuitive level, the emotional needs of a baby. "Why do you think the baby was crying?" I asked.

> It wasn't because he was unhappy, I knew that. I think maybe it was because he was feeling pain and was trying to tell me that. I worry about having to take medication. Do you think the baby can be affected by it a little? But I also wonder if the medication will help the baby's brain if he has my sickness. Maybe by the time he's born he won't have my sickness at all.

Noticing the degree of defensiveness that characterized Tiffany's last statement, I decided on a temporary midcourse correction, and I gently asked her to refocus her attention on the feelings she was shielding. I guided the conversation back to Tiffany's dream, asking her again why she thought the baby had been crying. She suggested that it might be because the baby felt hungry or uncomfortable, that its diaper might need changing, or that the baby might have been frightened or upset by something. I attempted to guide her to the discrete needs of her infant in a more concrete perspective; however, she focused grandly and unrealistically on a far-future element—diapers that might need changing—and this too, I feel, indicated a well of unsurfaced cognitive processes on the topic at hand. Tiffany admitted that these thoughts worried her considerably. "I want to be able to figure out what he needs." Her comment that the baby's crying might result from a variety of causes is also positive, indicating that she is beginning to envision the complexities posed by motherhood.

"I'll tell you another dream," she volunteered. "In the dream, I gave birth to a girl and a boy. They were very nicely dressed, which I liked. I think my husband was in the dream too, but I don't really remember. And I had another dream in which the baby was born—it just came right out of me without any pain." Tiffany appeared to perceive these babies as if they are dolls, further emphasizing the notion that the delivery process and its outcome may be a nonclimactic event, one in which she does not have to figure in the long term. Such distortion might be symptomatic of more unresolved magic thinking.

"I've been having dreams about the baby—and dreams with a lot of sexual stuff, also." Tiffany displayed some awkwardness about relating her sexual dreams. When we agreed that she could stop if she felt embarrassed, Tiffany continued:

> I had one dream about my brother. He and I were making love. I know that's really bad ... it's like incest, and no matter what happened in my family, there was no incest. I think I had that dream because he had called earlier that day. I have a lot of other sexual dreams, too. Before I was pregnant I used to dream about being pregnant with twins or triplets.

It is important to note the amorphousness of her references: As with the diffuse reference to diapers, the reference to twins and triplets is another example of the patient's indulgence in undifferentiated boundaries. Seamless flow from herself to her baby, from her present to her past, from her to other important people in her life, all these mark her inner concept of reality, but they rarely accord with objective reality. Resuming her account of the multiple-birth dream, Tiffany continued, "that was kind of sad, because I always dreamed that one of the babies was healthy and the other wasn't because of my medication." Here, she is previewing a healthy child as well as a sick one—a sign of her improving confidence. "Now sometimes I dream about being pretty again; you know, getting thin and having the blemishes go away so I'll be sexually attractive again. But mostly right now I dream about sexual things and about babies." Numerous nurturing figures appeared in the dreams she related during this session—her brother and husband as well as many infants. This meshing in such a casual way of "sexual 'things' and babies" is another urgent signpost along the road to boundary fusing.

"I'm glad you were able to share that material with me," I commented.

Tiffany was evidently startled. "It's not easy to explain so that one of us doesn't get embarrassed." The peculiar dislocation of this response reveals what could almost be deemed a thought disorder. She has little consciousness of the absurdity of suggesting that a therapist would become "embarrassed" by what she has said. And her relegating both herself and the therapist to a level of equivalent social interaction provides an archetypal example of her difficulty with boundaries and reality and ego differences. Tiffany seemed to mean this comment, and the exuberant exhibitionism of our first sessions was no longer evident.

Although I am still concerned about Tiffany's essential inability to visualize her infant as a healthy and a positive individual in her life, I am pleased that she is able to voice her fears and to gain confidence from the fact that her dreams indicate the infant is becoming more and more real to her and that she is successfully beginning to preview the baby's behavior.

## SESSION 6

As the session began, Tiffany noted that she now thought I should have access to a diary she had been keeping since the beginning of her pregnancy. Discussing this issue, I felt that the diary could be an important means of clarification and communication and hoped to read the diary together with her. It was an elaborately bound book with a quilted cover and the word *Baby* printed on it. She leaned forward, adopted a confidential tone, and told me that a close friend had made the book for her. I found her intimate tone indicative of the increasing therapeutic alliance between us.

"The diary is supposed to be a mutual project, but Frank won't write anything. I have to write things down for him." When I asked Tiffany to explain, she added, "Men don't talk about things that matter to them, do they? They suppress their emotions, and that hurts them. So then they turn around and hurt the women in their lives. You have to be very strong to be a woman. . . . I have become involved with many men like that. The only way to conquer a man is to give in to his weaknesses."

"Are you saying that when you feel a man is weak you give in?" I asked.

Tiffany nodded vigorously. "That's it. They think they want affection, but they don't when they feel weak. Men are more vulnerable because their genitals are outside their bodies." Here she expounded so knowledgeably—and did so several times—on male anatomy, that I suspect some defense against something she was trying desperately to suppress. "They're always protecting themselves by being assertive. They'd like women to be assertive, too," she assured me, but suddenly she seemed on less certain ground. In fact, this assertion proved some sort of wish or half-understood construct of hers that she used to contradict herself immediately ("sometimes, anyway..."), aware that her statement was not, after all, too defensible in real or factual terms. "But mostly they are threatened when women get like that," Tiffany continued, "they especially don't like it when women express their feelings too much." She concluded, "I think that boy babies get very concerned with their genitals and that influences the way they interact with the world. Anyway, this is the diary that my girlfriend gave me. I'll read you some of it."

Tiffany proceeded to read excerpts from about 20 pages of her book. Several of the entries described prenatal checkups or tests. In particular she described the sonogram she had received, not only the process and the instruments but her reaction and Frank's when they heard the baby's heartbeat. This commentary was filled with factual disclosures. A good deal of Tiffany's growing attachment to her unborn child was also revealed in this book, feelings of which she had given little or no indication during our therapy sessions:

> When I saw the baby move on the sonogram, I became so excited and happy! It really is alive! The baby feels so good inside me. It's warm and quiet, we curl up together on the bed and nap. I am beginning to imagine and like that. The baby kicks more when Frank is listening to him. I think he's lying in there thinking, "I know my daddy is listening. I'd better put on a good show!"

Tiffany's diary revealed a side of her personality I had previously only suspected. Her comments in the diary suggested a more emotional, almost sentimental woman who was beginning to derive pleasure from her pregnancy. Moreover, the comments in the diary also suggested that Tiffany possessed skills for viewing her experiences in an adaptive manner. Her description of the sonogram and the feelings it evoked, for example, indicated strong representational skills grounded in real experience.

"You seemed relieved when you got good test results on the baby," I said when Tiffany paused.

"Oh, yes. I'd like him to be normal. I don't want him to have my disease," she responded.

"It also seems as if you are starting to envision the baby as a real person. If you had to explain your emotional condition to the baby, what would you tell him or her?"

For a moment, Tiffany cast her eyes down to avoid my glance. "I don't know. I wouldn't just tell him. Maybe I won't have to tell him at all?" After a brief silence, Tiffany continued:

> Okay, I'd have to tell him at some point. If my child said, "Mommy, how come you're doing all those really strange things?" then I'd have to tell him. But I wouldn't say too much, either, since I wouldn't want him to say to his friends, "My mommy has this disease," because then they would go home and gossip about me. You know, people are really strange about emotional diseases. And maybe then they won't let their kids play with mine. But I hope I won't have to tell him at all.

Tiffany has continued to associate difficult interactions—such as talking about her emotional condition—with the gender of her infant. For the second time she predicted that she might have a conflict discussing her psychological condition with a son. This continuing concern for male "weakness," particularly when Tiffany herself may want to be the "weak" one, and her reservations about being unable to communicate with the infant suggest that Tiffany would be happier if the baby were female. Nevertheless, she now consistently referred to the baby as if it were male; perhaps this is a subtle way of negatively previewing about the child. Exploring Tiffany's fantasies and fears about explaining her sickness to her child will be an important goal of future sessions.

"Predicting in this way and planning for the future is good practice for you. It allows you to feel that you are in control of your life at the same time that it allows you to be in touch with your feelings," I told her.

After a pause, Tiffany smiled brightly and said she had been thinking about having a second child.

"What factors are influencing you to think about a second child now?" I asked her.

"Because I don't want to have children when I'm old. I want to have them now when I have the strength to take care of them. I want to go back to school and get a job; though I don't know about that, because I think Frank would rather that I stay home and take care of the children. My girlfriend just had a baby, and she's pregnant again, already." Tiffany sighed and slumped in her chair. Many elements are condensed here. Tiffany sets out a jumble of wants (to go back to school; to get a job; to be free of a little child, the reference to her girlfriend being "pregnant again, already"), but she is checked instantaneously by her fear of Frank's disagreeing with her independent plans. Beyond this unvoiced fear of her independence being checked, she sees with horror the reimpregnation of a girlfriend stand in for herself. This symbolizes her fear of loss of control, and for Tiffany, the key is to maintain control at all costs. She fears going haywire, and given her vulnerabilities, she would choose overprotection rather than a random determination of circumstances. Her body language actually symbolizes this sense of childlike powerlessness. She slumps over, defeated, scared. Indeed, once I realized to what extent her vulnerability caused her to feel incompetent, almost to the point of psychosis, I decided to support her inchoate plea to remain defended.

I concluded the session with a suggestion that we devote future sessions to a discussion of what having another child might mean to Tiffany. I also wanted to continue exploring the relationship Tiffany was forging with her baby.

## SESSION 7

Tiffany arrived punctually for our next session. She looked extremely confident, waved, as if welcoming me into her domain, and complimented me on my clothes. Clearly in a "take-charge" mood, Tiffany first inquired, "How do I look?" and then launched into an enthusiastic discussion of her two "big problems": her husband and the prospective infant.

"You know, I don't think I have an emotional sickness after all," Tiffany said, suddenly authoritative. "I think I have a sociological disorder and two problems: Frank and this baby." This particular comment about Frank is, in my view, a masked plea for me not to be "like" Frank; she wanted to warn me to beware of behaving in any way similar to Frank (or men in general who could strip her of her autonomy and control). Without explaining why she had characterized her husband and infant as "problems," Tiffany repeated that she thought her sickness was a product of environmental pressures. She launched into a rapid-fire and reasonably insightful discussion.

> Anyway, I don't think my baby is going to get my sickness through the genes. I think mentally ill people usually just don't want to be bothered with things, so they aren't very alert. But this baby kicks and moves . . . he's always alert, so I don't think he has my sickness. However, there is one thing," she added, pausing to convey some meaning. "I don't think the baby is very happy inside me. I'm always having to move around so he won't kick me. It's making me a little crazy."

"It sounds to me," I said, "as if you think the baby is taking control of your life again."

"Yes, I think that's the key," Tiffany said enthusiastically. "Not having control, *that's* what triggers my sickness. And if the baby is trying to control me, I could become sick again."

"Do you think your sickness gives you some degree of control?"

Tiffany stared blankly at me for a long moment, then said slowly, "when I'm sick it doesn't matter so much, I think. Maybe that's what it does for me: I know I'm going to get what I want no matter who's in control." Clearly, she was feeling more solid here, as evidenced by her delving into her self and sharing the insights with me. This is the productive result of having followed a more laid-back and reserved stance of not challenging her on those strongly defended issues. In essence, then, Tiffany's progress flowed from my subtle cues as I somehow communicated to her that I had no interest in using what insights she had to "blackmail" her with any information—on sensitive grounds—she might be willing to share with me.

Without giving me time to respond, Tiffany abruptly changed the subject. "Frank is jealous of the baby. His jealousy gives me delusions and paranoid feelings!"

"Gives you delusional and paranoid feelings?" I repeated.

Tiffany shrugged. "Frank has these mood swings; he feels like the baby and I are rejecting him. It's almost as if he thinks we're *plotting* against him." This last comment was made in an almost conspiratorial tone.

When I asked Tiffany how she was dealing with Frank's "feelings of rejection," she smiled broadly. "I threaten him with divorce to see how he'll react. That's how I'll know what he's really feeling. Otherwise, he hardly expresses his feelings to me."

Conveying some concern, I asked what would happen if Frank took her threats literally. "He won't," she said. "He needs me too much. But just let him try to leave me . . . let him!" she said, almost happily. "I'm prepared to be a career woman without a husband!" When I repeated my concern that threats might not be an effective way to get Frank to disclose his feelings, Tiffany shook her head, saying I did not understand. "Frank has been difficult," she insisted. She was convinced she had to shake him up and shock him. She had lately been calling him five or six times a day to make sure he was at work and not with another woman. In contrast to what had been accomplished earlier in the session, my intervention above questioning how Frank could cause delusions and paranoid feelings in Tiffany apparently challenged her by validating her seemingly offhand remark with the gravity of my professional consideration. This led, obviously, to some slippage with the patient and revealed how uncommonly sensitive she was to even the slightest suggestion of challenge.

"Do you think this is an effective way of getting Frank to understand your feelings about the pregnancy? Isn't it important to build harmony now that you are about to have a baby?" I asked. Tiffany would not let me continue, insisting that I did not understand. She became agitated, noting that in her opinion, Frank was seeing other women because he was jealous of her increasing bond with their unborn child. I suggested we might talk about how to make Frank a part of that bond, so that he would not have to feel jealous. Tiffany responded that she didn't want to; her husband "thinks that being pregnant is a picnic," and he "just doesn't understand what I'm going through." She added, "Besides, I like the idea of just me and the baby."

Thus, we have a reiteration of the preceding scenario displaying the patient's ongoing delusions and paranoia. "Frank" is, in this scenario, I believe, myself. Tiffany then is warning me against judgments and challenges. In so many words, she is coping with too much already, and rather than being congratulated or being at least left in peace with her struggles, she is being given the impression that her burden is slight, her accomplishment minimal. It is wise to note that she might be, in all this, reflecting views wholly manufactured by herself: Frank may not be, in fact, expressing any such attitude. The increased emotional lability Tiffany has displayed in this session forecasts ongoing disorganized thought processes.

I asked, "So what is bothering you is that you feel Frank doesn't appreciate your vulnerability?" Tiffany nodded. "Could you consider speaking with him and letting him know that he needs to be supportive of you?"

Tiffany leaned forward suddenly, stamping her feet. "No! Now is not the right time to talk about those feelings with him. I want to be in control. So he's a problem for me and so is the baby. They both make me so crazy! I could have another episode of my sickness."

Tiffany looked at me sideways, from under lowered eyelids. "Don't I deserve a break from all this worrying? It would be nice to go to a hospital just to take a rest."

"What if you explain your feelings to Frank, particularly your feelings about being jealous?" Tiffany shook her head "no" vehemently. I continued, "Are you saying that even if you talk with Frank, nothing will change?"

Tiffany nodded, then continued with challenging sarcasm: "You're so smart, Doctor! Or at least you think you are. Frank is afraid of rejection; I am afraid of knowing. So we can't change anything." She rose again. We had reached a dramatic turning point with the patient oscillating between trusting me enough to share what amounts to several years' worth of therapeutic insight and regression to previous delusional and destructive cognitive patterns. She leaned back. From Tiffany's increasingly disordered thought patterns today, I suspect that she has begun to perceive some of the developmental changes in her fetus as a threat to her own needs for nurturance. It appears that at least one underlying fear is that the baby, another obvious potential nurturer, might develop so quickly that she will lose the nurturance almost before she has secured it. One way for her to gain control now is to control as much of her relationship with her husband as she can. Part of this seems to entail predicting definitively negative outcomes for the marriage as well as for her pregnancy. This also raises the issue of triangulation. I believe that Tiffany is beginning to preview upcoming change and now realizes that she and her husband will both have to forge relationships with the baby while maintaining and strengthening their own somewhat tenuous relationship. These triangular interactions, entirely new to her thought patterns, are threatening to Tiffany.

When I suggested that she might be unnecessarily predicting negative outcomes for her marital relationship in much the same way that she had previously envisioned no positive outcomes for her pregnancy, Tiffany laughed. Her affect today seemed to be a sullen, forced "cheerfulness," a convenient cover for thoughts both disorganized and incoherent. I also posited that the imminence of the birth frightened Tiffany.

"What do you think Frank would tell me about you and your pregnancy if I were speaking with him?" I asked. "Would he know about the jealousy?"

"I don't think so. He would say that I'm doing good, but feel over-whelmed; that he has a hectic schedule and can't help me; that if I get too overwhelmed, he's going to take the baby away from me and give it to his mother—I can't talk for him any more." For Tiffany, the baby she is carrying has indeed become a metaphor for control. Another fundamental delusion that appears as a leitmotif throughout our sessions is that whoever is power-ful would come and make her lose control. Loss of power or control has evolved to an integral fulcrum of Tiffany's defensive mechanism for interact-ing with the outside world. Indeed, her own baby, sadly, has become a metaphor for this loss of control. To the extent, therefore, that she *has* the baby, Tiffany can be triumphantly *in control,* managing. Her wish to merge boundaries is thus a product of the magnitude of her fear of losing control, or fear of anything that would threaten loss of control, like separation or loss. Tiffany was apparently very angry now at the thought of having to re-linquish her baby to her mother-in-law. She blinked her eyes rapidly before saying that she was so angry she thought she would have another break-down. At this point she is ominously threatening to use her nuclear weapon: If she isn't handled delicately and with understanding, she'll revisit her worst nightmare on others (and also, problematically, on herself). If others fail their test of support, she can, she intimates, unravel in a twinkling. The manipulative behavior threatened here merely highlights the intensity of Tiffany's need to control, and, even more crucial, it reveals the state of mind to which Tiffany is subject in the dark corners of her insecure hold on her re-ality.

I inquired again about her feelings for the maturing fetus. Tiffany was now more than 5 months pregnant and had mentioned recently reading an article about fetal development.

"I suppose the changes he's experiencing are good for him, but it's scary to think all these things are going on inside of me," she said, again demon-strating how merged is her sense of the baby with herself. She insists that *she* feels the "insult" of the fetal changes, but at the same time seems oddly dis-sociated from her feelings. The fetus, not Tiffany, is undergoing changes. Although she accommodates the separate life within her, recognizing some boundaries by complaining about her discomfort, in focusing on her own narcissistic mirror, forgetting that the fetus is just going through the normal, optimal maturational process, the patient again reveals her tenuous hold on reality. Clearly, Tiffany still posits the fetus as a controlling, decision-making manipulator of the pregnancy.

In contrast to the disorganized thinking displayed thus far in the session, Tiffany made a seminal comment at the session's end: "I'm in control when I'm sick, because then other people have to take care of me. I'm not in control when I'm not sick, because then I have to take care of everyone else." Insights this clear were certainly not evident earlier in her therapy. I have commented before on Tiffany's belief that her psychotic episodes were empowering and thus paradoxically attractive to her. Accordingly, her final remark during this session summarizes that quality, validating several of my earlier conclusions. Certainly it is a positive sign that she is coming to understand how her sickness impinges on her and those around her. Whereas she understands on some level that her illness presents some danger to her unborn child, Tiffany is still clearly drawn to the seductive control she associates with being sick. I am greatly encouraged by her growing recognition and feel it presages an increased therapeutic awareness.

The important issues for Tiffany remain those of a negative versus a positive outcome in her life, from her marriage to the management of her sickness to her pregnancy. These issues are obviously interconnected, however, rendering it impossible for Tiffany to clearly predict a beneficial outcome for the relationships most important to her or to envision being a functioning member of a viable family. Thus, as she herself so cogently commented at the end of the session, she may well use her elated mood as a manipulative tool to forestall complex, ungovernable (for her) events and thereby to remain seemingly in control of her life.

## SESSION 8

Tiffany's first words were "I've been to the doctor today, and he thinks my blood sugar is too high." When I explored her concerns, she added that she and her doctor concurred that the anomaly was caused by her diet. She jubilantly added "that translates into they have to take care of me until the baby is born." Predictably, she sounded far more pleased by the necessary precautions than disturbed by the actual prospect of diabetes. Concomitantly, she mentioned nothing about having to control her diet herself. This avoidance is also *predicting,* in a way, her eventual difficulties with nurturance. Needing so much of it herself, obviously she will not have the resources or capability to be the caregiver to another even less nourished and even more vulnerable than herself.

"Aside from the blood sugar level, what else did your doctor say to you?" I asked her.

"Nothing much. The usual stuff. The baby is healthy, and I'm healthy except for my blood sugar. His heart is still beating strongly, so he's healthy. It makes me feel very good. I have to start going to the doctor every week from now on, though."

"Have our sessions made your pregnancy easier?"

She thought carefully before answering me.

> I think it's made it easier for me to talk about my feelings, especially about the baby. It's easier when the person you're talking to feels for you and listens to you. I think you're concerned about me—not just the baby or what I'm going through, but me as a person. Also, it's good to learn about the things I react to because I'm pregnant, and the things I react to because of my sickness. I'm learning to make that difference. I still have my fears . . . about being a mother, though. Having the baby scares me, and being a mother scares me. I didn't think about being a mother, only about having a baby. But now I realize the baby will be my responsibility and I don't know how I'll treat the baby. I am trying to love the baby, so that I'll love it when it's born.

These associations indicate that her sense of security (i.e., sense of being nurtured by the therapist) is such that she has here begun to realize the positive facets of the issue of nurturance; it need not be a horrendous burden to her. If I can make her feel secure in her role of maternal nurturer, she can then make that transferential resonance work on behalf of herself and her baby-to-be.

Tiffany is also now beginning to acknowledge the difference between her wishes (or fears) and reality (here, the real changes concomitant with advancing pregnancy). "How are you doing that? How are you preparing to care for the baby after the birth?" I asked.

> I talk to the baby, and I let the baby talk back to me. . . . Sometimes I imagine a conversation with the baby. I preview our conversations. So that's good. We're building a relationship. But also, the pregnancy has made me think about all these other things I didn't use to worry about, like what's going to happen to Frank and me after the baby is born. Sometimes I'm afraid he'll leave me for a woman who's better looking. But I know he really wants this baby. And then sometimes I'm afraid that maybe I'll get so involved with the baby I'll forget about Frank. [She paused, thinking] I also keep wondering if the baby knows about my sickness. I mean, what does it know in there? Earlier in the pregnancy, the baby was more hyper, too. I wonder if he was just responding to my state of mind. Can he sense those changes in my mood? Right now I think the baby may be tired, which is why he doesn't kick so much; I'm tired, too. It would be nice if the baby understood about my sickness, and I didn't have to tell him everything I've been through.

Here, already, is an oscillation of her anxiety about nurturance. She doesn't realize at this point how she places responsibility on the unborn infant for *her* difficulties. She displaces the burden of dealing with her sickness onto the unborn child.

"It's interesting to see that your concept of 'relationship' has many dimensions that you are just beginning to examine," I said. "For example, the birth will mean that you have to establish a relationship with the baby, and it will also affect your relationship with your husband."

"I know. I get concerned that I'm not patient enough to be a good parent. I don't know what I'll do when the baby cries, and I can't figure out what is making him cry. My hormones must be making me crazy. I don't know which of my feelings are normal, which are because of my hormones, and which are because of my sickness."

"Changes in your hormone levels are certainly contributing to your feelings; however, it is very important to determine what experiences in your life might also be contributing to your perceptions of relationship with the infant," I responded.

Tiffany frowned. "I never thought about how a baby would change the rest of my life, like my relationship with Frank. And I won't be able to go back to school for a long time. Lots of things have changed now that I'm going to be a mother."

Tiffany immediately vetoed my suggestion that she share these fears with her husband, insisting she had to "sort out" the answers before she confronted him. Despite the recent series of vacillations between accepting and rejecting responsibility for her own "sickness," she had been able to advance her status without undue dependency on her husband. She preferred to "work it out" for herself, laudably avoiding her husband's care as a crutch.

From my contact with Frank over the phone, I feel that he is more sympathetic to Tiffany's distress—and far more aware of her illness—than Tiffany believes. Despite the evident pool of sympathy available to her, Tiffany appears to be coping with the enormous burdens of pregnancy and mental illness virtually single-handedly, without reaching for spousal support. Although I admire her determination to "nurture" herself, I hope I can persuade her to share these feelings with her husband. Such sharing is a crucial way to maintain the intimacy bond that she and her husband have developed, even after their child's birth. Moreover, I believe that only by confiding in Frank can she eventually learn to negotiate two powerful, simultaneous emotional relationships.

"Do you think he would understand if you asked him for emotional support?" I assayed.

"He is supportive! He makes me stronger just by being around. And I think the baby will make me stronger, too; I'm just afraid that the baby may cause a rift between us. Frank said the other night that he was going to miss my affection when the baby is born." Interestingly, mention of jealousy or issues of other women have disappeared. Instead, Tiffany seems to be predicting a viable, real-life concern over Frank's eventual fit into the primary dyad once the child is born. Insofar as this is not an aspect of her illness but a concern that is valid for all new mothers, this rational train of thought shows progress.

With her perception of her own neediness, Tiffany's stridency in seeking nurturance seems to have abated. Her overall perception of the pregnancy and of her unborn child is vastly more realistic, although the wistful quality of her final comment at this session indicates that she still clings to the notion that the baby will "make her strong." Overall, Tiffany's comments and predictions were more realistic today than they have been. I sensed that her neediness springs from an appreciation of her own historic needs for support, as well as from a more realistic perception of her circumstances. Still, this shift in Tiffany's self-view is new and somewhat fragile; I wish to explore and encourage it in upcoming sessions.

## SESSION 9

Tiffany began today's session by talking about darkness—how much she disliked darkness, particularly in the winter and at night. "I don't know if I can keep coming to therapy in the winter," she said at last. "I don't like traveling in the dark, I get confused more easily, and I think my sickness comes out more." Although I asked her why she thought this happened, Tiffany could not explain, repeating that she just got more scared in the winter and that she did not think she could come for therapy in the winter.

She sagged forward and briefly put her chin in her hands, looking up at me. "I just don't know about this therapy any more," she said, using a slightly challenging tone I had not heard for several weeks. "About 80% of the time it's nice, and I feel we make real progress; and 20% of the time, it's not. I don't think therapy is really that useful." She went on to say that she didn't think she needed therapy. "Therapy just makes my life more difficult."

"Why do you feel that?" I asked, with concern in my voice.

> Before I come to therapy I plan what I want to talk about. But these days thinking about therapy is too much. This is maybe my last therapy session—you just make my life more confused. At least Dr. Bennett [her individual therapist] builds up my confidence. But here I always have to think about the future. . . . I have to preview what it will be like with the baby. I'm glad I learned that skill, but sometimes I wish I hadn't. I mean, when the baby comes, I'll plan then.

I was intrigued by Tiffany's need to invoke the name and therapeutic style of her other therapist during the session. Every time the subject has turned to something remotely personal or troubling, Tiffany has used these devices, and her anger, to deflect the threat, as if tempting me to reject her.

Tiffany refused to explain how her other therapist made her feel more comfortable. Instead, she stated firmly there was nothing wrong with people

having delusions like the ones she sometimes experienced. She denied ever having acted on her delusions. "Well, only when it's raining, because when it's raining I feel that God is closer to the earth," she said, qualifying her earlier answer. "You know, I never think about hurting myself, I just have this feeling that maybe God is going to take me closer to heaven when it rains." As she elaborated, Tiffany leaned back, her gaze flickering between me and a poster on the opposite wall. "I think a therapist should be more like a baby, you know? It's more beneficial to the therapy. But you put pressure on me to think about the future and what's going to happen next." She continued, explaining that babies were more open and curious about the events around them.

"Do you think your baby will be like that?" I asked.

Tiffany shrugged. "Sometimes." Evidently unsatisfied, she added, "I don't think I'll come to therapy any more. It's not beneficial." Her tone was challenging and mildly confrontational; but a moment later, she began to vacillate, saying all she needed was medication. "And when my baby is 4 years old I can tell her all the things I am telling you right now, only I'll make them simple for her to understand. If I stay in therapy with you, you have to make therapy more interesting for me. You know that you send my mind into other dimensions with your questions." This marks a decisive change in usage of pronouns. Over the past several sessions, Tiffany has used him/he/it to refer to her baby; suddenly she has shifted to the she/her usage. Coupled with her frequently asserted feelings about how difficult boys are, how they don't really have a true perspective on the real world (as opposed to females, who do), this shift suggests she might be choosing, if she has the option, for a baby girl. When I questioned Tiffany about the meaning of this remark, she could not explain it. It seemed clear that for today's session, as well as in the past, Tiffany becomes uncomfortable with questions that focus on emotional issues. She did not want to be "challenged," as she put it, and was attempting to avoid unpleasant feelings.

Tiffany then began to talk about how good her other therapist was in comparison to me. I spoke too elaborately, she said. She didn't understand me and stated that I sounded like her father. When I asked her to explain, she said merely, "I can't think right now."

After a few minutes, Tiffany calmed down. She reproached me for the tension during the session but then added that it had been a good one. "Today we made sure that you won't be so boring in the future," she said, chiding me.

After the considerable progress I had sensed at our last meeting, today's session was a definite disappointment. Tiffany seemed determined to derail the course of therapy from the substantive work we had achieved during our last meeting. Clearly, she is not yet comfortable discussing her innermost feelings. Frequently when these feelings become too strong she threatens to leave treatment, or she tries to distract us from the issues she herself has raised. I am, however, not entirely discouraged. In some respects, it is healthy for Tiffany to express her negative feelings for me. It was particularly significant for me to accept verbal chastising without "rejecting" her. I believe she was rehearsing with me a scene that may have actually been enacted with her husband.

## SESSION 10

Although Tiffany seemed eager to talk, she was not overexcited. A friend had driven her to the clinic, and she intended to take a taxi home: "I'm not taking any chances about getting lost," she said.

She began:

> I'm in good shape. I had another checkup yesterday. The doctor isn't so worried about my blood sugar any more; he says everything else is good. Frank and I decided to enroll in Lamaze classes, too, which makes me feel better. I'm not really crazy about the idea of natural childbirth, but I want to make sure that I can concentrate during the delivery, so I won't scream insults at people. They explain what's going on, so now I feel I understand it and won't be so scared. And, [she hesitated slightly] I'm glad Frank is going with me.

"What kind of things could make you feel scared?" I asked.

"The pain. Losing control and cursing. I've seen some things on TV lately about women who died during labor or gave birth to deformed children, and that scares me. I hardly eat right now because I'm afraid everything is going to be bad for the baby."

"How do you imagine the baby developing inside of you?" I asked.

Tiffany sat quietly for a moment, thinking about her response. When she answered, she smiled. "I think he's okay." She had followed my earlier suggestions and read a good deal about fetal development during the last few weeks. Reading these materials seemed to have calmed her considerably. Now she regarded her unborn baby's kicks as messages that all was well with her child.

"Are there any other changes that concern you?"

"Just that so many changes are coming so quickly it sometimes makes me sad. I'm working hard to build up my expectations, so that the changes aren't too hard. But I like the way things are with Frank and me now, and I hate to think of a change in our lives. I think both of us will have to make adjustments when the baby is born."

Tiffany continued on this topic for another few moments. When she paused, I asked if there were any other person in her life whom she would describe as "reserved." Almost without pausing she mentioned her father, saying that, although he had been physically demonstrative when she was a small child—almost oppressively so—she had always felt that his emotional behavior was in response to a series of affairs her mother had engaged in during that time. "Now that I'm an adult, both of my parents are very supportive. I don't think my father's behavior when my sister and I were little was abusive or anything, just a little too showy. But I do think that a lot of fathers take comfort from their daughters if their wives are not forthcoming." At this point Tiffany decided not to elaborate on this subject.

"Has the possibility that Frank might do the same thing crossed your mind?" I asked.

"No, but I understand that behavior." She retains the conviction that females are somehow stronger and more nurturing than males—a notion strengthened by her own experience during childhood as her father's comforter. Possibly Tiffany believes that one can only be nurtured or abused, and this perception may be one of the roots of her strong need to be nurtured. Her ambivalent relationship with her own parents may well interfere with her capacity to nurture her child as well. I wish that this material regarding possible maltreatment by her father had been disclosed earlier, since I believe it signals potential dangers, both for Tiffany and for her child. However, these issues can be addressed at a later date, as part of an ongoing treatment plan after the birth designed to improve Tiffany's overall adaptiveness as a parent.

> Frank and I got into a discussion the other day about whether we were ever going to have sex in the bedroom after the baby is born. I mean, the baby will sleep in our room. I don't think he'll hear or understand what's going on outside the crib, but you never know. And sooner or later you have to move the baby from the room—I don't think our sexual relations will bother the child before he's about 2 years old. It's more likely it would bother me or Frank. I'm a little afraid though.

She stopped. I encouraged her to pursue this line of thought, commenting that it was a positive sign that she and Frank were having such candid discussions. She continued to discuss the baby's imminent birth as a harbinger of her own reawakening sexuality, expressing fear about resuming sexual intimacy with Frank after the delivery.

"Have you envisioned the baby in dreams?"

"I had a dream that I saw the baby, I was holding it in my arms and it was healthy. I was happy and relieved, I felt glad it was all over."

"How old was the baby in the dream?"

"Two or 3 months old."

"And what sex was it?"

Tiffany smiled. "It was a girl. With curly hair and my complexion, which was fine. It also had my teeth, which I don't like because they're crooked, so she wasn't perfect. But she was beautiful and had a wise look in her eyes.

I had another dream in which the baby talked and sang like a bird, too."

"When you discovered the baby in the first dream had crooked teeth, how did you feel?" I asked.

"I was disappointed. I certainly don't want the baby to have my teeth. But I guess no baby is completely perfect."

"What do you think 'crooked teeth' meant?"

"Ummm . . . I don't know."

"Do you think that the crooked teeth may represent your fears about transmitting something bad to your child, such as your emotional disorder?"

"Maybe. And I also don't want things to change between me and Frank because I like them the way they are. It's going to be hard. I want things to stay the way they are now. You know," Tiffany said as she picked up her coat, "I am learning to deal with the world in a whole new way, with my entire life before me, as if I were someone new."

I had thought that this might be our last session, since Tiffany's baby was due the following week. At the end of this session, however, I arranged to see Tiffany at least once subsequent to the birth. Today I felt pleased with the progress Tiffany had made. The young woman whose dream imagery had been redolent with abortion and mutilation images at the beginning of our sessions now dreamt of an almost-perfect child. There were still areas in which her ability to be an adaptive parent was questionable, but she was by no means totally unstable. I believed that, despite her fears, Tiffany was committed to her child's welfare. Pivotal issues that continue to be of concern involve Tiffany's abilities to maintain close relationships with both her husband and child at the same time, and her capacity to prevent strange, angry, or distorted perceptions stemming from disease ideation that threaten to overwhelm her skills.

PRENATAL WRAP-UP

My overwhelming concern at the outset of Tiffany's therapy was that she might be prone to abusive behavior against herself or her child. I am now convinced that her initial ambivalence and the risk of destructive impulses directed against the infant or herself are substantially diminished. Tiffany neither terminated the pregnancy nor courted medical complications. In fact, throughout the term of treatment, her concern for her unborn child and her willingness to act in its best interests by monitoring her diet, abstaining from alcohol, and securing appropriate medical support increased. I believe this behavior profile reflects an overall increase in Tiffany's self-confidence as a prospective caregiver and in her own once-fragile self-esteem as well as enhanced ego boundary definitions.

Although the issue of nurturance is still central, she has relaxed her vigilance about it and seems to have found a middle ground in which mutual support, rather than complete dependency, is possible, particularly regarding her relationship with her husband. Tiffany no longer requires constant nurturance but is now willing to offer symbiotic (and symbolic) nurturance in exchange for empathic behavior.

As pleased as I am with these gains, I feel further intervention is warranted to strengthen Tiffany's skills in previewing and to reinforce her self-confidence as a competent caregiver. I would like to see Tiffany acquire a more realistic assessment of the role emotions play in her life and the lives of others. Because her disorder has resulted in hypomanic episodes in the past—periods of strongly if manipulatively empowering emotional upheaval—she tends to view (her own or others') strong displays of pleasure or anger with caution. Such avoidance of emotion may set up negative resonance in her relationship with her child if, for example, she suspects the infant's emotional displays are symptomatic of illness or disorder. Finally, I am intrigued and concerned with her revelations about possible abusive experiences during her childhood, particularly because such a past might reasonably be expected to influence her relationship with both her unborn child and the subsequent infant. Throughout the therapy it has been obvious that (baby) gender will play an important role in Tiffany's attitude toward her infant. This component will add substantial significance to an already emotion-laden subject.

## SESSION 11

Five days after our last session, Tiffany gave birth to a healthy baby girl. She named the baby Sheila. Two days after the birth, Tiffany called to give me the good news. She sounded tired but happy and arranged for postnatal follow-up. I was delighted when Tiffany said that Frank also wanted to participate. The day of the session, 3 weeks after Sheila's birth, was a sunny day in early spring. As I joined them, Tiffany was explaining to her husband what usually took place during a session. Frank, whom I was now meeting for the first time, was a tall, quiet man with a thoughtful manner and a slow, infectious smile. I was impressed with his calm demeanor.

At the outset of the session, I asked if I could be "introduced" to the baby. Sheila, asleep in her father's arms, was a well-developed infant with dark, curly hair. Frank held the infant out for my observation and, when the baby stirred and murmured, gently stroked her hand with a finger until the infant became quiet. He appeared to be highly sensitive to the baby's moods and knew how to comfort her.

"What is it like with the baby now?" I asked them.

Tiffany glanced first at her husband, then at her daughter. Frank seemed content to cradle his child and watch his wife as she talked. "Things are good. I'm just concentrating on adjusting to all the changes. For example, I'm teaching myself to know what the baby wants, you know? When she cries, I go through this list of 'Is she hungry? Is she wet? Is she uncomfortable? Is she scared?' I'm getting pretty good at figuring out what she wants, too. I think I'm a good mother." Tiffany made this last pronouncement with a combination of astonishment, pride, and defensiveness. I made it clear that I was impressed with her efforts at understanding her infant's cues. "You seem to be previewing very well," I noted.

The conversation now turned to the ways in which Frank and Tiffany were supportive of each other during this period of change. Frank noted that Tiffany was very good about letting him play with the baby when he got home from work, allowing him to share in nurturing Sheila. "It would be easy to be competitive about her, but we're trying not to be that way. We've both fallen in love with her, and she seems to need both of us. It has also brought Tiff and me closer," he noted. Tiffany said that Frank was doing his best to help her around the house and had arranged his work schedule so he could be around more. "I get jealous sometimes—it feels like he comes home just to be with Sheila, not me, you know?" said Tiffany. Both parents agreed they wanted to have another child soon, within a year or two.

"Sheila's easy. She eats well, she sleeps well, she seems to have her own schedule. She wakes up twice during the night to be fed, then goes right back to sleep," Tiffany said, not concealing her pride. She appeared to derive genuine pleasure from her daughter's "easy" temperament, viewing it as a sign of Sheila's "normality" as well as a source of pleasure in itself. We then discussed the characteristics customarily associated with an easy temperament—such as cycle predictability and a smooth transition between moods. Both parents felt this was an appropriate characterization of Sheila. Tiffany's long-standing suspicion of happiness as being a symptom of hypomania seemed to have disappeared, allowing her to believe that her daughter's happiness and even her own were permissible emotions.

I asked about Sheila's developmental changes in the weeks since her birth. "She's more alert. She's drinking more, you know, taking more food," Frank said.

When I asked about her thoughts on breast-feeding, Tiffany was firm, even a little defensive, saying she had two concerns. "I don't like the idea of exposing my breasts in public; it just makes me uncomfortable, and I don't want to stay indoors all the time. And there's my medication. We figure Sheila got some of that through the womb, and she doesn't need any more. The doctor said it would be all right, but we wanted to be especially careful." For these reasons they had jointly decided against breast-feeding.

"Frank understands my reasoning, but his mother doesn't," Tiffany said. "She's even hinting that I may be an unfit mother because I'm not breast-feeding." Tiffany looked at me soberly. "Do you think I'm a bad mother?"

Although Tiffany's confidence in her skills as a caregiver had improved considerably, from her question I saw that she still sought occasional reassurance that her parenting was adequate. The criticism she encountered from her mother-in-law contributed to that feeling, but I suspected that breast-feeding had deeper-level meanings for Tiffany as well. It might well symbolize a level of nurturance with which she is still not entirely comfortable. It may also be that Tiffany believes her breast milk might contaminate Sheila with her emotional illness or that her supply of milk might not be adequate, as in one of the dreams she had disclosed in one of her early sessions.

Tiffany appears to have learned how to manage many of her negative fantasies, but breast-feeding may somehow reevoke these negative perceptions. In this context, one of Tiffany's early dreams also dealt with milk inadequacy. It might very well be a fear Tiffany has that not only her breasts, but her symbolic "teat," her ability to mother a child, is suspect. She fears herself "poisoned" by medicine (transmissible through the breast) and less than perfect as a prospective mother. These nicely dovetail into fantasies about sparse nutrition flowing from her impaired or inadequate mothering apparatus. Although she has made considerable gains in the past few months, Tiffany clearly needs more time to become secure with her strategies for intervention and management, as well as with her previewing skills. Ability to cope with criticism of her competence as a caregiver also needs more work.

"I think you have made a very careful, well-considered decision," I said. Frank handed the sleeping baby to Tiffany, who accepted the infant in a clasp that supported both her head and neck, and cradled her against her breast. I was impressed with her adaptive gestures. For a moment Sheila stirred, opening her mouth several times as if tasting the air. Then she settled down and slept again.

Toward the end of the session, I asked the couple what thoughts they had had about any possible effects of Tiffany's emotional condition on Sheila.

"I don't worry about it," Frank said easily. "As long as Tiffany takes her medication when she begins to feel sick. I think when Sheila grows up and we tell her about her Mommy's sickness, she'll understand, because by then she will have become accustomed to both of us."

"I don't want to be sick again," Tiffany said definitely. "I have a baby to take care of now. I wish the sickness would go away completely so I didn't have to take medication, but until it does, I'll take it. I just like being with Sheila and Frank so much."

At the session's end, we discussed Frank's participation in the future; it was decided that Frank would participate intermittently when his schedule permitted. I also gave the couple two assignments for the coming months. The first task was to observe and track the changes that Sheila's arrival had caused in their own relationship; another part of the task was to chart the developmental changes Sheila exhibited in the upcoming months, including cognitive and affective changes. The second task was for them both to consider strategies for mutual support—particularly crucial for Tiffany, who was still at high risk for emotional dysfunction. It was assigned with the understanding that they could both involve themselves in this as a joint effort.

## Progress Notes and Further Postnatal Therapy

I continued to meet with Tiffany during the next several months, seeing her sometimes with her infant, sometimes without. During this time Tiffany's progress was considerable, although there were some setbacks. Tiffany's strategies to attain the support and nurturance so important to her varied widely during this period. She gradually became more realistic as therapy continued, however. We worked repeatedly on her previewing skills, so that she was able to stay one step ahead of her daughter. She also gained an awareness that, although she had multiple resources to rely on for support, to seek nurturance from her infant daughter was inappropriate; her parenting competence and responsiveness to her infant's signals both improved markedly as she came to accept her status as a mother.

Shortly after Tiffany and Frank brought their infant in for a family session, Tiffany's mood became volatile, swinging from overt flirtatiousness to clear defensiveness, and presaging a recurrence of her disorder. Her dreams during this time were rich with imagery. In the first session after Tiffany and Frank attended therapy jointly, she began by reporting a dream about her mother-in-law. In the dream, Tiffany's mother-in-law choked on some food. She became seriously ill and had to enter a hospital. Tiffany told me, "I know I should have been sad, but I wasn't. I was secretly happy she had gotten sick."

During the rest of this session, Tiffany continued to attribute her own feelings and observations to the baby.

"How are you getting along with Sheila?" I asked.

"Everything has been going beautifully!" Tiffany said enthusiastically. "She's so smart, so active!" Rather than go into detail about her daughter's growth and development, however, Tiffany questioned me about what had been done and said at the last meeting, commenting repeatedly that "the baby needed to be sure that I was paying attention" and would be "a good doctor for them." Her tone was playful, but I sensed that, underneath, she was serious.

In response to my renewed question about how she and her daughter were getting along, Tiffany stated in an annoyed tone that she believed her baby thought that she was "crazy." "She's saying, 'Mommy, I wish you'd relax and be more stable!' I can't cope when I think the baby doesn't accept me the way I am. Or when she says 'Mommy, I love you, I love you, I love you.' That really upsets me. I know I'm not doing a good job with her," she said.

"Do you think Sheila would say 'I love you' so much if you weren't doing a good job?" I asked.

Tiffany admitted sadly:

> I don't know. Of course, I just imagine her saying these things to me because she can't talk yet. When she looks at me I feel like she's saying these things, and I want to say, "Don't say that! Mommy is getting crazier and crazier every day" and she's saying "Mommy, you're so stupid." And now the baby is saying if I don't listen to my doctor she's going to cry and make me think she has colic. I just get so confused about it sometimes.

At the end of this session Tiffany disclosed another dream in which she, Frank, and Sheila had gone on a picnic. Sheila wandered away when Tiffany wasn't looking, and Frank began yelling at his wife. Tiffany then seemed to lose her train of thought.

Noting Tiffany's disorganized conversation and several other signs that she might be decompensating, I asked if she was taking her medication. Initially resisting the subject, she soon commented that the baby was telling her to "be good and take her medication." It worried her, she said, that the baby was "controlling her thoughts so much." But she added that she knew this apprehension was "just her sickness." When I responded that she had once told me she was able to control her father's thoughts, Tiffany agreed enthusiastically: "It's always the younger person who is able to control the older one's thoughts."

Despite the possibility that Tiffany's psychosis was reemerging, I felt that underneath she continued to have an ongoing concern for her baby and their relationship. Her dream about the baby wandering away suggested ambivalence as well as the fear that she was not, at this time, a good mother in her own estimation. She repeatedly asked for my reassurance that she was a good parent.

After this session, and with Tiffany's consent, I conferred with her regular therapist, whom I apprised of the patient's mental status. It was decided that Tiffany's medication needed to be increased. It was also decided that this proposal be shared with Frank to obtain his support and maximize compliance. Once Tiffany began the new dosage regimen, her condition became more balanced; although her manner continued to be energized and enthusiastic, her thought process and emotional lability stabilized. She appeared to have a new, deeper appreciation of her infant's recent developmental gains, reporting on them with pleasure.

"I'm so amazed," she said enthusiastically during one session. "Sheila just keeps growing and improving in her skills! She can recognize her hands—knows they're part of her—and she knows that Frank and I are different people. It's really great to watch her growing and to predict what will happen next." Genuine appreciation of her daughter's development did not, however, mean that change was solely a positive event for Tiffany, who continued strongly to equate any such maturational change with abandonment. Tiffany's ability to preview remained extremely tenuous, marked by a tendency to aggrandize and overpredict the infant's developmental potential on the one hand or to shy from supportive demonstrations with her child on the other.

I have found with Tiffany that a useful method for diagnosing and tracking the progress of her disorder in terms of previewing is to question her about her sense of time. For example, as Tiffany became more adept at previewing her infant's development, her ability to evaluate her daughter's progress realistically and the amount of time necessary to achieve a new skill notably improved. Consequently, over the next few weeks we discussed the milestone of crawling; Tiffany seemed both adept and realistic in her assessment of when this milestone would occur.

As her ability to preview grew, Tiffany's overall perception of developmental change as a positive event was strengthened. During one session, she indeed recognized the possible impact of her previously impaired perception. She expressed a fear that her sickness might interfere with proper appreciation of Sheila's growth and development:

> When I think she's going to learn something new, I just feel as if I can't wait. It's not that I need these changes to happen right away, I just don't want to miss a minute of it. I guess I'm anxious about waiting because I'm not sure that I won't be sick when something really important happens to Sheila, and I'll miss it.

She added that watching other parents with their children heightened her fear that important moments in her own daughter's development might be "stolen" from her by a possible relapse.

"I try not to think about my sickness. Most of the time I'm just fine, you know? So I don't want to think about getting sick. And having Sheila is such a pleasure on a daily basis. You know," she confided, leaning toward me, like two buddies about to share a secret, "sometimes I don't think about Frank at all."

This latter attitude was the cause of continuing conflict at home. Tiffany reported that despite her best efforts to include him, Frank felt excluded and neglected. He was making too many demands on her time and was jealous of her relationship with the baby. At this point in our therapeutic history, Tiffany could be highly productive in her verbalizations, elaborating on Frank's unreasonable demands, or her fears that he was seeing other women, and on her conviction that his family was conspiring to break up their marriage. She contrasted this family turmoil with her feelings for her baby. "I'm most impressed with the bond I feel with the baby. With all the trouble that's going on with Frank these days, at least if the marriage doesn't work out, I'll have the baby to remind me of Frank," Tiffany said somewhat sadly. She reported that she had threatened to leave Frank and had predicted that the marriage would fail. Although this material concerns possible divorce or separation, Tiffany's "sad" comment that the child would still "remind [her] of Frank" indicates her deep love for her husband, no matter what their current condition. She also opts for the sensible, natural order of things here: In a fight between Frank and her, versus her and the baby, she's adamant and clear on the necessary choice she has. She has zero doubt about where she'll put her loyalty: the baby. This doesn't eliminate her love for her husband. It does, however, reveal what she recognizes as her options and her decision-making capability.

Tiffany's position now is in stark contrast to the way she presented herself at intake, where she had very little interest in the baby except as an interference, nuisance, or handicap on many fronts, one that threatened her sexuality, her sense of her own independence, her ability to cope, and even (of course) imposed itself between loving partners. When I suggested that this kind of negative previewing was overly and unnecessarily pessimistic, Tiffany breezily indicated that she was far too involved with her infant "to be bothered with" developing a more realistic attitude toward her husband.

Over time, Tiffany's attitude regarding medication and her sickness became more pragmatic: "I don't want Sheila around me if I lose control. I was really grateful to come back to normal again [after a psychotic episode that led to the successful trial of specific medication] because of the baby. Having the baby makes me think more about how precious life is, because she's so little and so fragile. When I get sick I feel the same way."

Tiffany became quiet, even a little somber, as she spoke of her sickness and of her fears for her child. She admitted that, prior to her becoming pregnant, she had enjoyed the onset of each psychotic episode because of the "high" it would occasion. "Now I don't want [an episode] because if I can't control the high, I might do something to the baby without thinking about it and jeopardize her or our relationship."

Despite her increasing confidence in parenting, Tiffany continued to worry about when she and her child would have to discuss her sickness. This was demonstrated by a dream she reported when Sheila was 15 weeks old. In the dream, Tiffany was taking a test: "I was cheating on it. I'd written out a crib sheet for myself and was reading answers from it. I felt very guilty while I was doing it. Then I was caught. The teacher caught me. He caught two other girls who were cheating and made them leave the room, then he turned to me and said, 'Tiffany, you were cheating, you come, too.'"

"Let me ask you," I began. "Do you think the day-to-day interactions you have with Sheila are somehow testing you? That there are skills you had for dealing with her that you didn't know you would need or worry that you might not have? That some other mothers may be more prepared or better equipped than you?"

Tiffany reported that she was sometimes afraid that she misread the baby's signals or that the baby misconstrued her signals. Although confidence in her ability as an adaptive caregiver was higher than at any time during the therapy, Tiffany still retained some ambivalence with regard to her role. Further discussion strongly suggested that the issue of "cheating" had at least as much to do with Tiffany's wish to hide her illness—to secretly use her disorder as an excuse for behavior she perceived as beneficial to her private quest for nurturance—as it did with any feelings of insufficiency as a mother. The ultimate mothering "test," for Tiffany, would come when she would reveal her psychological condition to her child. This is an example of why she needs to continue further therapeutic intervention, since she is previewing difficulties years in advance. Only by close follow-up of her relationship with her infant will she be able to distinguish between her perceptions of future interactions and the real need for any particularly painful or troubling interface with her child. It will be years, obviously, before she will be able to share information intelligibly about her episodes of psychosis or long convalescence to her child.

During the same session in which she revealed the "cheating" dream, Tiffany recalled another dream in which her in-laws gave her a big black stuffed dog: "I guess it was pretty nice, but I didn't want it and I rejected it. My in-laws became very upset with me."

"Did your in-laws know that the black dog would upset you?" I asked.

Tiffany shook her head again. "In the dream, no. Actually, in real life they did bring Sheila a brown stuffed dog, brown, not black. But in the dream, the gift was for me—not the baby—and it scared me a lot."

At this point I reminded Tiffany of the dream of the dismembered dog she had reported early in our sessions. "I seem to remember that when you had the dream with your dog you felt distressed and sad when you realized that the dog was dismembered."

Tiffany shook her head in agreement, sitting up very straight. "Yes . . . when I think of that image, nothing fit together, all the parts were fragmented." She felt and remembered that dream, but she had progressed far enough beyond it so she could view it in a long lens of perspective.

"Do you think that your recent dream involves your fear that Sheila's grandparents may have realized there is something wrong with you—and because of that, Sheila may need another object to whom to become attached?"

Tiffany was silent a long time, considering my question. I suggested that perhaps this feeling was something she had picked up from her own mother. Tiffany agreed that perhaps this was so. On a recent visit, for example,

Frank's parents had been well-behaved, not making comments that would upset her. Nevertheless, Tiffany usually felt that Frank's parents judged Sheila negatively as compared with their other grandchildren, thus subtly or overtly disparaging Tiffany's ability as a mother and wife. "They're sneaky about it; they talk in opposites. When they say I'm looking good, that means they think I look terrible." She added that she believed her husband's family was also jealous of Tiffany, Frank, and Sheila as a family unit.

It was particularly intriguing to hear Tiffany recall her dream about the dog and for her to interpret this dream in the context of her life experiences. Her rejection of the dog—a strong symbol from the prenatal period when she harbored substantial ambivalence toward her fetus—suggested to me that Tiffany was attempting to reject both her troubled past and her illness. In conjunction with the "cheating" dream, I felt that the "stuffed dog" dream indicated a new attitude toward her illness: being sick was no longer perceived as a safe or desirable state but one that should be summarily rejected. As therapy continued, Tiffany reported several dreams in which the imagery suggested that she no longer viewed her disorder as an acceptable retreat from responsibility or as a guarantee of nurturance. In the past, retreat into psychosis had been a quick (though costly) way to assert control over her life and the people around her, by thrusting responsibility for her nurturance onto others—onto Frank, her parents, even her infant. Now, she spoke less of controlling or being controlled by her infant daughter, her father, or her husband. Her comments increasingly indicated that she resented the "control" her disorder had over her and that she viewed the therapy as a tool with which to remove that control. Moreover, her comments indicated that she was becoming increasingly eager to nurture her infant daughter.

In the last session of our 7 months together, Tiffany reported a dream in which she again confronted God. He had offered her something to eat, and thereafter she had had to concentrate and think "strongly." She was unable to describe what the precise meaning of this change was but indicated that in the dream her efforts had not been unsuccessful. Despite the ambiguity of the offering and its disposition by Tiffany, compared to the postnatal dream in which her daughter had actually wandered off, ostensibly because she was a bad parent, this dream seemed rich with a sense of potential and competence and portended an individual who could make choices, not merely react to them. Indeed, Tiffany's new dream showed a character well on its way to actualization, without the leftovers of half-realized wants and desires.

# CHAPTER 5

# Deborah: The Effects of Postpartum Depression on the Mother-Infant Relationship

GIVING BIRTH has always been viewed as one of the most significant events in a woman's life. Indeed, until relatively recently, in many cultures a woman's primary role in life was to be a wife and mother and to produce as many children in the span of a marriage as possible. Moreover, childbirth was a universally celebrated event. The pregnant woman achieved status and respect. Whereas the variety of life-cycle roles women have played in various cultures emphatically did not find champions in literature or society at large, and whereas older, nonfertile, low-estate, and young women were either derided or viewed as necessary adjuncts to male functions, the single undisputed time women seemed to achieve respect and status was when they produced children. In some societies, the more offspring produced, the more respect was accorded. This attitude does not speak to the overall deplorable low esteem in which the other nonchildbearing women were held. But in recent decades, theorists have begun to question this image of motherhood, replacing it with a more objective, balanced view.

Clinicians now recognize that a majority of women who give birth may experience some form of subdued or depressed mood both immediately before pregnancy and shortly after birth. For example, it is now commonly recognized that some form of dysphoria often follows the delivery (Lee, 1983). Popularly labeled "maternal blues" or "baby blues," these responses encompass a broad spectrum of reactions, ranging from a mild disappointment to a pervasive and seemingly inexplicable veil of profound sadness. The incidence of postpartum depression (PPD) is approximately in the range of 10% to 20% of births (Kennerly & Gath, 1985). This muted affective mood may last for a few days to weeks or even months. In almost all cases, the mood gradually lifts, but the mother and her physician may be left to wonder about the effect of this maternal gloom on the psyche and persona of the baby. Although in many instances, and across cultural lines, men (intimate partners of the new mother) also experience substantial affective vicissitudes, their impact on the new infant is so much less noted in comparison to the exceedingly tight mother-infant dyadic bond that the child's sense of the father's emotional disarray is tangential and of far less consequence.

In cases in which the normal course of mothering is interrupted by illness or psychiatric insufficiency, fathers will usually play a much more significant role. These particular instances, moreover, provide clinicians with a much more fertile ground for examination of the father-child interaction.

The precise medical etiology of PPD is unknown. For many years, clinicians believed that the dramatic changes in hormonal status that women experience after birth contribute, in part, to their altered psychological status. Interestingly, however, it has also been found that adoptive mothers and fathers can undergo a similar emotional disorientation when their newly adopted infant is brought into the home, suggesting that at least some of the etiology of PPD may lie in external, rather than biological, factors that involve changes in life-style, social circumstances, social stress, and family relationships (Bittman & Zalk, 1978). Thus, theorists have recently focused on environmental factors, such as the significant changes in daily routine and marital valences caused by an infant's arrival in any household, and on the social support given the caregiver (Atkinson & Rickel, 1984; O'Hara, 1986). Social support in this regard includes the woman's spouse or significant other, other children in the family, other family members—particularly those who might be involved in the care of the child—and a network of friends. In one society, however, life-event stress and social support were not found correlated to PPD; rather, infant-related stressors including medical complications and maternal perceptions of infant temperament were related to depression (Hopkins, Campbell, & Marcus, 1987). In general, different levels of PPD, ranging from mild "baby blues" to full-fledged clinical depression, have different causes (Landy, Montgomery, & Walsh, 1989).

Saks et al. (1985) found a high correlation between PPD and such antenatal factors as lack of social support, ambivalence toward the expectant mother's own original caregiver, and the mother's unresolved emotional process in having a child who might be unwanted or accidental. These findings provide the obstetrician or therapist with a rich vein of other psychological areas to explore when predicting whether a particular woman may be a candidate for PPD.

In addition, Cutrona and Troutman (1986) found a direct correlation between the child's "difficult" temperament and maternal PPD. A mother's early efforts to bond with her infant may thus be frustrated if the infant manifests a "difficult" temperament. A problematic interaction of this type may be sufficient to trigger a PPD episode. The social-support assessment performed by these researchers indicated that mothers with high levels of social support tended to have more positive perceptions of their skills and consequently experienced a significantly lower level of antenatal and postpartum emotional distress than counterparts lacking comparable support. Thus, both infant temperament and social support have an impact on the mother's perceived efficacy in her parenting role. This means that, whereas "normal" parenting creates a sense of "perceived efficacy" and maternal mastery of the caregiving role, both unusual ("difficult") temperament and weak or absent social support would substantially attenuate the experience of competent motherhood.

Regardless of its etiological origin, however, PPD and its less extreme forms of dysphoria can wreak havoc on the necessary formation of an adaptive rapport between caregiver and infant (Lyons-Ruth, Zoll, Connell, & Grunebaum, 1986). Searle (1987) identified PPD as a significant contributing factor to "insensitive" mothering and nonresponsive interactional patterns. This is manifested by the mother's suffering from the condition.

The primal mother-infant rapport serves as the foundation for the future course of infant development (Klaus & Kennel, 1976). There are many reasons put forth for why this maternal-infant bond is so crucial. Several examples come to mind. During the first years of life the infant must attain physical mastery over body functions, acquire the capacity to communicate through language, and formulate a coherent sense of self with an intact personality. For these maturational events to occur adaptively, the caregiver should be available to provide the infant with a maximally nurturing environment that communicates the message that the external world is a controllable and predictable domain. Furthermore, it is essential for the caregiver to act as partner in guiding the infant's efforts toward developmental achievement. Searle (1987) has found evidence linking insecure attachments, significant delays in developmental mastery, and eventual primary child abuse to maternal PPD.

When Winnicott (1960) said "there is no such thing as an infant," the theorist meant that the infant and caregiver are an indivisible unit during the early years. Psychotherapeutic techniques addressed to the dyadic unit are helpful when internal maladaptive behaviors begin to be entrenched and when the problem is not sudden but, rather, one of gradual deterioration. This type of maladaptation involves a systemic breakdown that incapacitates both dyadic members. Such maladaptation doubtless has repercussions for the infant's smooth acquisition of developmental skills. Because dysfunction is not the result of a specific precipitating event—as is the case with a developmentally disabled infant—the need for treatment is often not perceived, and the dyad often fails to present for treatment until the maladaptive patterns become habitual. In these postpartum caregiver-infant pairs, early signs of secure attachment may be absent—for example, the infant may fail to rely on the caregiver as a social referencing partner—or absence of affect attunement and imitative behavior will be noted. Moreover, previewing skills will be absent. These and similar deviations from adaptive behavior suggest that dysfunctional patterns are becoming entrenched within the dyad, thwarting the infant's capacity to assert competence over vital developmental functions.

Particularly important to the infant's ability to experience mastery in this regard is exposure to contingency relationships. Without this experience, infants will most likely not learn how to predict the behaviors manifested by the caregiver who will, in turn, fail to learn how to make predictions about the skills the child is likely to articulate in the near future. When predictive skills are not fostered, the interpersonal world becomes an unpredictable and uncontrollable domain for the infant and eventually for the caregiving adult. The infant is bombarded with stimuli from the external environment and from his or her own emerging skills. Failure to control these skills results in the perception of inadequacy and helplessness. Untreated, such chronic depression produces in adults debilitating emotions that may culminate in long-term, full-fledged depression. In infants, some researchers have hypothesized a similar short-term outcome (Trad, 1986, 1987), although with less certainty of long-term sequelae. What is certain, however, is that continual and habitual exposure to caregiver depression is likely to leave an indelible imprint on the course of infant development and on the infant's predictive capacities.

The caregiver must also be alert to the infant's responsivity. Because an infant is so exquisitely sensitive to environmental shifts, the mother's fledgling depression may initially be reflected or mirrored in the infant's behavior. For instance, the infant may withdraw from harmonious interaction, may retract its normally diverse emotional spectrum, or may discontinue an entrenched pattern of imitation. The child will cope with the depression affects by, perhaps, adopting a new (and most likely undesirable) disharmonious behavior pattern. If any of these changes occur, either from the mother's perspective or in terms of infant behavior, the mother should seek therapeutic assistance both to prevent a future depressive episode and to ensure reinstatement of adaptive patterns. Therapists who treat mothers who suffer from PPD should periodically monitor these caregivers for at least a year after the depression remits to ensure that adaptive patterns have been successfully reinstated.

Caregiver depression is also frequently associated with an absence of previewing behavior. As noted earlier, previewing refers to the process by which the caregiver introduces the infant to imminent developmental achievement through particular parental representations and loving behaviors (Trad, 1990, 1992b). In effect, the caregiver envisions imminent developmental skills that the infant will soon experience and then devises behaviors or scenarios to introduce him or her to the sensations and interpersonal implications of these new skills. Caregivers who are depressed, however, fail to preview properly or to rehearse both the infant's future development and their own future relationship with the infant.

Cohn and Tronick (1983), pioneers in the area of maternal depression, have summarized the repercussions of maternal depression by noting that the infants of these impaired caregivers are at risk for a wide array of developmental disorders from earliest maturation. Cohn, Matias, Tronick, Connell, and Lyons-Ruth (1986) have reported that the Bayley scores of infants of depressed mothers, at 12 months of age, lag behind those of normal neonatal infants, whereas Sameroff, Seifer, and Zax (1982) have documented such Bayley score differences in infants of 18 months, correlating these results with maternal depression. Overall, such infants are less dynamic and more withdrawn, listless, and apathetic than counterparts who have been continuously exposed to adaptive caregivers. In short, infants of depressed mothers appear to be distinctly less enthusiastic about all potential and upcoming development. They are, as a group, marked by general apathy.

Several factors may predict PPD. First, research shows that women who have already experienced such depression face a heightened risk of recurrence with a subsequent pregnancy, and such women may also be at increased risk for experiencing generalized clinical depression (Boyd & Weissman, 1981). In addition, Buesching, Glasser, and Frate (1986) found that mothers with high scores on prenatal depression assays were three times more likely to report a past history of depression and twice as likely to have high levels of dysphoric affect at 6 weeks postpartum. McNeil (1986) has reported that postpartum psychotic episodes were significantly related to a previous psychiatric hospitalization of lengthy duration and often to active mental disturbance just prior to pregnancy. A history of previous depression and the presence of depression in first-degree relatives are two further risk factors for susceptibility to a postpartum depressive episode, according to Frank, Kupfer, Jacob, Blumenthal, and Jarrett (1987). Kennerly and Gath (1985) emphasize that the close correlation between PPD and affective disorders at other times in the individual's life indicates that a similar etiology may be operating in both situations.

Researchers have in the past 5 years outlined the symptomatology of PPD. According to Bonime (1982), depressed individuals often suffer from episodes of intense anxiety and display a subdued or severely muted affect. Weepiness may be a key indicator. Yalom, Lunde, Moos, and Hamburg (1968) reported bouts of weeping in 50% to 80% of newly delivered mothers. Interestingly, in particular, they noted that new mothers may be tearful without feeling depressed and may manifest extreme feelings of joy or sentimentality—or both—during periods of weeping. Davidson and Liebert (1972) comment that this form of weeping in new mothers often acts as an outlet for expressing tension and irritability, rather than attributing it to a depressed mood. The fluctuations of hormone levels and the reinstitution of prepregnancy hormone levels also play a role in the new mother's disturbed affect. Most mothers, for example, experience brief weeping episodes associated with happiness and oversensitivity shortly after a birth. A certain role is played, too, by the relief of pent-up gestational pressures and subconscious tensions acting on the pregnant mother for the term of pregnancy.

Another symptom of postbirth depression is marked mood lability: Moods may fluctuate from elation to irritability, often with dramatic mood swings occurring several times during the day. Kennerly and Gath (1985) distinguished between two types of weeping in new mothers. For many mothers, the more common form of weeping is brief weeping. Furthermore, these circumscribed periods of crying generally occur in the absence of depressed mood and may be attributed to hormonal alteration. Less common, but more significant diagnostically, is severe, prolonged weeping—over weeks or months—which is virtually always accompanied by a depressed mood and a lugubrious emotional tone. Health care professionals should be able to distinguish between these two forms of weeping and remain particularly alert to the more severe, prolonged variety.

According to Robin (1962), elation, an emotion far more intense and extreme than ordinary happiness, often occurs on the first day after childbirth. The adverse is also common: New mothers frequently describe feelings of confusion, with a concomitant lack of concentration, with distractibility and frequent absentmindedness, although psychological batteries have produced no evidence of cognitive impairment despite the roller coaster of emotions experienced in the first few postpartum days.

Even if no atypical emotional symptoms are evident during the pregnancy itself or immediately following birth, the emotional lability commonly referred to as PPD may surface during the early puerperium period. Clinicians should be sensitive to these symptoms from several weeks to several months after birth, because these emotional changes will interfere with the caregiver's ability to establish a consistent rapport with the infant. Paffenbarger, Steinmetz, Pooler, and Hyde (1961), in an early survey exploring the incidence of PPD, found the prevalence of psychiatric disorders dramatically increased during the early puerperium, especially in the first month. Mild-to-moderate depressive episodes requiring intervention may occur in anywhere from 3% to as many as 50% of all new mothers. These findings underscore the significance of taking a complete medical and psychiatric history of the mother, including pertinent data on the psychiatric history of first-degree relatives. Obstetricians should also inquire on a regular basis about the mother's moods and her attitudes toward her infant. Objective data in these instances are probably of less value than subjective reporting.

When PPD first surfaces, confirmatory behaviors and responses should be identified as soon as possible. Identifying PPD may be challenging: A genuine emotional disorder that may be a precursor of PPD is difficult to distinguish from the normal emotional vicissitudes of pregnancy. Research suggests that psychological and physiological alterations—including ambivalence, past conflict, dependency, loss of control, fantasies involving infant health, nausea, weight gain, and maternal insomnia—are for the most part to be found on the spectrum of normal response experienced by most puerperal women (Benedek, 1959a,b; Condon, 1987; Ottinger & Simmons, 1963). The normal maturational process replicated during pregnancy necessarily brings dramatic alterations in psychological attitude (Lester & Notman, 1988). Nevertheless, excessive emotional response during pregnancy may be abnormal and may signify an incipient affective disorder that will only bloom as a postpartum disorder. Thus, close monitoring of emotional fluctuations is strongly advised.

It has been suggested that the key to diagnosing an abnormal response lies in the proportionality or appropriateness of the woman's reaction. If the woman manifests exaggerated emotional reactions—whether in the form of excessive irritability, anger, withdrawal, or lack of concern—the clinician should carefully examine whether these responses result from what can be classified as normal fluctuations of pregnancy or attributed to an abnormal response (Raphael-Leff, 1986). In addition to the disproportionality of response, therapists should ascertain the duration of any evident emotional symptoms. Although pregnant women are often quite labile emotionally, a quality that may be attributed in part to dramatic hormonal changes typical of pregnancy, the persistence of extreme emotional symptoms may yield insight about whether these manifestations are normal or pathological. In other words, since pregnant women are ordinarily expected to exhibit some emotional lability, a woman who evinces a depressed mood or, conversely, "manic" behavior consistently throughout the pregnancy may be displaying a marker of her inability to regulate her emotions in general in a manner typical of an adjusted personality during a routine pregnancy.

To ascertain whether the woman's emotional response is within normal range during pregnancy, the therapist should pose open-ended questions followed by more probing specific inquiries. The woman should be asked to map her emotional status, to attach a specific label to symptoms, such as whether she feels depressed, anxious, angry, or apathetic, and should be questioned about the duration of each of these moods. It is important to ascertain if previous episodes of emotional distress have occurred in the woman's life and to detail the patient's family history, sexual history, suicidal ideation, and child-abuse potential (insofar as it relates to her evident lack of emotional stability).

One way to determine emotional distress is to monitor the mother's early interactions with the infant. During the first few months of life, mothers exhibit a myriad of intuitive responses designed to elicit adaptive modes of interaction from the infant, to assuage the infant's discomfort and minister to his or her needs, and to initiate and carry forward a harmonious exchange between mother and child. These maternal behaviors occur on a level that is often imperceptible during direct observation. But the gross outlines of such behaviors can be observed if maternal visual cuing, vocal communication, appropriate bodily contact, and feeding competence are witnessed, or if the mother manifests such early mechanisms as infant-adaptive responsiveness, emotional regulation, and mimetic capacities. New mothers will sensitively use these skills both to respond to the infant's behaviors and to begin laying the groundwork for a long-term pattern of adaptive communication. Depressed mothers lack these skills and will also often express their apathy, dysphoria, and anxiety directly to family members or medical personnel.

Once postpartum depression has been diagnosed, the next step is to formulate intervention strategies for both mother and infant that should be designed first around the infant's need for early interaction with a consistent caregiver. If the mother is unable to provide the infant with this stable stimulation, if she interacts only on a sporadic basis, or if she omits visual and vocal cuing and appropriate holding behavior from her repertoire, the infant may either experience deprivation or be exposed to a pattern of early non-contingency, which—if sustained—may have devastating developmental repercussions. Although researchers have found that infants are highly resilient in their capacity to "catch up" if early interaction is inadequate, it is nonetheless advisable to attempt to avert these deprivations associated with maternal PPD. This avoidance may be achieved by early diagnosis and the rapid designation of another family member who is psychologically capable of serving as a surrogate caregiver during the mother's recuperation. Although the most logical candidate to assume this position is the infant's father, he will likely feel the burden of and be the chief resource for the mother's psychological difficulties. Thus, the father may need extra guidance to maintain adaptive interactions with the infant beyond what he would ordinarily do. Indeed, some fathers may even resent intimate bonding and interacting with the newborn, who might be viewed as the cause of their wife's distress. This ideation should be corrected as soon as possible, since the postpartum process is often independent of the particular child.

Once provision has been made for the infant, the next step in managing an episode of PPD involves formulating an appropriate treatment regimen for the mother. Antidepressant medication is often recommended in these cases, with particular caveats to the mother to avoid breast-feeding during the period of medication. Most researchers have found, however, that individual psychotherapy is also beneficial for resolving the emotionally debilitating feelings the mother is experiencing. Moreover, even in severe cases, mother-infant psychotherapy may be used effectively, thereby avoiding unnecessary hospitalization (Jacoby-Miller, 1985).

Reduced to its essentials, psychotherapy for maternal depression is a four-step process. Initially, the therapist should assess the overall dyadic interaction to formulate an accurate diagnosis and to evaluate the deficit or deficits emerging during exchange between the caregiver and infant; this takes place through observation and inquiry. During assessment, a therapeutic alliance is forged by adopting an empathic and nonjudgmental attitude that conveys to the caregiver that the therapist understands and accepts her depression. Conveying acceptance is particularly important with postpartum mothers who might feel guilty about their behavior or who believe it somehow socially unacceptable to manifest so little affection for the infant. Diagnosis of dyadic interaction is only then shared with the caregiver. Following this discussion, the therapist channels the caregiver's agenda into more positive, adaptive interactions with her infant. This positive rechanneling allows the caregiver to begin enacting adaptive gains derived from the treatment within the context of dyadic exchange with the infant. Progress in the psychotherapeutic process may be hampered by conflict and resistance that surface during each phase of the process. But in the case of a caregiver who is experiencing persistent or recurring bouts of depression, intensive psychotherapy offers one of the most effective strategies for reestablishing adaptive interaction with the infant. Other strategies include, of course, drug (pharmacological) or chemical interventions. However, we are concerned only with the psychotherapeutic dynamic.

Once the cause of the distress has been discovered, many mothers make rapid progress, and eventually in most cases these PPD episodes recede and finally remit. When a remission has been achieved, the next step in treatment involves reinstating or beginning an adaptive interaction between caregiver and infant. The primary strategy is to motivate the mother to perform certain tasks involving intuitive behaviors (e.g., gazing, feeding, holding) during interaction with the infant. As fundamental skills are encouraged, then enhanced, the mother acquires confidence, and the therapist should begin to stress some of the more abstract goals of interaction, including the provision of adequate stimulation and support of the infant's integrative processes through exposing the infant to sufficient contingency experiences. One convenient method for monitoring the mother's progress is to ask her to interpret her infant's behavior. This form of meaning attribution becomes a convenient barometer for evaluating the caregiver's emotional attitude toward the infant. I have found that previewing techniques that focus the mother on adaptive behaviors are often highly effective exercises for overcoming the mother's depression and helping her reassert adaptive interaction.

The following case history explores these issues in detail.

# Patient Identification

Deborah was a 22-year-old woman who had recently given birth for the second time. She had been referred by her obstetrician because her overall sadness and preoccupation with the morbid that had surfaced immediately after the birth had persisted. Initially, the obstetrician was convinced that this dramatic change in Deborah's mood was an instance of "maternity blues" that would remit within a few weeks. When no improvement occurred after nearly 6 weeks, her obstetrician referred her to me for a consultation.

## DESCRIPTION OF MALADAPTIVE BEHAVIOR

When asked to describe why she had come for a consultation, Deborah commented that her obstetrician had recommended a meeting. She complained of sleeplessness, nightmares, forgetfulness and short attention span, loss of appetite, and other classic symptoms of depression. In particular, she reported a growing inability to sleep because she feared that she would die in her sleep. She explained that both her mother and husband had persuaded her that her symptoms were severe enough to warrant evaluation by a therapist. Deborah diagnosed her condition as "baby blues" but said that she had recently grown "more anxious" because "the feelings just aren't going away." She said she had no problems or concerns regarding Liza, noting that her daughter was a good baby, which was "lucky, considering my problems." Deborah's insight into her own condition would prove of value during the treatment.

## FAMILY HISTORY

Deborah, her husband George, their older child, 2-year-old Mark, and Liza live in a middle-income housing project in what Deborah described as a "used-to-be-nice" area of the city. She reported increasing signs of deterioration in the neighborhood, including homeless people camping out in the project's playground and strangers she suspected were drug dealers. "No one does anything about it," she added, shaking her head. George, owner of his own house-painting firm, hoped they would soon be able to buy a house in the suburbs, but Deborah seemed skeptical, commenting that until she returned to work and could supplement the family income it was unlikely they would be able to afford the move. She emphasized that although George earned a comfortable living, for a variety of reasons she felt pressure to return to work as soon as possible.

Deborah had been born and raised in another city, where her mother and older sister still lived; her father had died when she was 10. She reported that he had been an alcoholic and, when he drank, had been verbally—although not physically—abusive to her mother, her sister, and to her. She avoided discussing her father, making it clear that this was a painful topic. At first she seemed more forthcoming in talking about her mother, saying that she and her mother had been very close when they had lived in the same city. A few minutes later, however, she qualified the statement, saying, "no, that's really not true; my mother isn't close to anyone." This switch from discussing her own feelings (about her mother) to discussing her mother's feelings about the daughter, herself, shows the presence of residual strong emotions that were to play a vital part in Deborah's competency as a new parent. Although Deborah's mother had worked hard for the first 6 years of her widowhood to provide for Deborah and her sister and to sustain a stable home for them, neither daughter felt much intimacy with her mother. "And in the last 6 years Mom has basically fallen apart. She lives on insurance and social security and, I don't know . . . I think she takes pills," said Deborah. Both Deborah and her sister had married at a young age, according to Deborah, in order to leave home.

Deborah had met George when he was visiting friends in her city. George, then 26, extended his trip so that he could get to know 18-year-old Deborah; by the end of his visit, they had decided to become engaged. Deborah continued living with her mother long enough to finish high school and obtain a certificate in business skills from a local secretarial college. She then relocated to George's city, where they were married. Mark was born 10 months later, just before Deborah's 20th birthday. She reported that she had not been depressed after her son's birth. Although she thoroughly enjoyed her role as caregiver, family finances at the time made it essential for Deborah to find a job within 2 months of Mark's birth. The baby stayed with George's mother while Deborah went to her job at the offices of a large magazine. Showing a flair for organization and production management, in the 2½ years following Mark's birth, she was promoted several times. The work was "hectic and demanding, but enjoyable," and her proven competence at work had given her a "tremendous sense of confidence." Then she added tellingly, "Of course, that was back in the days when I used to be competent."

George was the youngest of three children. According to Deborah, his parents had been strict disciplinarians. As a result, she believed that George had an "authority problem," which was why, Deborah posited, he had started his own business: "He loves being his own boss because of this, I guess." Although Deborah did not have the benefit of a great deal of formal education, obviously she is both intelligent and insightful. Many more highly educated people would not have come to this conclusion or have stated it so economically.

The predictive aspects of, first, her analysis of her mother's affective dysfunction, and then her insight about her husband's parental difficulties, reveal this patient's keen ability and sensitivity to problems involving parent-ing. This insightfullness has value, furthermore, in terms of presaging future predictive ability. Deborah described her husband as jovial and friendly and described his relationship with both Mark and Liza as very affectionate. "Because he runs his own business, he doesn't have much time to spend with us, though," she added. She said that she felt their relationship had, over the past year, become lackluster and static but that George was a good husband and a good provider, and she did not want to cause problems in the family. For that reason, she had not spoken to him about the deteriorat-ing quality in their relationship. She still loved George, Deborah stressed; she simply felt disassociated from him. "I had Mark and my job to keep me happy, and George had Mark and his company, so I guess we were about even," she summarized, her insight again, right on the mark, her affect flat and bleak.

When she had discovered that she was pregnant again, Deborah had arranged to take a 3-month maternity leave, beginning in her 9th month. By her first session with me, her maternity leave had almost expired, but she was not at all certain that she would be able to handle her job again. During the last trimester, Deborah said, she had begun to experience a series of un-settling nightmares in which she was either dying or being murdered. One persistent dream involved a disembodied voice that repeated over and over, "You are going to die. You are going to die." These dreams had intensified after Liza's birth, and for the past month Deborah had been afraid to go to sleep. As a consequence, she noted that she was "tired all the time, which makes it easier for me to get depressed. Everything is just so hard right now, and it used to be so easy." It was interesting to note that the normal woman's fear of dying in childbirth was not even considered by Deborah, since she re-ports the death dreams intensified *after* birth (when many women would be profoundly relieved of their fear of such an eventuality). My sense of the sig-nificance of these death dreams is that they masked something far more fun-damental to Deborah's psyche than fear of perinatal mortality. In Deborah's case, it would seem plausible that they masked unresolved suicidal urges.

Although she had only vague memories of her daughter's birth, Deborah told the therapist later that she believed these strange feelings had started in the first moments of Liza's life. Because she had already acknowledged that these dreams ("strange feelings," to Deborah) had begun prior to Liza's birth and worsened thereafter, it is significant to see that she is at this point almost blaming Liza (these feelings had "started in the first moments of Liza's life") for what infant Liza certainly had no responsibility for or culpability in. These bizarre feelings are also juxtaposed to the feelings of elation she had felt immediately following Mark's birth. "When Mark was born, I was so elated, I felt incredible. But this time I was totally exhausted. They put the baby on my stomach, and I looked at her and just didn't care. I assumed it was the medication they had given me, but when they brought Liza to me later to nurse, I still felt unexcited inside, and I kept feeling that way. It was as if I had no strong feelings about this baby."

Deborah related that she felt and continued to feel guilty about her inability to react joyously to her daughter's birth, but during her hospitalization, she did not discuss these feelings with anyone. She brought her infant daughter home from the hospital, persuading herself that her lack of feeling toward the baby would change in familiar surroundings, when she was responsible for the care of her daughter. Evident here is that Deborah sees herself performing mechanically, as if on "automatic pilot": She doesn't provide for the normal process necessary to occur between herself and her child, or between herself and her husband. At this point she may indeed be indifferent to the process of interaction of any kind. She expects the joy and connectedness to come without any involvement on her part, simply as a consequence of having given birth. This perception might be a way of dealing with her unresolved negative memories of her own past. If she can hurriedly brush off the process of reaching joy in her new baby's birth, she can continue to deny her own disturbing childhood memories.

Deborah found that her apathy, instead of resolving, became more pervasive and now extended to her relationships with both her son and husband. She described the sensation of "going through the motions," of duly doing what was expected of her without experiencing any sense of emotional connectedness. For about a year prior to her pregnancy, and during the pregnancy itself, Deborah reported, her relationship with her husband had begun to grow lackluster, but after the birth of their daughter, although her husband appeared willing to be more involved with their home life, Deborah felt herself slowly withdrawing. "It was as if I were shutting down emotionally," she said with her characteristic insight. My interventions at this point were aimed at exploring the implications of her apathy when she was dealing with her new child and at enlightening Deborah about the nexus of apathy to depression. It was clear that she had failed to note the connection between the two. It was further apparent to me that, even if she did see a connection, she did not perceive the apathy as being a severe threat to the development of her adjusted, functional, normal child.

Insofar as her relationship with her husband was concerned, Deborah felt such apathy that it was indeed possible she would not be surprised if this spousal apathy proved "contagious" and spread to her relationship with her child, as well. Although efforts at clarifying her apathy to her husband and its emotional relatedness to her inability to respond to her baby were made by me, it was clear that Deborah didn't feel comfortable exploring these issues at this juncture.

MENTAL HEALTH STATUS EXAMINATION

At our first interview, Deborah was red-eyed and seemed depleted of all energy, as if arriving on time for the appointment had taxed her strength to the limit. An attractive woman of African-American background whose clothes and accessories were expensive and tasteful, Deborah nonetheless appeared disheveled and ill-groomed. For example, her hair, although neatly arranged in front, was tangled and untended in the back, and her blouse was buttoned incorrectly. Her voice throughout our conversation was high-pitched, though soft; her manner was subdued and somewhat diffident, as if she were embarrassed to seek treatment and disliked taking up the therapist's time. Deborah carried her 6-week-old daughter Liza in her arms. Liza was a beautiful infant with dark, serious eyes, warmly dressed in a haphazard collection of expensive baby clothes. The infant wore several layers of handwoven and appliquéd pullovers and costly crocheted cardigans. Some items of the baby's outfit were, however, clearly too large for her, whereas others were inappropriate given the rather warm weather.

# Therapy

SESSIONS 1 AND 2

My intentions during these two sessions were to observe intently the dyadic interaction between mother and infant and to explore Deborah's feelings. During our initial session, Deborah had left her children with her mother-in-law. In later sessions, however, she often brought the baby with her, which I encouraged. Deborah reported that she felt little or no "talent" in caring for her baby, although she was aware of the infant's physical needs and could minister to her in a reasonably adaptive manner. Nevertheless, Deborah's inability to cast off her depression further compromised her self-image as a competent caregiver. She emanated apathy when interacting with Liza, and although she seemed aware of the need to provide adequate care for her baby, it was clear that providing such care required considerable effort and concentration on her part. There was little natural free-flowing or spontaneous interaction between Deborah and Liza. Emotionally, she had almost totally distanced herself from her daughter.

During our early sessions, Deborah emerged as an intelligent and well-spoken woman. She reported no delusional symptoms and denied active suicidal ideation—although she did say that she sometimes wondered if she "was any good to anyone now" and speculated whether Liza, Mark, and George would not be better off without her. In my office, Deborah exhibited impaired facility at focusing and maintaining attention. Instead, she frequently seemed like someone forced to muster all her strength just to attend to routine matters at hand, whether ministering to her daughter's needs or continuing a conversation. Deborah's affect during sessions ranged from sadness to exhaustion as she appeared to retreat further into herself and the bleakness of her despair. At the first interview, she mentioned her concern about the effect her depressed attitude might have on her children, particularly her infant, adding, "If I didn't know I had to care, I don't think I would. I just feel so empty."

In contrast to her mother, 6-week-old Liza was an alert, curious infant who was captivated by new stimuli, particularly voices and lively colors. Deborah noted that Liza's favorite object was a brightly colored stuffed clown hanging beside her crib. "She stares at it all the time," said Deborah listlessly. Liza's psychomotor functioning was appropriate for her age; she had begun to reach out actively for objects that caught her eye. Her interactions with her mother, however, already displayed a quality of wariness or caution; Deborah spoke of the baby "watching [her], as if she's trying to figure out what [her mother is] feeling. It's as if she has to monitor [her] before she can act." For example, as Liza lay in her mother's arms, the therapist offered her a brightly colored plastic ring. After a moment the infant smiled broadly, waving her arms in an effort to grasp it. She looked at the ring, then toward her mother, as if inviting Deborah to share her pleasure in the toy or to participate in the interaction. When her mother's response was not forthcoming, however, Liza's mood turned somber. Deborah's expression was blank, and her head moved as if she hadn't even noticed her daughter's delighted antics at all. Immediately, Liza's expression became neutral and her gurgling ceased; as she continued to gaze alternately at the toy and at her mother, the sense of spontaneous joy that had characterized her initial reaction receded, then vanished entirely. When the therapist commented "Liza thinks you don't like the toy," Deborah seemed startled and admitted she had hardly noticed the toy or her daughter's reaction to it.

Despite this example and Deborah's stated sense of her own "incompetence," some of the interaction observed between Deborah and her daughter was adaptive, despite so much of the exchange being negatively affected by Deborah's apathy. Although Deborah seemed to lack the energy and enthusiasm to vocalize with Liza or to play with her, her holding and feeding techniques were appropriate (if somewhat automatic), and she displayed a moderate ability to read Liza's signals and anticipate her needs. Her failure to be more attuned to her daughter appeared to be a function of her overall apathy and of an inability to focus rather than a deficit of intuitive understanding or basic skill. Although she expressed difficulty in predicting the future course of Liza's development, when pressed, Deborah was able to make accurate and thoughtful predictions about her daughter's imminent physical and cognitive skills, predictions that seemed rooted in her understanding of basic infant development. She was nonetheless unable to attribute these forecasts to her own competence as a parent. "It's just stuff I remember from having Mark," she said in a flat, self-negating tone.

During our second meeting, as Deborah spoke with the therapist, she held the sleeping Liza against her shoulder. When Liza began to wake, Deborah bounced her absently for a moment, gently soothing the baby's transition from sleep to a waking state; however, Deborah did not turn her head toward or otherwise shift her focus to the baby, as if to do so would exhaust her. As Liza awoke, she made mild noises of distress and moved her head with some evidence of discomfort until her mother turned to look at her, asking, "What is it now, Lee?" in a gentle, if slightly exasperated, tone. Apparently satisfied at having attracted her mother's attention, Liza ceased fussing, rested her head on Deborah's shoulder, and peered curiously out at the room. In contrast to my initial concern about Deborah's apathy, it does appear here as if the dyadic pair are beginning to reciprocate: The baby wakes, gets some reassurance, then feels secure enough to stop fretting and begin to explore her environment. It appeared that, even at such a young age, this adaptive infant had begun to develop successful strategies for eliciting the contact she needed. Whether this skill would manage to shield Liza from her mother's apathy and sadness depends significantly on Deborah's continued efforts to overcome those feelings and to encourage Liza's development.

During our first two sessions, I had felt that Deborah had been candid and forthright about her emotional status after Liza's birth. In addition, Deborah had provided a good deal of background information concerning her childhood, her aspirations for the future, and her relationship with her husband. We had nevertheless spent relatively little time discussing Deborah's experience during her second pregnancy. In this regard, I was interested in several issues. First, had this pregnancy been more difficult or in any way different from the first pregnancy experience? I was also interested in whether Deborah had noticed changes in her emotional response based on the phase of the pregnancy. Researchers have reported that women undergo different emotional reactions depending on the trimester of pregnancy. The most vivid artifacts of these fluctuating emotions are the woman's fantasies and dreams. Fantasies include the daytime reveries the woman experiences; the imagery contained in dreams is also part of this fantasy world. We may refer back, in this context, to the "death dreams" that had plagued Deborah before and after Liza's birth. The emotions reflected in such dreams reveal her intensely negative fantasy world, suggesting deeply rooted feelings of worthlessness and fragmentation.

In contrast to the latent content of the original material, with the eventual cessation of these death dreams, Deborah had begun to assimilate our therapeutic sessions in a helpful way and had to some extent begun to resolve the lingering emotional residue from her own childhood.

## SESSION 3

When Deborah arrived, I sensed the same emotional listlessness that had intruded on our previous sessions. Deborah seemed to lack the physical energy to engage in even the most basic of tasks; she sighed frequently and spoke in a monotone. Using slow, labored gestures, she began removing Liza's snowsuit. Although her gestures were appropriate, she seemed to lack the energy to convey any emotional support to her daughter. She did what had to be done in a mechanical fashion.

When she was settled, I asked her reaction on learning she was pregnant for a second time. Deborah expelled a deep sigh and gazed at her hands. "Mark's pregnancy had been planned, this one wasn't," she said barely audible. "George and I had both agreed that we would wait a few years before I got pregnant again. We had all sorts of concerns. Some were financial, and some had to do with our careers. Anyway, we were both happy with that decision." Deborah lapsed into a brooding silence.

"How did you feel when you learned of this pregnancy?" I asked.

> I was frantic. At first, I thought about an abortion. What upset me the most was that I knew George would be disappointed. We had promised each other that we would wait, and I felt I had let him down. It wasn't fair. I was so guilty. At first, I wasn't even going to tell him I was pregnant. But then I decided it wouldn't be fair to keep the news from him, especially if we wanted to consider an abortion.

Her mode of dispensing with uncomfortable thoughts (or events in her past) permits her to view these events as if they just "happened" to her without her collusion. At the time of her conceiving Liza, Deborah admitted she was "sloppy" in the use of contraception. The result was, and should have been, no surprise. But Deborah perceived this conception as yet another untoward event in her life. At the same time, her husband's "disappointment" in her pregnancy warrants consideration: If he so much wanted to avoid a pregnancy, she appears to be indicating, he had the option to do something more than rely on his wife's haphazard contraceptive methods.

"So you told him?"

"Not at first. At first I didn't tell anyone. I even tried to convince myself that I wasn't pregnant . . . that the test was wrong and somehow, they had made a mistake . . . that I wasn't experiencing morning sickness, even though I was. But after a few days, even George could tell that something was wrong. I finally told him."

"What was his reaction?" I asked.

"I thought he would be angry at first, but he wasn't. He was just kind of . . . sad. That's the only word to describe it, and, of course, that only made me feel even worse." After a long pause, she continued. "George is very religious, and he wouldn't even consider the idea of an abortion. So we both resigned ourselves to having the baby. But we didn't have the same joy we had experienced when I was pregnant with Mark. I think that's because on a very deep level I had disappointed George." But had she really "disappointed" him? Or was this her own distorted and defensive reaction? George, as I said above, was aware of his options. If he had felt so strongly that he wanted no more children at this point, he should have assumed some of the burden of contraception. But letting her assume the bulk of responsibility for the second pregnancy created a fait accompli, shifting the burden of guilt and anxiety entirely on Deborah.

I asked Deborah if she could explain what she meant by "disappointed." She commented that there had always been an unspoken trust between herself and her husband. "But when I got pregnant again, it was as if it were my fault, and I had broken that trust. As a result, I guess I started to believe that I was not as close to George as I had imagined. I haven't really thought about this much, but now I realize that the sense of closeness just wasn't there." The factors that Deborah had been discussing—her unplanned pregnancy, her husband having been upset by the pregnancy, the increasing distance between herself and her husband—suggested that social factors, perhaps more than biological factors, might be implicated in Deborah's depression. Moreover, these same factors might influence the way Deborah bonded with Liza.

"Can you describe more about how you felt at that time?" I asked.

I began to have a very hard time physically. The morning sickness was terrible with this pregnancy. I gained a lot of weight very quickly. I had never completely lost all the weight from my first pregnancy, and then, as I began to gain weight with the second pregnancy, I started to feel like a beached whale. It was terrible. Also, my very close girlfriend moved to Chicago in the middle of all of this. She was one of the few people I could confide in. And since George had become more distant with this pregnancy, I began to feel terribly alone, and fat and ugly.

Deborah paused, deep in reflection. I sat silently listening, sensing that she had a good deal more to say.

The situation at my job didn't make it easier either. I think I mentioned that I worked for a magazine. Well, everyone is very fashion conscious, and I was getting fatter and fatter, and feeling sick all the time. My work began to slip. At first, my boss was understanding. But by the time I was in my sixth month, I think he had had it. Fortunately, my doctor recommended that I take a leave of absence because my blood pressure was skyrocketing. It was a great excuse. I think the company was very eager to get rid of me for a while.

Deborah, then, was clearly evidencing a markedly depressed affect several months prior to Liza's birth, and this 3-month period of melancholia certainly predisposed her to an additional depressive episode postpartum. Suffering from the mild form of postpartum depression known as "baby blues" or "maternity blues" in itself is not unusual. But it was clear that Deborah's double layer of depression left her ill-equipped to expose Liza to the experience of previewing or to share with the infant perceptions of upcoming development. Here again, the infant is at risk for being exposed to the kind of deprivation that can exert a debilitating effect on development, and thus it is essential to assist the mother to develop effective clinical strategies for coping with her ongoing stress.

It will be essential to focus in detail on Deborah's postpartum depression, especially to delve into causative factors and to use it as a model for introducing therapeutic techniques. As is well known in cases of postpartum depression, the following scenario is evident: If Liza fails to experience sufficient stimulation in early life, she may ultimately fail to establish a secure attachment, leaving her ill-equipped to use Deborah as a secure base from which to explore the external world. Deborah, unresponsive to most of her infant's cues, may for her part also fail to provide Liza with an intact social referencing system that enables her to experiment with the environment while using the caregiver to signal hidden dangers, so that she can begin to develop a coherent sense of self. Deborah's support and encouragement are essential for Liza's complexity of personality to emerge and to receive satisfactory validation.

## SESSION 4

At the outset of the session, Deborah seemed slightly more energized than during our previous meetings. "I thought a lot about our meeting last week," she said, "and it brought back a host of feelings I thought I had forgotten." Since I had not treated Deborah during her pregnancy, inquiries about this period in her life were especially important. I asked her to expand on her comment.

"You reminded me of all the fantasies and dreams I had during my pregnancy," Deborah said. "This pregnancy wasn't like my pregnancy with Mark. That one was relatively uneventful. I remember having a few weird thoughts every now and then, but most of those feelings went away quickly. Besides, George was so supportive then. But this time, with Liza, it was different." Lack of a previous experience of such depression reinforced the possibility that Deborah's condition might result primarily from social factors rather than biological ones.

"Can you describe for me how it was different?" I asked, referring to her second pregnancy. "For one thing, it was the fantasies. They were almost like flashbacks," she said. "I guess they started a few weeks after I learned I was pregnant. I began to have memories of myself as a teenager . . . my first date . . . the way I felt about my body changing," Deborah paused and looked down.

"It is important to remember the content of these fantasies because they may help us to understand why you are feeling sad now," I encouraged. "These kinds of fantasies are not unusual, and talking about them will, I believe, help you to make sense of them and feel more in control."

Taking a deep breath, Deborah commented, "I know. It's just hard to talk about these things. And before you brought all this up last week, I didn't realize how significant these fantasies were. Now that I've started to remember them, I want to share them." She took another deep breath, then said, "I think it started during my second month, the fantasies about high school. I began thinking about how my body had changed when I was a teenager and how close I had felt to some of my girlfriends. We would sit around and talk, mostly about boys. It was so much fun, and I felt so close to them."

"So you enjoyed reexperiencing these memories?" I asked.

"Well, not really," Deborah said. "You see," she explained, "when I was a teenager and having fantasies like that, I could always share them with my friends. But now that I was pregnant, George, the person I had always shared my secrets with, had become distant, as if he weren't interested in how I felt. I tried to tell him these things sometimes, but he just didn't seem interested. So I stopped communicating with him." She paused here for a long while as though contemplating how very isolated she felt.

"I can understand that you felt sad about not sharing these fantasies with George," I said, "but the fantasies themselves from your adolescence don't seem painful or unpleasant."

"They are frightening fantasies, though," Deborah explained. "Adolescence is a scary and intimidating time. You want very much to share your feelings with someone you feel close to. I thought I had that kind of relationship with George, but he just turned away from me, and that hurt." Deborah's "fantasies," of themselves, are not so much "frightening" or "weird" as they are a signal that she is feeling cornered by a marriage she has no idea how to handle at the same time she is grappling with a new infant whom she doesn't "recognize" because she has lost her mooring—a sense of herself in her marriage. Together, these set the stage for what to Deborah represents an ominous and terrifying (clearly her nightmares can be categorized as more than just anxiety-producing) confluence of events from which escape onto the dulled emotional plane of depression represents the only means of relief. Moreover, she attributes "fright" to the content of these high school flashbacks because, although she is distraught, she is still afraid to directly raise the troublesome material with me. Deborah's nightmares, then, are nocturnal anxiety attacks.

Perhaps, too, this material represents a displacement: I did not understand some of the undisclosed message she was trying to convey to me of her feelings of being out of touch with both her husband and her own needs for support. By using verbal subterfuge, in other words, Deborah was here masking her true concerns about her current adult life with talk of high school events and imagery.

"Did that attitude continue throughout the pregnancy?" I asked.

"Not really. As time went on, I had other fantasies. I began to have dreams about my mother. I particularly remember some dreams that involved fights with my mother. My mother is a very tough lady," Deborah stated and looked directly at me. "She was in charge of the household, and she didn't put up with any nonsense from anyone. I remember wondering if I were going to be as good a mother to my baby as my mother had been to me. I also remember thinking that it was weird for me to have those fantasies." In future sessions, we explore the connection in Deborah's mind between being a "good" mother and a "tough lady," as she so vividly characterized her mother.

Deborah obviously did not report any of these episodes to her obstetrician, and he was the only doctor she was consulting at the time. Even if she had brought the material up, the obstetrician would not have dealt with such material on a psychodynamic level, and thus she really had not confided the material to anyone in a position to understand its significance or, with the skill of a therapist, to effectively establish a therapeutic communication. I am uncertain of the strategy any other doctor would have pursued. Moreover, these kinds of fantasies are frequently experienced among pregnant women. Thus, I needed to understand how to distinguish between the typical emotional lability of pregnancy and the postpartum period and responses that are aberrational and indicative of disorder. "Why did you characterize those fantasies as 'weird'?" I asked.

"For one thing, my mother lives in a different city. So it wasn't as if she were sitting over my shoulder, observing the way I behaved with the baby. But even more significantly, I don't remember having those kinds of fantasies at all during my first pregnancy. Of course, with my first pregnancy I worked almost until the time I gave birth."

"Do you remember any other differences that occurred with your first pregnancy that might have affected the kind of fantasies you were experiencing?" I asked.

"As I mentioned before, my relationship with George was different. During the first pregnancy, George was eager to know how I felt and to share my feelings with me. He was as excited about the baby as I was. He went to almost every obstetric visit and Lamaze class with me. We talked about the pregnancy continuously, and I told him everything. I felt as if he supported me in every respect." She paused and then added in a quiet voice, "but this changed dramatically with the second pregnancy."

"Can you tell me how it changed?" I asked.

For starters, I think the fact that the pregnancy wasn't planned really affected George in a negative way. I sensed that he felt betrayed after that, as if he could never trust me completely again. Also, his business wasn't doing as well then. When Mark was born, George had more time on his hands. But during Liza's pregnancy, he was continually attracting new clients and the business was thriving. I had very intense fantasies during the day when he was at work.

"Were they the kinds of fantasies you were telling me about before?" I asked.

Deborah responded:

Yes and no. The fantasies really became terrible during the last few months of the pregnancy. I started having horrible dreams almost every night. They were more like nightmares. In these dreams, the baby was born dead or deformed. Once, I fell asleep on the sofa in the afternoon and dreamt I gave birth to a kind of monster. It was like something out of *Rosemary's Baby*. I remember waking up in a cold sweat, trembling all over and calling for George. But he wasn't there.

The manifest message of her connection to *Rosemary's Baby* may have been, as Deborah suggests, the nightmarish or monstrous baby given birth to by the beset heroine of the film. The latent message, however, is much more to the point. In that film, the husband has pulled away from his wife, making pacts beyond the marital contract with other beings. He is cold to his wife; he is unfeeling, and as the film progresses, he consistently misreads and mis-directs the wife's cries for attention and understanding.

Here, in contrast to the previous dream or fantasy report given by Deborah—where I had difficulty in definitively placing her meaning—she is nearing the true issue that terrifies her: withdrawn spousal understanding and support. Deborah had lost the emotional support of her biological father as a child at age 10; vulnerable now with the impending birth of her second infant, she is terrified at the nightmarish prospect of losing her substitute emotional ballast, her husband George. Thus, we may trace the roots of Deborah's current sadness to an intense childhood fear of abandonment with all its anxiety-provoking potential.

Concurrently, the mother in *Rosemary's Baby* had no feeling for her baby, had not yet bonded with the infant, and could in a sense be seen as having no affect for the child. I was most interested in assessing whether Deborah was making a parallel between the film's dyad—Rosemary and her absent "monster child"—and Deborah's own new child.

"Did you tell George about these dreams eventually?" I asked.

It was hard to share these dreams with him because he was hardly ever home. When he was home, I felt he didn't want to talk about those things. I just began to stay up very, very late at night, to avoid having to go to sleep. I would finally fall asleep out of exhaustion at about four or five in the morning. Of course, I had to sleep downstairs, because George needed to go to sleep by midnight. He couldn't stay awake in bed with me thrashing around, and he made it clear that he didn't want to listen to my fantasies any more.

Again, very similarly to the wife and mother of the movie, Deborah too becomes chronically "exhausted" from staying up until all hours. Like that heroine, she isolates herself from her husband, or he from her, while sleeping at night in a sort of unspoken broken marital bond. The wife in both instances seems to be considerate of the husband's need to rest for work, but in both cases, much more was going on subliminally than either couple acknowledged aloud. This whole film reference is both startling and amazingly apt for the difficulties experienced by Deborah.

"It sounds as though he was unsympathetic," I said.

That's not entirely true. He was sympathetic, but up to a point. At first he listened and tried to comfort me. Then he suggested that we both discuss the dreams with the obstetrician. But because his business was thriving, we could never seem to find a convenient time when both of us could set up a doctor's appointment. Finally, he seemed to lose interest and became frustrated. So I started to keep the fantasies to myself. I just kept the nightmares inside and prayed they would stop after I gave birth.

Thus, by presenting her material as nightmare scenarios in this way, Deborah is creating of her normal baby a monster, such as the one in the horror film. She thereby exonerates herself from any responsibility. The aberrant act was done *to* her. Her husband is culpable, and she need assume no responsibility. In Deborah's defensive fantasy, then, she has had no hand in the whole birthing process, but she has encouraged an ever-growing welter of fears and obsessions, giving rise to her current troubled relationships and perhaps a host of practical difficulties involving trust and communication where her marriage was concerned.

This aspect of Deborah's line of defense deserves a great deal of examination. Her tenuous relationship with her mother as well as her rapidly disintegrating relationship with her husband form a triangulation to be explored in further sessions.

## SESSION 5

We had spent the two previous sessions discussing Deborah's experiences during her pregnancy, so I wanted to spend this session talking about her first response to the infant. I felt it was important to explore how

Deborah felt about the baby on a very primal level because these deep feelings might help explain her apathy and might serve to motivate a more adaptive response.

"Deborah, last week you described the kinds of fantasies you had during your pregnancy with Liza," I began. "I wanted to emphasize for you that although some of these fantasies might have seemed extreme at the time, they are, in many respects, not unlike many of the fantasies that have been reported by healthy and adaptive mothers. In fact, numerous studies have shown that adaptive mothers have very similar fantasies." I paused, noticing that Deborah wanted to express something.

"But they were so vivid and, at times, frightening. Often I would wake up sweating or trembling all over. And what really upset me was that I had not experienced these kinds of fantasies during my first pregnancy," Deborah said.

I noted:

> It's important to remember that every pregnancy is different. You mentioned that during this second pregnancy George was not as available to you because of responsibilities at work. The fact that the pregnancy was unplanned may also have contributed to your distress. In general, it sounds as if it was a difficult time for you, quite different from the situation during your first pregnancy. But again I want to emphasize that your experience and the fantasies you were having are not unusual or bizarre.

"You mean other women fantasize about giving birth to deformed babies?" Deborah sounded incredulous.

"Yes. I know it seems strange, but that kind of fantasy is actually quite common, particularly for a woman in the last trimester." I paused, then added, "But today I wanted to review a related issue. Specifically, do you remember how you felt when Liza was first born? Were you excited about the fact that she was a girl and your first baby was a boy? Did you want to see her right away? Were you eager to nurse her?" I explained to Deborah that she should take her time in responding to these inquiries. There were no "right answers," I told her, only truthful answers that reflected her consideration of the questions, and these would help us both understand her current reaction to the baby.

Deborah sighed deeply.

> It's very hard to talk about this, because I am embarrassed about my first response to Liza, and I feel so guilty about it. When Mark was born, I was so excited. It was like a miracle. I remember feeling a kind of pure joy . . . I was exuberant. After the birth, I felt as if I had truly accomplished something meaningful for the first time in my life. I wanted so much to be close to Mark. When the nurse brought him to me for the first time, I remember feeling how helpless and vulnerable he looked. He needed me so much and that was a wonderful feeling. All I wanted to do was take care of him.

Deborah lapsed into deep thought. After several minutes, I said, "It seems as if you felt differently after Liza's birth. Can you explain how you felt?" Because I had used an empathic and nonjudgmental approach, Deborah seemed to believe that I accepted her situation and attitude. Now, she has become more accessible than in earlier sessions. I was working, throughout, toward engaging her in direct discussion of her concerns. Thus, here, when she was able to discuss her joy at taking care of her first child, she became undefended and not bound up in the obsessional fantasies that had clouded the issue previously. It is significant, furthermore, that Deborah described the arrival of her first child as an empowering event, one that would enable her to play the active role of nurturer. The birth of her second child, however, left her helpless and desolate, a victim of her own despair.

She exhaled deeply.

> I felt very different. First of all, I was so physically exhausted after I gave birth to Liza. It wasn't because of a long labor, either. With both pregnancies, I was fairly lucky. But after Liza was born, I was physically and emotionally depleted. I had no sense of energy or excitement. I just wanted to sleep. It was almost exactly opposite the response I had when Mark was born. There was no excitement or sense of accomplishment. And I just couldn't shake the weariness.

Deborah then reported intermittent episodes of lengthy weeping.

"Can you describe how you felt when they brought Liza in?" I asked.

> I felt very sad suddenly. I sensed that she was helpless, just as Mark had been, and that she needed me very much. But I also knew I couldn't "be there" for her . . . that I wasn't any good for her at that time. It was as if I had no desire to get to know her or to "bond" with her . . . I think that's the word they usually use. I just didn't have strong feelings for her. At first I thought if I just waited, I would start feeling close to her after a few days. But it didn't happen.

Deborah's sense of alienation from her infant was an obvious source of distress to her.

"Have you had any feeling of close bonding toward the infant to this point?" I asked.

"Not really," Deborah said. "I keep trying to tell myself that it will come. I should be patient. But so far, nothing. It's as if I feel absolutely nothing for this baby," her voice trailed off in a welter of despair.

"How does that affect the way you care for her?" I asked.

"It's strange," said Deborah. "I can take care of her. I bottle-feed her; I change her diapers, and I can hold her. It's as if I know exactly what to do. But it's as if I am going through the motions like an automaton. There is no emotion behind my actions."

Sadly the impaired social interaction of the dyad appeared to cause developmental deficits to surface early in Liza. Certainly, material exchanges with the infant were characterized by an increased number of negative interactions and fewer opportunities for shared emotion between them. The negative affect apparent during such interactions colored other developmental dimensions as well, exerting a proliferative effect that had a negative impact on the baby's emotional expression. And yet, the mother can now recognize and deal cognitively with the issue of her current difficulty of closeness with her child without shielding or displacing her fears to the metaphor of horror films (or monsters, spells, and evil happenstance).

"Do you think the baby knows you are not feeling any strong emotions?" I asked.

"It's hard to say," Deborah commented. "Sometimes I feel as if my life is a dream, and I am not really there, as if I am a machine caring for Liza." Note again the mechanical, automaton association she evinces here.

> At first the doctor said these feelings would go away in a few days; then he extended it to weeks. But it's been over 2 months and I just can't get rid of this empty feeling. I'm not motivated to do anything. Whenever I think about doing something, I say, "What's the point?" And I guess what should upset me is that I feel that way about all kinds of things. Little things . . . like cleaning the house, and big things . . . like taking care of the baby. It's as if I've become a very mechanical person.

Deborah's sense of despair here is very real, and her plea to me to help to release her from the emotionally flat landscape of her robotlike existence is painfully poignant. Also, we have here for the first time a clear exposition of the problem: Deborah lacked the ability to share emotions with her infant. My original question was dangerous, because it probed too deeply into the subject, instead of proceeding more gradually into its depths. Deborah was clearly not yet ready to deal with the causative factors of her affective disorder; my approach could be calibrated very closely to win her assurance and cooperation.

"Do you have any idea why you are having these feelings?" I asked.

> The doctor told me that "baby blues" or "maternity blues" are common. She explained that during the pregnancy your hormones keep increasing at a steady pace, but after the birth, your hormones just shut off suddenly, without warning. They plummet. That's the word she used—"plummet." That explanation made sense to me. She also said I should just be patient, and eventually my normal feelings would come back.

Deborah also reported that an aunt and a cousin of hers each had two episodes of "baby blues" that had eventually remitted.

> But I've been waiting now for more than 2 months, and it hasn't happened. I would panic, except that I don't feel anything that strongly. It's as if all the passion and strong feeling has gone out of my life. But now I'm beginning to be

afraid, because none of my feelings are coming back. One of the things that's most frightening is that I can't feel any passion for George. I'm so afraid that eventually he will become frustrated and want to leave me and the kids. *That* terrifies me.

Though I realized the immediacy of her concerns vis-à-vis her marriage, because of the recent experience of having her slide away from direct questioning, I decided not to address these pointed matters now but to come back to them at a later time. My assessment was that, because she was focusing on her marriage and husband, she would be most likely to respond without defenses to considerations of proper care for Liza.

It was clear that for Liza's sake a surrogate caregiver would be necessary until Deborah's "baby blues" remitted. This form of surrogate care would enable Liza to bond with an attachment figure and begin experiencing contingent responses. Deborah reported that her mother-in-law was more than eager to function in this surrogate capacity; the following week, she moved into the home to care for both Liza and Deborah. Although Deborah seems passively receptive about accepting this surrogacy arrangement, in fact her acceptance of the need for such a circumstance is a heartening development. The agreement is a representation that she knows and accepts her limitations as a caregiver for the time being.

Since our session time was up, I told Deborah we would continue discussing these issues at our next meeting.

## SESSION 6

I began our session by asking Deborah to describe how she felt emotionally. "The same as last week," she said bleakly. "Sometimes I just don't know how I can go on: What's the point?"

"Deborah," I said, "your previous doctor reminded you that overcoming your depression might be a long and difficult process." I didn't say that I, too, had repeatedly reminded her how patient she'd have to be to overcome this depression.

"But it's unbearable." Tears began to roll down Deborah's cheeks. "I don't even see the light at the end of the tunnel." It is obvious that it had become crucial to institute an effective interventive regimen with Deborah and Liza, one that would reawaken enthusiasm about developmental trends. The goal of therapy here is to initiate adaptive patterns of exchange in the dyad. Therapists who minister to depressed mothers must often undo the habitual patterns of dysfunction that the dyadic members have come to accept as normal. In addition, my task was to provide Deborah with the insight and skill for initiating adaptive patterns within the context of the caregiver-infant dyad. At this stage, I felt the time was ripe for introducing prospective strategies because I saw enough movement in Deborah to warrant a trial in this intervention. I saw her as open to my suggestions and free of overt defenses. The surrogacy issue (that might remove some of her remaining power and control as primary caregiver) is potent in its implications, and I felt that introducing a "task" connecting Deborah to her infant could reinforce her vital role and provide her with reasons for continuing to be involved in an active way in the development of her daughter.

One means of treating depressed caregivers such as Deborah may be to teach them how to engage in previewing behaviors with their infants. Strategies such as representing upcoming developmental milestones may be taught, and caregivers may also be guided in methods for enacting behavioral sequences designed to introduce the infant to upcoming change. For caregivers who have difficulty learning these techniques, the therapist may use modeling strategies, such as showing videotapes.

"I have had many patients in similar situations, Deborah," I commented. "As best as I can, I understand and empathize with the feelings of agony and the hopelessness. But I have also developed a method that may be of some help." I then went on to explain the concept of previewing to her.

I explained to Deborah that previewing persuades the infant that both the external world and the maturational changes within his or her own body are, to a certain extent, predictable and capable of being mastered. Second, previewing behaviors would reinforce for Liza the perception that development was cumulative. In other words, one skill gradually emerges from an earlier skill. Thus, a sense of continuity infuses itself into the maturational processes. Third, Deborah's attentive ministrations during previewing exercises would help Liza to internalize the experience of being nurtured, allowing the infant to gain perceptions of mastery and competence, within a loving (or at least supportive) environment, over the developmental changes occurring inside. Deborah would also naturally experience an intimate communication with Liza during this process. My view all along has been that when there is conflict, there cannot be previewing because the conflict preempts and subsumes all other emotional development. Now that Deborah's turbulent conflict seems to be at an ebb, it is an ideal time to introduce the concept.

Deborah had been listening attentively, particularly as I described the previewing process. "That sounds so familiar," she said. "It's what I used to do with Mark all the time, and I enjoyed it so much. I would always watch Mark carefully to see if I could figure out the kind of skills he would be showing next. Sharing those new skills with him and helping him learn how to use his body was so exciting." She paused. "But that's just a dim memory. What makes me feel even sadder is that I don't know if I will be able to experience those feelings with Liza."

At this point I focused on encouraging her to use her native previewing skills, skills she had already demonstrated adaptively with her first infant. "Previewing," I explained to her, "seems to depend on a group of behaviors most mothers engage in naturally. For example, new mothers seem to be particularly fascinated with watching the baby, monitoring the baby with their eyes. That kind of monitoring is called 'visual cuing.' Another behavior that new mothers engage in is 'vocal cuing.' The most common form of vocal cuing is 'baby talk.'"

> This is bringing back so many memories. I remember with Mark, I would be fascinated just watching him. I would get so excited when our eyes met, and especially when he was old enough to follow my eyes. I also liked baby talk. I know it sounds very silly, but I used to love making up sounds to practice with him. He would follow me with his eyes and then just giggle. I never thought I would behave that way with my baby. I mean, I've seen other parents doing it with their babies, but I never thought I would do it with mine.

I assured her:

> Many people say that. It's very strange to see other people previewing with their babies. No parent ever thinks she will do it herself, but she does, and she seems to do it automatically. There are also other kinds of previewing behaviors. For example, mothers who preview tend to hold their infants in a very supportive way. Another significant behavior that has been associated with previewing is feeding behavior. I know you realize that feeding is one of the most vital tasks a mother performs for the infant. After all, it's the way the mother conveys emotional closeness and affection, as well as provides the infant with needed nutrition. Finally, adaptive mothers seem to know exactly how much stimulation is appropriate for the baby. Mothers then use this information to initiate episodes of play with the infant so that they can demonstrate their affection.

"It all sounds so complicated. I remember doing those things with Mark, but that was when my spirits were optimistic and I looked forward to every day I could spend with him. Everything has changed now. I just don't feel the same about Liza, and ... recognizing that makes me feel even more guilty, as if I am depriving her of the experiences she needs to grow and be healthy."

> There may be a way to circumvent that problem. Since these feelings aren't coming from you spontaneously, we can work on prompting you so that you behave in this manner, anyway. For example, we can spend some of our time during sessions observing Liza and trying to determine her needs. It may take some time, but I think gradually we can both figure out Liza's needs. Then we can devise some behaviors you can engage in to help her to achieve her needs. It may be slow going at first, but gradually, I think we can do it.

At this point we should recognize that there is a chronic dimension in Deborah's makeup that pushes her consistently in the line of "guilt and sadness," sadness and guilt over her treatment (or nontreatment) of Liza. Despite this Calvinist inclination, Deborah is truly interested in helping and enlightening and even *enjoying* her child. She is far less self-absorbed than many other depressed mothers are in her position, and I have treated some who actually repel any attempt to ameliorate their depressive state.

If the mother cannot nurture the infant during the first few months of life, one suggestion is to provide an interactive partner who can guide the mother in the nuances of early infant exchange. This partner performs a modeling function by conveying basic skills for instilling adaptive development, such as visual cuing and vocal communication, initiating positive body contact, and dispensing such basic skills as appropriate feeding and nurturance. I now proposed that I, as the therapist, could serve this role during therapy sessions, and Deborah's husband and mother-in-law could be interactive partners with her at home.

Deborah sighed, "That just might work. But I feel depleted so much of the time. I don't have the energy to focus on Liza."

At this point I attempted to provide as much encouragement for previewing behavior as possible, since a residual effect of this kind of depression may have been Deborah's experiences of vulnerability and incompetence with respect to caring for Liza. Indeed, during this period she may have convinced herself that she was, for all intents and purposes, forever incapable of forging an adaptive relationship with the infant.

"Everything you are saying makes sense," Deborah said. "But I'm not sure how to start, and besides, how can you help me to start previewing for Liza when I just have no desire to develop this skill with her?"

> I know it sounds difficult, but one of the things that sometimes helps is to predict what's coming up next for your infant. You would spend some time each week watching Liza carefully. We could then discuss your predictions and see what they meant. You wouldn't have to interact with her if you didn't want to, but this would require you to observe and identify carefully the precursory behaviors Liza will be displaying.

"What do you mean by precursory behaviors?" Deborah asked.

"Precursory behaviors are behaviors that precede full-fledged developmental changes. For example, kicking gestures may be precursory forms of crawling, and grasping gestures may be precursory to being able to perform finger-thumb apposition. Let's try to pay attention to your observations, and let me know if you see any of these behaviors when we meet next week."

"I'll try . . . I don't know if it will work, but I'll try," Deborah promised. That the therapeutic alliance between Deborah and me seems to be working is demonstrated by her repeated efforts to go along with my suggested interventions and tasks despite her ongoing sense of deep depression.

## SESSION 7

When I entered the treatment room, I felt a sudden surge of energy. For the first time since Deborah had been meeting with me, she met my gaze directly as we began the session.

"Your mood seems a little different today than it has been in previous sessions," I began.

"Yes," Deborah said. "Something is different. I still feel very depressed. But this week I tried to follow your advice." As Deborah began to hone her adaptive interactive skills, a shift had begun to occur with respect to attributional tendencies toward Liza, so that she viewed the infant's needs and cues more realistically and attributed more positive emotions to the infant. She described her week this way:

> I watched Liza very carefully. At first, I didn't really notice anything. I just became even more depressed when I realized that. But I kept at it, the way you told me to. After a few days, I began to notice some things and, more than that, I began to sense that Liza was trying to communicate with me. For the first time in months, I felt reinvigorated. I became fascinated with watching her, all of her gestures and little signals. She has a new toy—a rattle that plays different melodies. You have to shake the rattle in a certain way to get it to play these melodies. Well, I know Liza is only 2½ months old, but she seems to have figured this out by herself. Anyway, she reaches out with her hand, and sometimes she manages to hit the rattle in a certain way so that the melody starts playing. She seems so happy when she is able to do it on her own. Her whole face changes and she starts smiling.

"It sounds as if you were extremely observant in this instance and that you noticed her responding to a contingency response," I said. This was both a way to support Deborah's new found maternal visual cuing as well as a way to introduce to her the term "contingency response" in a natural way.

"What do you mean by a contingency?" Deborah asked.

> In general terms, a contingency is a cause-effect reaction. One very basic contingency that all infants seem to learn at an early age relates to feeding. It works in this fashion: Infants cry when they are hungry, and then their caregivers feed them. This pattern is repeated over and over again, and eventually the pattern becomes familiar to the infant. That is, the infant comes to understand that if he or she cries, the mother will provide food. Stimulus-response, cause-effect. Essentially, that's what a contingency is: Two events are connected in a cause-effect sequence.

"It really is fascinating," Deborah replied thoughtfully.

"Contingencies are important for a variety of reasons," I noted. "By understanding the meaning of a contingency, the infant begins to comprehend that he or she can use behaviors to exercise control over the external environment, as well as control over the diverse changes of his or her body."

"So contingencies help the infant to understand about control and communicating their needs to the world," Deborah repeated, partly to herself. It is interesting to note that as she speculates about her infant daughter's growing ability to control the environment, Deborah, too, is learning to control her own affect.

"That's right," I agreed. "Contingencies are one way in which the infant learns about control in the world around him or her. But there are lots of other ways in which the infant learns about control, as well. Probably the most important way involves the behavioral cues the caregiver provides for the infant."

"Can you explain that a little bit more?" asked Deborah.

The best way to understand it is to realize that, from the very first days of life, infants try to communicate with the world. They do this in a variety of ways. At first, it's very difficult, because they are at the mercy of their physical functions, such as sleeping and eating. It takes them quite a while to move beyond what we might call the "body's prerogatives." But you would be amazed at how quickly they begin to assert themselves and gain control over their bodies. Of course, babies can't communicate through language. So they start using their eyes, gestures, and sounds to attract attention and communicate their needs. Probably the most important thing during this time is the caregiver's response. The infant needs to understand, at some time during the first few months of life, that a consistent, supportive other person is available to respond to his or her needs—someone who will try to read his or her messages, as incoherent as they may seem to be. By reading the infant's messages, the caregiver communicates that the infant "makes sense." Eventually, the infant understands this message.

Deborah looked down at her hands. "Some of what you are saying is making me sad," she said. "I feel very inadequate. As if I am not being an adequate mother for my baby, even though I'm trying."

"You shouldn't feel that way. It's very important to understand the difficult time you had with the pregnancy and the prevalence of postpartum depression. As we've discussed before, you are far from alone in this experience. Besides, we have also talked about how helpful George has been recently. But it's equally important for you to maintain hope, to recognize that your condition is temporary and not your fault."

"I know, but it's hard," Deborah said faintly.

The best way to cope is to continue focusing on Liza's developing skills and to try to understand—as best you can—how she is changing and growing. I know this sounds like a very difficult thing to do. It certainly is a challenge, and it will continue to be difficult. But the one thought that can sustain you in many ways is that your "baby blues"—this inexplicable feeling of sadness that you are now experiencing—almost always go away.

Deborah replied:

> I have been trying. I still feel sad and apathetic much of the time. But I'm find-
> ing that I can focus my attention for longer periods of time on Liza and her
> skills. Sometimes I'm so amazed by her. She's ingenious. It's as if she knows
> she can't talk, but there are so many ways she tries to communicate with me. I
> get so absorbed in trying to understand her that I forget about myself and my
> own feelings. Then the sadness just fades—at least for a few minutes.

The observations she is describing here are true discoveries for Deborah.
Although she evidently experienced these feelings and insights with her first
child, she is being gradually reintroduced to them now and weaned away
from the flat, nonresponsive affect of her deep depression. These exchanges
are heartening for me as therapist and show very acceptable levels of response after so few sessions.

"It sounds as if you are describing the gradual lifting of your depression.
What's most exciting is that you are also focusing so intently on Liza," I
noted.

> Yes. This past week I started to feel as if I had missed being with Liza. It began
> pretty suddenly. But I just started looking forward to my time with Liza. You
> know my mother-in-law has been helping out since I brought Liza home from
> the hospital and . . . since I've been feeling so depressed. But I've improved so
> much that recently we've started having lunch together, and then both my
> mother-in-law and I play with the baby all afternoon. It's so enjoyable. It's also
> exciting because my mother-in-law describes what George was like as a baby.
> I've never heard these stories before. I feel as if a special closeness is developing
> between the generations of my family.

In contrast to the isolation she had described earlier with respect to her husband and her relationship with him, Deborah here uses the term *my family* to
indicate the family of George, showing she loves, is acknowledging, and accepting of them. With this pronoun, she has traveled quite a distance. The
word *my*, too, conveys considerable information about her growing sense of
ego awareness.

"How does that make you feel?" I asked.

"Happier and stronger. By watching my mother-in-law and baby together, I feel stronger. It also motivates me to interact with Liza," said
Deborah.

"This sounds very positive. We can continue discussing these events next
week," I added, concluding the session.


SESSION 8

When Deborah entered the treatment room this week, her stride was
strong, her posture erect, and her facial expression pleasant. Needless to say,
as the postpartum depression lifts, the mother's relationship with the thera-

pist is eventually terminated. But termination should not be abrupt. I particularly stressed, in Deborah's case, that if a problem arose, she should not hesitate to contact me again. Studies have revealed that women who experience this kind of depressive disturbance are at an increased risk for suffering another episode of depression. Given this heightened susceptibility, an important final step in the treatment of this form of depression is to emphasize that the mother herself should learn to be alert to symptoms indicating a recurrence. Such symptoms may affect her functioning and may result in a failure to provide adequate stimulation for her infant.

Deborah held Liza in her arms, and I noticed the sensitivity with which she used her gestures to soothe and comfort the baby.

"Hi," she said, in a strong voice, "I think we've arrived early today."

"That's fine," I said. "You seem to be in a great mood today. It's very nice to see you holding Liza so well."

"I feel much better this week," Deborah began. "In fact, earlier this week, I took Liza out for a stroll. I was with my mother. We all felt so good. At first, we were just going around the block once. My mother thought that might be a good start. But we had such a good time that we just continued and went to the park. We went to the lake. Liza saw the ducks, and she got so excited. It was as if she were trying to convey her joy to us. I felt so close to her, and we weren't even talking, just communicating with gestures and laughter."

"It sounds wonderful," I agreed, "as if you are beginning to consolidate some warm and intimate feelings in the family."

"Yes," said Deborah. She added:

Of course, every now and then I'm still aware of the depression. But I'm beginning to put it into perspective. What you kept telling me when I was so down— "This will pass"—is turning out to be true. Now I've gained some perspective. I realize that after Liza's birth I was physically exhausted and that may well have been caused by the late hours I was keeping as well as by the abrupt changes in my hormones. I know I didn't experience any depression with my first pregnancy, but that could be for any number of reasons. In fact, we've even discussed some of those issues in treatment, such as the fact that the pregnancy was unplanned, my problems with George, and my alienation from my mother. I was also leaving a job I truly enjoyed. All of these may have contributed to my depression. And now that I'm beginning to come out of it, I am discovering that I have a beautiful daughter and a wonderful husband and family. I'm really looking forward to the next few months.

At this point we must be aware of the limitations of short-term intervention. Here, quite clearly, although our immediate goals of helping a new mother "ride out" and emerge from an episode of postpartum depression have been achieved, are presented issues calling for further discussion and exploration—the patient's "alienation" from her mother, her undiscussed unhappiness about leaving a well-liked job, her "problems" with George (still unspecified), her "decision" to "stop feeling so guilty" (as if this emotion could be decided on from one day to the next!). But the issue at hand, postpartum depression and its manifestation in one problematical new mother, has been successfully resolved.

"I'm so pleased to hear of your progress," I said. "Can you tell me what's coming up in the next few months? You mentioned earlier that you've arranged for a leave of absence from work. Will you be spending time with Liza and Mark?"

"Yes," Deborah agreed, "I'm very excited. I've arranged to take some extra time off from work. George and I had a long discussion about it. We understand that since the depression is receding, it's not fair for me to miss this special time with Liza. I am experiencing a lot of the things I would have experienced had I not undergone the episode of depression," she said with her characteristic deep insight.

"Can you give me some examples?" I asked.

"Earlier this week I noticed that Liza was beginning to twist her body to turn over. I think she will be crawling soon. I've helped her and have been encouraging her efforts, previewing for her. George and I can't help but wonder what my relationship with Liza would be like if I had not been depressed. Probably I would have been previewing for her all along, the way I was able to do with Mark. As a result, we both think it's important for me to catch up on some of the time we've missed." Thus, as Deborah's depression lifts, we can see a positive ripple effect of her new-found enthusiasm and previewing skills as they serve to reenergize all of the dynamic relationships in Deborah's life. Casting a bright light over her difficulties with her new-born has helped to illuminate some concomitant dark spots in her relationship with her husband and presages well for an improvement in their marital dyad.

"I'm truly delighted that the depression has begun to recede," I told Deborah, "but when you were sad, was there anything that kept you going?"

Two things in particular. The knowledge that most women overcome this condition. You reminded me of that often, and knowing that fact gave me hope. Also, focusing on Liza in such a way as to preview her upcoming development was a great help. Those behaviors were of enormous benefit as I tried to concentrate on Liza. By displacing all of my energy to the baby—however minimal my energy was—I removed the obsessive attention I had on myself. That displacement of energy helped me to see how quickly Liza was developing and, that in turn, motivated me to improve and begin interacting to establish my own relationship with her. I remember in one of our first sessions you focused my attention on Liza's emotions, her thoughts, and her motivations. If I hadn't been undergoing an episode of depression, I would probably be doing that automatically, the way I did with Mark. By coaxing me to preview, you reminded me of those skills and, I believe, reawakened them for me. I am very grateful.

The case of Deborah is a prime example of how short-term intervention can be effective, even where psychopathology is prominent. It also shows that the postpartum depression evidenced here was not unicellular. Intermingled in it were the patient's difficulties with her mother, her anxiety over her husband and her marriage, her loss of daily esteem with the removal of her job, and unresolved conflicts surrounding childhood abandonment—all colluding to complicate a sometimes intractable conflict. The patient herself was both cooperative and particularly insightful and thus helped to resolve her difficulties by efforts extended beyond those many patients have in them to dispense.

# CHAPTER 6

## *Barbara: The Advent of a New Skill Causes Crisis in the Mother-Infant Relationship*

DEVELOPMENTAL CHANGE in the infant will be the most challenging issue new parents confront. Most parents respond to the infant's maturational growth in a fundamental way. They comment, for example, on their infant's progress in a variety of ways without great difficulty: "Someday soon he'll walk" or "Before you know it, she'll be talking." In contrast, however, some parents (specifically, mothers) are not equipped to confront the emotional dislocation that attends an infant's physical development. During pregnancy, after all, the boundaries between self and other become blurred as mother and infant merge on a physical and psychological level (Blos, 1980; Lester & Notman, 1988). Birth is but the first act of separation; from then on, the infant continues to separate from the mother. In particular, the infant's continual acquisition of new skills necessitates that the parents' relationship with the infant must change, perhaps undercutting past intimacy. Such change is not necessarily provoked by a single event. Rather, the perception is that someday the infant will assert increasing autonomy and make overt efforts to separate physically from the parent.

How is autonomy defined? Infants are dependent creatures, relying on their caregivers for food, clothing, shelter, and nurturance. Within a short time, however, the parent recognizes how rapidly the infant changes. At first, most parents celebrate the infant's growth. Adaptive parents in particular know growth means that the infant will master new skills, and that these will enable the infant to communicate on a more consistent and intimate level. Recognizing these skills, however, is a corollary to acknowledging the infant's gradual attainment of autonomous functioning, and thus, a concomitant diminution of dependency.

As the infant continues to develop, however, the parent may see that dawning autonomy also alters the primary relationship with the infant.

Once the baby begins to explore the world beyond the secure orbit of the parental relationship, some parents find this new independence traumatic, threatening, even disruptive. Theorists believe that the closer the mother and child are, the more this type of parent is troubled by the infant's growth. The infant's evolving independence threatens the deeply intimate relationship.

The association between dyadic intimacy and developmental mastery is not difficult to understand. Parents who share a flexible relationship with the infant will frequently be enthusiastic about describing the pleasure of this rapport. Indeed, many parents, especially mothers, will comment that the emotional exchange shared with the infant is one of the most rewarding relationships they have ever experienced. In fact, the parent may be reluctant to relinquish the close bond with the infant precisely because she recognizes that the infant's continued development almost depends on the severing of the intimacy between them. Where the infant's early maturational progress was once celebrated, the sensitized caregiver may now become upset at the slightest indication of infant change.

Adaptive mothers respond to this situation in a variety of ways. First, they may attempt to deny the infant's continued developmental progress. Denial enables them to preserve their relationship with the infant. Mothers find it hard to maintain this stance, since it soon becomes evident that the infant is not going to stop growing and will continue to assert autonomy. Unless the caregiver can reconcile her feelings with the objective reality of the infant's ongoing development, psychosocial problems are to be expected. In particular, the caregiver may manifest resentfulness with the infant's relentless maturation that steadily erodes their intimacy. Some caregivers may withdraw from the infant, no longer providing the encouragement that is vital for optimal development. Development of autonomy itself may be hindered by this lack of enthusiasm, since its emergence depends, in part, on the emotional support the infant receives from the caregiver (Berlin & Cassidy, 1990; Heinicke, 1990; Ward, Brinckerhoff, et al., 1990; Ward, Carlson, et al., 1990). The infant, accustomed to adaptive interpersonal exchange, may become confused by the unexpected about-face in the caregivers' behavior and lose confidence.

As mentioned in chapters 1 and 2, a mother overly concerned with the effect the infant's development is having on their relationship may also paradoxically promote precocious behavior in the infant. Rather than accommodating the change, the mother panics, believing that any evolution will sever the intimacy within the dyad. She thus thrusts the infant away, both literally and figuratively, by encouraging independence far beyond the infant's capacity. Previously, the caregiver was available and accessible, serving as a supportive partner. Now, however, the infant is precipitously left to his or her own devices, expected to achieve new developmental skills on his or her own.

A third response to change occurs with extraordinarily sensitive caregivers. Although they are painfully aware that the infant's burgeoning development has caused shifts in their feelings about their child, they also feel guilty about the resentment they harbor toward the baby. Rather than resenting the infant directly, however, they implode (direct their frustration inward) and often experience a full-fledged episode of depression brought on by their suppressed guilt.

Each of these scenarios is relatively common. Moreover, in each case the dyadic rapport that existed before the crisis was generally highly adaptive. It is ironic that the caregiver's skills of adaptation and sensitivity may give rise to an attitude that later interferes with the infant's maturation. If the caregiver attempts either to rein in the infant's development or to push him or her ahead precociously, the infant will learn the wrong message about development both times. If the mother succumbs to depression, she will inevitably damage the interpersonal relationship shared with the infant. Skillful therapeutic intervention, however, may avert a crisis and reestablish rapport between mother and infant.

The following case examines this issue. Mother and infant shared a highly adaptive and rewarding relationship characterized by emotional reciprocity (Brazelton, Koslowski, & Main, 1974) and attunement (Stern, 1985). Nonetheless, the mother sought treatment to learn more about her infant's developmental trends. From the beginning of treatment, the mother expressed excessive enthusiasm about breast-feeding the infant and spoke of the intimacy she experienced with the infant during these feedings. A problem arose, however, when the infant spontaneously weaned herself before the mother had predicted this behavior. Weaning triggered depression in the mother, which was resolved by the exploration of issues of loss, and by a minor surgical procedure that allowed the mother to purge symbolically her guilt at the infant for continuing to grow and change.

## Patient Identification

Barbara, a 34-year-old first-time mother, had been referred for a consultation by her pediatrician because she had displayed slight overconcern about her infant's development. The mother was well educated and articulate. Her pleasant manner exuded curiosity. Prior to her pregnancy, Barbara had been a rehabilitation counselor, and her soft but firm manner conveyed an empathic quality. Her most striking features were her candor and eloquence. She not only appeared to possess keen insights about her condition but also manifested a desire to understand her emotions. As a result of her sensitivity, Barbara had created a rich emotional environment for herself and her daughter.

Barbara's 4-month-old daughter, Kim, was an active and inquisitive baby. She babbled and laughed as she scrutinized her surroundings and reached out often to grasp at objects that caught her interest: a toy, a shadow, or a stranger's face. Barbara seemed adept at holding her infant and responding to her visual and vocal cues.

## DESCRIPTION OF INTERACTIVE BEHAVIOR

Although Barbara voiced no specific complaints about Kim's behavior or her relationship with the infant—reporting that she and her daughter "had a terrific rapport"—Barbara was intensely interested in learning more about the subtle changes occurring in Kim's development. She also expressed some uneasiness about weaning, saying that she was afraid the experience would be difficult for her because her relationship with the infant was so close. Barbara noted that food was a significant issue for her. She had been overweight since adolescence and was always trying to "lose just 20 pounds." Kim's hearty appetite vaguely concerned Barbara. "I hope she hasn't inherited my weight problem," her mother said. Barbara's statement of concern as well as its phrasing were revealing: one does not inherit a "weight *problem.*" One can only inherit a proclivity to weight gain. Surely as a rehabilitation counselor Barbara knew this, but her wording suggested the etiology of a potential problem that would undoubtedly bear investigation.

I was particularly attentive to Barbara's feelings and perception of feeding, nurturance, and weaning from this point onward, since her provocative statement didn't sit well with me and seemed, in essence, to be forecasting a crucial point for this highly educated, competent woman whose ability to articulate her perceptions and experience still provided her little or no protection from maladaptive reactions that could only damage the healthy mother-infant dyad.

## FAMILY HISTORY

Barbara, Kim, and Rob, Barbara's husband, lived in a one-family house in a prosperous suburb. Until her pregnancy, Barbara had worked as a rehabilitation counselor specializing in sports injuries, especially those of children and adolescents. Barbara had worked through the seventh month of her pregnancy, and, although she considered her work fulfilling, she expressed no regret about putting her career temporarily on hold to care for Kim. "When Kim was ready for school," she said she would return to work again. For now, she enjoyed spending time with her daughter, watching her development, and cementing their relationship. She also reported a mutually supportive bond with Rob, explaining that he was as involved in parenting as his architectural career permitted. Although the marriage occasionally felt the "normal pressures of parenting," Barbara reported that neither she nor Rob "felt overwhelmed." Yet, it is telling that, in a circumstance calling for any one of a number of more neutral terms, Barbara chose to say "overwhelmed." Her usage of this word led me to note the potential direction for future investigation: Was she at this early point in the therapy pinpointing by denial the very emotion she was experiencing?

The second of three children, Barbara had been raised in a family that had emphasized emotional closeness. "I think that's one reason Rob and I waited 4 years to start a family," she told me. "We wanted to get our careers off the ground so we would have a solid financial foundation." She reported "a normal childhood," although the family had moved several times because of her father's military job. Some of these moves were sudden and unexpected. As she entered high school, however, Barbara's family settled in the suburb where her parents still lived. She described her mother as being "very involved" in her children's lives. Barbara said she wanted to emulate her mother's parenting style in her relationship with her own children, including a "genuine enthusiasm about the activities that interest [her] kids." She described her father as affectionate but "traditional" and considerably less involved in child rearing than her mother had been. Barbara said that she found attractive her husband's "nontraditional" attitude, exemplified in his willingness to help her to raise Kim.

According to Barbara, Rob, 35 years old, had been raised by his father after his mother's death when he was 9. "Rob had the perfect model of a nurturing father," Barbara said. She noted that sometimes it was hard to ask Rob for help when he had just returned from a long workday but added that she thought it was important for him to share in Kim's upbringing.

Barbara's pregnancy and labor had been uneventful. Her obstetrician had performed amniocentesis, so the couple knew in advance that their baby was a girl. "The emotional satisfaction of having Kim is something I couldn't have imagined." Barbara then volunteered emphatically that of all the activities she had had in her career, breast-feeding was "the most rewarding experience of [her] life." The sense of warmth with her daughter that breast-feeding provided was particularly important to her, as was her competence as a caregiver, which she said was also at its peak when Kim was breast-feeding. At this point there was no indication that the patient was experiencing any sense of overinvolvement with her infant on a conscious level.

## MENTAL HEALTH STATUS EXAMINATION

During the intake interview, Barbara appeared to be a highly adaptive parent. She displayed attunement, reciprocity, and intuition about Kim's developmental trends. Vocal and visual cuing, for example, appropriate holding behaviors, and frequent stimulation through soothing gestures were common in her interactions with her daughter. Barbara's physical handling of her infant was also extremely adaptive. Even when Kim was in her carriage, Barbara gazed at her daughter and intermittently addressed comments to her. When holding Kim, she cradled the infant to facilitate feeding and direct eye contact. Barbara's sense of when the baby wanted to play or be cuddled, as well as when Kim had reached the limits of stimulation, seemed to be accurate. She gracefully eased her daughter's transitions from one state to another. In addition, Barbara was particularly adept at previewing: encouraging her infant to experience the sensation of upcoming developmental capabilities. Rather than shying away from new infant skills, Barbara anticipated these capacities eagerly. In one instance, she told me how eager she was for Kim to speak so that they could share perceptions on many subjects. We hadn't yet formally broached the subject of previewing, but Barbara seemed highly receptive to predicting Kim's upcoming skills.

Kim was an active infant whose psychomotor development was within normal range, but toward the advanced side of the spectrum. At 5 months of age, she sat up with her mother's support; at 6 months, she sat without support; by 7 months, she was crawling. While Kim attended to Barbara's voice, she was friendly and curious with other adults, and by her squeals and hand waving, the infant indicated that she enjoyed playing with others. When distressed, Kim immediately returned to her mother for comfort and reassurance. This pattern of easy exploration during play, mingled with a return to the mother during times of uncertainty or danger, suggested a normal secure attachment relationship between the pair.

## Therapy

### SESSION 1

I observed mother and infant in the waiting area prior to our session. Barbara, I noticed, was quite plump. Both mother and child appeared well groomed, and Kim seemed both alert and good-humored. When I greeted Barbara and leaned down to address Kim, the infant smiled. Barbara laughed and said her daughter was "a big smiler. She seems to be at the stage where she wants to interact with everyone."

"How is Kim doing developmentally?" I asked.

Barbara looked thoughtfully at her daughter. "She does things . . . uses gestures and sounds to attract my attention . . . in a very deliberate way. I think she knows what she's doing."

"Do you think she has specific intentions and tries to express them to you?" I asked.

"Absolutely! Her physical agility has improved lately, so I understand her messages better. She can hold her head up when she's lying on her stomach. . . . When I put her on the floor on her stomach, she moves backward. She's not so good at going forward yet, though."

"That's quite a list," I said. Barbara added that her daughter's interest in the external world appeared to be increasing every day and that each day she studied her daughter for progress. Barbara's ability to observe Kim's developmental attainments is impressive, and her gentle handling and responsiveness suggest that she is highly attuned to her infant.

At this point, I explained the concept of previewing to Barbara, emphasizing that it was a form of developmental rehearsal: Both mother and infant practice skills that are just emerging in the infant. As a result of these rehearsals, abilities are refined, and the baby experiences how its relationship with the mother will change once the new skill is achieved. Barbara's questions about previewing suggested that she was integrating the concept into her nurturing style.

Barbara then described how much she enjoyed breast-feeding. She noted that, although she was breast-feeding, she produced and expressed enough milk for at least one extra bottle in the morning, so that if Rob wanted to feed the baby, it was possible for him to give Kim a bottle. At this point Barbara also noted with an embarrassed laugh that she had always had a weight problem—"even during childhood"—and that she hoped her daughter's healthy appetite did not mean that Kim would also be susceptible to weight gain.

Essentially, by defining "the big pleasure [as] feeding" and declaring the breast-feeding of her infant to be the "most pleasurable experience of [her] life," Barbara has delineated the parameters of her problem. Feeding—the actual process and its implications—appears to be at the core of what definitely threatens to become a nonnormative pattern with her child.

Certainly, educated people, especially those in the health care professions such as Barbara, realize that overfeeding an infant produces discrete fat cells that are potential sources of lifelong adult fat. Yet Barbara, educated and professional as she is, appears not to know or not to deem applicable to her infant current basic nutritional theories. Instead, anxiety around the subjects of feeding and eating seems to be establishing a pattern that ignores the reality of potential overfeeding and fat cell formation. As noted, feeding behavior seems to be of particular significance to this mother who is effusive about breast-feeding. Her reiteration and focus on this topic point to a nonnormative preoccupation with feeding. Pertinent here is the fact that Barbara mentioned her weight problem and expressed more than once the wish that Kim not inherit it. Yet there might also be, perhaps, a suggestion that, paradoxically, Barbara *wants* her child to be overweight, as she is, as part of a misguided mother-child identification. Unconsciously, then, she'd be prone to overfeed her daughter consistently so that she would mirror her own image (of overweight).

As Barbara was speaking, Kim suddenly became irritable, crying insistently. Barbara reached for her tote bag, commenting that these were hunger signals. For the first time during the session, I felt that Barbara was using an authoritarian tone. This behavior, coupled with her earlier discussion of feeding, suggested that feeding behavior may be a potentially conflicted issue for this mother. Barbara is in fact saying, "I know when the baby is hungry. I know how to interpret her signals." The assertive tone soon vanished, however, as Barbara settled Kim in the crook of her arm. And, once she had brought the bottle into Kim's line of sight, the baby calmed down, the rigidity left her body, and she grasped for the nipple eagerly. The baby's initial rigidity, however, suggested something beyond the usual. Kim's body tension was higher than average for a seemingly well-adjusted infant. I will be focusing more closely in the future on this pattern as another index of the dyadic dynamic between Barbara and infant Kim. While feeding Kim, Barbara gazed at her; Kim, for her part, frequently gazed reciprocally at her mother's face.

After feeding the baby, Barbara draped her over her shoulder, alternately patting and rubbing her back. "She's a shoulder baby," Barbara said, explaining that she thought the pressure of her shoulder on Kim's stomach helped burp the baby. We have demonstrated here unusual insight on the part of the mother, who has created a specialized vocabulary—"a shoulder baby"—around this particular infant system; she does not employ a special vocabulary for her infant's sleeping or excreting functions, just for her feeding response. Barbara is highly sensitized and aware of anything connected with this realm of feeding and all the rituals associated with it. Indeed, feeding has become a highly symbolized act for her. Her needs gratified, Kim now appeared comfortable. "She needs a little rocking, I think," Barbara said. The mother stood, shifted Kim in her arms so that the baby could gaze around the room, and began to rock.

Kim slept in a relaxed state on her mother's shoulder, while Barbara rocked her. As the session was ending, Kim awoke, and Barbara stroked her daughter's head gently. This physical gesture smoothed the infant's transition from a sleeping to a waking state. At this moment Barbara seemed to personify an adaptive, nurturing mother. When Barbara's feeding behaviors are evaluated, however, they suggest a pattern of maternal overinvolvement and dependency. The issue of feeding will be probed further.

## SESSION 2

Barbara and Kim seemed in good spirits, although Kim was more subdued than last week. "She's a little grumpy today," Barbara noted, adding that the infant had been incredibly "needy" over the past few days. I asked whether being "needy" to Barbara meant that Kim wanted more attention.

In addition, I asked if Kim's neediness might be in response to an emotional signal she was picking up from Barbara. Barbara said she wasn't sure. "I had a stomachache the other day and felt pretty lousy, and Kim wanted more attention than usual. It was as if she wanted to make sure the change in me wouldn't affect her," Barbara responded. Significantly, she attributes adult sentiments and motives to her infant. Kim, at only a few months of age, would be unlikely to sense her mother's subjective perceptions to that degree, although she might be attuned to general modulations in mood. Thus, evidence is accumulating that this is not the idyllic adaptive situation it appeared to be on the surface but one of a more disguised or defended nature.

Barbara held Kim in a sitting position, comfortably supported. The physical interaction between mother and child was casual, yet the intermittent cooing Barbara emitted suggested a deep affection. Barbara's conversation was punctuated by Kim's murmurs as she peered at me, then up at her mother.

"I hold her so she can see what's going on, on my lap or on my shoulder," Barbara noted, "but I also try to keep up a conversation with her." When I observed that Barbara seemed to sense Kim's need, the mother said simply, "I can usually figure out what she needs. I'm aware of her needs most of the time. I guess I'm lucky because Kim's not a crier, and I seem to know instinctively what she needs."

Barbara's perception of Kim's needs and the behaviors she uses to meet those needs are indeed impressive. The efficiency and affection with which she attends to her child convey her self-confidence, and Kim clearly benefits from being in a relationship in which her cues are reciprocated. Barbara's keen understanding of her daughter's needs has also made it easier for the baby to grasp perceptions of contingency and attunement, and so on a very basic level we can see that the communication between mother and child is indeed fulfilling.

I asked whether Barbara had noticed any new developmental changes.

"Not this week," Barbara said. "Some of the things she was doing last week are falling into place a little more."

Later, when Kim displayed the same signs of hunger Barbara had noticed at the last session, the mother produced a bottle and began to feed her daughter. During feeding episodes mother and infant seemed quite intimate. Barbara continued to talk. Within a few minutes, Kim pushed the bottle away, but Barbara did not remove it. I began to wonder precisely how sensitive Barbara really was to Kim's true feeding needs, among others. Normally so sensitive to her infant's signals, Barbara failed to respond when Kim indicated that she was finished and wanted the bottle removed. Only after Kim kicked her legs did Barbara pull the bottle back so that Kim could explore it with her fingertips. When Kim indicated that she wanted to nurse again by grabbing the bottle, Barbara readily returned the nipple to the baby's mouth.

I was slightly disturbed by the enmeshed pattern exhibited during these feedings. Although I clearly felt the affection between mother and daughter during the feeding sequence, I also noticed a mechanical quality in Barbara's handling of the bottle, as if she were manipulating her hand. Since Barbara normally breast-feeds her daughter, it is possible that these bottle feedings are a form of previewing the next developmental phase for Kim: It is almost as if her mother is preparing her for this next stage by announcing, "This is the next source from which your nourishment will come." Permitting Kim to hold the bottle herself certainly previews self-feeding. Viewed in this light, Barbara's dissociation from the bottle suggests that previewing a source of food other than the breast may evoke difficult-to-handle emotions for her. The direction of inquiry I am determined to pursue is to address the issue of weaning with Barbara in upcoming sessions.

## SESSION 3

At the beginning of the third session, Barbara announced with pleasure that Kim had learned a new trick. "It just began this week: she's able to turn over."

Barbara's enthusiasm for her daughter's new developmental skill was almost palpable. I asked when she had noticed this new skill. In all areas outside of the nourishment realm, Barbara displays a generous, spontaneously enthusiastic delight in her daughter's new and emerging attainments. She also appears personally enhanced by such new skills as opposed to her evidencing concern that growing independence in self-feeding threatens her equilibrium.

"About 3 days ago," was Barbara's prompt response. "She's been experimenting for a while, and sometimes I helped her. She turned her head and sort of kicked her legs, and, presto, she flipped over, without any help from me."

"How did Kim react?" I asked.

"I think she was surprised. She looked surprised. I just laughed. She was so proud of herself. Every time she does it now, she laughs. It must be so exciting to interact with the environment without me or Rob to help her!" Kim is now 23 weeks old; her ability to roll over is an age-appropriate developmental milestone.

Kim grasped a lock of her mother's hair and craned her body outward, fixing her gaze on several toys. "You want to go down, pumpkin?" Barbara asked, placing Kim on the floor. The mother then produced several small toys from her tote bag.

After several minutes, Kim began to look at one of the toys. As we watched, Kim rolled over from her stomach and reached with her upper body until she had rolled again, this time onto her stomach. The infant crowed with pleasure at her accomplishment and then began to wriggle purposefully toward the toy.

While on her back, Kim reached upward to her mother as if to sit up, then rocked backward. She smiled broadly at her mother, as if inviting her to share her accomplishment. Barbara returned her smile, saying "Yes, yes!"

Barbara was previewing another milestone here—sitting. As we talked, periodically she would offer her daughter some fingers and allow Kim to pull herself up to a sitting position using the fingers. I was also pleased to hear that Barbara had begun to recognize her own previewing skills as well as to coordinate previewing techniques into her nurturing of Kim.

As the conversation continued, Barbara mentioned that Kim would be the perfect baby except that sometimes she demonstrated a "temper." "What circumstances trigger this temper?"

"When she doesn't get her way or when things aren't happening as quickly as she wants. For example, if she's really hungry she can get very angry at me."

I asked Barbara how she knew when Kim was angry.

"Her expression becomes angry. She kicks differently. And she has an unpleasant, nasty screech. She gets angry if I'm getting ready to breast-feed her and it takes me too long to get settled. I guess she knows food is coming, and from her point of view I'm teasing her by not feeding her right away." Significantly, this is the third instance Barbara has used intensely negative language and associations of rupture and violence ("angry expression," "kicking," "unpleasant, nasty screech") to describe breast-feeding her infant, the very experience she has already termed "the most meaningful" of her life. In a fleeting moment of awareness, Barbara appears to recognize that her previous perceptions of an idyllic bonding situation are somewhat flawed. It appears as though the fine equilibrium between this mother-infant dyad definitely has another less idyllic side. Here, despite Barbara's best efforts, the child's anger has manifested itself, leading to an awareness that what the mother has previously called a "perfect baby"—and, by extension, symbol of a perfect mother-child bonding—is not perfect, at least with respect to the feeding arena. Furthermore, given her lifelong history of mild obesity, it is probably symptomatic of Barbara to project anger (or other adult feelings) into food-disparity situations.

"How do you deal with her when she acts that way?"

"I try to convey that I am feeding her as quickly as possible."

I was intrigued by Barbara's comments about Kim's "temper" in relation to feeding. Barbara cannot control this area of the infant's life, and her inability to assert control appears to frustrate her. Barbara's observations suggest that, when deprived of food, Kim quickly becomes frustrated. Thus, Barbara may be endowing Kim with the potential for the same ambivalence, even anger, in the nurturance situation that she herself may experience when weaning occurs.

I then raised the issue of weaning. "I wanted to ask you about weaning," I said. "Kim is progressing so well, we can even preview signs of walking with her. Given all this progress, I wonder if you have given any thought to weaning."

Barbara's face went blank. Then Kim cried out suddenly and Barbara glanced at her watch. "I guess we should discuss that next time," she said, "because it's time for us to go." She looked down with embarrassment, as if she knew she was avoiding a difficult issue. Her behavior distinctly suggested that despite Barbara's attunement and skill at previewing, the issue of feeding—particularly weaning—is definitely one that arouses conflict. It will be important to explore this aspect in upcoming sessions, since weaning is an essential component of the separation between this mother and infant. Her withdrawal—one could say flight—from the scene just as we were about to explore the sensitive topic of weaning permits Barbara to elude the subject of separation for now. But her refusal to delve into its meaning represents a denial that clearly serves as an impediment to the effective exploration of an issue that holds deep conflictual meaning for this patient. Although the overall picture of the mother-infant dyad is very positive, from the outset of our therapy there were evidences of a problem. Further sessions have revealed the patient's potential for maladaptive interaction with her infant surrounding the feeding experience. Breast-feeding has become a major construct for this patient, and weaning has become her greatest threat to continued peace and intimacy with baby Kim.

## SESSION 4

I was surprised at how somber Kim somehow appeared today, until Barbara explained that they had visited the pediatrician that morning for a routine checkup. Kim had had an inoculation that morning, and the experience had been upsetting for both mother and infant. Distress after a pediatric visit is something I have encountered previously in adaptive caregivers. These caregivers seem to have difficulty previewing negative events, partly because rehearsing these events is unpleasant, and perhaps because the previewing is obviously more difficult for the mother than it would be for the infant.

During the first part of the session, Kim sat quietly on her mother's lap. She seemed serious, although there was no sign of fear or wariness in her behavior. As the session continued, the infant began to babble, and her curiosity reasserted itself. About midway through the session, she signaled by moving her legs that she wanted to be let down from her mother's lap.

"Down you go!" Barbara said, positioning Kim on the floor. As in earlier sessions, Barbara placed several toys near her daughter. Kim grasped a rattle with several rings. She waved one of the rings, gurgling happily. Barbara continued to talk. Suddenly a car outside backfired loudly. Kim froze, all expression wiped from her face. Gazing around as if searching for her mother, the infant began to cry. Kim would probably have been less distressed by the noise if she had not already been upset by the pediatric visit.

Barbara seemed to welcome the opportunity to comfort her child. She picked Kim up and rocked her gently. Kim's tears and rigid posture continued for a moment; then she relaxed, rubbing her cheek along Barbara's neck. The mother's soothing attitude verified for the infant that something untoward had happened but that the situation was now under control. By responding as she did, Barbara was in effect previewing for Kim the notion that in a world of sudden loud noises everything could be made fine, and by extension she was conveying that frightening events in the environment could be controlled. Kim recovered from the noise quickly, as if assimilating her mother's message. A few minutes later, she was returned to the floor and began to explore the toys, glancing referentially at her mother from time to time.

"Kim seems to be exhibiting social referencing behavior," I said to Barbara. When the mother looked at me quizzically, I added that infants who were securely attached tended to check visually with the mother during perceived stress or danger situations.

Barbara added another new item in Kim's list of skills: "She can actually get things into her mouth now. Before, she could bring her hand to her mouth, but her motor coordination didn't allow her to put her fingers into her mouth. Sometimes I think: Today it's her fingers, tomorrow it's everything else in the house." Since Barbara seemed so in control of her emotions, I decided to reraise the issue of weaning. "You seem so skillful with Kim," I began, "that I was wondering if we could talk about weaning? Last week you were troubled by the issue. I am a little confused by your response, because weaning is, after all, a natural aspect of development and separation, and you seem so pleased with Kim's other achievements." By this point my original suspicions regarding the dyadic impairment had been confirmed. Accumulating evidence revealed that not everything was as straightforward as it had initially appeared. Given the patient's ability and willingness to articulate her feelings, I here used the term "confused" as a gentle entrée to get the patient to explore the concept of weaning in a nonjudgmental and sympathetic manner.

"I know," Barbara said. "It confuses me. It's just that . . . breast-feeding is so special. I feel so close to her when I feed her. I'm afraid of losing that feeling when she weans. I have this horrible premonition that our whole relationship will change." Barbara lapsed into silence. Yet again we have an extremely negative word intruding into Barbara's beatific relationship. In fact, the word *horrible* is unusual in Barbara's lexicon. By using such a negative and powerfully emotive description, she provides insight into her innermost feelings. The linkage between her infant and herself is so important to Barbara that any threat to its integrity will bring down the image of the ideal that she has constructed of their dyadic union. Her ability to begin discussing weaning at this point is a positive sign. In addition, she has recognized that some of her behaviors may be contradictory. Recognition of this conflict may lead to a positive change concerning a difficult issue. We agreed to return to the weaning issue in ensuing sessions.

## SESSION 5

I began the session by asking if Barbara had noticed any developmental changes. "She's started on solid food," Barbara announced, adding that the transition was one reason why they were both so tired. I asked Barbara to elaborate on the connection between her fatigue and Kim's new diet.

She laughed. "Everything! Earlier this week Kim started waking up in the middle of the night. Two or three hours of sleep, then she was awake. She didn't want to nurse. So, yesterday afternoon I gave her some solid food, and she ate it. She ate only a teaspoonful, but what a difference. Last night she went right to sleep and slept through the night. I guess she was ready." Barbara added that it had been a difficult week because her family was visiting. "My family insists upon hospitality at mealtimes," she said suggestively. I continued to sense the special significance of food for Barbara. She indicated that her family meals conformed to a cultural stereotype: "You know, Mom says, 'Eat, eat!'" Her very sense of perception lacks objectivity when food is around. Although her relatives are staying with her, are guests in her home, something about her behavior around food has evoked criticism of her, which is why she says "my family insists on hospitality at mealtimes." There is the implicit suggestion that Barbara *hasn't* been quite hospitable, that her behavior has somewhat been blameworthy. So her food problem with Kim is echoed by her larger problem around food, even with adults, especially with the adults of her own family.

Perhaps it's not surprising then that the one area in which Barbara is incapable of preview involves feeding. The source of the overwhelming significance of food and eating to Barbara is now apparent. As a child she had been subject to the parental blandishments ("Eat! Eat!"), and this probably has led her to her current overdependence on food, her "weight problem," and her enmeshment with breast-feeding. Food may now be a symbol of control in Barbara's life. Note that, whereas she successfully predicted Kim's approaching mastery of sitting behavior, she has repeatedly denied her daughter's ability to self-feed. For now, the implications of weaning may be too traumatic for Barbara to face. She is, nonetheless, on some level beginning to acknowledge this issue of residual conflict. Barbara confronts any non-breast-feeding nurturing experience of her daughter as if it were troublesome: When she discussed how Kim began eating solid foods, themes of turmoil entered her conversation, yet she was able to concede that the baby slept well after solid food. I am encouraged that these feelings are being raised by Barbara and view this as a healthy confrontation by the patient with deeply rooted conflictual forces.

## SESSION 6

During this session, Kim was teething on her rattle. Although Barbara supported Kim with a hand at her waist, the baby's posture was notably stronger, and she appeared ready to sit without support. The choreography of movements within the dyad as Kim approaches the milestone of sitting is intriguing. Barbara conveys substantial affection with her gestures. At the same time, the mother does not forget that she is the leader with certain responsibilities for Kim's welfare. Barbara seems to understand that motherhood requires her to guide the infant's development. Thus, there is an appropriateness to these interchanges as each reinforces the other's behavior.

At almost 7 months of age, Kim's skill in manipulating any small object, such as a toy, has improved markedly. Her movements are quick and strong. Several of Kim's psychomotor skills seem to have consolidated during the past week. Moreover, Barbara previews these new skills adeptly. As I commented on her daughter's developmental progress, Barbara noted that Kim was now accomplished at "testing" new objects by mouthing them. "I think it gives her a sense of accomplishment. When she first discovered where her mouth was, all she could do was put her hand in there. She used to lick her hand. Then she put it in her mouth. Now she can get a toy into her mouth and test it."

"That's certainly one change that has occurred since we began," I commented.

Kim gurgled. "Well, that's new," Barbara said. "I think Rob taught her that noise, and she seems to use it to say, 'Look at ME.'" Barbara gently shook one of Kim's feet. "'Pay attention to me, Mom!'" Kim responded with another gurgling noise. I commented that this was an enjoyable exchange to watch. Barbara reported that Kim had an entire repertoire of "attention-getting noises," many of which had specific meanings, such as: I'm hungry; I'm wet; I'm lonely.

I intentionally did not raise the weaning issue during this session. Since this issue is of concern to Barbara, I continue to feel it important that the mother broach the topic herself. I also felt that Barbara deserved to bask in her accomplishments as an adaptive mother encouraging her infant's skill.

And I told her that, in my considered judgment, her adaptive skills at mothering were exemplary.

## SESSION 7

By now Kim had developed an exuberant personality, and for this session she greeted me with a big smile, echoed by Barbara's smile. Gazing up at me from the floor and lying on her stomach, Kim rolled onto her side. After I clapped and then commented on how advanced Kim's balance had become, the baby smiled. Her evident self-confidence in exhibiting a new skill was highly advanced for her age. Overall, there is a heightened sense of the child as an autonomous social being and an increased playfulness in the dyad. I sensed Barbara's enthusiasm for her daughter's skill during this process.

"She's gained a lot of ground developmentally," I commented. Barbara agreed proudly, adding that Kim's mobility meant that she had to keep a sharper eye on her daughter or else the child might "crawl away and hurt herself."

Both of us focused on Kim; then Barbara asked, "Do babies dream?"

"What made you ask that question?" I responded.

"Sometimes when she sleeps I see her eyelids flickering, and I wondered if babies dream."

Our discussion led easily to my asking Barbara about her own dreams. Recently, the mother confided, she had dreamed that Kim had two teeth. "They just appeared. There was no teething, no pain for her, and I thought, 'This is really terrific!' We just wake up one day and she has teeth." That the infant acquires teeth almost miraculously, without undergoing the process of teething, suggests that Barbara wishes that Kim's weaning be accomplished with minimal emotional pain. It is intriguing as well that Barbara's dream (in that complex way that dreams permit one subject to symbolize several layers of meaning) allows her to preview teething in a manner that avoids pain for Kim.

As noted earlier, adaptive caregivers seem to have little success when previewing negative events for their infants. This teething issue has two elements insofar as Barbara is concerned. As an adaptive mother, first, she envisions a pain-free, easy scenario for Kim's inevitable teething process. But secondly, and perhaps of greater significance, the dream indicates the latent content in the whole issue surrounding teething. The process represents, inevitably, maturation, reliance on solid food, a growing autonomy of a child away from the sealed loop of breast milk and mother-child feedings. For Barbara, the content of the dream underscores both her insecurities and the need for exploration of this material in the future.

Barbara added that Kim had "adult teeth" in the dream. She seems to be previewing far into the future as a strategy for defending herself against predicted changes in her daughter. By making an extreme prediction, Barbara can then retreat to a less threatening image of Kim with baby teeth.

"Was there any fear about being hurt by her teeth?" I asked.

"Oh, no!" Barbara said. She insisted there was nothing painful associated with the teeth in her dream and adamantly denied it symbolized any hostility from Kim directed toward her. I commented that teething was an important developmental milestone and signaled many other events. In general, however, the dream might be used to explore Barbara's reaction to upcoming changes in Kim.

"How would Kim's new teeth represent a change in your relationship with her? After all, teething is a demonstrative sign of her change," I said.

"I suppose," Barbara said pensively, "I must have some ambivalent feelings about Kim changing. Even though it's very exciting to see new skills, sometimes it's scary too, because I'm afraid I'll lose her. Maybe I dreamed that she changed overnight so I wouldn't have to experience the change with her." Because Barbara and Kim share such a secure attachment, it is not surprising that harbingers of developmental change disturb this mother. Her use of the phrase "I'm afraid I'll lose her" indicates the extent to which her exaggerated enmeshment reaches. She refers to her husband only when the infant and she are on utterly secure grounds. She fears "losing" her daughter at the merest hint of teeth or the too-rapid advance of skills she otherwise celebrates. We will be further examining the concentric relationships evident here: Barbara with her baby; Barbara with her husband.

"What events may have evoked this dream?" I asked.

Barbara answered, "Two weeks ago I felt little bumps on Kim's gums. She's not teething yet, but soon she will be. The pediatrician confirmed my suspicions. Maybe the dream was a way of preparing myself for that event." The dream suggests that Barbara's pleasure in her daughter's progress may not be entirely without misgiving, and, although Barbara does not associate weaning with this dream, I am convinced that she is exploring this issue on some level. A baby with teeth, for example, cannot suck at the breast without causing the mother pain. Moreover, such a child has generally completed the weaning process.

As Barbara protectively placed Kim on her lap and pulled her close, I wondered if she was at some unconscious level troubled by discussing the dream and its latest hints of separation.

"There seems to be a strong continuity in your relationship with Kim. No developmental event has disrupted your relationship with her?" I asked.

Barbara nodded. "Her new skills change our relationship—she doesn't need me to move her around as much. But disrupt it? Not really."

Tellingly, her response here is a flat statement of denial that serves as an impediment to the effective exploration of issues that are conflicted for this patient. She does in fact speak of the various interruptions she gets from Kim's increasing independence, especially, mobility. But although these bother her, the really crushing changes relate to self-nourishing behaviors in Kim—grabbing a bottle, rejecting the breast, short attention span—she only permits them to surface through the protective layers of her dreams.

## SESSION 8

When I arrived for this session, Barbara was already settled in a chair, feeding Kim. The infant lay relaxed in her mother's arms, her gaze rapt on Barbara's face. Except for a brief smile at me, Barbara's attention was wholly focused on her daughter.

Barbara and I began to talk about Kim's relationship with Rob and how it differed from her relationship with Kim. When Barbara attempted to move the sleeping baby, I offered to hold Kim. She agreed and carefully handed me the baby. I was pleased that she had no trepidation about my holding her daughter. Kim slept soundly during the session. Barbara appeared to be pleased that I could hold Kim without disturbing her sleep. Yet I continued to hold reservations about this portrayal of ideal maternal serenity. Despite her relaxed posture, I sensed that the mother continued to monitor her daughter. As soon as Kim stirred in my arms, Barbara immediately rose to take her daughter back.

Whereas I was pleased that Barbara intervened protectively on her daughter's behalf, nonetheless, I felt that her possessiveness might interfere with Kim's assertion of autonomy. I also felt that this episode demonstrated a transference reaction to me. Because Barbara trusts me, she allowed me to hold her infant, although she displayed some wariness. Underneath that, Barbara's protectiveness indicates at base a less-than-adaptive response. It is reminiscent of the vaguely authoritarian attitude that Barbara exhibited early in our sessions.

According to Barbara's descriptions, new developmental changes had not been observed during the previous week, yet the mother's "hypervigilance" throughout this session was evident. We have another indication, then, that, although in most respects Barbara is an adaptive caregiver, evidently she has still not negotiated the issue of Kim's autonomy. The contrast between "not noticing" new developmental changes during the preceding week and Barbara's evident observational alacrity in this session really showed two sides of the same subtly countertherapeutic force. Once again, my suspicions were substantiated that Barbara was beginning to experience observational and coping difficulties vis-à-vis her infant's growing independence.

## SESSION 9

Barbara and Kim both appeared exceptionally serene at this session. As I have said earlier, adaptive caregivers frequently become possessive as the infant manifests skills indicative of separation. At these times, the caregiver may become unusually close to the infant, apparently unwilling to relinquish the intimate relationship.

Today, mother and daughter wore matching outfits that Barbara had sewn herself, obvious evidence of the mother's enforced closeness. So difficult is the upcoming separation for her to contemplate that she must physically reunite herself and her daughter under a veil of single fabric in a symbolic gestation! It is almost as if Barbara is using her sewing skills to stitch up the boundaries between the two of them and generate one personality for herself and Kim.

Responding to Kim's gurgling during my conversation with her mother, I smiled; Kim smiled. When my expression became one of mock ferocity, the infant smiled and gurgled. Despite Barbara's subtle but constant efforts to deemphasize Kim's development and maturity, that Kim could notice my "pretend ferocity" was a good sign. Kim was clearly well within normal range for an infant of her age.

"How is Kim's development progressing?" I asked.

"Very well," said Barbara. "She's almost sitting up, crawling, and rolling. But everything is changing so quickly," she added with a negative inflection. When I asked Barbara to explain what she meant, she continued: "Mobility introduces an entirely new dimension. Suddenly I have to be everywhere. Her new skills make her very demanding." Barbara discussed efforts to childproof her house. Her concern with childproofing, although legitimate, may also be symbolic of her unwillingness to relinquish intimacy with her daughter and let Kim explore on her own.

Although Kim signaled clearly that she wanted to play on the floor, in this session Barbara kept her firmly on her lap. The mother's behavior seemed strange in light of Barbara's customary response to Kim's signals. Finally, Barbara lifted Kim so that the infant was "standing" in her lap. The baby grabbed for her mother's face, squealing triumphantly.

Throughout this session, however, Barbara forbore to put her daughter down to play; again, this response was most unusual considering both the diversity of Kim's new skills and Barbara's previous willingness to let the baby explore. It seemed as if she did not want to spend this session monitoring the infant, but by keeping Kim in a controlled condition, Barbara was definitely trying to rein in her daughter's autonomy. The mother had noted previously that her closeness with Kim might be expected to make separation difficult for her. Certainly, each developmental milestone Kim attained foreshadowed the child's growing autonomy and separation from the mother.

At last Barbara settled the baby and reached for a bottle of juice. Kim clearly recognized the bottle: She sat straight up and followed Barbara's movements as her mother removed the lid of the bottle and brought it close.

"She can't manage by herself yet," Barbara said, more to convince herself than me. Clearly the issue of feeding continues to raise conflicts for this mother and she consistently manages to avoid the milestone of self-feeding. Although Barbara is correct that Kim does not yet have the strength to hold her bottle, with any other developmental change, Barbara would most likely be saying, "Kim will be trying soon," rather than "she can't manage by herself." Barbara seemed determined to ignore Kim's feeding progress. Still, the self-feeding milestone appeared imminent, and Barbara's unusual closeness with her daughter may well have signaled her continuing inability to accept this new skill. Although obviously proud of her daughter's physical and developmental growth, she still appeared reluctant to relinquish control over the child's feeding habits.

## SESSION 10

Kim was now almost 8 months old. Virtually every week had brought new developmental accomplishments. Our initial conversation focused on Kim's new skills. Barbara seemed at ease about discussing Kim's increasing ability to sit and crawl. "It's a very different world for her now," she said. "I try to imagine things from her perspective. Being able to move around and approach objects that interest her probably changes her whole perspective. When she's sitting up her view of the world must be different too. You can see it in her face when she changes position."

Barbara continued. "It's amazing to watch her. She knows what she wants to accomplish and how it ought to be done. Each time she gets halfway up, she beams ecstatically because she's fulfilling her intentions."

As we spoke, Kim maintained eye contact with her mother. As soon as she had met her mother's gaze, Kim's body relaxed. This may be a form of "social referencing," by which the baby checks with the parent (usually the mother) to verify that everything is all right before further exploring the environment. Then Kim looked around her with avid curiosity. At this stage, the infant needs to feel her caregiver will be available when she returns from adventure. Similarly, it is as if Barbara needs to be persuaded that Kim will return to her. Several times while I was talking, Kim gurgled at the sound of my voice. She punctuated her mother's statements with slightly different sounds but always added a megawatt smile.

It is intriguing to watch the reciprocal "dance" of signals between this mother and infant. At times, Kim initiates a previewing episode by demonstrating already consolidated skills and rehearsing talents that are beginning to emerge. She seemed to be telling her mother, "We have come this far—what's next?" Barbara is enthusiastic about Kim's new skills and previews precursory abilities for her infant. It is furthermore evident that the previewing process has served to enhance the intimacy for both mother and child. Yet what Barbara seems to want is a perfect, adult alignment of two-person empathy—an unrealistic assessment of any baby's abilities, to be sure.

I asked Barbara if she had any thoughts about an upcoming trip to the Midwest that she had mentioned. She stated that she was a little apprehensive because she couldn't tell how Kim would weather the rigors of traveling. Here again Barbara is ascribing more knowledgeability to her child than is possible, since Kim clearly won't be traveling alone and Barbara will be there to minister to her needs throughout. Kim's problems with the projected travel are more probably Barbara's projections of her own fears about the trip. On a more conflicted level, Barbara is worried about Kim's "journeying" toward more independence and away from her. So the "weathering of rigors" will be Barbara's own.

## SESSION 11

Because of the family's trip, Barbara had canceled three sessions. Noticing that Kim greeted me with a big smile, I thanked her formally for her welcome and said I felt she had recognized me.

"Oh, yes, I think she recognizes you now," Barbara agreed. "She's getting very adept at recognizing people we see frequently." Barbara spontaneously reported that their trip had been extremely rewarding and without any complications. Kim had apparently been the center of attention for family members. Barbara also mentioned that Kim had demonstrated great flexibility in adjusting to altered schedules and an ability to "roll with the punches."

I asked whether Barbara had noticed any new developmental skills in her daughter. At first she said no; Kim was honing the skills she had already acquired. However, when Barbara placed the child on the floor, she did so in such a way that Kim stood briefly on her own before she was lowered to a crawling position. Then Barbara looked startled and said, "Of course, there is something new. We haven't seen you for almost a month." Kim, she noted, was now standing on her own, using a chair or table to pull herself up to a standing position.

After I asked Barbara how she felt about Kim's new accomplishment, Barbara said in an obviously jubilant tone, "I'm very proud of her. I expected to see Kim sitting and walking, all the milestones the books talk about. What I didn't anticipate, though, is her ingenuity. Pulling herself up and down on a piece of furniture. I can see her integrating skills almost before my eyes. Sometimes I feel as if I'm learning new skills along with Kim."

I shared with Barbara a contemplative sense that indicated an awareness of loss—of leaving something behind—even as both she and her daughter were advancing to new stages. This note of sadness intermingled with her obvious pride and joy in her daughter's achievements was evidence that Kim's ongoing development was still evoking troublesome aspects from Barbara's past. Yet these comments suggested that the conflict around Kim's self-feeding was beginning to resolve. Not only did Barbara explicitly describe some imminent milestones in very positive terms, but her ability to preview was fluid, and the adaptive momentum between the dyad was unimpeded.

After a pause she added, "For the last week or so I've also been feeling a little sad, though." Barbara was quiet for a moment. "I've had a sense of loss about Kim. I really loved having my baby, and now I sense the end of her infancy." Barbara sounded as if she were near tears. "The newborn is gone, I guess. I'm proud of the way Kim is growing, and her sense of accomplishment is infectious, but I get a little sad sometimes, too. At first I didn't want to talk about these things. I thought maybe the sadness would go away."

"How do these changes affect Kim's relationship with her father, and yours to him?" I asked.

"As Kim gets more independent, their bond seems deeper. For a while I was jealous when I saw the incredible smiles he elicited from her. Now I get the same kind of 'royal treatment.' I think it's because she's so mobile. When she looks at me, it's as if she's really happy to see me. I don't direct my jealousy to Rob anymore."

"Can you elaborate on these feelings?" I inquired.

Barbara looked uncomfortable. "I don't think Rob ever realized my feelings, but I was aware that part of me resented him for being so special to Kim. I'm the one who really cares for Kim, and I know this sounds terrible, but sometimes I feel I'm not appreciated. But now Kim is starting to make a big fuss over me the way she does with Rob. So I don't feel left out anymore. I may miss the intense closeness we had, but there's a new, dynamic closeness." Barbara here has almost renegotiated the emotional contract between herself and her baby. Whereas earlier what she had expected emotionally from her child was unhealthily excessive, now she has worked out a new but satisfactory contract: Barbara is nourished by Kim's huge smiles and bountiful affect.

I was pleased to find both that Barbara was able to continue feeling intimate with her daughter even though their relationship had changed and that she was consciously aware of and able to articulate this growth. Her sadness at losing some intimacy with Kim and her slight jealousy of her husband's relationship with Kim are typical responses even in cases where the dyadic maternal dependency is not so pronounced. Expressing these emotions during treatment may help to resolve them, and just as her daughter is using newfound abilities to navigate *her* environment, Barbara is now using her psychological maturity to master the situation. Kim's growing sophistication in communicating to her mother compensates Barbara as well for the intimacy that has been lost now that nursing behavior is diminishing. Barbara has indeed learned her lessons of previewing well.

After a few minutes of play, Kim began to fuss. Barbara reached for a bottle of juice. As at our preceding meeting, Kim became calm as soon as she saw the bottle. Barbara placed the baby on the floor on her back and positioned the bottle in Kim's hands. "She's learning to hold the bottle by herself, but she doesn't really have the strength. In this position she can just manage it." Kim clutched the bottle and sucked eagerly. Barbara sat with elbows on her knees, leaning forward, ready to come to her child's aid if Kim had trouble with the bottle. I was careful to observe whether, behind all of these helpful repositionings and assists, there wasn't also a subtle effort to sabotage the baby's feeding autonomy.

As if to validate my suspicions, almost before Kim had loosened her grip on the bottle, Barbara removed it and said, "This is the way it goes these days: almost before she's finished eating, she wants to explore. It happens even when I'm breast-feeding. We used to cuddle after feedings, but now she seems more interested in exploring." The infant herself, then, has begun to exert some control over her feedings, in the process confronting the overprotective nature Barbara has tried to impose on the dyad.

As if to confirm Barbara's words, Kim began crawling toward a chair. With her mother's help, she pulled herself up to a standing position. I asked Barbara her feelings about this particular skill.

"It's another change that makes me feel a little sad, I suppose." Then, with more conviction, she added, "Nursing has always been special for me. But the best thing I can do is learn from these sessions and begin looking to other skills that will compensate for the closeness I'm losing," she said a little abjectly.

"What 'other' kinds of skills come to mind?" I asked.

"I look forward to Kim's being able to talk because that will allow me to communicate better with her," she said, sounding somewhat lost in her willingness to compromise "down" future intimacy from verbal communication for the intimacy relinquished as her baby gives up nursing.

## SESSION 12

"We just came from my mother-in-law's," Barbara commented at the start of our session. "She was having a party," Barbara concluded. Both she and Kim were elaborately dressed.

"How did Kim respond to the party?" I asked.

"I was surprised," Barbara said. "She was shy! I think it was because there were other children there, but she's never reacted like this before. When the other children looked at her, she clung to me and hid under my arm. But the minute they looked away, she peeked out. Every time one of the other children made a noise, she looked for its source; then she would look at me to make sure things were all right. With the adults she was fine; just the kids made her shy. Not what I would have expected." Then Barbara added, "Sometimes I forget to look at the world from her point of view. The experience of meeting a lot of new people must be scary for her. She doesn't spend much time with other children yet. Most of the people she encounters are adults. She knows kids are different. Maybe she is more accustomed to adults."

Interestingly, by the age of 8 months, Kim has not been exposed by her mother to interactive situations with other children, either informally in a park-playground setting or in a formalized playgroup situation. This mother, in her attempt to reinforce the dyadic bond, has restrained her daughter's social development to some degree. I told Barbara that I was not particularly concerned about Kim's behavior, although now might be the time for Barbara to investigate joining a mother-infant playgroup, so that Kim could be exposed to other infants of varying ages. I mentioned that this group might also benefit Barbara, who would be able to discuss issues such as weaning with other new mothers. As we spoke, Kim began to explore the room.

"See what I mean about her getting around? I spend most of my day following her. I feel like I'm constantly rescuing the baby."

Despite Barbara's vigilance with Kim, I also sensed that some of her earlier possessiveness had faded. She added that she didn't understand how women with more than one infant managed. She and Rob often discussed having a second child, but neither of them thought it would be practical while Kim was still a toddler. Despite Barbara's nostalgia for her daughter's dependency, neither she nor her husband view a second pregnancy as a way to recapture that closeness: "I want to give Kim time to become an independent person before I have another baby," she said. Barbara's attitude is one way of acknowledging her daughter's independent status.

I commented on the growing sophistication of Kim's communications. Barbara agreed and added that Kim was undergoing so many changes it was hard to keep up with her.

"Can you describe your feelings in more detail?" I asked.

Barbara selected her words carefully. "When Kim was a newborn, it was just Kim and me; now it's Kim and the whole world. I'm just a small part of it. I have to compete for her attention along with everyone else. But I've become accustomed to her changes and understand how her skills have helped me to be closer to her. By about 2 months of age, Kim discovered the world; by 4 months she was becoming a part of that world. Now she's so independent!" It is impossible to ignore here that, although Barbara has progressed very far in attempts to establish a more healthy and balanced dyadic relationship with her daughter, she still defines her emotional landscape by connection with Kim. I reflected that for adaptive caregivers it often becomes more difficult to describe the infant's developmental changes as separation grows imminent. But although such caregivers frequently fail to note intricate developmental details, they generally regain their equilibrium once the developmental event about which they are conflicted has occurred. I am encouraged by Barbara's use of empathy to understand her daughter. Developing this empathy may ultimately help her to move beyond the disappointment she is experiencing now.

Barbara continued, "I'm looking forward to the time Kim will walk on her own. From these sessions I've learned to represent that milestone, so I'll appreciate it." By "represent," Barbara clearly means "picture the milestone" in her mind's eye.

Kim suddenly became extremely active, grabbing at her mother's dress and pulling her hair. When I offered her a toy, Kim showed it to her mother. Her activity increased until Barbara said, "I know what you want," and produced a bottle of apple juice. As she had in previous sessions, the baby grabbed the bottle herself. While Kim's grasp appeared firm, Barbara maintained a loose grip on the bottle. Once Kim's initial thirst had abated, the baby turned her head, dislodging the nipple. When Barbara withdrew the bottle, however, Kim grabbed immediately for the bottle, pulling the nipple back to her mouth. Barbara laughed and said, "Okay, so you're not finished yet," and returned the nipple to Kim's mouth.

Barbara's motions definitely seemed more relaxed than the last time I had watched her withdraw a bottle from Kim. When I noted this to her, she said, "You're right. I'm trying hard to understand this weaning process from Kim's perspective. I don't think she wants to lose the closeness she has with me, but propping up the bottle by herself must be exhilarating. So I'm trying to understand her pleasure." Barbara here is still demonstrating remnants of her old dereistic thinking patterns and ascribing thought processes to her infant that really reflect Barbara's own concerns. Clearly, the infant does not think in terms of "losing her closeness with her mother," and Barbara's projection is continued evidence of ascribing adult motivations to her infant. Similarly, she is rationalizing in her use of the words *understand* her pleasure" instead of simply *acknowledging* the child's pleasure.

As Kim continued nursing, Barbara noted that in about 3 weeks, she would start Kim on whole milk. "It will represent the beginning of weaning. I'll let her nurse in the morning and at night, but it will be so much more convenient to give her a bottle." Barbara said that she didn't anticipate any trouble weaning her daughter. Then, she added strangely, "About once a week she wants to nurse all day long." Whereas before Barbara's complaints had involved a fall-off state between the baby and herself, now she suddenly seemed to be complaining that the baby wanted *more* closeness. Since it is unusual, in my experience, for an infant to "nurse all day," this statement likely reflects Barbara's lingering desires for total bonding despite her contention that she would relish Kim's new independence.

"When you say that she wants to nurse all day long, how do you know that?"

"She pulls at my sweater all day. Roots—you know."

"So weaning will be a relief?" I asked.

Barbara smiled. "A mixed blessing," she said wistfully.

Despite her practical attitude about weaning Kim, Barbara's reluctance about discussing weaning is evident. She's indulging in fairly evident denial. Faced with the initiatory rite of weaning, Barbara goes to lengths to defend the child's hunger for continued care and feeding in this way: Thus, we have Barbara's (odd) assertion that Kim wants to "nurse all day" and that she "roots around" for her nipples in public, seeking to be nursed. Barbara is still clearly in conflict about the whole area of weaning and its implications for her future relationship with her daughter. Clearly, Kim's recent accomplishments may be metaphors for the loss of the "special closeness" Barbara is anticipating. Still Barbara seems to be defusing the anxiety she feels about weaning by verbally rehearsing it during our sessions.

## SESSION 13

During the first minutes of the session, the infant played quietly on the floor. She had gained almost a pound since her last pediatric exam and had grown almost half an inch. Now 36 weeks old, Kim's length was catching up with her weight. The doctor had told Barbara that Kim appeared healthy and thriving. Barbara was pleased with her daughter's progress.

As we talked, Kim hoisted herself up until she was standing, using the chair for support. For several seconds she stood without any support. Observing this, Barbara exclaimed, "That's a first! She's never done that before." She clapped her hands, saying, "Hooray." Barbara's positive response was spontaneous. It appeared that Kim realized she was standing without support, and she too was pleased with her new ability. Then her expression became sober. She immediately reached out and caught the top of the chair. Seeing and hearing her mother's happy response, Kim smiled. Her positive emotional tone was infectious and evidently in response to her mother's positive response.

"Have you been thinking about weaning since our last session?" I asked.

Barbara sighed. "I started her on whole milk. She's only 8½ months old, and everyone told me not to start milk until the baby was at least 9 months old, but it's only a 2-week difference. Since we're going to visit Rob's grandmother in a few weeks, I think it would be easier to feed her milk." Barbara added that Kim seemed wholly untroubled by the change. "I'm still breast-feeding, but now her attention span is too short for me to breast-feed during the day." Barbara hesitated, then added, "I still have some ambivalent feelings about it."

"Could you talk about those feelings?" I asked.

"During the day, she is simply filled with energy and doesn't want to lie there that long. It's more work for her, I guess. I can't just sit there for an hour and a half letting her feed. So I suppose moving to a bottle is good for both of us. It's a good decision from a practical standpoint, but emotionally . . . " Barbara's voice trailed off.

"How do you interpret these changes . . . do you feel that curbing your breast-feeding has facilitated her functioning?" I asked.

"Yes," Barbara said, dismissing the issue. She then sounded nostalgic and noted that it had always been a lovely time for her and Kim. By cutting back to twice a day, she thought it would remain that way. "I'm considering keeping the morning and evening feedings going until she's a year or so." This strategy appeared to be a way for Barbara to stretch out the experience of breast-feeding for a little longer.

There was silence for several minutes, as if Barbara were suddenly uncomfortable. Finally I asked if there had been any more episodes during breast-feeding when Kim had turned away from her. "No," Barbara said firmly. Kim had only turned away on a few occasions. "In fact," Barbara said tersely, "at one point she bit me and, boy, did that hurt."

"How did you convince her not to bite you?" I said.

Barbara reported that after the first biting episode, she had consulted her friends. "Basically, by putting her down on the floor, and by saying in a firm voice, 'No biting!'" Barbara winced. "It wasn't fun, but it seems to convey the message effectively."

"How did you feel when Kim bit you?" I asked.

Barbara laughed. "Annoyed and angry. It hurt! I was also surprised. There we were, and suddenly I'm being bitten. It's not fun." Now, Barbara said, she was occasionally nervous that Kim would bite again. "I don't trust her sometimes. I think she intended to bite me. I know that's silly," Barbara added defensively, "but sometimes I attribute adult feelings to her." Although it is not surprising that she attributes intentionality to Kim, there is a vague sense of anger in Barbara's tone. By her own admission, breast-feeding had been a time of intense emotional closeness with Kim. Understandably Barbara regarded Kim's biting as a betrayal, an action that has made it difficult for her to trust her baby completely.

"Do you think she meant to hurt you?" I asked.

Barbara shook her head. "No. But I think she thought, 'I wonder what will happen if I chomp down on Mommy?'" She laughed. "I'm just kidding. I think it was a reflex." Barbara lifted her daughter to her lap and kissed her cheek, as if to deny her anger toward Kim's development.

"So you don't think Kim bit you intentionally?" I asked.

"Absolutely not!" Barbara settled Kim against her chest. "She hasn't bitten in weeks, but I don't completely trust her. That first time, I sat very still after it happened, then I brought her in to Rob and told him that if he wanted to see his daughter go to college he had better put her to bed that night. I was so shaken up, and it hurt! Later, I cried." Although the rational part of Barbara knew that Kim did not intentionally bite her, her emotional side was clearly saying, "How could you hurt me and reject me after all the love I've given you?" Even though Barbara was evidently distressed by this episode, I was reassured to find that her attribution of intention to Kim was reasonable and that she had maintained a sense of humor about her conflict concerning weaning.

At the end of the session, Barbara sat with Kim in her arms. She repeated that she wanted to reduce the breast-feeding but admitted she would miss the experience.

"I guess I am exchanging that closeness for a new freedom for Kim and for me. Of course," she perked up, "I won't miss the biting!" By infusing breast-feeding with a negative association, then, the biting episode may actually help Barbara to accelerate and accept the weaning process. The biting episode also underscored for Barbara that Kim was a person with her own likes and dislikes—a person separate and apart from her mother. It is almost as if the infant and natural developmental processes had undertaken to initiate the very weaning process the mother had been so reluctant to accept.

The evolution of Kim's development and of Barbara's conflict about the weaning process has occurred almost as predicted. Although the distress this caregiver had been experiencing and would experience as she weaned her daughter was evident, I believed that Barbara would adjust. Certainly her willingness to preview milestones for Kim and her encouragement of each of her daughter's newly acquired skills have helped to foster a more healthy dyadic relationship. I remain convinced, however, that without my interventions Barbara's adjustments to increasing separation from her infant would have been much slower and vastly more strained.

## SESSION 14

When I next saw Barbara and Kim, the infant had just passed her 9-month birthday. As I entered the room, Kim, who had been playing on the floor, looked up and smiled broadly. Barbara smiled cautiously. I sensed something wrong.

I began by asking about their trip to visit Rob's relatives. Barbara reviewed the itinerary, talking about the perils of air travel with a 9-month-old, and said that Kim had behaved like a seasoned traveler. A dissonance was evident in Barbara's emotional tone, however. She sat with her legs crossed and arms folded tightly, as if holding her emotions in check. Her body angled away from her daughter, and although she monitored Kim, her smiles felt forced.

Kim played actively on the floor. In addition to rehearsing new skills, she was now able to stand unsupported for several seconds, after which she would occasionally tumble to the ground. Barbara's response to this behavior was a big smile, but her responses lacked enthusiasm. One of Barbara's most consistent behaviors had been her ability to share Kim's mastery of new skills, a capacity referred to as "validation." Validation begins when the mother or father recognizes the new skill the infant has mastered. To acknowledge the skill, the parent applauds, smiles, and generally displays positive response. But Barbara was clearly unable to empathize with Kim today.

"Kim can hold her bottle herself now without support," Barbara volunteered, sadness emanating from her even more strongly.

"How do you feel about this new development?" I probed, attempting to target the mother's depression.

After a brief silence Barbara shook her head. "Kim sort of weaned herself on the trip," she said finally, in a quiet voice.

"Can you tell me what happened?" I asked.

"I had decided to cut down to two breast-feedings—in the morning and right before bedtime," Barbara said. "One morning I was going to feed her, but she pushed my breast away and turned her head. . . . At first I thought she wasn't hungry. So I put her down on the bed, and the diaper bag with a bottle of juice was nearby. She just reached into the bag . . . she seemed to know just where the bottle was . . . and pulled it out. She started drinking from it until she finished it!"

"So from that point on Kim did not breast-feed?" I asked.

Barbara shook her head. "Not that day. The next day she did. But since then, nothing. So I guess I have to accept the fact that the breast-feeding experience is over."

"How did you feel about these changes?" I asked.

"When I started thinking about it, I decided it was better that the decision to stop was made by Kim, rather than by me. I don't like the idea of forcing her to stop something. This way the decision was on her terms. I'm grateful about that. But I feel emotionally devastated."

"Do you think," I asked gently, "that Kim picked up nonverbal cues indicating that the time for weaning had arrived and that both of you negotiated this process together?"

"You mean, was the decision more of a joint one than I realized?" Barbara smiled. "Maybe. I know that this step seems to give her tremendous pleasure. Now that she can hold her own bottle, she seems to have achieved a sense of self-sufficiency."

After several minutes of silence, during which both of us watched Kim, I told Barbara that regardless of her distress, it was obvious that she was a skilled interpreter of her daughter's skills. "You are very adept at sensing new accomplishments—previewing—and rehearsing these skills with Kim. You help her to negotiate developmental transitions, making her independence a bold reality."

"I really needed to hear something like that. If it's a mutual choice then I don't have to feel as if I pushed her away. The trouble is, I feel pushed away," she said somewhat sadly.

"What is it about breast-feeding Kim that you miss?" I asked.

"The closeness. Since Kim was born, that was always our time together, to cuddle each other physically. Rob says that the way she had been for about the last month was probably a sign that Kim was preparing to wean. I have to admit he's probably right. I become so upset when I realize that I could lose the intimacy in our relationship, and for a few days I thought that was going to happen." Barbara laughed. "As if tomorrow morning Kim was going to get up from her crib and say, 'Thanks for all the meals, Mom; I'm going off to college,' and disappear!"

"How long have you felt this way?" I asked.

"Six days, since she stopped nursing," she indicated with some sadness. "So I've had some time to deal with this emptiness. Anyway, I finally realized that my part in Kim's life won't end when breast-feeding stops. Of course it will continue to be important for her to get close to me. Sometimes I will approach her for a cuddle, rather than her coming to me."

At this point Barbara began to cry. The depths of this new mother's sadness reflect the disproportionate emotional attachment and gratification she was now being forced to relinquish. The infant occasionally glanced at her mother, smiling tentatively, then more fully when Barbara returned her smile. Kim crawled to her mother and raised herself to display one of the blocks she held. Barbara caressed her infant's forehead.

Barbara felt she had weathered the worst of her reaction to Kim's weaning, but I was not entirely convinced. Although Kim still seemed able to evoke positive emotions in Barbara, even when her mother was upset, she also seemed aware of her mother's depression. Barbara tried not to let her reaction have an impact on Kim—to give Kim the reassurance that she needed. However, it was an effort. For the first time in our 5 months of treatment, I noticed that Barbara's reactions were not fluid and reciprocal but were, instead, cautious and measured.

I felt that the caregiver's strong efforts to prevent her depression from exacting a toll on her previewing behaviors for Kim were the most encouraging signs of this dyad's continuing health. When a mother stops thinking of her own emotional effect on the child—obliterating thereby the infant's point of view—then, the potential for trouble becomes real. Thus far, Barbara was making obvious efforts to manage her reaction to this separation without penalizing Kim. Allowing these feelings to emerge now might have a cathartic effect. In other words, since Barbara was beginning to express her feelings candidly, it might now be possible to deal with her negative emotions overtly.

I commented:

> Kim is starting to exert some control over her environment. She is beginning to understand that she can change her point of view by standing or sitting. She's also learning that she has some control over what happens to her—weaning and feeding herself are techniques she can use to express that control. It's very commendable that you are allowing her to experience this control. Sometimes, shifting the locus of control from you to your infant can be difficult. Many mothers feel this way, especially sensitive and adept mothers who are so attuned to their baby's changes.

Barbara seemed grateful for my words of understanding, although her affect remained sad.


## SESSION 15

Barbara's emotional tone and mood seemed little changed since the preceding week. She was uncharacteristically drab in dress, whereas Kim appeared joyful and exuberant. Barbara, by contrast, seemed depressed and subdued.

For several minutes Barbara said nothing, watching Kim. The infant had discovered a full-length mirror behind one of the chairs and was reacting to her reflection. I commented on the importance of this mirror interaction, noting that Kim's enthusiasm when she recognized herself was a very positive response that suggested her awareness of her "self" as an individual. Kim grasped both sides of the mirror, while giggling and smiling.

At last, I asked if there were any changes with regard to the weaning behavior.

Barbara sighed. "She's definitely weaned. I thought after our last session that I had finally adapted. For the rest of that day I felt good. But the next day it hit me hard. I sometimes feel as if my whole life has been deprived of meaning. I'm afraid that the bond I had with Kim is lost." After a brief pause she continued, "There are other things I'm concerned about, too."

Barbara went on to explain that she had a cyst on her hand and was preparing to have it surgically removed. "The day after tomorrow I have the surgery. I'm a little more upset by the operation than I expected to be." The cyst was not malignant or painful, Barbara explained, and it had been on her hand for many years. She felt that the time had come to have it removed. For her it represented another symbolic weaning or removal.

"You say you've had this cyst for many years. Why do you want it removed now?" I persisted.

Barbara shrugged. "I couldn't have it removed before because the anesthesia might have contaminated my milk. Now that Kim has weaned, my milk is not an issue, so I decided to have it done. The doctor says it's a simple operation. Basically, they just drain the fluid."

I am intrigued both by Barbara's decision to have her cyst removed at this time and by her verbal association between experiencing surgery and weaning. The timing strikes me as being more than coincidental. Could it be that in having this voluntary procedure now Barbara is perhaps symbolically excising her "breast," which no longer attracts her child? Or perhaps in "rejecting" the cyst, Barbara is symbolically rejecting Kim, responding to the implied rejection by her daughter and thereby gaining control through her own behavior. It is not farfetched to suggest that for Barbara the fluid-filled cyst may symbolize the breast filled with milk. According to that scenario, draining the cyst may serve several purposes. On one level, she is punishing Kim by depriving her of "milk," but she is doing so in a way that won't hurt Kim. By excising this symbolic part of herself that Kim is now rejecting, Barbara may also be punishing herself for having these negative feelings.

"It's not a big deal," Barbara continued. "Having your tonsils out is riskier—but I guess I wasn't as emotionally vulnerable when I had my tonsils removed."

"Do you feel vulnerable now?" I asked.

"Yes. Being with people helps, but I feel as if I'm operating at half-speed. After our last session, when all these feelings about Kim's weaning behavior hit me, I just wanted to . . . eat 16 quarts of chocolate ice cream or buy myself something extravagant. I rarely act impulsively, but it was hard to prevent myself. I'm really experiencing overwhelming sadness because of Kim's weaning."

"Does anything help you to contain these impulses?" I asked.

Barbara smiled wryly. "I drove around town aimlessly and fantasized that I would be in a car accident. I also had a series of strange dreams."

Disturbed as I was about Barbara's ideation of self-inflicted injury, I wanted to seize the immediacy of exploring her dreams. I urged Barbara to describe her dreams. "In the first one, I was sitting in my kitchen with an old friend from grade school whom I hadn't seen in years. She was persuading me to go to this party. She kept telling me it wasn't that expensive, that I'd enjoy it."

"How did the dream end?" I asked.

"I only remember the part about my conversation with my friend. We were very close when I was 12 or 13. We were best friends almost from the moment my family moved to that town." Barbara shrugged. "We moved around so much then, I was always leaving friends behind. But this friend, April, was very special to me. She and I had our first periods at the same time. We used to talk about how much our lives were going to change when we grew up. We shared all our secrets and aspirations. We promised to remain friends when we grew up. But, of course, eventually we lost touch with one another, and remembering that makes me feel so sad."

When asked to interpret the dream, Barbara suggested that her relationship with April might be symbolic of mourning the changes in her relationship with Kim. "Something ends, and something else begins. My relationship with April ended abruptly. Her parents used to have terrible fights. One day, April told me her parents were getting divorced, and a few weeks later, she and her mother left town suddenly. I never saw or heard from her again. I felt a terrible sense of loss." Significantly, Barbara's relationship with her childhood friend was abruptly ruptured—much as Kim ruptured the breast-feeding relationship by biting her mother's nipple—prematurely for Barbara.

"Do you feel that your relationship with Kim has ended in the same way your relationship with April ended?" I asked.

"No, of course not. But I do feel as if I'm mourning for something precious that has been lost. Thinking about April made me more depressed." Barbara continued. "I had another dream, about Tania, a high school friend. All of a sudden Tania stopped coming to school. She had pneumonia and died. It was strange because no one went to see her in the hospital. She was the first person I ever knew who died. Two days ago I had a dream in which I was worrying about whether to call her family. I hadn't thought of either of those people, Tania or April, for years." The dreams and sadness Barbara reported may be expected, particularly since losses apparently form a pervasive theme of her own early childhood history. But for Barbara, both dreams symbolize the finality of shattered hopes and aspirations. There is a theme of terrible helplessness and finality common to both dream scenarios.

"More experiences of loss," I commented here. Barbara nodded. "You said that you're in mourning. Is that for the loss of breast-feeding and the closeness that you associate with breast-feeding Kim?" I asked.

Barbara shook her head. "Yes, the loss of the intimacy. For that tiny baby who really needed me. She's growing so fast, every time I look at her she's doing something new, moving away from me. I expected to have some difficulty about weaning, but nothing as shattering as this."

When Barbara paused, I said, "It seems that you're working hard to keep your own needs from interfering with Kim's development. The fact that Kim is so independent is due in part to your determination not to hold her back and to the encouragement you have given each time she exhibits a new developmental skill. Have you ever had fantasies of asking her not to change?"

"I have this image of putting a kind of hat on her head so that she can't grow any bigger." Barbara laughed. "Sure, I have fantasies about it, but I've learned that it's natural to feel this way—to a certain extent. I know that Kim's entitled to her own development, though, and that I will have to get over these feelings. The mature part of me doesn't want to interfere with her progress. Even though I may want to keep her just the way she was, I won't. That would be unfair to Kim, and ultimately to myself." Barbara sighed. "I just feel sad and lonely. What I really want right now is to be a little mothered myself . . . and then there is the surgery. I'm just sad." When she finished speaking Barbara sank into her chair and watched Kim playing. I was struck by how much the mother now resembled a small child.

"Have you ever felt this kind of sadness before?" I asked.

"We were always moving when I was a kid, so I had to learn about change—pulling up roots and saying good-bye to people. You'd think I'd be able to handle it by now, but I can't. I find change frightening. I don't like not knowing what's next. Learning to preview has helped me. At least I can predict how Kim will change developmentally, but it's still hard to deal with the feeling of loss."

I explained to Barbara that the friends in her dreams—the girl she was talking to, and the girl who died when she was in high school—represented losses in her life. I continued:

> There seems to be a pattern of losses because of your family's continual moving. But don't forget, those relationships were temporary, whereas your relationship with Kim is permanent. Your relationship with Kim has definitely changed, but Kim still needs you. That relationship is still very real, to both of you. You've got every right to mourn the passing of a special aspect of the relationship, but this change should not erode the rest of your relationship with Kim. Keep in mind that it's important for both of you to capitalize on the exciting changes Kim is now experiencing.

Barbara nodded. "I've been worried that I would convey my negative emotions to Kim. I'm trying not to. Maybe she senses some of my depression and that's why she's been so needy. Between her neediness and my feelings, all I've done this week is sleep and cuddle the baby."

"Then obviously the physical closeness you prize is still intact," I said.

Barbara looked startled. "Yes. That's certain." She smiled, as if she had been caught saying something. "I'm still sorting this whole thing out."

I reminded Barbara of Kim's behavior with the mirror earlier—noting that it was her ability to recognize Kim as a separate individual—that was helping the infant to define herself. "That's probably the most formidable task a young child has to accomplish—establishing an identity. Think of how much will be gained when Kim can express herself as an individual. There will be so much for you to share."

Barbara nodded. "I want her to be her own person. I didn't think it would affect me so much, but I'm glad she's becoming an individual."

Despite her depression, it seems that Barbara's ability to read and observe her child remains intact. Because this adaptive mother has previously manifested highly competent skills, I have reason to hope that her depression will have only short-term effects.

## SESSION 16

Because of Barbara's surgery last week, we missed a session. When we met next, I sensed an improvement. Barbara seemed to be her old self, smiling and full of energy. Kim, after a moment of bouncing to signal her pleasure, began playing. Barbara brought me up to date about her surgery. Everything had gone as expected; the relatively simple operation had taken place at her doctor's office. "Kim gave me this big smile and a kiss when I came back," Barbara reported, "and there was hardly any pain. I even like the way my hand feels without the cyst."

After the first 5 or 10 minutes of the session, when Kim, Barbara, and I played in front of the mirror, I asked Barbara if she had any further thoughts about her weaning experience or her bout with depression.

> I've stopped thinking about my feelings in terms of depression. I guess that's what I was experiencing. But I've been focusing on how Kim picks up my moods, how deep our emotional connection runs. That made me think about how attuned to her I am and how much she's attuned to me. We should be tuned in to each other. It will help me to keep out of her way when she needs to explore and to remain with her when she needs me. Our relationship has gotten more intimate in so many ways. The closeness I used to feel from breast-feeding I now feel because of our improved verbal and emotional communication. About the weaning . . . I think my moods are still a bit off kilter. I still have brief periods when I'm pretty down, but I'm 85% functional. Most of my energy is back, and we're getting along fine again. I think eventually our relationship will be better than before.

"Have you experienced any changes in your attitudes about breast-feeding?" I asked.

> I've gotten to a point where I feel that nursing is the way Kim and I used to interact. It was a wonderful experience when it happened. There's a residual sadness . . . but only slightly. I'm beginning to think about what you mentioned in the last session . . . all the incredible new skills—walking, talking, and things like that. I don't want to rush any of them, but I'm learning to welcome them. I think that weaning made me aware there is nothing simple about interacting with a baby, and I shouldn't lose sight of that.

"Have you shared your experiences with Rob?" I asked.

"Oh, yes. He didn't go through the emotional distress I went through, so he was a great source of support during this transition."

"I think that one lesson to take home from this experience is that you can ask Rob to serve as a buffer for developmental transitions by providing continuity in the relationship with Kim. In this particular case," I said, "it sounds like the three of you have behaved like a real family."

Barbara nodded eagerly and said:

It's interesting. As I was listening to you I remembered a dream I had the night after our last session. I had just returned from the hospital after giving birth to Kim. As I was preparing to breast-feed Kim, the phone rang ... the ring sounded different. For a split second I thought of not answering it, but I did. It was one of Dr. Roth's assistants—he's my obstetrician. He wanted to know if everything was okay. I mentioned that I had discomfort in my lower abdomen. Apparently this assistant had been told by Dr. Roth that if I reported that sensation I had to go back to the hospital to make sure no remnants of the placenta had remained inside. Isn't that an odd dream?

I then asked her what *she* thought of the dream.

"Since the dream took place a few days before the cyst was removed from my hand, it may support the notion that I felt I needed some outside help to deal with the imminent separation I previewed with weaning Kim."

"The dream sounds like a way of representing the conflict. It's interesting that when you had a dream about breast-feeding, an 'alarm' went off. It's as if you were telling yourself not to get 'stuck' in the conflict, but to relinquish it." I went on to add that in her latest dream Barbara had the "weaning" or attachment to her baby removed for her in a completed process. Life is usually not as easy and neat, I added.

After a few minutes of silence, Barbara mentioned that she had followed my earlier recommendation and started taking Kim to an activities group, which they were both enjoying enormously. Kim loved it, she said: There were lots of games geared to children her age. There were older kids, too, for her to emulate and lots of different stimuli.

"In fact," Barbara said, "I'm beginning to think about terminating therapy. I've got through the worst of the weaning, I think. There's so much to do that I have to be increasingly choosy about how we're spending our days. I feel that if we go on too much longer, I am going to stop seeing the forest for the trees. I want to be spontaneous and attuned to Kim. I think this playgroup is the next stage for us. Kim's beginning to learn some social skills— such as the fact that it's not good to pull the other children's hair or poke them in the eye. I think it may be time to end these sessions."

I commented to Barbara that we should discuss this issue in the following session so that we could better address terminating the therapy.

## SESSION 17

My final session with Kim and Barbara was extremely gratifying. Barbara was beginning to find time to do some of the writing that she had hoped to do for some time. "Kim does have down times when I can work." She paused.

"The thing I'm working on remembering—what I learned from our sessions—is that I'm entitled to my feelings, whatever they are. That doesn't mean I should clutter up Kim's life with them, but I'm entitled to have them. Feeling that way makes it easier to let those fantasies go once I identify them, and that makes it easier to keep my relationship with Kim uncomplicated."

Barbara's significant conflict over her infant's achievement of weaning is, for all intents and purposes, resolved. At its root was one of the crucial questions that adaptive mothers face in confronting separation: When my infant becomes an independent person, will he or she be able to see me as a person, too? Will my baby be able to understand my emotion? More significantly, will developmental progress mean that the intimacy they share will be lost or that the closeness of the first months of life will be irrevocably lost? Because the bond between caregiver and infant is so close, it demands reciprocity—an assurance on both sides that the experience will be meaningful to the other.

In the case of Barbara and Kim, I think this question has been answered affirmatively. Barbara has come to understand that development is an ongoing and cumulative process: Perpetual change continues as does the renewal of intimacy. For the time being, Barbara has mastered the circumscribed area of conflict denoted at the start of her therapy. There is still some ground of unresolution, as should be clear from Barbara's evident difficulties with letting Kim go about her explorations without constantly referring to her and with her recurrent dreams symbolizing separation. But the overall outlook here is one of optimistic interaction and adjustment.

# CHAPTER 7

## Laura: Compounding the Dyadic Failure by Marital Distress

B OTH CAREGIVER and infant contribute to the interpersonal patterns that characterize their relationship. In cases of maladaptive interpersonal exchange, therapists must discern the factors that precipitate problematic interaction. On one hand, these factors may lie primarily in the domain of the caregiver. For example, caregivers suffering from a psychiatric illness (e.g., postpartum depression) may be unable to interact with their infant in an adaptive fashion. On the other hand, the infant's constitutional disposition may also contribute to the development of negative interpersonal patterns. The caregiver-infant relationship may also be adversely affected by a temperamental mismatch between the dyadic partners. Whereas these factors address individual characteristics, another potential factor that predicts the nature of the relationship between caregiver and infant is the caregiver's relationship with the spouse.

As family theorists have observed, marital partners both bring to the marriage a certain amount of "unfinished business" from their family of origin (Freeman, 1992). Eventually these aspects can precipitate conflict within the marital relationship. For example, one person may marry in order to escape feelings of neglect engendered in relationships within the family of origin. Frequently, however, the marital relationship cannot compensate for past deficits (Paris & Guzder, 1989). Conflict usually surfaces during times of transition or stress. Thus, it is not surprising that the birth of an infant may cause latent conflict in the marital relationship to emerge, or may exacerbate extant conflict.

Fleming, Ruble, Flett, and Van Wagner (1990) interviewed 32 mothers at 1, 3, and 16 months postpartum and observed differences in the evolution of the mother's feelings about the infant and her husband. Whereas positive feelings about the infant tended to increase linearly, the curve depicting positive feelings about the spouse had a U shape. The least positive feelings for the spouse were noted at the first and third months following the birth. These findings suggest that the infant's birth may have a sizable effect on the marital relationship in the months immediately following this event. Framo (1981) has observed that the infant may be viewed as a metaphor for the parents' relationship. If the parents are in conflict, it is likely that conflict has been or will be displaced onto the infant (Lask, 1982). Under these circumstances, the marital relationship may have an impact on the nature of dyadic exchange. Moreover, the infant's perception of the caregiver's distress may evoke powerful feelings in the infant. Over time, the infant may become a scapegoat—a repository for the parents' conflict. Parents cite the infant's problematic behavior as the source of their conflict when, in fact, it is actually the product of marital distress. Infants are particularly susceptible to becoming scapegoats because they have not yet developed sophisticated strategies or defenses for parental projections.

Marital distress may have a more subtle impact on the caregiver-infant relationship in cases in which the infant does not witness conflict between the parents. It may be expected that caregivers who are experiencing distress in their marital relationship are more likely than caregivers with a strong marital relationship to experience negative moods and even depression, both of which may affect the relationship with the child. Jouriles, Murphy, and O'Leary (1989) examined the effects of mothers' moods on interactions with their sons who were 46 to 72 months old. These researchers found that mothers experiencing a negative mood prior to interacting with their children delivered fewer positive statements toward the children and generally engaged in less verbal interaction. Moreover, these children were found to be less compliant with their mother's requests.

Kochanska, Kuczynski, and Maguire (1989) compared the differences between depressed and nondepressed mothers in the strategies they used to control the behavior of their children at toddler age and then at 5 years. When the children were toddlers, the nondepressed mothers were observed to use more direct commands and reprimands, as well as to provide more explanations, than depressed mothers. Moreover, nondepressed mothers who reported a negative mood immediately prior to the interaction were observed to use decreased directness in controlling the behavior of their toddlers. Depressed mothers with a negative mood tended to give fewer explanations. Thus, nondepressed mothers of toddlers are more capable of firm limit-setting than depressed mothers.

Subsequently, when the children were 5 years of age, the researchers observed that nondepressed mothers used fewer direct commands than depressed mothers, although directness increased if these mothers reported a negative mood prior to interaction. These observations may suggest that nondepressed mothers are less intrusive than their depressed counterparts.

In cases in which adaptive dyadic exchange is thwarted by marital conflict, therapeutic interventions should first alert the caregivers to the impact it has on the infant. The therapist may then explore the source of the marital conflict, which frequently resides in each spouse's family of origin. In this regard, it is important to note how the infant resurrects latent conflict. For example, a caregiver who views his or her family of origin as being neglectful may also misrepresent the infant's behaviors as being neglectful. Misrepresentations of the origins of problematic infant behavior may cause the caregiver to view developmental change in a negative fashion. Thus, it is important for the therapist to introduce the caregiver to normative trends of development and the implications of developmental change for the dyadic relationship. The positive effects of promoting adaptive development in the infant may translate into the relationship with the spouse, thereby promoting more positive interpersonal exchanges in the couple. Positive interactions between husband and wife promote positive interactions between caregiver and infant.

The following case examines the effects of marital distress on the caregiver-infant relationship. Because her husband was not compensating for her past "neglect," their relationship suffered from a significant amount of conflict. This conflict contributed to their toddler's apparent "hyperactive" behavior. Previewing was used to alter the caregiver's representation of her child and to promote more adaptive interpersonal exchange. Moreover, the caregiver came to understand how her representations of past relationships in her family of origin and of her current relationship with her husband were having an impact on her son's behavior and development.

## Patient Identification

Laura presented as a thin woman in her late 30s with a tight, reserved manner. At our first meeting she was dressed professionally in a tailored suit and silk blouse appropriate for a college associate professor specializing in foreign languages. Laura's outward manner was mildly friendly but directive; underneath a veneer of friendliness, she appeared constrained and resistant. Laura tended to flaunt her impressive vocabulary during our conversation and appeared to be somewhat impatient if not outrightly contemptuous of the interview process. At 14 months, Teddie, her first child, was a robust toddler whose high activity level frequently appeared less a matter of enthusiasm than an industrious outpouring of nervous energy. Despite the distant manner of his mother, Teddie occasionally showed flashes of warmth as well as signs of anxiety and shyness.

## DESCRIPTION OF THE DYAD'S MALADAPTIVE BEHAVIOR

Teddie and his mother had been referred to the clinic by Teddie's pediatrician for evaluation of the infant's possible hyperactivity. In addition to the pediatrician's concerns, Laura characterized her son as "tense" and "easily agitated," adding that she felt he was different from other children. According to Laura, Teddie required "constant stimulation." When not the center of attention, Laura said, Teddie would whine and scream. Consequent to a minor physical trauma that had occurred at Teddie's birth, Laura feared that her son might have sustained brain damage and that his apparent hyperactivity might be symptomatic of that trauma. Laura seemed convinced that her son was not normal, and she voiced this viewpoint repeatedly.

## FAMILY HISTORY

From the outset, Laura aggressively took charge of our first session. "Once Clark and I decided to start a family," she said, "I did my research." "I read dozens of books on pregnancy and infant development." Unhappily she had sustained two miscarriages before her successful pregnancy, and she asserted that her troubled obstetric history had only reinforced her determination to be a "successful" parent. Considering the trouble she had had in carrying to term as well as her present age of 37, Laura acknowledged that it might not be possible to have more children, although both she and her husband had hoped for another child. "So it's especially important that we make Teddie's childhood everything it should be. Or at least," she added with some degree of anxiety as well as with some melodrama-tinged resignation, "whatever it can be, given his impairment."

Laura had grown up in the Midwest the eldest of five children, "my mother's second-in-command." Her father had been a sales representative for a national company. Laura described him as kindly, hardworking, and very religious; both he and Laura's mother were actively involved with their church. "My parents were older parents by local standards. My mother was 33 when I was born, and Dad was 38. Because I was the oldest, I did a lot of 'secondary parenting,' watching out for the younger kids." Laura's mother had been hospitalized several times during Laura's childhood and adolescence, with operations to contain breast cancer, ovarian cancer, and gastric ulcers; she is now a semi-invalid. Laura's recollection is that her mother had been "terribly mean" to her throughout her childhood, behavior she now attributes, rather bitterly, to "all the pain Momma was going through. Momma cried and yelled all the time; when she yelled, she yelled at me." The first respite from her mother's "verbal abuse" occurred when Laura went away to college.

Laura performed exceptionally well in college. Enrolled in an accelerated program, she completed the requirements for her undergraduate degree in 3 years and began work in a Master's program immediately. At the same time, she tutored high school students and worked at a part-time job. "I don't know that I've ever felt as alive as I did when I was in college," she comments. At that time, she also had her first relationship with a man, which lasted almost 3 years. During that time she became pregnant, but she chose to terminate the pregnancy. Typically, her explanation is both forthright and defensive: "The relationship was beginning to unravel, and I didn't want to have a child, considering how young we were and our professional status at the time." At the time, she apparently felt no adverse emotional reaction to the abortion, but she admitted that more recently, after her miscarriages, she had begun to wonder if the abortion had somehow compromised her ability to bear a child.

When she was 25, Laura met Clark. After dating for 2 years, they were married but made the decision to wait until they were both financially secure before starting a family. Originally, when Laura became pregnant, they had planned that she would take a leave of absence from teaching at the college and return to teaching within 6 months. During the pregnancy, however, she reevaluated her feelings and ultimately decided to resign her post. She said that returning to her old position, where she had been on track for tenure, would be virtually impossible and seriously thought that she might have to start from scratch in rebuilding her career. "I have no regrets about it; I want to be a better mother for Teddie than my mother was for me," she added forcefully.

Like Laura, her husband Clark—an executive for a major corporation—was also the oldest of five children. Whereas Laura's family had been close-knit albeit reserved, however, Clark's family, according to Laura, was not close. "Everyone in Clark's family is always vying for position. It's part of the reason Clark is so reserved." Laura explained that one of the qualities that had attracted her to her husband initially was Clark's very reserve that she felt counterbalanced her own assertiveness. Although he had expressed considerable reservations about starting a family, Laura reported that he now "adored" Teddie. She characterized her husband as "quiet, rather short-tempered, and impatient."

After two miscarriages, Laura's third pregnancy was uneventful; she delivered after just a few hours of labor. At birth there was meconium-stained amniotic fluid, and Teddie had been suctioned. Within 6 hours of his birth, a rapid respiration rate was noted, and he had been transferred to the intensive care nursery, where he was given 100% oxygen for a short time. Antibiotics were also administered at that time. Within 3 days Teddie was weaned from the oxygen, and within 8 days he was discharged from the hospital and allowed to go home. Since that time, Teddie has had no other physical ailments. His pediatrician has consistently reported him to be in good health and has noted that there is no evidence of any birth trauma.

Despite her husband's affection for their son, Laura reported that Teddie's birth had placed severe strains on their already tenuous relationship. The infant's "demands" had exhausted both parents, and neither could seem to find the time or summon the energy to focus on their primary relationship. Furthermore, Laura noted that Clark did not take seriously her concerns about Teddie's health and the trauma he had suffered at birth. In fact by now he was so "fed up" hearing Laura's comments on the subject that he refused to hear her talk about it at all.

## DYADIC MENTAL HEALTH STATUS EXAMINATION

The mother was 37 years old, well-educated, and appeared highly intelligent and verbal. She had twice undergone psychotherapy for mild depression, once during her 20s prior to her marriage and once shortly thereafter. Laura was neatly groomed, with her soft brown hair pulled austerely back into a bun. A first impression yielded the sense that she suffered from mild dysphoria and depression combined with almost uncontrolled anxiety and sustained fatigue. As a mother, Laura initially appeared to be particularly attuned and assiduous to her infant's needs. Yet Laura was overly officious: She seemed to anticipate his need for a bottle or a change of diaper merely by glancing at him. When interacting with Teddie, although her manner was attentive and affectionate, she seemed constantly poised to swoop down and pull her son away from people who threatened social interaction. As Laura watched her son at play, her pleasure seemed muted by concern. In this regard, she displayed a distinct reluctance to encourage her toddler's exploratory interests, and she seemed particularly uneasy when Teddie was held or cuddled by anyone else except Clark, her husband. Laura's general emotional affect was one of edgy exhaustion and wary apprehension.

When I entered the room, Teddie was dashing frenetically from one chair to another. He stopped momentarily when I entered, then turned, and raced to his mother's chair. Laura looked up and smiled, a genuine but ambivalent smile. Throughout the session, her eyes followed her son, as if she half-expected some unpredictable crisis to erupt.

A handsome toddler with large brown eyes and rosy cheeks, Teddie was tall for his age and a trifle awkward, as if his weight had not kept pace with his height. Teddie's fine and gross motor skills and language abilities were all age appropriate. He could walk, run, stand steadily, and climb over low objects with considerable ease. In addition, he displayed good coordination when transferring small blocks into a bucket or engaging in other play activities. When he spoke to me, it was in a halting manner, as if he were trying to become my friend. When left to his own devices, Teddie evidenced joy and interest in his play. This pleasure, however, was occasionally marred with an apprehensive aspect that culminated when he stopped what he was doing and turned to find his mother. Frequently, during the session Teddie would go to his mother, take her hand, and attempt to pull her out of her seat—a behavior his mother seemed to encourage. Overall, Teddie's reactions seemed intense and exaggerated, his attention span low, his distractibility high, and his ability to contend with new stimuli only minimal. Teddie was willing to play with me—a "friendly" stranger—as long as his mother was included in the game; otherwise, Teddie appeared to be withdrawn and overwhelmed. For her part, Laura was zealously intrusive; she never let him *be* for a moment.

The interaction between mother and child was characterized by affection, but an affection charged with an anxious despair on one side, and with confusion on the other. It appeared as if mother and son were both compensating for the fact that there was something wrong. At times, it also seemed as if the relationship between mother and toddler were overly intense, too fused, and lacking the appropriate ego boundaries.

## DIAGNOSTIC IMPRESSION AND RECOMMENDATIONS

At the outset, Laura's tightly controlled demeanor and her parental solicitousness, together with Teddie's age-appropriate development, had conveyed an impression that the problems of this family unit were not particularly severe. By the end of the session, however, I had revised that assessment. Laura and Teddie were, if not at a crisis point, then rapidly approaching one: Each progressive milestone in Teddie's development was slowly eroded by Laura's insistence that her son was somehow damaged, handicapped, and condemned to underachieve by the incidents surrounding his birth. She appeared obsessed with this idea and continually returned to it. In discussing those incidents, Laura revealed her absolute conviction that her son had been traumatized, perhaps deliberately, at birth. She appeared adamant and resolute in this belief. The use of the term "deliberately" is bizarre here, but it was not used again in the treatment by Laura. Certainly it indicates a peculiar presumption of conspiracy. The fact that again and again throughout her treatment Laura returns to her own trauma and to the alleged evils of the birth is revelatory of her own distorted sense of reality. Her delusionary mind-set would go so far as to charge medical professionals with willfully and knowingly traumatizing a child they had no reason to know or relate to except as one of thousands of infants delivered with their hands and through their care.

It may be that this sense of ready victimization of her baby had made it easier for Laura, a victim of her mother's illness who had been robbed of her own childhood, to identify with her infant. Each of Teddie's developmental gains clearly contradicted Laura's theory about her son's retardation and abnormality, which in turn threatened the established order (of impairment/repair) of this dysfunctional dyadic enmeshment. Laura's personal agenda seemed to frustrate all momentum toward development in her son and to maintain their maladaptive and co-dependent status, regardless of the effect her behavior would presumably have on Teddie's psychosocial development. Of special concern was this paradoxical condition of Laura's: Although highly educated, she seemed unable (or unwilling) to apply logic or what common sense any man in the street would automatically apply to any situation. She was, for all her degrees and schooling, blind to the basic ramifications of the fundamental mother-child relationship and to the unhealthy implications of her inability to separate from her own child.

In some cases, substantial progress in a maladaptive mother-infant dyad can be accomplished over several weeks. Because the conflicts evoked by clear-cut developmental changes (such as those experienced by infants) can be examined and analyzed discretely, they can sometimes be resolved before the next developmental milestone occurs. With this case, which I regard as a model for short-term crisis intervention, my primary goal was to foster developmental momentum in the relationship between Laura and Teddie while breaking the pattern of pathological enmeshment binding the dyad and probably inhibiting full child development.

# Therapy

## SESSION 1

At the first session Laura described her complaints at great length, dwelling on details of Teddie's birth and her feeling that the physicians and nurses attending it had mishandled her son and perhaps damaged him in the first days of his life. When I attempted to attract Teddie's attention by calling his name, Laura interrupted softly and said, "he doesn't listen a lot," when Teddie failed to respond after the second call. Teddie, who had been edging around the back of a chair opposite mine, turned and looked shyly in my direction but did not approach. "He's a little shy with strangers," Laura apologized. It became evident that in all our preliminary interactions, where Laura's maneuverings and histrionics "ran the show" for both the therapist (in a sense) and the infant, the patterning was already well established: This child appeared resigned to his mother's carrying-ons.

Throughout the first half-hour of the session, Teddie scuttled about the room at increasing speed, running, sitting, investigating briefly, and then moving on. He never persevered in any one pursuit for more than a few seconds, returning every few minutes to his mother, whom he pulled at often;

not so much to establish contact reassuringly with her, as to engage her in play. As the session continued, an increasingly anxious quality marked his activity; when he could not get Laura to respond, or when an activity did not satisfy him, Teddie would begin a low, rhythmic keening, "uh-uh-uhuh-uh-uhuh." This noise elicited noticeable distress in Laura, although she appeared unable to soothe or quiet her son. The two appear to be in a bipartite collusion, with the mother being the leader, complete with (secret) codes and (manifest) behaviors, playing a constant game of provocation and response, endlessly ping-ponging action and reaction no matter where or whom the drama was played out in front of.

"It's hard to talk about Teddie's birth," Laura began, her voice becoming shrill. "It gets more upsetting every time I describe it. I just can't believe what those people did to my child." When I encouraged her to expand on her provocative accusation, Laura took a deep breath and began anew:

> You wouldn't believe what I went through to have this child! Even after I'd made it plain I wanted a child, Clark resisted it. And then we had a hard time conceiving. When I finally managed to become pregnant, I had to endure two miscarriages—so when it finally began to look as though I was going to carry Teddie clearly to term, I was overjoyed.

"And your husband? What do you think Clark felt?" I asked.

> Until Teddie was born, Clark was basically against the whole idea. Now he's really crazy about the baby and enjoys being a father. Then we had doctor problems—we belonged to an HMO, and I never really had my own doctor, just got handed around from one person to the next each time I had to see a doctor. That's why I think no one really cared about what happened to us when Teddie was born.

She then reiterated the circumstances of Teddie's birth. Laura sighed and asked me abruptly:

> Do you think my son is healthy? I don't know. I don't think anyone can tell me. I've seen some books that tell pediatricians not to tell parents if their children have brain damage, so the parents won't restrict the expectations they have for the child. I just never feel like I'm getting a straight answer.

She said she had taken Teddie to his doctor several times since his birth for nonroutine checkups when she feared there were signs of neurological damage. "They always say it's nothing. I just wish someone would tell me the truth."

Laura's weary statement, "I just wish someone would tell me the truth," indicates the desperation with which she disbelieved any input that went against what she *wanted* to believe, that is, that her son was defective at birth, owing to errors in medical procedure. "I know something must be wrong, though. I want Teddie to be happy and to live up to his potential. He's just so . . . tense. I think it's because he was roughed up at birth by the doctors and nurses. I want him to relax; then I could relax a little, too," she added as a poignant afterthought. I perceived from these comments that she didn't trust my observations. But as I was concerned (in light of her extreme defensiveness) that she might not yield to the therapeutic intervention, I suggested she consult another practitioner for a second opinion.

"What do you mean by 'tense'?" I asked.

"He—he just seems wrought up and anxious all the time. And if we don't keep him amused all the time he cries dreadfully. It just tears my heart whenever I hear him cry. He whines; it's this horrible sound."

Laura then changed the topic abruptly, noting that her pediatrician had spoken to her about the "need to separate more from" Teddie, to have time for herself as well as for her son. "If I could find a real baby-sitter, one I could trust . . . but I can't. Besides, Teddie needs me," she said with conviction. This again distances the mother-child unit from others and makes of her dyad an outsider couple against the world.

For several minutes Laura was quiet, watching her son apprehensively as he tottered around the room. Finally, I asked her what she hoped to achieve from this therapy.

Her response was both revelatory and indicative of her confused reality orientation and awareness of what constitutes a functional versus a dysfunctional maternal-child interaction dynamic. "I'd like to stop always worrying that there's something wrong with Teddie. I know he's bright—everyone says that—but I just can't stop thinking about it. I think maybe he's brain damaged, though. They say we have to set more limits with him." She laughed shrilly. "How do you set limits without being too strict? My mother was a tough disciplinarian, and I don't want to be that way with Teddie. From the minute we got him home from the hospital I guess we've been too easy with him. If he's damaged, though, why shouldn't we be easier with him?"

Her sequence of fallacious reasoning provides an invitation to the child to be enmeshed with her. Obviously, if she'd set limits and be appropriately firm with him, he'd be less likely to be so intertwined with her. In short, this mother's weak interactive behavior patterns constitute seduction. The seductive quality of her thought processes becomes increasingly obvious as she continues, "I just can't bear ignoring him, not after all he went through at the birth. I'm tense because my childhood was horrible," Laura adds plaintively. "My goal for both of us is to be relaxed. If Teddie relaxes, then I'll relax." Laura sighed audibly and sank deeper into her chair.

It seems to me that Laura may be manufacturing crises. Even in the best of situations, all Laura's meaningful interactions seem to relate to crisis, as if she needs to exaggerate events in order for them to be meaningful. "If anything's wrong with Teddie, I'm not sure I want to live," she suddenly announced histrionically. A clear-eyed assessment must dismiss the suicidal intent blatant on the surface of her threat. Underlying this, however, remains the fear that the therapist might, in focusing on Teddie's problems too thoroughly, withdraw attention from her. Her false claim to suicidal urge is more or less a plea for the therapist to take note of her needs and wishes.

I asked Laura to clarify her statement.

"I expect him to be smart [here Laura became overtly more agitated]. I don't want him to be shortchanged by experiencing the kind of childhood I had. My childhood was awful, and I don't want him to go through the kinds of things I experienced."

Teddie himself reflects exquisite sensitivity to his mother's moods. For several minutes, as Laura's own level of tension had fluctuated, Teddie's behavior also shifted. His movements had a more compulsive quality, and he was able to maintain his interest for less time as he played. As he turned to establish his mother's proximity, and occasionally returned to her, his movements were less frantic only when she became calmer.

One of the more remarkable aspects of this session was the visible emotional change that took place in Teddie when his mother finally relaxed. Throughout the first half of the session, when Laura spoke defensively about what she perceived Teddie's problems to be as well as the "damage" he had sustained at birth, Teddie flew around the room, flitting from one activity to another. As noted earlier, Laura sounded shrill and agitated when discussing these issues. Toward the end of the session, however, Laura modulated her speech and spoke of issues not connected with the birth experience. Laura's change in tone—to one far less fraught—was reflected in Teddie's level of reactivity; he visibly slowed, concentrated longer at each toy or game, and even sat on his mother's lap for several minutes.

Despite Laura's reports of Teddie's "hyperactivity" and other symptoms, there is no hard evidence suggesting attention-deficit hyperactivity disorder. On the other hand, Teddie does show classic signs of a "difficult" temperament—irregular rhythmicity, inflexibility, high responsiveness, and a tendency toward negativity.

I then began to explain the concept of temperament to Laura. I noted that temperament refers to an individual's characteristic style of behavior and that most theorists believe in three basic temperamental types, including the "easy" temperament characterized by a regularity of mood and body functions; the "slow-to-warm-up" temperament characterized by a reticence or hesitancy in mixing with others; and the "difficult" temperament, characterized by high sensitivity that at times borders on irritability. I suggested that Laura might simply be misinterpreting Teddie's behavior and that in actuality he might simply have a "difficult" temperament. She did not seem particularly receptive to this idea, and soon thereafter our session ended. She is currently so vested in the syndrome of her son's "birth" defects and traumatized level of functioning that one couldn't realistically expect anything like receptivity from her at this point. She has already invested 18 months elaborating on this misadventure; she's not likely to abandon its pathologically nourishing, if debilitating, embrace.

The patient's distorted perceptions, then, place me in the curious position of having to compare notes of my observations with her own flawed perceptions. It appears that this therapeutic enterprise will be as much about examining Laura's fears as it will be about helping Teddie to regulate his distress. Over the next few sessions, I would contrast Laura's apprehensions about her son with solid medical information about his status in hopes of allaying those fears. At the same time I want to explore the significance his mother's crises have for Teddie. Finally, I want to work with Laura to observe the effect a more relaxed demeanor would have on her son's behavior. This is where I began to strategize interventions whereby the child's responses could be modulated if handled correctly. Thus, I created a series of scenarios in succeeding sessions where when Laura, or Laura and her husband Clark, become agitated, Teddie would be encouraged to leave and return when the atmosphere was somewhat fresher or clarified of its intense agitation or anxiety.

## SESSION 2

As I arrived, I found Teddie pacing around the perimeter of the circle of chairs in the interview room. He bore a large Band-Aid across his forehead. On my entrance, Laura said hello. She looked as anxious as she had at the last session and even more fatigued.

Once I had settled into a chair, Teddie began to move around the room again, running from one area to the next, iterating the frenetic behavior he had displayed at our previous session. His movements seemed somewhat forced, and he rarely stayed in one place or investigated one object for more than a few moments. Twice he ran to his mother, pulled at her hand until she stood, and then seemingly forgot what he had wanted. Laura reacted to her son's behavior with vague embarrassment; however, she made no attempt to resist his demands or to calm him down.

I noticed the gash on Teddie's face and asked, "What happened to Teddie's forehead?"

Laura launched into a long explanation. The family had gone to visit her husband's mother out of state. While there, Teddie had cut his forehead on an open kitchen cabinet. "I took him to two different hospitals," Laura explained. "The first place just cleaned the cut and put a Band-Aid on it. After I left, I thought to myself, I don't want him to have a scar from this. So I went to another hospital, and they put a new dressing on and told me that it didn't look like he'd have a scar."

This episode provides another example of the patient's search for corroboration (or validation) of her need to manufacture a problem (or crisis) where one might not in fact exist. Having been assured by doctors at the first hospital that things were "all right," she actively went in search of another institution that would identify an area of concern to validate her *readiness* to obsess. It would be interesting to know in the future whether Laura would continue in her ploys of seeking out insults or imagined damages, or whether my intervention will ultimately help to stem this particular destructive behavior pattern. "I hope they're right," she said gloomily at this point. "I'm so skeptical about hospitals and doctors after what happened at Teddie's birth."

"How did you feel for the rest of the trip?" I asked.

"I tried to set some limits." Laura's face contorted briefly, almost as if she were about to cry. "I guess I don't know how to do that, though. I can't stand it when Teddie screams or whines. We usually let him do whatever he wants, unless it's dangerous for him. And when he doesn't get what he wants, he whines." At this point Laura imitated her son's low "uh-uh." "It sounds as if he's being abused, and I just can't stand it. It reminds me of the fact that he's damaged."

Remarking that this was the second time Laura has described her son's whine in that way, I asked why she associated the cry with abuse. Laura shook her head vehemently, without answering. Then she said, "It's not that he's being abused, because he isn't. It's just this dreadful cry."

As she spoke, Laura's voice rose to a thin shrill, and Teddie ran to her, clambering into her lap. Once there, the toddler whined and agitated for attention. Laura crooned indulgently, "What do you want, huh? What is it?" before she turned back to me and commented that she could never tell what it was that made Teddie behave this way.

"Perhaps," I ventured, "he sensed the tension in your voice and came seeking reassurance."

Laura shook her head, "Yes, maybe, but—" before Teddie slid off her lap, "how much can we give him? He's got every toy on the market, all the clothes—everything." She became silent again as though she were pondering the implications of her last statement as reflective of a pattern—more of the same inadequate parenting. She must be aware that a chest full of toys will not replace a consistent, unfrantic relationship with her child. The continual accretion of more and more material objects, "things," serves to sidestep (in fact becomes symbolic of) the emotional *gridlock* she feels because of her own (as well as her husband's) unresolved conflicts.

I suggested gently:

> Do you ever think that you may be placing an unnecessary burden on Teddie? I think he's responding to a number of things, including the moods he picks up from you. This *is* his temperament, after all. You may be communicating your

fears to him; then, for example, if you are afraid of brain damage, you may unconsciously expect Teddie to move erratically, to be less coordinated than he actually is. For this reason, Teddie may be overabounding with energy and overly active to reassure you that all is well. He may be trying to tell you that your negative expectations are incorrect. There is no hard medical evidence to think that there has been any lasting trauma. We need to explore what will help him to channel his energies and calm down. We need to help him learn your limits—which can be learned best by setting limits for him.

Softly stroking her son's forehead, Laura nodded. As she responded to my comments, Teddie slid to the floor and began to investigate a few of the toys. From this point on in the interview, the toddler's movements and emotional tone were far less frenetic, more relaxed and curious.

We were following the established pattern of last week, the moment Laura became more subdued, her son also calmed down. "That's more like it," Laura said at last.

"What do you mean?" I asked.

"That's more like the way babies are supposed to behave—sort of serene and 'babylike.' Teddie has never been like that. Isn't that what a baby is supposed to be like?"

I acknowledged her statement by saying, "Not entirely. Babies are very busy people, learning how to handle their bodies, learning how to interact with their parents, beginning to figure out who they are as individuals in relation to their parents and the world. There's a lot of work involved in those tasks, and some of it isn't particularly easy."

"But I want him to be normal. My childhood certainly wasn't normal."

Again she fails to comprehend that what has been pointed out as the baby's "work" is normal and developmental and that Teddie's various affects are therefore normal—certainly within the range of the normative spectrum. Moreover, Laura again uses her complaint about wanting Teddie to be idyllically "normal" as a springboard for her real agenda, her fear of re-creating her own dysfunctional past. Here she reiterates the leitmotif we have come to identify with subjective recall of her own past: "My childhood certainly wasn't normal." *This* is Laura's primary complaint—what she responds to time and time again. She is obsessing over rehearsal of her own tainted childhood, frantically attempting to re-create it by convulsive efforts and ploys vis-à-vis her perceptually "damaged" but, in reality, perfectly normal child.

"At the next session we should talk about what it means 'to be normal' and how you define it, Laura," I concluded.

Just as the session was ending, Laura tellingly commented that her mother had physically abused several of Laura's younger siblings when she was young. In Laura's mind her mother's abusive behavior was associated with the "abuses" of the doctors who had handled Teddie after birth. Laura concluded the session by indicating she believed she was still being abused, now by her husband, Clark, whose "neglect" she feels deeply. She associates this neglect with a form of abandonment abuse perhaps symbolic of the abandonment of Laura the child by a sick mother who herself lacked the emotional resources to guarantee her daughter a normal childhood. Thus, Laura might be expecting Teddie, her child/symbolic parent to abuse her. Obviously, Laura, too, feels she sustained abuse as did her siblings. The wounds of this childhood abuse are very open and raw. She feels "still" abused from the circumstances of her youth and now feels an evocation of that abuse from her current circumstances, chiefly her husband's neglect and her child's unruly disposition.

I was pleased to note that even since the first session Laura has grown more reflective about the past and its consequences for Teddie; it appears she is trying to develop her predictive capacities. She still has a long way to go, however. I feel that Teddie remains as distractible as he is because Laura is not able to focus on his behavior objectively or on his present attainments; she is still rooted in the past, *her* past, and sees her son not as he actually is, but as a projection of what she needs to see.

In a case such as this one, the predictive and diagnostic work that previewing can accomplish must frequently be deferred until the sense of crisis is under control. Laura herself has so far proven almost incapable of previewing; instead of focusing on upcoming development, she is obsessed with the situational "abuses" of her own—and Teddie's—past. Perhaps by focusing more closely on the traumatic aspects of Teddie's birth we can begin to resolve this obsession and improve Laura's developmental awareness and predictive capacities.

## SESSION 3

Laura appeared calmer and less tense than she had at previous meetings, but her grasp on Teddie, although gentle and affectionate, seemed to have a definite clinging quality.

"So," I began, "how was your week? Did you try any experiments with limit setting?"

Laura's words gushed out. "Things were okay. I thought he was really getting better, until 2 days ago, and then we had another episode. It was terrible, I can't imagine what people think I'm doing to my child!" The fact that she is concerned with "what other people think" reveals that she still considers other people—even strangers—as a part of her own ego support system; perhaps her fused way of functioning is incrementally loosening.

"What do you think people think you could be doing to your child?" I asked mildly.

Laura looked as if my question had confused her and continued her story without responding directly:

Two days ago we went to the beach. Teddie was fine when he was playing with other kids and I was there, but when I wanted to take him into the water, he went crazy—he screamed and clung to me—it sounded like I was trying to hurt him, and even when I brought him out of the water, he just kept screaming. We had to take him home because of the way he was screaming. Then, when I got him home, he ran all over the house, wouldn't eat his dinner, was just really crazy. I was so embarrassed. All those other mothers must have thought I was abusing him.

We have here more proof that Laura lacks the rudiments of sensitivity on normal day-to-day behavior for a toddler. Considering Laura's education level and the fact that she has read extensively on infant and child rearing, her inability to recognize a normative toddler response to overstimulation (in this case being immersed in the ocean with a mother who questions her own ability to protect him) is startling. As evidenced in her exasperation at the beach, Laura's inability to preview makes clashes such as this one inevitable, because she fails to evidence any forethought in an adaptive fashion before events erupt into potential crises.

Further, her acute fear of being embarrassed in front of "all those other mothers" is crucially significant. It reflects a definite wish projection for the times when she and her siblings had been abused by *their* mother and no one came to their aid.

As she spoke, the pitch of Laura's voice grew higher and more strident; her words came faster and faster. Teddie, who had slid from her shoulder to her lap and was now seated there, began to rock rhythmically, turning his head as if to root through her clothing. "When I tried to get him to slow down and eat some dinner, he started crying again until I couldn't stand it! It really makes me crazy! It sounds like someone is killing him. I feel so helpless, and I can't take that. Feeling helpless makes me feel so angry!" Her voice was now so high-pitched she was almost shrieking.

"I have an observation," I stated. "You've made several comments about Teddie's crying, saying that it sounds like someone is trying to hurt him. But I've also gotten the feeling that if the crying goes on for too long, you're afraid *you* might hurt him. Could this be true?" A flicker of insight passed across Laura's face following my guided question: She is beginning to see her own potential—perhaps—for child abuse. We have seen the first glimmer of positive growth for the patient.

Then Laura slumped back in her chair, regarding her son bleakly. Teddie, who had been wriggling for some time during her comments on his crying, ceased wriggling now and slid quickly from his mother's lap to the floor, where he began to explore the room, finally settling beside a pile of toys and investigating them.

It is remarkable to observe the rhythm of this dyad—Laura's anxiety as it becomes transmitted to her son, who then becomes pressured in his play and vocalizations. Concomitantly, each time Laura relaxes, Teddie, too, relaxes.

"It's as if he can't behave well for too long," Laura said at last. "I keep waiting for him to become normal, so I can relax, finally, but I never can. Whenever Teddie starts to cry like that it triggers a scene. I get so upset, because I know that his crying isn't normal, and then I seem to lose control." She emphasized this word strongly. "And Clark just folds his lips and ignores me, like he doesn't care that this happened to his son, his own son!"

Here again Laura seems so fixed on the possible consequences of a birth trauma that she fails to note that others respond to Teddie on an immediate, current level. The thrust of this and future sessions will be to focus much more on this particular aspect of the patient's problem with reality bases and time orientation.

Laura's voice became strident, suddenly as she returned to her husband. "It makes me really angry. I really resent him because he has no regard for either of us; he neglects us just like 'they' did Teddie when he was born!"

"Do you think," I asked at last, "at least, in part, that the problem you're dealing with is Teddie's crying, or your reaction when he behaves this way?"

"I'm afraid of the crying. I start worrying that maybe he has water on the brain or some other kind of damage. It's also—it's also difficult for me because my mother cried throughout my entire childhood. It's like—like I'm making my baby into my mother."

We finally have open expression of the conflict she's been repressing for so long. For the first time, Laura has confronted this important historical issue and has finally confronted why Teddie's whining and moaning drive her to near madness. For Laura, caught in a confusion of generational swirls, the shrieks and sobs of her baby echo the wails and moans of her own mother in pain so many years ago. She expresses this realization rather graphically: "It's like I'm making my baby into my mother." Beyond that, this is the first time she has a clear transferential insight about her mother and her mother's crying connected through the corridors of time to her own baby's crying so piteously. For several minutes Laura was quiet, watching her son, who now played by himself with only an occasional glance around to refer to her. The toddler's vocalizations were still made in staccato, high-pitched tones, but they no longer had the tense, pressured quality of his earlier noises.

"Maybe it's hard for him to hear me talk this way," Laura said at last. "I just get so frantic . . . but that probably upsets him."

"Which isn't great for either of you," I added. I then suggested:

One way to think about it is that when he calls for you, says "Mommy" and "Daddy," as you've said he does, you must understand he's practicing his language skills. That's an excellent sign as well as a healthy one. It means he's attached to you and turns to you at any sign of danger or distress. Realizing that should make those cries a little less threatening for you, especially when you consider that Teddie's ease with language is further indication he isn't brain damaged. Can you envision what Teddie's going to be like in 3 months or 6 months? Do you find yourself making any predictions about his behavior then?

"I just have such strong premonitions of disaster. I know things are going to go wrong because my brother was abused," Laura replied. I asked Laura to explain what she meant, but rather than explaining, she said, "My mother was always sticking things in my brother's mouth—washing his mouth out with soap—as a punishment for being too loud. And I used to get smacked for making too much noise, too. I guess that's why intense noises get me so upset." In view of Laura's mother having punished her and her siblings for making "loud" noises, this comment by Laura on Teddie's "intense" noises "making her upset" can be construed as a transferential reaction. She is re-capitulating her childhood memory by becoming upset, too, at these unto-ward sounds. Teddie's cries represent for her a kind of warning bell; Laura's own child is evoking long-repressed, traumatic memories, as well as pre-senting situational material she has to deal with face to face. Since the trans-ference is now only sporadic and inconstant, Laura must be encouraged both to recognize and to deal with this emotionally charged material. After a few minutes of silence, during which the mother and I watched Teddie play, I handed a soft foam ball to Laura. "Here," I suggested. "Try playing catch with him."

Laura brightened. "He really loves ball games." She lobbed the ball gently past Teddie, who immediately turned, smiling broadly, then chased the ball. The crisis in this family is acute, but I sensed that Laura was becoming more receptive to change and to understanding that her own behavior might be unrealistic. In time, I believe she will be able to relinquish her obsessive be-havior. This does not mean that Laura's problems will be easily vanquished. We have seen the elaborate labyrinths and barriers she has created to avoid confronting emotionally painful issues.

"I can see he loves games," I commented. "By throwing the ball away from you, you're encouraging him to explore on his own, to go away from you and come back again. I think that's very important to Teddie right now."

For the rest of the session, even though Laura frequently became ani-mated about what she was saying, her voice did not reach that higher, stri-dent pitch. Teddie went back and forth between playing quietly on his own and sitting on his mother's lap, where he was content to be engaged in self-play. On such occasions he would smile broadly, chortling with pleasure. Laura returned twice more to the incidents surrounding Teddie's birth, once to say "I blame my husband for what happened to Teddie—his neglect of me during the pregnancy and now." Although Laura admitted several times that her husband was good with the baby and "adored" him, she accused him just as often of neglecting her and being insensitive to her needs. Now that she is confronted more and more with the child, and even coping more or less satisfactorily with some of the conflicts brought up by dealing with her child, she is unconsciously beginning to seek other avenues of transference, where she can displace her dammed-up conflicts and avoid the difficult psychological work she must know lies ahead. Thus, her unfortunate finger-pointing at Clark, who is entirely innocent of culpability in Teddie's birth.

Near the end of the session, Laura began to discuss her own family background once again. She disclosed that her father had died of a stroke that had initially been misdiagnosed as acute alcoholism. Although she admitted that her father had been an alcoholic, she felt that his death, too, had been a direct result of medical neglect (again the familiar refrain)—"just like Teddie's birth. I know it's silly, but it's almost as if there is a hex on my family."

It is evident that everyone Laura has cared for—her mother and father, her son, Clark, as well as she, herself—is perceived by Laura as a victim. As she recites the "facts," I begin to discern a pattern: Her mother was sickly, her father died as a result of "medical neglect," her husband was a victim of his emotionally withholding family, her son was damaged at birth, and Laura herself has been the victim in almost all her interactions. It is clear to me that victimization is a quality that Laura views as being unavoidable, even desirable on some level. Being a victim allows Laura to become fused with another; in the case of the dyad, with her son Teddie. One might say that early separation from her own caregiver (her father) left her with a wound, and Laura's whole life has been devoted to finding another person with a "matching" wound so that she might become whole again. Here is another reminder of the potential Laura has demonstrated in small ways for being abusive. It is also important to see how far Laura's definition of victimization extends. As we see, everyone with whom she has had contact, from her parents to her siblings to outside people, and finally her husband, has been victim or victimized. She appears in some way mesmerized by victimization. Separation—particularly the appropriate separation a toddler requires for adaptive development—may thus be a devastating event for Laura; it is no wonder she finds it difficult to preview anything but disaster for her son's future. She has experienced only progressive variations of disaster in her own life thus far.

At the end of the session, Laura agreed to arrange for Clark to attend our next session. My purpose in asking Clark to join his wife and son was twofold: First, it is exceedingly important to see how both parents interact with a child when attempting to understand the child's emotional or behavior topography. Second, given Laura's tendency to dramatize, I needed to see how she behaved with her husband in order to evaluate realistically her ability to view her situation with any degree of objectivity. I looked forward to Clark's participation, not only for the fresh insight he might provide into

Teddie's behavior, but moreover, because I suspected that, beyond the damaged dyad, additional parental dysfunction lies at the root of much of Teddie's behavioral patterns.

## SESSION 4

Laura, Teddie, and Clark were punctual for their appointment. Clark, a conservatively dressed man in his early 40s, has a calm, deliberate manner that nonetheless hints at undercurrents of frustration and impatience. His manner to Teddie was attentive and affectionate, and I was at first impressed by his seeming sensitivity. Over the course of the hour, however, I had the impression more than once that Clark's involvement with his son enabled him to avoid his wife's highly emotional outbursts.

I began by asking Clark to describe the chief issue confronting the family. "The critical issue, I think, is that Laura can't stop blaming me for what she calls Teddie's 'condition'—her mixed-up idea that Teddie was somehow injured at birth. She has actually told me that I tried to kill Teddie before he was born by my treatment of her when she was pregnant. How am I supposed to respond to that?" he asked, frustration in his voice.

Laura turned to her husband angrily. "How can you respond? You can't, not after what you did! I don't know what to do with my anger—I'm sure it affects Teddie, and that's your fault, too." She turned to me, saying that her husband had no respect for her. Clark's face turned red, and he looked frustrated and sullen. As Laura continued, she became more and more agitated, her voice rising, her face angrily contorted as she vented a rambling, confused jumble of grievances concerning Clark's neglect of her, her rage at the mishaps of Teddie's birth, her anger at the pregnancy of one of Clark's sisters. She appeared particularly angry in her prediction that her sister-in-law would receive excellent medical care and have an easy birth, in contrast to her own delivery, which had "been botched."

I was pleased to have Clark at the session because he temporarily diverted Laura's transference reaction with me—I had begun to predict that the transference in this case would be so powerful and regressive that Laura would eventually try to enmesh me in another smothering relationship, similar to the kind of relationship she had established with her son and husband. Certainly Laura regressed in Clark's presence, and many of the gains I had felt were achieved in the first three sessions were not apparent during today's meeting. Laura was, for example, far less objective about her perceptions.

"I can't believe, I can't," Laura cried, almost screaming. "I hate her—your whole family thinks she's so great, they hate me—she should feel the agony I've felt!" Resentment appears to be a major character component for Laura.

Clark, who had been playing with his son, seemed embarrassed by his wife's display of emotion. He was clearly making an effort to sound reasonable, to temper his wife's emotionality. However, his calm had a masklike quality, as if whatever feelings Laura's confused and vitriolic words evoked could not be true and were being rigorously suppressed. He conceded that Laura was correct in some of her statements about his family, particularly in her assessment of his mother, whom he characterized as "dominating," but he added that Laura had a tendency to "exaggerate to the extreme." An undemonstrative man of few words and even fewer emotional outbursts, Clark struck me as being quite angry and actively attempting to squelch his frustration to prevent adding fuel to Laura's conflagration. Clark's emotional coolness appeared understandable in light of his evident discomfort at and desire to avoid compounding the problems of his wife and child. About Teddie he said, "I think he's basically an intelligent little boy. A little high-strung and, as Laura says, tense. But I think a lot of the tension comes from what he picks up from Laura and her moods." He added that he felt he did his share, working full-time and taking care of the baby when he came home; "Laura's always exhausted, so the load falls on me." I am convinced Teddie's parents need marital counseling in addition to mother-child psychotherapy to work out their unresolved problems.

During the parental exchanges, particularly when Laura was crying and yelling, Teddie shuttled back and forth between his mother and father. His motions had a staccato quality, as if he could not fully control his body, and his vocalizations were both mechanical and rhythmic. During Laura's tirade, Teddie approached his mother, but he never actually touched her. When his mother's rage reached its peak, however, Teddie crumpled and buried his face into his father's legs in a gesture indicating supplication and a desperation for mollification. The infant's face was tense, with brows knit and mouth drawn. It was clear he relied on his father to quell or dissipate the emotionality of the situation.

"You see what this does to him?" Clark pointed out to me. For the first time during the session, he evidenced anger. "Laura claims she's so concerned for Teddie, but when it comes to either expressing herself or protecting her son from her anger, she insists on putting her own feelings first."

Teddie now appeared in front of his father, grabbing his hand and tugging, repeating "Dah, Dahdee" in low-pitched rhythmic cries. With an air of finality, as if he had said all he intended to, Clark rose and accompanied his son out of the room and into the corridor.

Laura appeared not to take notice of the fact that they had left and continued to vent her anger at her husband, doctors, and family, automatically repeating that she wanted Teddie to have a father but could not stand much more of Clark's treatment. By the time Clark and Teddie returned to the room, Laura was considerably calmer, although her statements were still discernibly exaggerated. Now Teddie approached his mother, who smiled and talked to him, greeting him affectionately. He took her hand and pulled her to her feet, as he had done with his father minutes before. This time Teddie's manner and vocalizations were somewhat less stressed, as if his walk with Clark had calmed him. Laura followed meekly as Teddie propelled her out of the room. She did not resist.

When his son and wife had left, Clark sighed deeply and sank into his chair. When I asked him for a response to Laura's complaints, he rubbed his eyes and began to answer in a tired voice:

> It's true I don't have much empathy with her about the business of Teddie's birth. These things happen, and I honestly don't think Teddie is any the worse for it. In fact, the doctors reassured us that Teddie is all right. I certainly don't think there's any brain damage. Laura's always criticizing me, blaming me—that ridiculous claim that I tried to hurt her or the baby when she was pregnant! It's just crazy.

Clark said that he thought Teddie was calmer with him than with Laura, but he added that he didn't think either of them was providing the right emotional environment for his son.

At this point Teddie and his mother returned. From both father and mother I learned with no surprise that Laura already had some history of obsessive behavior—in college she became convinced that one of her professors was sabotaging her academic program. Even 5 years later, when Clark and Laura met, she vividly recalled her distress and anger over this alleged academic sabotage. Although many things were said at this juncture, largely touching on the marriage and relations between the parents, rather than on Teddie, the discussion remained calm.

## SESSION 5

After two successive cancellations, Laura and Teddie returned to the clinic without Clark. The 3 weeks since the last session had been "one long fight," Laura reported. Only during a 4-day business trip Clark had made to the West Coast, on which he had taken his family, had the fighting ceased.

"I just don't know what to do. I've reached the end of my rope," Laura said flatly. "I'd leave in a minute if it were up to me, but Teddie and his father are close, and I don't want to break that up. Also, I couldn't support Teddie if I were by myself, since I left my job after he was born." Her lavish hyperbole appears to be an elaborate smoke screen in asking the therapist for attention, reassurance, and unconditional love.

I asked about the arguments that had gone on during those 3 weeks. Had Teddie witnessed any of them? The fights had been "loud and violent," Laura reported. She added that she thought her husband believed in violence "when he thinks it's warranted." And the quarrels had taken place almost exclusively in front of Teddie.

"I know it's not good; I'd leave him in a minute if I had the money and the emotional support," Laura repeated more to herself than to me. As Laura became somewhat agitated describing the fights that she and Clark had had, Teddie began to rock back and forth frenetically, then he seemed to sink down or crouch between his mother's legs.

My observations and impressions of these two last sessions were interpreted on two levels—objective and symbolic—to accommodate the intense and stormy scenarios acted out before my eyes. The agitation and heated exchanges of the married couple would wax and wane, in tandem with the frenzy of their son, whose tendentiousness was a mirror of his parents' rage and bickering.

After a brief silence I asked Laura if she had noticed any new developmental changes in her son.

"His development is going well, I think. He's learning words a mile a minute, and he's getting very agile. He loves to climb stairs." For the first time that afternoon, Laura smiled at some memory of her son and took evident pleasure in his progress. Almost immediately, however, she raised the specter of new problems. "But he still won't eat when I put food in front of him. He drinks from a bottle. Isn't there something wrong with that? I mean, he's over 16 months old now. Why does he still drink from a bottle? And," she added, before I could respond, "he's still screaming and whining like an abused child. My brother was beaten when we were small, I think I told you that." When she speaks of her son's tantrums and negative behavior, I continue to feel that Laura harbors unresolved explosiveness. Laura has said that she fears an "explosion" from Teddie, but I suspect this description is a projection of her own rage. Laura then jumped erratically from the subject of her brother's abuse, to her problems with Clark's family and her own, to the subject of Teddie's birth, finishing with "I just have to know how badly hurt he is."

"To the best of my knowledge, the information I have received from the hospital and Teddie's pediatrician shows no evidence that Teddie suffered any lasting physical damage at birth," I assayed. None of my assurances with regard to Teddie's developmental and emotional progress, however, seemed to allay her fears.

Instead, she reiterated her oft-stated old notions of damage.

It is important for a therapist to know when to challenge such fears—and I felt today was not the time. "I would like you to explore if you think these arguments with Clark have any effect on Teddie, especially when you argue in front of him," I offered.

Laura shrugged. "I don't suppose that helps him." To the extent that she acknowledges damage if she argues in Teddie's presence, Laura is learning to recognize inappropriate events and not to cast blame off on Clark or the therapist or other medical staff attendant at Teddie's birth.

At the end of the session, I mentioned to Laura that Clark's presence at sessions was important in order for me to begin formulating a formal recommendation for the entire family. I also suggested that Laura consider becoming a member of our mother-infant group, which focused on raising awareness of developmental issues. Attending such a group would doubtless help her to gain perspective on Teddie's behavior and status in the maturational continuum. Laura's response to this suggestion was indifferent and unenthusiastic. Nonetheless, I will continue to recommend her participation in the group.

## SESSION 6

Teddie and Laura were waiting for me in the treatment room. As I entered the room, Teddie took up playing with the wooden animals that had fascinated him the week before, naming each of them as he picked it up. His manner was notably more relaxed and carefree than at our last meeting. Laura sat nearby, a somewhat dejected look on her face; she made an effort to brighten up when we began to converse.

"He's still not eating," Laura reported unhappily. "He'll throw food, or play with it—he certainly won't let me feed him. But he won't eat it himself."

"Nothing at all?" I asked with a tone of skepticism.

"Well, he'll eat some special things—when Clark picks up this vegetable souffle from a specialty store in the city, Teddie will eat that. He'll eat boiled shrimp, too. He likes expensive food."

"Do you think he perceives he is getting a different kind of attention when he eats special foods?" I asked.

Laura shrugged, then advanced one of her typically overreactive hypotheses. "Maybe. It just worries me. I start thinking there is something wrong with his digestive tract." Over the next 10 minutes, a familiar pattern ensued. As Laura returned to the subject of her perceived problems, her tone became shrill and angry. Teddie grew more agitated, standing beside her, sucking from his bottle, pawing at the ground with one foot. Finally he threw his bottle away, as if temporarily to break the flow of Laura's angry conversation. "I still worry about the way he eats. I've read some articles lately about meconium aspiration leading to sleeping and eating disorders."

"Do you feel that his current eating habits correlate with the distress at birth?" I interrupted.

Laura looked unsure. "Well, maybe. I just don't know, you see." She admitted that Teddie had no trouble sleeping, but she repeated her worries about Teddie's feeding behaviors, which led her again to focus on the incidents surrounding his birth. Well launched into this topic, she broke off, nodded toward her son, and exclaimed, "Look at that!" Indeed, she appears afraid of dealing with a "perfect" (i.e., not damaged) child and maneuvers in every way possible to suggest that Teddie is not well, positing "meconium aspiration" and "poor eating habits" to maintain him as "damaged" in her eyes. For if he were to become "perfect" (i.e., normal), then her own poor parenting would be exposed unacceptably.

Interestingly, because a good deal of our discussion centered on Teddie's feeding habits, his play today involved pretend feeding games that were highly adaptive. Teddie had found a new toy, an enormous stuffed panda almost twice his height; he had rocked it back so that it was lying on the floor and was pretending to feed the panda by holding his bottle to the panda's mouth. Laura clapped her hands, and Teddie beamed at both his mother and me. After a few minutes of feeding the panda, Teddie approached his mother with the bottle and proffered it. Laura understood immediately that she was to feed the panda and participate in this pretend game. Teddie clapped and laughed as he watched his mother hold the bottle for the panda. Finally Laura sat up again and said, "All gone now!" to Teddie, and put the bottle back in her tote bag. Teddie seemed perfectly satisfied with this resolution to the game and began to play with the wooden animals again. This sequence reflected a highly adaptive exchange for the dyad. One aspect of this is that since in the game he'd already been "fed," Teddie could afford to nurture his mother. From the mother's point of view, Laura was promoting this nurturing behavior—she claps and laughs as he performs—and the transition from one game scenario to another was a smooth one, reflecting the internal cohesiveness, and, one could almost say, harmony, between the two.

"Have you thought about what it's going to be like when Teddie increases his exploratory activities? Can you imagine what that will be like for you?" I asked. Laura looked at me blankly. "I'll tell you why I'm asking," I continued. "For a lot of mothers, the hardest thing about dealing with their child's development is coming to terms with the realization that the more the child learns, the more the child gains autonomy. How do you feel when you think about Teddie's increasing autonomy?" I asked.

At first Laura strenuously denied that separation frightened or troubled her in any way. "But Teddie had a lot of trauma when he was born, so he needs a lot of attention," she added. Whether he's moving toward greater independence or not, her statement seems to indicate she *sees* him as limited to his birth-trauma-initiated dysfunctionality. If he were able to write a note denying he had any difficulties, she would find it hard to acknowledge—so vested is she in her fixation on his trauma and dependency, and her outrage and need for thwarted nourishment. After several minutes, she said, "I've been dedicating myself to him for 18 months, you know." She paused. "Maybe that's where some of the tension comes from."

"Where do you think the tension originates?" I asked.

Laura smiled. "In both of us, I guess. But he's getting better lately; I really think so. I'm beginning to think maybe Teddie isn't hyperactive after all. Maybe . . . well, maybe there wasn't much damage at the birth, and I was overreacting." Here, finally after much work is the dividend of my prior restraint: As a result of feeling "safe," the patient can actually share this rather amazing insight about her situation, an insight I find all the more satisfying because only a few moments earlier she had still been protesting about Teddie's alleged birth trauma. The repeated evidence is strong that letting this patient have her way beyond a certain point yields unusually rich results in terms of "rewarding" personal insight.

"The reason I brought up the issue of separation is that Teddie's birth and the possible trauma he received at that time are excuses you could use to keep Teddie from separating," I commented. Then I added:

> By saying Teddie is damaged, you are keeping Teddie close and protected beyond the time when he needs that kind of closeness and protection from you. I've seen reports from all the doctors, and I must say that I agree with them—I don't think there is evidence to support the idea of a developmental deficit or damage at birth. Teddie is a healthy, happy little boy who is trying to deal with tension in his life. I think Teddie has what we call a "difficult" temperament, and I've explained that concept to you before. But that's something you can learn to work with, and it is not a deficit.

Laura seemed genuinely surprised by my statements about Teddie's status and even more surprised when I mentioned that I agreed with the previous doctor's reports stating that Teddie had suffered no damage. This demonstrates how obtuse she had been in terms of listening either to me, the therapist, or even to herself. Often great swings in patient insight come in waves, receding as well as advancing. What Laura exhibits is a typical oscillation in these matters; still, her power to divorce herself from reality and shut down her perceptive abilities from moment to moment is challenging to me. Maddeningly, she can still be obdurately resistant to true and meaningful change.

From comments that Laura made as we were ending the session, it appeared that she and Clark had been making an effort recently to keep their disputes private from their son and also that Laura had been trying to monitor the effect her mood swings had on her son. The results are noteworthy: Teddie today was able to take risks confidently and to play adaptively. Nonetheless, Teddie's changes are demonstrative of short-term adaptations. The effect of his mother's mercurial oscillations of temper near and around

Teddie, however, leave his long-term adaptation with a guarded prognosis, since the long-term effects of this maternal variability are quite hard to gauge.

## SESSION 7

Clark joined his wife and son for today's session. Laura greeted me quietly with a mixture of politeness and exhaustion and immediately returned to watching Teddie at play. At the outset the atmosphere in the session room was somewhat tense, but not overwhelmingly so. The readiness for overt hostility between the parents seemed to have decreased. In fact, both laughed freely, albeit nervously, and appeared to be striving to find shelter in the "humorous" aspects of their situation. They seemed to be serious in their resolve of not fighting with each other. Only Teddie himself seemed unconvinced by his parents' efforts at creating a more reasonable atmosphere: In many ways his behavior resembled the behavior he had displayed at our earlier meeting with both parents. Even when discussion between Laura and Clark was ostensibly calm and amicable, Teddie fidgeted, often trying to pull one parent or the other out of the room. But when his parents spoke with me, Teddie seemed content to play by himself, occasionally showing a toy to one or the other, but not attempting to break into the conversation.

Laura stated that she was experiencing increasing disciplinary problems with Teddie. Typically, her predictions are all dire. "I don't know what to do—he doesn't listen to me at all. I'm really worried about what he's going to be like when he starts school—or even the playgroup we've enrolled in for the next month." Forced more and more to yield up her cherished defenses, in these instances she resorts to disguised hostility in ways both subtle and overt. Here, I feel that she is overtly testing me: When I had asked about when or whether she would join a mother-child group, she had retorted "I haven't thought about it." But she *has* had the time and energy, it appears, to invest heavily (in terms of emotion, time, and probably money) in a playgroup she enrolled in "for the next month."

I noted aloud that the couple seemed more at ease with each other. Clark admitted that things were easier at home these days. "I don't feel as if Laura's blaming me all the time for what happened at Teddie's birth, and that helps me." This change had convinced him of the benefits of treatment, although he still felt seeing a "shrink" was "unmanly" and unnecessary. "I don't think it's necessary for strangers to know our problems," he revealed. We briefly discussed the meaning of "unmanliness" for Clark: It combined a sense of vulnerability and an unwillingness to ask for help as the strongest associations he could identify. There is reason to suspect that Clark is also uneasy about the alliances that have been formed in this therapy. Can he side with me against Laura? Are she and I united against him? Have I established a bond with Teddie? He is plainly curious about what Laura has said about him during these sessions.

Teddie was the one who most clearly demonstrated his feelings directly today. I noticed his perceptiveness always includes the moods of both parents, and he serves as a barometer for the tension level in the room. As the parents sparred back and forth, Teddie, who had been nervous throughout the prior exchange, made a strong effort to pull his father from his chair and lead him out of the room. Clark told his son firmly he couldn't play now. Despite Clark's calm tone when talking to Teddie, the tension between Laura and Clark escalated. Teddie next tried to pull his mother away from the conversation; she too told her son that she could not play with him now. When Teddie realized his efforts were being frustrated, he stood virtually equidistant from his parents, looking from one to the other, whining softly. Then he began to run around the room frenetically, as if to attract his parents' attention.

By now the toddler had raced out into the hallway. For a moment it seemed that the child's attempt to disrupt his parents' conversation had succeeded. Both rose to bring Teddie back, until they were firmly reassured by me that there was a clinic aide in the hallway who would look after Teddie. Although both parents seemed slightly ill at ease, they remained seated and continued their discussion. After playing in the hallway for only a few minutes Teddie returned and stood by the door, peering in at his parents, an alert expression on his face, almost as if he were sniffing the air for danger or anxiety. Apparently satisfied to discover that the mood between his parents was once more peaceful, Teddie reentered our room. The tension created for this child by the continual oscillations in his parents' moods must be very great.

The discussion now revolved around Clark's relationship with his family. Although Clark admitted that his mother exerted a "divisive and negative" influence on his marriage, he also insisted that Laura exaggerated that influence. Laura, for her part, expanded at great length on her mother-in-law's influence on Clark, recounting several "negative" comments Clark's mother had made to her and Teddie. As she continued and her stream of thought became faster, Laura's voice became higher and shriller. Teddie, still seated on his mother's lap, immediately became restless. At first he made protesting sounds, then reached up to put his fingers across her mouth, clearly trying to stem the flow of emotionally charged vocalization. Again we see repeated the pattern of provocative outbursts of one parent eliciting explosive reactions by the other, almost immediately to be superseded by a wave of pseudocalm until the next tidal wave of emotion is ready to crash forth on Teddie's beach.

"Earlier, you said that you were having disciplinary problems with

Teddie," I said. Distracted from her tirade about Clark's family, Laura agreed that she was concerned about Teddie's response to instructions and discipline. "He never listens to me. Most times, I have to shout at him. I can't just tell him something once. It scares me. This could be some sort of a real behavioral problem, and," Laura hesitated, "I know both you and Clark disagree with this, but I'm convinced it's evidence of the damage he sustained at birth."

"You may have noted in the literature you have been reading that most 16-month-old infants display this kind of behavior," I said. "Teddie is at the stage when he's exploring the environment. It seems as if he is going against your directions and testing the limits, as is the case with most toddlers of his age."

"But the way he's acting can't be normal," Laura protested. She recounted a shopping trip during which she had battled to get Teddie into his car seat for the trip home. "I wound up screaming at him and fighting with him—it was awful."

Rigid in her position, at this point Laura will not yield to me or my views, although common sense would indicate the completely normative behavior of her toddler at this developmental stage. "A child of that age can be very difficult, particularly if he doesn't understand what is happening next," I explained to Laura. "When you're feeling irritated, you may want to show Teddie what will be happening next, so he can begin to realize the consequences before it is too late. It's important for him to exercise his skills in predicting at this time," I continued.

"I do that. I told him, 'Now we're going to get ice cream; then we're going to go see Daddy.' But he just doesn't listen to me!" Laura's voice rose again angrily.

> I think two things may be happening here. One is that you've said more than once that significant people in your life—your mother, Clark—don't listen to you. You're expecting Teddie to listen to you the way an adult would, and then you're transferring your anger at adults onto Teddie. But he's just not capable of that kind of behavior yet. That's one observation. The other is that I think you're concerned by how to provide more structure in Teddie's life. You seem to tell him what you're doing now, instead of what will happen in the near future. It's a subtle distinction, but you need to give him a chance to prepare or rehearse for the next change through previewing. . . . "Soon we're going to get into the car and drive home," for example. You are saying "we're getting ice cream and then we'll see Daddy," which starts out in the present and provides Teddie with information about the future.

Clark, who had been silent for some minutes, spoke now. "Maybe Teddie just doesn't want to go home because he thinks he'll encounter fighting there." He said this simply, without a trace of the mocking cynicism that had colored many of his earlier comments. After discussion, Clark agreed to attend some sessions with his family. I think it particularly important to work with this family as a unit, in order to assess the ability of both parents to evaluate and preview developmental progress for Teddie. That the tension in their marriage is clearly a source of great tension for Teddie cannot be ignored. In a sense, Teddie's acting-out behavior may be viewed as a metaphor for the marriage itself: Laura sees Teddie as "out of control," but it is *the marriage* that is out of control.

At the end of the session Laura said she intended to join the mother-infant group, in accordance with my earlier suggestions. I was pleased to note that Clark seemed more willing to participate and become involved than he had in our first meeting.

## SESSION 8

When I joined the family, they looked like a coherent unit. So long as the conversation around him stayed low-key and relaxed, Teddie was evidently happy to play and to explore the toys in the cabinet in behaviors that were entirely age appropriate. But when Laura, discussing her week and her relationship with Clark, became more shrill, Teddie immediately attempted to interact with her, first by throwing toys from the cabinet onto the floor, then by throwing the wooden cow toward his mother so she would have to stop talking and pick it up.

"He always throws things when I'm upset," Laura said, acknowledging for perhaps the first time the connection between her moods and Teddie's behavior.

"Can you tell me about the fights?" I asked.

"They seem endless sometimes," Laura began. As she talked, Teddie wandered away and discovered a low wooden cradle. He climbed in and tried to stand, balancing precariously. Laura stopped what she was saying and went to supervise her son, allowing him to stand in the cradle, rocking himself gently back and forth, as long as she monitored him. Laura then continued her previous narrative, which concerned a phone call Clark had received from his mother. As she became increasingly agitated, describing the phone call, her voice rose steadily. In response, Teddie threw himself out of the cradle and tried urgently to pull his mother out of the room by yanking at her arm. One of his emerging traits is that he's become prematurely adept at forecasting the conflicts erupting around him. I reminded Laura that she had to set the limits; she shook her head and said gently, "Mommy's going to stay here and talk a while, Teddie, so please stop it." Teddie returned to the cradle and played again for a few minutes, attended to by both Laura and me, while Clark sat back and watched the three of us.

Interestingly, when offered a bottle of juice, Teddie became upset. Kneeling on the floor, he buried his head in his arms and wailed forlornly until his mother took the offending juice bottle away and replaced it with one containing milk. Laura noted that he loved his milk, almost never drank juice, and still ate hardly any solid food. "I'm at my wit's end about that. I can't believe this is normal." Then she corrected herself and added, "Well, maybe it's normal for Teddie." At this juncture Laura is making a significant move toward recognition of reality, especially as very recently she protested quite routine toddler stubbornness as "not normal." The changes in Laura's awareness are gradual from session to session, but words used in this way are encouraging of future growth in insight.

For now, Laura's deficits are still causing disruptions in the continuity of the baby's experience. As we noted earlier, such disruptions are difficult to quantify, assess, and correct, leaving the long-term effects on the child's development under some doubt.

I again reassured her that Teddie was healthy and normal. "From what you have described, I suspect that he gets more solid food than you realize. I believe Teddie will probably start eating more solid food naturally."

When he was finished with his bottle, Teddie returned to the toy cabinet and played happily. Laura began to discuss Clark and his interaction with his family. At first her speech was neutral and fairly unemotional. When I noted that Clark shared many of her views about his mother and her attempts to undermine their marriage, however, Laura bristled.

"Now he agrees! Sort of, maybe! I've been telling him these things for 7 years now, and he's only beginning to understand."

"Do you think that it might be hard for Clark to change his outlook, given your attitude?" I asked. "It's hard to change the way you've looked at someone as central to your life as your mother. It doesn't happen overnight. But it sounds as if Clark is willing to consider your perspective. That attitude should encourage you and help you try to see his perspective." Clark sat without comment, watching his wife.

After a long silence Laura admitted, "I guess I have too much anger in me to be fair and objective about it." She described her feelings graphically by saying she felt like the top of her head was "coming off," as if she could "blow a hole in the ceiling with her anger." Her tone became increasingly shriller until suddenly Teddie turned from the toy cabinet and once again tried to run out of the room. "Also, I know now that I'm not really angry at Teddie or Clark and shouldn't take it out on them," Laura added crucially. I went to the door and asked one of the clinic aides to watch Teddie. Returning to Laura, I explained that this was Teddie's most effective way of escaping his mother's explosive (and for Teddie, frightening) emotions.

"It's all that tension he has, as if he's all wired up," she responded as if it were her child who had just confessed to anger great enough to torpedo a hole in the office ceiling. "I guess that comes from living with Clark and me, although we really have been trying not to fight in front of Teddie."

Whereas interaction with her husband still remains turbulent, some of the interactions between Laura and Teddie have become a true joy to watch. For example, at the end of the session, Teddie accidentally tripped and fell. Laura was well-attuned to the nuances of her son's distress and calmed him with her actions. She threw up her hands, saying "BOOM!" loudly, then asking, "Are you okay? Yes, you're okay." When I commented on the way she had handled the mishap, I noted that she had not immediately ascribed the fall to "neurological damage" but was instead able to call it an accident. This was one of the most positive signs I had seen in Laura's interaction with her son.

"I've been trying to develop more realistic perceptions," she responded simply.

By contrast, Teddie's reactions continue to be intense, a learned response I believe that is attributable to the continuing intensity of his environment. As that environment becomes steadily less stressful, Teddie will continue to relax and start moving toward independence. I see in Teddie a growing awareness that there is more than one way to be with his mother, that it is not necessary for him to intervene to protect her good mood. As he finds other ways of coping (such as leaving the room), Teddie stretches the boundaries of his enmeshed relationship with his mother. I am pleased with the progress of both mother and son.

Whereas he participated in today's session, Clark was quiet and watchful; I believe he is still watching for alliances and may be baffled because I have not formed one with Teddie or with Laura. Perhaps, despite my dispassionate stance as therapist, Clark *does* perceive alliances, against my best efforts to prevent any from forming. The strategies I had planned to take to counter this were to see them together more often and to set tasks for Laura that would reinforce Clark's sense that alliance was not my goal but, rather, progress versus conflict in the dyad.


SESSION 9

When I joined the family today, I sensed that Laura had something important to talk about. She was polite but impatient as I greeted the family. The toddler sat near his mother's chair, playing quietly with half a dozen small toys from a plastic bag his mother had brought. Laura then announced that she had started the mother-infant group this week. "And something is definitely wrong with Teddie!" she added emphatically.

"Something is wrong with Teddie?" I repeated. The toddler sat on the floor, playing calmly with his toys, piling them atop each other. Periodically, he would glance up at his mother, then return to his play. He looked entirely normal and healthy. Laura shared her impressions from the mother-infant group, stating:

It's incredibly upsetting. He's so clingy, not like the other kids at all. Now I'm beginning to think he's backward for his age. He clings to me, doesn't want to play with the other kids, and wants to suck on a bottle all the time. All the other children his age are off the bottle by now. I am so embarrassed for him! There was one little girl in the group who was very aggressive! Of course, according to her mother, she had a healthy birth and has always been perfect!

We have here a perfect example of how Laura's obsession becomes manifest: She is exceptionally ego dystonic and ferrets out of anyone around a possible parallel to her own obsessive style. Her yardstick remains the birth trauma. "The girl went up to Teddie and started hitting his bottle, and Teddie got mad and pushed her away," Laura continued. "That was last week; we went in yesterday and found that the girl and her mother have left the group. I'm afraid we drove them away. Teddie was too aggressive and negative to her." We must note the grandiosity in her presumption that one child, hers, "drove" away another by virtue of unexceptional (frankly, typical) childish behavior. Laura is locked in a pattern of relating all problems to her own instead of recognizing the spectrum of differences.

"Could you tell me more about the little girl's aggressive behavior?" I asked.

"I was afraid that she and Teddie would be labeled the bullies of the group. Though I don't know why she should be—she was absolutely perfect! And Teddie! We brought his toys to the group," she pointed to the bag from which Teddie was pulling more toys, "and the other children wanted to play with the toys—I mean, it's only natural. Well Teddie became enraged. It was horrible! I'm afraid we'll be asked to leave unless I can teach Teddie to behave and share his toys. I still feel as if I can't discipline him!"

As Laura's voice rose steadily with distress, Teddie edged backward until he was noisily hitting two blocks together. Not until Laura calmed down somewhat did Teddie's posture and expression relent, at which point he also stopped banging the toys together. Teddie was displaying a response to Laura's stress that I had not seen in him for several weeks.

"Children Teddie's age don't really play together yet," I explained. "They're not ready to share their toys. They're too young to have developed that kind of social skill. Teddie's a forceful little boy, and he's intense; we've commented on that before. A review of Teddie's current behavior sounds well within the normal range for a child of 16 months. I think you simply overreacted, Laura."

My observations mollified Laura somewhat, although she returned several times during the session to the subject of the aggressive little girl who had had a "perfect" birth, as well as to her concerns about Teddie's interaction with other children. In Teddie's recent behavior I observe a regression to an earlier level of enmeshment with his mother. By trying to protect his mother from emotions that agitate her (and thus protect himself from her overwhelming responses), Teddie effectively establishes a boundary between Laura's internal chaos and the external world.

Clark, who had been silent for much of the session, now described several "successful" interactions with Laura during the past week. They had both made a special effort to keep their arguments away from the baby, Clark noted. He had also been trying to take Teddie "off Laura's hands" and give her a little time to herself. Laura commented that she had been trying to talk to Clark about specific, defined issues, as opposed to rehashing her litany of complaints about the damage her son had experienced.

"I know I promised not to raise this theme, but I still can't help feeling that Teddie's behavioral problems were caused by the meconium aspiration and the birth trauma. He's just not like most of the other children," she said, returning to a familiar theme. "But didn't you tell me that the other child who was difficult and aggressive had a 'perfect' birth? How do you explain her behavior if she didn't have any birth trauma?" I asked.

Laura sighed. "I don't know. Maybe that little girl is spoiled. I know we've spoiled Teddie, and I keep trying to stop. I just don't know how. Maybe her parents feel the same way."

I suggested another alternative. Maybe both children had "difficult" temperaments, and their behavior was largely attributable to this factor rather than to "spoiling" or an accident at birth. In truth, I harbored more than a suspicion that Teddie's behavior may actually suggest that he has grown accustomed to the kind of attention he receives from his mother because she is convinced he is "damaged." "Infants with difficult temperaments have a hard time adapting to changes," I reminded Laura.

"But he's so hostile. I mean, not being able to share his toys!" Laura said once again imputing pathology to totally normative toddler behavior. Indeed, with this "hostility" remark, she's imputing, once again, adult motivation to a child's pattern of behavior.

"You probably were focusing exclusively on Teddie, but if you had watched the other children in the group carefully, you would have seen similar behavior," I explained to Laura. "Teddie might be an aggressive child, and maybe the little girl is too, but that aggression could be a reaction to a wide range of environmental factors, particularly to hostility or aggression in the home. Besides, children of that age tend to be very action-oriented, particularly in new environments."

Clark then related a recent incident. Teddie's increasing vocabulary included the word "more" and he would frequently ask for "more milk" or "more play." A few nights earlier, Clark had told Laura that the fact that Teddie never saw his parents "being nice to each other" probably exerted a negative effect on their son. "She told me to come give her a kiss, and I went over and kissed her on the cheek," Clark said. "Teddie was watching. He clapped his hands and called out, 'More! More!' He seemed genuinely happy to see this form of affection taking place between us."

This session marked a turning point in Laura's treatment from a number of points of view: First, she has joined a mother-infant group, although she quickly rejected the realities of other members of the group as they fail to support her obsession. Her negative construction for every behavior shown by her son means she can continue to excuse her own failure to perform adequately. By the same token, she is unable to discipline her child and looks for excuses in the child's "flawed" makeup. In addition, son and mother continue to oscillate with their respective waxing and waning tension(s). But on the positive side, Laura has been trying rather hard to monitor her own responses. Attempting to exit from her neurotic pattern, she has been working on ways to restructure her marital link, although when the relationship with her husband and child fail to achieve security she becomes prone to regression back to the old obsession. Then, although she is earnest about wanting to react well, she continues to evoke the flawed or neurotic symptomatology to help herself "reality test." Finally, we see that Laura globalizes the limited problems she is confronting and thereby limits her future success.

My thrust for upcoming sessions will be to continue to help Laura reality-test her perceptions and—most of all—to support her efforts to try to establish proper functioning with her crucial primary relationships, her baby and her husband, that will allow her to discard her histrionic prop of Teddie's "birth trauma." When the important linkage of enhanced reality-based communication finally takes place, I expect to see the marker of a successful transition. It would mean a clear diminution of her overt reliance on the obsession with her baby's "trauma at birth" and rejection of her feeling that her husband just doesn't understand the "truth" of her experience.

## SESSION 10

When I joined them today, Teddie stood next to his mother with his back to the door, inspecting a picture book Laura held. Laura looked particularly weary, as if she had not slept in days. Teddie kept his back turned for the first 10 minutes or so of the session, as if trying to consolidate the secure unit formed by himself and his mother. Evidently, he might be trying to exclude me. Clark, however, seemed at ease and more comfortable than on previous occasions.

Laura reported that it had been a tough week. Clark's father—from whom her husband had been estranged for almost 15 years—had arrived for an unannounced visit and had stayed for 5 days. During that time the atmosphere in their usually tense household had been "unbelievably charged with emotion." Laura expressed some sympathy for Clark's father because she felt that Clark had made little or no attempt to relate to him. "So I had to entertain him. As usual," Laura announced sarcastically.

"How did Teddie react to the visit?" I asked.

"He's always upset after family visits," Laura reported. "My family, Clark's family, it hardly matters. So he's been very clingy. I mean, I do feel sorry for James [Clark's father]. But on the other hand, all he did was drink scotch and criticize Clark, which was hard for me to take. I kept trying to be hospitable to him, but how do you do that with someone who just wants to get drunk and criticize?"

As Laura's description became shriller, Teddie's transition from usually normal age-appropriate behavior to regressive behaviors, particularly in speech, became more pronounced. However daunting this behavior appears at first glance, I still regard it as evidence that Teddie is learning to self-nurture: He took care of his own needs today, despite the fact that doing so resulted in an independence that was frightening for him. In the next weeks I hoped to see a gradual upsurge of self-nurturing from Teddie, with fewer tantrums as he becomes more secure in caring for himself and exhibiting the full repertoire of his developmental skills.

Laura then acknowledged that she still wasn't certain what she wanted to do about her marriage. As she spoke, Teddie became increasingly agitated, attempting to remove his mother from her chair and physically drag her from the room. Though Laura refused to go initially, ultimately she did rise and follow her son into the hallway, and he resisted with whining and tears when Laura attempted to return to my office. Failing, still, to set limits, Laura passively goes along with Teddie's agenda and fails to impose restrictions on her child. He in this instance takes up the slack for her: She "needs" him as a failure. Teddie's behavior can continue to be used as a "proof" of her "birth-trauma" contention. For almost 15 minutes, they stayed in the hallway, as Teddie threatened a tantrum each time Laura approached the treatment room. Even a brief return to the treatment room to retrieve their coats and Laura's handbag had Teddie in tears, whining and pulling on his mother's hand to make her leave. Although Laura didn't seem pleased with Teddie's behavior, she made no real effort to resist. His whining did not stop until they were together in the elevator.

The session had moved us therapeutically forward, however. The visit by Clark's father proved symbolic to Laura for her increasing anxiety over an incipient separation from her husband (and child). The visit had stirred turmoil, resentment, and anxiety in all three family members: Teddie had promptly regressed in affect; Laura had used the visit as an occasion for projection; and Clark had remained angry and silent.

Hence, the direction of my future focus will be to unhook these three from their enmeshed bounds by "unregressing" the mother and child by further anchoring the mother's objective-reality awareness, by encouraging

Clark to reinvest in his wife's trust, and by being supportive to the child who is almost lost amid all this stormy fighting.

I believe there is great value in the work we are doing together, but I continue to feel that Laura is in strong need of individual treatment without Teddie present. This would give her a forum for personal and marital issues and perhaps allow us, during our sessions, to focus more on issues affecting Teddie's development. When I made this suggestion to Laura, she nodded and agreed listlessly. She has become completely passive about major areas of her life—waiting, for instance, until it is financially "convenient" seriously to consider divorce and then spending money wildly or unwisely to make herself feel better, thereby compromising the family's financial stability. She is, in fact, so deeply enmeshed with the failures of the past that it is still almost impossible to get her to consider the future seriously. To be considered en route to recovery, it will be essential for her to confront the implications of Teddie's development and to form a workable new alliance with Clark.

## SESSION 11

At the beginning of today's session, Teddie played actively in the middle of the floor, putting small plastic toys into the wooden cradle there, then removing them again. He smiled when I entered the room, and continued playing. Clark, in a business suit and tie, seemed at ease. This calm atmosphere was a dramatic change from our last session. I looked forward to learning what had engendered this family transformation.

At the beginning of the session, I posed a question to Clark. "Is it difficult for you to come to these sessions when Laura is so often critical and negative about you and your relationship? How do you feel when she speaks this way about you?"

Both parents looked startled by this question. Clark shrugged, smiled slightly, and responded that it was certainly difficult, but that he was used to Laura's criticism. "I just close off; that makes it easier." Then I asked what, if anything, would mitigate the defensiveness and withdrawal with which Clark commonly responded when in the treatment room. Clark thought for several minutes, and finally answered that he would have to think about the issue further. "I think that Laura feels pretty safe talking about the issues that are important to her here, and I want to make sure that you feel that way as well," I commented.

Both parents agreed that it had been an easier week. Clark insisted that he had not changed, that Laura had become more relaxed, less accusatory this week. They had even managed to share some enjoyable times together as a family. "She didn't harp on that issue of damage to Teddie," Clark said. Following my earlier suggestions, Laura said, they had found a baby-sitter at last. It had taken some of the pressure off her, which was "terrific." "So perhaps part of the reason that Teddie is so relaxed and cheerful today is that the whole family is more relaxed and cheerful together," I concluded.

Clark mentioned that, at Laura's request, he had attended a lecture entitled "Intimacy in Marriage."

"What would you both like to improve in your relationship?" I asked.

Laura shrugged. "Hope. I wish we both had a better sense of optimism about the future."

Clark looked at his wife, surprised that their wishes were so similar. "I'd like to be more positive, more optimistic about the marriage and about each other," he said openly. "With our history—all the bad feelings—it's hard to maintain any kind of optimism, and without that, I don't suppose there's much point in trying to solve anything else. But on another level, I think we have a lot to be thankful for and a lot to be happy about."

Toward the end of the session Teddie passed from one of us to the next, handing out little wooden fishes to each of us. His mother received the most fishes—twice what either Clark or I received. I commented that "Mother needs a lot of fishes—a lot of nurturing." Laura, looking at me over her son's head, smiled ruefully and said, "No kidding!" Teddie has proven that he is capable of nurturing his mother, but he is no longer fixed on doing so to the exclusion of taking care of himself and developing his own autonomy. At first impression, the family's new "peacefulness" had a great deal to do with the departure of Clark's father. The family, now regrouped, is much more in touch with each other.

We began to realize the source of Teddie's remarkable "closing off" (shutting down emotionally) when we watched Clark. He shrugs, stays silent, and withdraws. When he's upset, Teddie does the same thing as his father, and Clark's angry silence serves as an object lesson for Teddie. Yet as this session progresses, they all seem more attuned to one another's moods. There is a reciprocal and adaptive approach that had been lacking before.

For the first time, here in this session, we see that Teddie is less eager to fall into the *trap* of his mother's regression. As I work toward reestablishing the mother's autonomy, it becomes clearer to her that any regression being done is not of the baby's doing, but of hers. It is clearer to all concerned that Teddie has been a convenient life jacket for Laura to pull along with her when she broke from reality.

For Clark, merely enrolling in a marital lecture course is evidence of substantial progress. And when the couple together speak about confidence in the future—it's a very good sign. One of my contentions is that couples having problems hardly talk, and always do so in the past or present. Once, however, they do see a future, we have a very optimistic sign, and greater intimacy usually ensues.

For his part, Teddie's native ability to relate at the same time with both parents is wonderful and far in advance of his years: Indeed, he is exhibiting pseudomaturity. Seeing Teddie behave like this makes it difficult to imagine how Laura could ever believe that her son had developmental or behavioral problems. At one point, Clark had said Laura's insistence that he was somehow to blame for the incidents surrounding Teddie's birth was a heavy burden on him, functioning as a barrier to their communication. Laura had responded by saying that she only wanted to know what had happened; that was why she repeatedly kept bringing the subject up. Now she said she was genuinely sorry if Clark had been upset by her comments. Although I could not get her to agree to stop directing such accusations at Clark, she seemed less perturbed about this normally incendiary topic than I had ever seen her. This itself registered as promising progress.

## SESSION 12

At the end of our previous session, I had requested that Clark bring a list of 10 things he wanted to achieve from the marriage and relationship, feeling that he was the one who most needed encouragement to voice his feelings and needs; I was pleased to see that he had completed his "assignment" and brought the list. When I first arrived, Teddie was a little diffident with me, which both Laura and I attributed to the fact that he had just come from a birthday party during which he had been physically active. As expected, he warmed up considerably as the session progressed.

When Clark announced that he had brought the list of the things he wanted from his marriage, Laura's defensiveness became immediately apparent. She glanced briefly at the paper her husband held and said something deprecatory about its brevity. When he actually read some of the items on his list, she protested each one, rather than listening to her husband's comments. Whereas it was plain that Laura was on the defensive, her manner was more voluble and explanatory than angry. I noticed that her voice and manner did not become shrill. As Clark went through his list and Laura denied or contradicted each point, Teddie was playing with me, and to many—if not all—of his father's remarks, responded "NO!"

"That's his favorite word right now," Laura remarked ruefully. "He loves to say 'no.'"

As the discussion progressed and Teddie continued playing, he would occasionally give his parents toys as a way to break the edginess that was soon evident between them. Teddie seemed to be playing the role of mediator very well.

Clark only read 5 of his 10 items during the session because of the time spent discussing each point. These items included: that the couple had to work to control expenditures; that Clark wanted to hear no further criticism of his mother and other relatives; that he did not want to hear further accusations that he was somehow responsible for the trauma surrounding

Teddie's birth; that he wanted no further discussion within Teddie's earshot of possible damage that the infant had sustained at birth; and that the couple had to control wastefulness around the house.

After each point, Laura interrupted to defend herself, and frequently the discussion would be sidetracked to include the familiar topics of Clark's family and the circumstances of Teddie's birth. As in the past week's session, although the birth trauma continues to be an important issue to Laura, she indicated that she was not interested in making Clark the culprit, only in finding out what had happened. Nonetheless, Laura is beginning to discuss these emotionally charged issues in a mature and more rational fashion. Interestingly, when Laura criticized Clark during this session, she said, "He's just like my mother that way." The subject of Clark's family came up, but Laura seemed less concerned with his relationship with his mother than with the alleged similarities between his behavior and that of her own mother while Laura had been growing up. I mentioned that I thought Laura was beginning to work with the transferential aspects of her relationship with Clark and explained how important this would be in improving their relationship.

At one point I said: "It sounds as if you have both tacitly agreed to stay together, as if you've made a commitment to each other and to the marriage. Am I right?" They looked at each other warily, as if this question was something neither had expected, but each agreed that it was "probably" so and that they were committed to resolving their problems.

I was enormously impressed with Teddie's behavior today. Despite his initial fatigue and shyness, he'd settled down to explore and play confidently on his own. When it was necessary for him to defuse the tension of the situation by removing a parent (in this case, his father) from the room, he did so. Teddie's ability to gauge his own tolerance and to find remedies for distress is really relatively sophisticated; whereas I lament the necessity that has made this so, I am nevertheless impressed by it. Overall, I think the prognosis for Teddie is positive.

Laura had moved, by this time, from the troubling subject of doctors and Teddie's birth to her son's current status. I asked if the reports she had received in the past year—including my own favorable evaluation of Teddie's behavioral and cognitive status—had not assuaged her fears somewhat. She agreed that it all looked hopeful but voiced her fear that something horrible would turn up in the future. "How long do I have to worry about this?" she asked plaintively.

I think that's up to you. I will tell you that Teddie's saying "NO" all the time and the temper tantrums he has sometimes are all age appropriate. These behaviors are not very surprising in a child with a temperament like your son's. Perhaps one of the things you need to focus on is how to interpret his needs and attend to them in a way that makes him feel these tantrums aren't necessary. You need to convey to him that he can elicit your attention and affection in a much less dramatic fashion. You know, listening is a big problem in this family.

Laura nodded her head and would have agreed aloud, but I continued:

If the parents don't listen to each other—and that means Laura listening to Clark, as well as vice versa—you don't have much chance of improving your marriage. And if you don't listen to each other, Teddie is going to grow up expecting that he won't be listened to either, unless he has a tantrum or screams "NO!" You see, a lot of Teddie's behavior, as well as your own behavior, is really within your capacity to control.

Today's therapy felt like a marriage-counseling session to me, but I think some valuable information was imparted to the family. The subject of listening—an important theme for Laura, who feels she has never been sufficiently listened to by her own family, by Clark, or by Clark's family—has been extended to include Clark and even Teddie. I hope Laura begins to understand that listening is a two-way street. In reviewing the management of finances, I hope to have given this couple a model for resolving some of their difficulties in a more practical, less fervid manner. And in all instances, I have tried to make clear to them how their relationship influences their son.

Today was my last session with this family, although I have encouraged Laura to continue with the mother-infant group. In any case, the immediate crisis with Teddie has been resolved. He is much better able to handle his own emotions and those of his parents, and he has begun to separate from his mother appropriately. Laura's obsession with Teddie's "damage" has now abated, and, even when it crops up, she is able to acknowledge that there is no real evidence to substantiate her fears. My goals, as they evolved through the course of therapy, have been to relieve the immediate pressure on Teddie; to persuade the family to hire a baby-sitter at least on a part-time basis, relieving some of the pressure on Laura; to see Laura and Teddie join a mother-infant therapy group; and to persuade Laura to seek individual counseling. All of these goals have been met—Laura has already had one individual session with a therapist and said she was interested in continuing in order to finally rid herself of all of her negative thoughts. I also suggested in passing that Clark and Laura might want to find a couples counselor to work on the issues affecting their marriage.

I am still concerned about Laura and the effect her obsession with Teddie's birth could still have on her son. Although she occasionally predicted all the way through therapy that "something horrible" would happen to Teddie, overall her focus is much more on the future, on what is upcoming, rather than on the past. Teddie's separation may be threatening to her, but she has still accepted the inevitability of the process. I sense that, overall, Laura is working hard to change and to deal with the issues this therapy has raised. That a transference from her mother to Clark has emerged so clearly indicates that many things are surfacing for her in a positive way. I think that individual therapy will make the most of Laura's willingness to explore the relevant issues.

At session's end today, I accompanied the family downstairs to the clinic lobby. Teddie walked with me, casting an occasional glance backward at his parents, who walked side by side behind us, chatting about a planned trip they would take as a family. Once downstairs, Teddie took his mother's hand, but remained easy and friendly with me. As they left, Teddie took his father's hand as well, and the three walked out as an intact family.

# CHAPTER 8

## Deirdre: The Recurrence of Conflict During the First Two Years of Life

RECENT FINDINGS suggest that children whose parents suffer from a psychiatric disorder are more likely than children of healthy parents to experience psychopathology later in life (Grigoroiu-Serbanescu et al., 1991). In part this finding is the consequence of the genetic transmission of psychiatric disorders from one generation to the next. However, psychopathology also arises as a result of conflict deriving from maladaptive interactions with the caregiver or caregivers. Although the genetic transmission of many psychiatric disorders may constrain them, psychotherapeutic interventions are an effective means for preventing the emergence of maladaptive patterns of interaction in the parent-child exchanges.

Four parameters that may have an impact on the ability of a caregiver suffering from a psychiatric condition to minister to her infant appropriately are the symptoms that characterize her illness; the medication or medications she may be taking; the nature of her interpersonal relationships with individuals in her family of origin and with the infant's father; and the effectiveness of the social support available to her. Therapeutic interventions with these caregivers are designed to predict the potential effects of the caregiver's illness on her relationship with her infant and to avert potentially harmful outcomes. Thus, it is beneficial to see the caregiver both during her pregnancy and after she has given birth in order to begin assessing the effects her illness may have for her parenting skills.

In attempting to assess the potential effects of the caregiver's symptoms on the infant, the therapist should consider her behaviors. For example, if the caregiver tends to engage in self-destructive or other violent forms of behavior, the therapist should attempt to predict whether these violent behaviors will be transferred to the relationship with the infant. In addition, the therapist should assess the caregiver's representations. Caregivers who are unable to represent their infant's affective, cognitive, and motivational abilities may tend to view the infant's abilities in a distorted fashion and may, consequently, be more likely to impose their own perceptions in a somewhat inflexible manner. Or, for example, if the patient suffers from hallucinations, the therapist should explore whether the caregiver attributes these hallucinations to the infant. In such cases, the caregiver may represent the infant as exerting control over her.

Although there is debate over whether medication should be used in the treatment of pregnant women, some type of medication appears to assist the progress of therapy in cases of severe symptomatology or in cases where mild symptomatology overlaps with a more chronic disturbance such as personality disorder (Wyman & Rittenberg, 1992). In this regard, the use of medication may enhance the patient's participation in the treatment by improving deficits in the patient's sleep patterns, affects, impulsive behavior, and object relations (Akiskal, 1981, 1983; Bellak & Rosenberg, 1966). However, there are also drawbacks to using medication in the treatment setting. For one thing, medication may interfere with the patient-physician transference because it affects the patient's perceptions of the therapist. Moreover, medication may have various side effects: sedation, overstimulation, physical side effects, and so on. More research is needed in this area, therefore, in order to assess fully the costs and benefits of using medication as an intervention.

Prior to the infant's birth, caregivers who are taking medication to treat their psychiatric disorder should be educated about the potential effects any such medication may have on their unborn infant. After the birth, it is also advisable to educate the caregiver about the likelihood of transferring medication through breast-feeding. In addition to the physical effects of the medication, the caregiver should also be alerted as to how its attendant pharmacological effects may impinge on the relationship with her infant. For example, if her medication should render her either sedated or overstimulated, it is important for her to be aware of how to overcome such effects in order to provide the infant with appropriate amounts of care and stimulation. This is important for the infant's eventual facility for experiencing feelings of mastery and competence. Caregivers who do not respond to an infant's requests for interaction or quiescence may cause the infant to experience feelings of helplessness and depression.

Another area to be explored is the relationships the caregiver has formed with individuals in her family of origin and with her spouse. Because past attachment patterns tend to influence contemporaneous and future relationships, it is important for the therapist to assess whether the caregiver will repeat the attachment patterns experienced in her family of origin or attempt to alter these patterns in order to compensate for a perceived deficit in the attachment relationship. For example, a caregiver who experienced an inse-

cure attachment with her parent may fail to bond appropriately with her infant, or she may form an "enmeshed relationship" with the infant in an attempt to fulfill a need that had not been met in the past. In turn, assessing
the nature of the relationship with the infant's father is particularly important because individuals tend to marry a person who they believe will fulfill
a need that was not met by the attachment relationship with their own caregiver (Paris & Guzder, 1989).

The family of origin and spouse frequently constitute the caregiver's primary forms of social support. In many cases, it may be helpful to augment
this support through participation in a caregiver-infant group. Such groups
expose the caregiver to infants at various developmental levels and to a variety of temperaments and interpersonal styles. Moreover, the caregiver has
the opportunity to interact with other caregivers undergoing similar life experiences.

Assessment of these parameters can optimally begin during the pregnancy period. At this time, the therapist can explore the caregiver's thoughts
and fantasies regarding various facets of her life—including any psychiatric
disorder—that might have an impact on her relationship with her unborn
child. At these times, the caregiver is oriented toward the future as she attempts to make predictions. The caregiver's inability to engage in representational exercises and reports of representations of a maladaptive relationship may signal the presence of conflict. However, because the birth has not
yet occurred, the therapist has the opportunity to assist the caregiver in
forming adaptive representations of future interpersonal outcome. The therapist can also verify that the caregiver is aware of the developmental
timetable so that she may predict the emergence of various developmental
milestones and interact with the infant in a way sensitive to his or her developmental status.

Many times, however, the caregiver may not present for treatment until
after the infant's birth. Moreover, having the infant in treatment with the
caregiver affords the therapist the valuable opportunity of observing their
dyadic interaction and assessing the potential effects the caregiver's emotional status has on her child. Again, it is beneficial to orient the caregiver toward future developmental change in order to predict the effects her expectations may have on the symbiosis with her child. In addition to engaging in
representational exercises, the therapist can assist the caregiver in engaging
in behavioral exercises designed to help her to predict the effects of her behaviors on the infant.

It may seem that some caregivers suffering from psychiatric disorders or ill-
nesses are unable to engage in adaptive patterns of interaction. Nevertheless,
promoting adaptive interaction through the use of previewing is effective in
these cases because previewing calls on intuitive skills that virtually all caregivers exhibit to some degree. As the caregiver becomes aware of and

rehearses a developmental change with the infant, she allows the infant to experience the sensations of future mastery and competence in the here and now. The positive affect the infant manifests in response to these sensations is automatically resonant with the emotions of the caregiver, who, in turn, also experiences positive affect. Thus caregiver and infant are motivated to seek each other out for interpersonal exchange. By the same token, the caregiver is thus less likely to engage in maladaptive patterns of interaction with the infant.

Deirdre's case addresses these issues. Deirdre, with a history of prior psychotic (and destructive) episodes, was currently taking medication to control her mood swings and auditory hallucinations. Her visits took place during the pregnancy and following the birth of her son Patrick. Because of her history of self-destructive behavior, it was feared that she might engage in violent behaviors with (or toward) her infant. Indeed, when Deirdre was seen prenatally, she expressed no feelings regarding her pregnancy and reported that she had no fantasies regarding what the baby would be like after the birth. This suggested that she might have ideated the baby less as a person than as inanimate object—and thus that she might be more likely to abuse him. The sessions following the birth focused on helping Deirdre to become more attuned to her son's development and his sensitivity to her moods. Moreover, the therapist carefully monitored Deirdre's representations of and interactions with Patrick to ensure that Deirdre did not act out the rage she frequently felt. Thus, previewing served here to predict the potential effects of Deirdre's illness and of her personality traits on her relationship with her son as well as to introduce the dyad to adaptive patterns of interaction.

## Patient Identification

On a gray day in October, I was scheduled to interview a new patient who had been referred to me by a colleague affiliated with the hospital. Seated in a chair that had been moved away from the others in the waiting room, her shoulders hunched and head down, she presented in an attitude of classic dejection. This somber portrait was my first impression of Deirdre.

As I approached, Deirdre sat up, as if startled, and smiled hesitantly. She was a tall and attractive woman of 23, casually dressed in faded jeans. Her auburn hair reached to her shoulders and frequently swept across her face as if to veil it. She had high cheekbones and large, expressive eyes. Her unhappy facial expression shifted abruptly from a sad and wistful one to one of cold anger. Despite the fact that she was at this time almost 6 months pregnant, her condition was not readily apparent until she stood; during most of the interview she slouched in her chair, her body slightly averted, one arm draped over her swollen abdomen.

According to the notes forwarded by Deirdre's psychiatrist, the patient had a distinct history of psychiatric disturbance. My colleague was concerned about the effect of pregnancy on Deirdre and of the problems that this clearly troubled young woman might encounter as a mother. Deirdre initially had made no connection between her infant and what she termed "my craziness"; however, as the interview progressed, she revealed concern about the effects that her psychiatric history might have on her parenting skills and her ability to nurture a child.

## FAMILY HISTORY

Deirdre's first psychotic episode had occurred when she was 14. During this episode she had heard voices commanding her to cut her face with broken glass. This incident occurred shortly after the family had returned to the United States following a 7-year residence in Ireland. At that time, Deirdre had been hospitalized for 2 months until the symptoms abated. When she was 18, a second episode again required hospitalization; this episode appeared to have been precipitated by a highly dramatic breakup with a boyfriend. This second episode had also evoked a self-mutilation, and Deirdre had hacked off all her hair. She told me about the episode with a curiously diminished affect, shrugging and laughing inappropriately. She had received supportive psychotherapy at the time and was instructed to take neuroleptic medication but had refused to do so. Subsequently Deirdre was placed on a maintenance dose of Stelazine, which controlled her auditory hallucinations. She was still on Stelazine when I met her.

Deirdre's father, an Irish immigrant, worked for a company headquartered in Dublin. The family had lived in Dublin from the time Deirdre was 7 until their return to the United States when she was 14. Asked about her father, Deirdre discussed him with a deprecating shrug as being "okay," adding that he was a cold and unemotional man. Her mother, by comparison, was highly emotional. Deirdre reported that her mother had "hated every minute" of the family's stay in Ireland and while there had started to "drink heavily." The family's return to the United States did not put an end to her mother's alcohol abuse, and Deirdre said that eventually this behavior caused her parents to separate when she was 17. When her father returned to Ireland, Deirdre remained with her mother. Beginning at this time, Deirdre's relationship with her mother, always highly emotional and stormy, deteriorated. Within 6 months, Deirdre moved out to live with a boyfriend. When she finished high school, she spent one semester at a junior college before dropping out to get a job as salesclerk in a boutique.

As a result of her psychotic episodes, Deirdre was diagnosed as suffering from a bipolar disorder. In addition, she began abusing alcohol, marijuana, LSD, and cocaine by the age of 16 and had been in several relationships with men who were substance abusers. When she was 23, she met Mike. Within a month she had moved into his apartment. For several months they were involved in heavy substance abuse, which finally ended when both enrolled in Alcoholics Anonymous (AA), a decision of which Deirdre was proud. At the time of her entrance to therapy Dierdre was no longer a substance abuser or a user of alcohol.

Shortly after the couple began at AA, Deirdre discovered she was pregnant. The pregnancy was unplanned, although Deirdre reported that she had not been particularly surprised to learn of it, since she and Mike had been "real casual" about the use of birth control. The couple had discussed abortion, although not with any real seriousness: Mike's main concerns, Deirdre stated, had been financial. He liked the idea of having a child and had proposed marriage.

During Deirdre's fourth month of pregnancy Mike lost the lease on his apartment, and the couple was forced to move into the home of Deirdre's mother. Unfortunately, the move renewed the old friction between Deirdre and her mother. Deirdre reported that her mother was alternately thrilled at the prospect of a grandchild and increasingly resentful, "really hard to live with." She added that although her mother did not actively discourage her involvement in AA, Deirdre sensed both resentment and jealousy: "I guess because she drinks, she thinks we're pointing the finger at her because we're going to meetings and she's not," Deirdre said.

Before her pregnancy Deirdre had held a series of jobs that supplemented the Social Security disability payments she received because of her psychiatric condition. When she discovered that she was pregnant, Deirdre stopped working. She said she planned to stay at home with her baby. Mike, the prospective father, was 27 years old, the third of five children, but the only son, in a Midwestern family. He worked as a technical draftsman for a computer company. Like Deirdre, he, too, had a long history of alcohol abuse and had been attending AA meetings for almost 2 years.


MENTAL HEALTH STATUS EXAMINATION

Deirdre first presented for an assessment when she was in her second trimester of pregnancy. She appeared to be calm and in control of her emotions. She was neatly but casually dressed and resembled a teenager more than an expectant mother in her late 20s. Deirdre spoke slowly, as if verbalization was not her preferred medium of communication. Often, upon being asked a question, she would lapse into silence or comment, "I don't know what you mean." In general, she seemed to have difficulty communicating her thoughts and establishing interpersonal connection.

# Therapy

## SESSION 1

During the first session Deirdre sat quietly, volunteered little, and maintained almost a self-imposed stance of isolation. She was not overtly uncooperative but indicated that she just wasn't "much for talking," reinforcing by her behavior her physical positioning in the waiting room. During this session Deirdre appeared well oriented. Although her responses were unpolished, she demonstrated intelligence and good insight into her psychiatric history and condition. Although she reported no recent delusional episodes, Deirdre's fantasies suggested a degree of self-destructive ideation, which, when matched with her generally subdued affect, gave cause for some alarm.

When questioned about her psychiatric history, Deirdre was obviously uncomfortable. Her first response was, "Didn't Dr. Meade [the referring therapist] tell you all that?" When encouraged to share her experience in her own words, Deirdre shrugged and tersely described both psychotic episodes. She resisted when I asked her to elaborate, physically retreating into her chair and giving short, flat replies to every question. Throughout the interview, but especially when asked questions she apparently experienced as stressful, she tapped her foot compulsively.

As the session proceeded, it became obvious that Deirdre's reluctance to examine her past experiences was not limited to her psychiatric history. When questioned about her pregnancy, Deirdre was voluble about physical details, her due date, how much weight she had gained, her obstetrician's clinical observations. But when asked to discuss how she felt about being pregnant and her plans and hopes for her unborn child, her profound discomfort became apparent. At first she denied thinking much about the pregnancy or her unborn child at all, saying blandly, "Yes, I'm having a baby." And although she repeated that the pregnancy had been unplanned and that she had reservations about having a child, she denied that she had felt any anxiety on learning about her pregnancy, even when she and Mike were discussing possible termination of the pregnancy. Here her selective denial appears to overlie a more basic dysphoria that Deirdre assumes as a defensive mask to cover an underlying sense of vast hopelessness.

Deirdre's inability to express her feelings about the pregnancy was mirrored in her seeming disinterest in the child she was carrying. The only question regarding the child that she answered with any degree of ease was whether she wanted a boy or girl. "A boy," she said emphatically, then smiled nervously. "I get along better with boys. You don't have to tell them as much as girls," she said flatly.

Throughout the interview Deirdre insisted that she had no fantasies about her infant. In fact, she could not envision the baby or predict anything about its looks, characteristics, behaviors, or her own response to it. "I guess I'll love it," she said uncertainly. When pressed, she said she would like "a nice quiet little baby" and grinned inappropriately, as if she had said something embarrassing. Deirdre's distinct emotional detachment, here, coupled with her paucity of ideation about the new life emerging within her, are emblematic of her disorder. The very flatness of her replies in response to continued questioning, almost prodding, about her infant highlights an underlying amorphous dysphoria and presages an inability to relate in a normative fashion once the baby is born.

Yet, despite her seeming detachment, Deirdre was able to vocalize her feelings about the effects of the pregnancy itself on her physically. "I feel like a whale," she complained. "I feel huge." She shrugged and added, "I guess everyone says that, right?" Although she indicated that she felt well, she made it clear that she resented the physical discomforts of pregnancy. She added that she felt the pregnancy had activated a good deal of anger and hostility in her, a change she attributed to "hormones." Interestingly, while discussing these feelings of anger, Deirdre gave evidence of thinking about her infant as an individual for the first time. "Sometimes I think that these feelings are going to affect the baby. When I get angry," she said, "I'm afraid I could hurt the baby." When asked what she thought might happen to the infant, she vaguely responded, "Hurt it somehow." Deirdre's masquerade of indifference seemed to dissolve suddenly as she confessed that, although she felt she was coping with these fears, at other times she wanted to "punch walls." These statements greatly concerned me. Deirdre might well be tempted to harm either herself or the infant. How would this young mother cope with the stresses of parenthood when she so clearly had problems mastering the stresses of her own life?

At the end of the session I briefly outlined how our future therapy sessions might be structured. I specifically described the concept of previewing to the patient and noted that it would be beneficial to discuss developmental events after the infant's birth. I provided this outline to encourage the patient to start reflecting on the process of therapy and her own participation in it. In essence, I was attempting to preview the therapeutic experience for Deirdre. We agreed that our sessions would begin at the time of her child's birth because Deirdre was scheduled to visit with relatives in Germany until shortly before the birth. Given that Deirdre's emotions in connection with her pregnancy ranged from seeming indifference to definite negativity, would she prove incapable of involving herself in the joy of an anticipated birth?

## SESSION 2

I looked forward to my first official session with Deirdre and her new-born son, Patrick. Deirdre's sad and curiously vulnerable demeanor had left a strong impression on me several months earlier, and I was interested to see if the birth of her child had changed her in any way. I arrived to find Deirdre unwrapping her infant from several blankets; she herself was red-cheeked from the wind. Almost immediately I had a sense that this mother was not behaving typically. Not only did Deirdre not offer to "show off" her son, but when I asked to see him, she tensed, then shrugged and said, "Why not?" She pulled back a blanket to reveal Patrick, almost 4 weeks old, sleeping soundly. When I commented that he was a handsome baby, she smiled and said that everyone told her so. "He looks like, I don't know, a baby, I guess," she added. In fact, Patrick was a well-developed and attractive infant. He was wrapped in so many layers against the cold that even when most of his outerwear was removed, he still appeared larger than he was. I sensed an ambivalence on Deirdre's part even to having her infant son be observed. Whether this ambivalence extended specifically to me or included everyone, I had yet to determine.

As the session began, Deirdre settled Patrick in his carriage, then sat down in a chair several feet away. She made no effort to move the baby's carriage closer to her or to shift the position of her chair so she could monitor him as she spoke with me. She slumped low in her chair and looked out from behind her long hair. Throughout the session, Deirdre maintained only the most casual contact with her infant. She rarely spoke to him directly, and her gaze was almost always directed away from him. These distancing be-haviors underscored the alienation she projected. Because Deirdre's aware-ness of her son's states appeared to be minimal, it would be important for me to increase that awareness as well as to improve the quality of her inter-actions with her son. I was troubled by what effect Deirdre's distant and de-pressed affect could have on her infant, as well as by the evident fatigue and sadness that so clearly characterized her emotional life and its potential dele-terious influence these could have on her son.

When discussing Patrick's birth, Deirdre showed resistance. The birth had been "easy," she reported; labor had lasted less than 2 hours. She denied any special memories about the birth—either negative or positive—and de-nied feeling any immediate bond with the infant. "It just wasn't a big deal for me. I was out of the hospital in 2 days," was her response when pressed. Her tone suggested that Patrick's birth was not a special event but more like a momentary inconvenience in her ordinary life.

I asked Deirdre what she could tell me about the changes and gains she had observed in Patrick during the past week. Specifically, had she observed any developmental changes in Patrick from the time of his birth until this meeting? Deirdre said that she had not noticed anything unusual. "He's gotten bigger, I guess," she supplied at last. She did not report noticing any motor, cognitive, or emotional changes, dismissing the issue by saying Patrick was "basically good." I encouraged her to reflect on changes in the future, such as those in appetite, sleeping, elimination, and sensitivity patterns. Although she did not display a great deal of sensitivity to the signs of Patrick's development, Deirdre had developed a rudimentary sense of her baby's personality. He was "mellow, like me, and he doesn't say much." She added that she thought he became bored easily. Whereas I was certain this "boredom" was his mother's ready defense against long-term therapy, I was also planning to focus attention on Deirdre's perceptions of Patrick's individuation as well as to continue to bring out his personality in the face of the onslaught presented by Deirdre's "sickness" and her overwhelming needs in and outside of therapy.

"Can you describe his behavior when he gets bored?" I asked.

"He screams. Then I bounce him around." She giggled tentatively. Although she did not admit to any frustration at the powerlessness to which motherhood had brought her—her occasional inability to soothe her baby's cries—her laughter and shrugs seemed false and inappropriate. She could distinguish between his noises, she said, and knew which sound meant that Patrick was hungry or sleepy. In general, Deirdre's observations seemed to relate almost exclusively to Patrick's physical states; with the exception of anger and frustration, she did not seem comfortable in identifying his emotions. "I think he knows my voice," she said finally with a weary apathy.

"How long did you breast-feed?" I asked.

"Two weeks. I knew I was going to just try it and see if I liked it, but it was very draining and inconvenient. I got headaches after the feedings. Somehow I thought it would be easier, you know: 'natural.' But it just wasn't."

When I asked if she had needed to make an emotional adjustment when she stopped breast-feeding, Deirdre merely shook her head. "I heard there was supposed to be a bonding when you breast-feed, but I never felt it." As she spoke, Deirdre watched me, apparently searching for signs of disapproval.

"Did the change seem to make any difference to Patrick?" I asked.

"None. He eats more now, in fact." Again, Deirdre seemed better able to focus on the infant's physical state, rather than his emotional state. When asked what Patrick's next developmental milestone would be, she shrugged and answered, "I don't know. Maybe eating solid food?"

I was struck by Deirdre's evident apathy to engage in predictions about her child's development. One important goal in the coming weeks would be to heighten her awareness of Patrick's developmental achievements. In particular, I hoped to sensitize Deirdre to the various aspects of Patrick's perception. For example, I intended to discuss aspects of psychomotor, socioaffective, and cognitive maturation with her. To that end, I offered to show her a series of videotapes on development during the next few weeks. Although Dierdre did not appear enthusiastic about my suggestion, she agreed to view and discuss the tapes.

## SESSION 3

Deirdre and Patrick were in the waiting area, and I enjoyed my first clear look at Deirdre's 4-week-old son. As the session began, Deirdre turned Patrick, who had been cradled in her arms, his face away from me, so that he now lay against her shoulder. She did not support the baby's head, which lolled to one side, and kept him pressed against her shoulder with her hand. Neither mother nor child looked comfortable. Deirdre's reluctance to let me view Patrick may indeed reflect her own ambivalence about revealing her genuine emotions to me during therapy.

Deirdre was first asked about observations she had made of Patrick over the past week, particularly about changes that might indicate advancing maturational skills. Although we had discussed the importance of such observations in our previous session, she looked blank.

"Nothing's really different," she said at last. After a long pause she amended her statement, saying that Patrick had "decided" to change his schedule around and was up all night now.

"Is that different from before?" I asked.

She considered. "Well, last week he was awake a little more at night, but this week he just lies fussing all night. And now he wants to play sometimes."

"These changes, and the increasing fussiness, may have something to do with Patrick's basic temperament," I said. I briefly outlined the parameters of "easy," "difficult," and "slow-to-warm-up" temperaments. Deirdre listened and said that all of those qualities sounded like Patrick to her.

"You said, a few minutes ago, that Patrick wants to play sometimes. How do you know?" I asked.

"He fusses, and it's not because he gets hungry or needs changing. He's just bored and wants to be carried around or held." Deirdre now gained confidence in reporting on changes in her son's life. "He's not crazy about the formula I give him either," she said then. Asked how she knew, she responded, "He just won't suck." She reported that she persuaded him to drink from the bottle by "just sort of popping it in his mouth. After a little while he stops fussing and starts sucking." She continued to hold the baby against her shoulder, patting his back absently with sharp rapid taps. Once again Deirdre's casual demeanor and her lack of concern for the effect this cavalier attitude might have on her son concerned me. An infant of that age has many considerations and impinging realities, but the "boredom" she attributes to Patrick is not generally one of an infant's repertory of emotions or interactive styles. Deirdre's interpretations, then, clearly represent a projection of her own internal state rather than an accurate representation of an infant's cognitive and emotive mind-set. Similarly, she eliminates from her consideration how lonely and unloved the man who fathered Patrick must feel. The universe for Deirdre consists exclusively of *her* feelings and projections; no one and nothing else, at this point, seem to permeate her consciousness, characterized by its drab emotional topography.

Deirdre then placed Patrick back in his carriage and pulled a blanket around him, moving the carriage slightly. There was a furtiveness to her actions as she did this, as if suddenly she were afraid that her care of her baby were being evaluated. Once the baby was settled, Deirdre moved her chair until it was almost 2 feet away from the carriage; from time to time as she talked, she would reach one arm out and rest it on Patrick's carriage. From her posture, it definitely seemed as though Deirdre were disassociating herself from her son. Throughout the rest of the interview, amazingly, she made no physical or verbal reference to Patrick at all, maintaining contact with him only through her vague hand motion.

During this session, no reciprocal interaction whatsoever occurred between mother and infant; Deirdre did not once spontaneously play with her son, nor did she cuddle him. The closest to an affectionate touch seemed to be the rather abrupt patting she displayed when she held Patrick against her shoulder. In fact, Deirdre's behavior conveyed the impression that Patrick was like a dissociated inanimate object to her rather than an individual, indeed her own flesh and blood.

When encouraged to speak about her experiences as a mother, Deirdre volunteered very little, preferring, as was her wont, to comment superficially. For example, when asked "Are there times when you don't know what your baby wants?" Deirdre nodded with a sense of vague apathy. "He gets stomachaches," she began at one point. When asked how she knew that stomachaches were the source of her child's discomfort, Deirdre responded with an array of signs indicating a higher level of attunement, at least to Patrick's physical state, than had been previously expected. She could hear his stomach rumbling at such times, Deirdre said; and he burped repeatedly and fussed.

"What do you do when Patrick gets stomachaches?" I asked.

Deirdre smiled inappropriately and announced matter-of-factly, "I let him cry it out. Nothing I do is going to help, so I let him scream for a few minutes, until he's tired."

"Doesn't it bother you when the baby screams?"

"Yes. Especially when I'm home with him. Sometimes Mike gets home from work, and I just hand him the baby and say, 'You take him. I can't.'"

Her boyfriend, Mike, continued to be very good with their son, she reported. Since Mike got home from his job half an hour or so before Patrick went to sleep at night, the baby was usually at his most irritable then. "Mike doesn't mind. He just plays with him, and after a while, Patrick suddenly isn't crying. It's like a safety valve," she said.

"What would happen if that safety valve weren't there?" I asked.

Deirdre grinned and waved her hands. "Kaboom!" Then, with an abrupt turn of face, "Probably nothing, I guess," she added. Deirdre's allusions to destructive behavior concern me. She apparently has sufficient "safety valves" to check her anger and manage her turmoil at present; however, if Deirdre's perceptions of Patrick's fussiness increase, this behavior may significantly stress her ability to cope. I feel these issues must be raised in future sessions to give her the best opportunity to overcome her turbulent feelings and their possible consequences.

In the last few minutes of the session, Deirdre grew increasingly withdrawn and apathetic. She slouched in her chair; she also turned at an awkward angle away from both therapist and infant. She jiggled one foot and averted her gaze from me. Asked if she were uncomfortable, Deirdre replied that sometimes therapy seemed "too personal" and focused on her.

I wondered if perhaps Deirdre's increasing discomfort were not caused by a picture of adaptive parenting revealed to her through my questions. Does Deirdre feel that the questions I ask about her relationship with Patrick suggest her parenting style is at odds with a more competent caregiving, and, if so, does this dichotomy bother her? Because her handling of her infant is currently so impersonal and brusque, two of my goals are to demonstrate physically adept behaviors and to help Deirdre to ideate and preview behavioral alternatives.

## SESSION 4

As I entered the room for our next session, I sensed Deirdre's unspoken hopelessness. I had planned to show Deirdre a videotape on feeding behaviors today and hoped to imbue her with a sense of the opportunity feeding afforded her for bonding with her son. At the same time, I had planned to observe her reactions to the tape for cues indicating specific problems with nurturing abilities. It was my hope that the tape would form a basis for our discussion that day.

Deirdre was feeding Patrick when I entered the room. Rather than being absorbed in responding to the infant who was so clearly dependent on her, her attention was clearly elsewhere, and she was staring out the window as I entered. She did not look at her infant at all until she felt, by the weight of the bottle, that it was almost empty. During this time her son's attention was on her face, or rather, on Deirdre's chin, which sadly may have been all the infant could see of his mother. I found myself wondering what Patrick was feeling as his mother looked away from him in this manner.

"Do you think Patrick associates the bottle with you?" I asked.

Deirdre shrugged, apparently unaware that she had shifted Patrick into an awkward position with his head only half-supported. The bottle fell from his mouth, and she replaced it without looking, almost with disinterest. "I think he just makes the connection about the bottle and food. He doesn't care who's holding it," Deirdre remarked impersonally, giving another example of her distorted projections. Her infant son is successively given "hard, sharp raps" when being burped; he is not given loving looks while feeding; he is not looked at even cursorily during sessions. Can the infant possibly be "uncaring" about these seminal interactions? Clearly the answer lies in the mother's ill-disguised transference of her own muted affect to that of her infant son. Obviously, the one who "doesn't care" is not Patrick but Deirdre herself. One of my strategies is gradually to test this hypothesis and to work slowly toward Deirdre's recognition of these attitudinal blockages.

When the infant's bottle was empty, Deirdre removed it, dabbed briskly at Patrick's mouth, then placed a towel across her shoulder and methodically draped her son there. She held him with one palm flat on his back, tapping rhythmically to burp him. This entire process was accomplished almost mechanically, with no murmured vocalizations or affectionate episodes of eye contact on Deirdre's part at all.

At this point the subject of the videotape was introduced. As she watched the tape, Deirdre responded neutrally, rarely in a positive manner. When the film dealt with the emotional bond associated with feeding, Deirdre slumped in her chair with a blank expression. During the film Patrick grew fussy, wiggling in protest on his mother's shoulder. This provided me an opportunity to observe how Deirdre handled her infant's distress. Deirdre repositioned the infant in her arms again and popped a nipple into his mouth. After a few exploratory sucks, however, Patrick protested, making it plain this was not what he wanted. He began waving his arms and legs, face contorted in an unhappy grimace.

When the tape was over and she was asked for her comments, Deirdre shrugged vaguely and replied that she had seen "nothing new." From the moment the tape stopped, Patrick began fussing. Deirdre placed him in her lap in a "feeding position," but rather than offering him the bottle, she began shaking Patrick's whole body. This quieted the baby for only a moment.

"Do you know what he wants?" I asked.

"He doesn't know what he wants," she replied. When I asked if I could assist, Deirdre shook her head. "He probably just wants to walk around."

I suggested that she might walk the baby around the room.

"He gets walked around plenty at home" Deirdre said. Finally, she cradled her infant in her arms and brought him closer to her face. For the first time during the session, he had an unobstructed view of her. For several minutes, while he had her in his view, the tension in his body dissipated. This relative quiet lasted for about 10 minutes. Then Patrick began to fuss again. Deirdre engaged in her customary routine of feeding and patting, but when it was obvious that Patrick was not being soothed, she plunked her son on her lap and held him by his shoulders in a sitting position that left his head unsupported. She reiterated her earlier statement that the baby didn't know what he wanted.

"Why do you think that?" I asked.

She shrugged. "Because he's a boy, maybe?" When asked to explain, she said that girls were more attuned to their bodies. "Boys aren't." Her answer is revelatory of Deirdre's blunted interactional capacity. Her responses are almost ludicrously simplistic and mechanical and couldn't possibly reflect real thought, yet she persists in these superficial platitudes rather than focus her fractionated skills of interpersonal reaction, persists in naive attempts to mollify the therapist with trite platitudes.

In observing this dyad, I was moved yet again by the insubstantial nature of the relationship between mother and infant. Given the dysfunctional status of this relationship, it is perhaps understandable that Deirdre cannot preview Patrick's future developmental accomplishments.

"I'd like to try something," I suggested. "I would like to interact with Patrick myself, if you're comfortable with that. While I interact with Patrick, I'd like you to tell me what you see happening."

She handed her son to me. I settled Patrick in the crook of my arm with his head supported, and began to interact with him, smiling and repeating, "Patrick!" This continued for several minutes, but while Patrick stared at me with interest, Deirdre made no comments.

"What do you see me doing?" I asked at last.

She smiled vaguely. "You were talking and making faces. He wasn't doing anything." When pressed, she acknowledged that Patrick had been watching my face. When I asked her to again narrate as Patrick and I played, Deirdre frowned impatiently, but agreed. But this second attempt failed to evoke any greater response from her. Whereas Deirdre was able to recount the superficial physical details of the interaction, she seemed unable to describe any interpersonal interaction between her son and me. At last I returned Patrick to his mother saying that I hoped we could try this experiment again.

## SESSION 5

When I entered the room, I went to look into the carriage and admire Deirdre's baby, commenting on his growth, a remark his mother shrugged aside with apparent disinterest. Patrick is large for his 7 weeks; Deirdre told me he weighed 10 pounds, 7 ounces, and ate "all the time." Throughout the session, Patrick slept soundly. Occasionally, Deirdre would look over to check on him; when she did so, however, her facial expression went blank and still.

As the session began, Deirdre volunteered a description of her son's changes over the past week. She said Patrick seemed to be getting fixed in his patterns. He was now awake for most of the day and asleep for 5 or 6 hours a night. I was delighted that Deirdre volunteered this information but wondered if she were aware of changes in Patrick's overall development or noticed changes because they simply made her life somewhat easier. "Do you see any changes in his patterns?"

"I think his patterns are more and more his own. He likes to eat often, many times a day. He's more alert, too," she said. "He watches what's going on more, even if he doesn't understand it. He keeps trying to smile. And he makes these faces." She wrinkled her nose to imitate one of her son's faces. This simulated face was a blended mask: the upper two-thirds was a contorted look of annoyance, impatience, and disgust, but the lower third showed something resembling a smile, though it seemed evident to me that the "smile" was a learned response of quasipropitiation to the certain anger of the infant's care provider. Although Deirdre called the expression a "mean face," in reality it was much more a plea face, a request and preupset face. In short, "meanness" had nothing at all to do with the expression as I saw it. Deirdre mechanically denied that Patrick's interaction with her appeared different from his interaction with others. "We're all the same to him, I guess," she added weakly.

Deirdre seemed determined to turn any responsibility for thoughts and feelings about her child away from herself. Whereas most mothers of young infants would state unequivocally that their child smiled for them or directed his or her cries toward them, Deirdre steadfastly denied this quality in Patrick.

Things at home were difficult for her, Deirdre continued, because she and Mike had been fighting a lot. She acknowledged that the presence of an infant in the house had made it difficult for her and Mike to find time alone together and that many small problems in their relationship had been magnified by the baby's presence. Deirdre's life revolved around "watching" Patrick during the day and attending AA meetings in the evening; Mike's life revolved around his work and AA meetings. These activities did not leave much time for their private relationship.

After several minutes of silence, Deirdre said rather loudly, "I want to say something: I thought about the film on feeding behavior you showed me last week." She continued in an aggrieved tone, stating that she thought the film had been intimidating and condescending. There was anger behind her words. "Do you know how hard is it to feed a baby?" she asked. "You give him the bottle, you wipe him up, and then you burp him." This was certainly an accurate description of her own terse feeding style. Deirdre clearly wasn't willing to have her parenting skills questioned or explored—perhaps because she sensed they were maladaptive.

I repeated her objections to the feeding film, then asked if Deirdre ever felt similarly intimidated. Did her mother, for example, try to correct her parenting behavior or impose her own views? Did Mike? The only time she ever felt uncomfortably scrutinized, she finally said, was when she and Mike took Patrick to AA meetings. "We have to take him because we both have to be there, and many nights Mom can't baby-sit [Deirdre had few illusions about her mother as an adequate caregiver]. If Patrick's quiet there's no problem, but if he starts fussing, I have to take him out in the hall. I'd really like to start an AA group just for parents with small children, because everyone would understand if your baby started screaming in the middle of things."

"Do you have any thoughts about leaving Patrick with an unfamiliar adult?" I asked.

Deirdre seemed perplexed. "No. Why would I?"

"Some parents fear that harm might come to their children with a babysitter. Just as some adults occasionally have fantasies of how they might accidentally hurt the child. Have you ever had such fantasies?"

"No," Deirdre said flatly, and then, "What do you mean by fantasies?"

I asked Deirdre if she had ever had fantasies about hurting her son, and she replied abruptly, "Yes, I have some, but I don't want to talk about them."

"They're frightening, those kinds of fantasies," I responded. "But I would like you to try to talk about them. That will help you from acting them out." I related an abusive fantasy in which one mother had fantasized that as she dressed her infant in his snowsuit she had pulled the drawstrings on the hood tighter and tighter until she had suffocated him. "Such fantasies don't mean that a parent doesn't love her child. In fact, this mother loved her infant very much." Despite encouragement and the assurance that none of her fantasies could be as dreadful as she herself imagined, Deirdre refused to disclose them. This refusal to discuss important relevant dream material indicated to me that Deirdre's resistance was strongly entrenched. Her blatant refusal indicated a desire to put increased distance between herself and her therapist.

## SESSION 6

In sharing her observations of Patrick's accomplishments during the week for this session, Deirdre noted that he had begun to feed more regularly, taking as much as 4 ounces at a feeding. When I asked at what point she intended to introduce solids into Patrick's diet, Deirdre said she hadn't thought about it; nor could she envision Patrick feeding himself. She also reported that he was beginning to imitate sounds. He had managed to make "a sound that sounded like 'Hi'" the day before. Asked how she had felt when she discovered that Patrick was imitating sounds, she gave her by now characteristic shrug and said, "It was funny. He got a strange look on his face, and then the sound came out. He looked as if he couldn't figure out where it had come from. Mike thought it was hysterical."

"In the future, he'll be talking and telling us what he feels and thinks," I commented.

"Maybe he'll be like me, not into talking," Deirdre replied. I have the distinct feeling that the more "retarded" or slow in development she can make the baby appear, the less responsibility she has to assume. It's "not her fault": The baby might just be laconic and taciturn and, thus, *not* able to tell the world what he wants and needs. This defense also has a lot to do with Deirdre's desire not to be challenged. She doesn't have to worry about *growing with the baby*, since if the baby is backward or slow or taciturn, he evidently *won't* grow speedily.

I wonder if Deirdre senses a link between Patrick's new imitation of sounds and her own terseness. I also wonder about the seeming connection between her dismissal of Patrick's future verbal skills and her inability to envision Patrick feeding himself. Saying that her son may be "like her" and dislike talking not only strengthens their identification, but it defuses the threat that Patrick will one day speak for himself, without needing his mother to speak for him. In much the same way, Deirdre may be reluctant to imagine the day when he is able to feed himself without her assistance. This suggests that she may be forming an enmeshed relationship with her son. Although she's maximally disinclined to investing emotion in him, she still denies his growing away from her (which his feeding himself would imply) and his eventual autonomy.

After a moment or two, I asked Deirdre to tell me about the visit to the pediatrician. She replied with her characteristic terseness, "Patrick is as strong as a horse. He's big for his age." Deirdre commented that in addition to his examination, Patrick had received some shots that day. When I noted that physical examinations could be potentially frightening for infants— "He's in a room with a stranger, without any control over the situation. Can you imagine being so small and helpless?"—Deirdre nodded. "It must be scary ... not understanding the world around you and not being able to get away from things," she said. "He doesn't know that what's going on now isn't going to last forever. He just knows what's happening to him right now." It was intriguing to me that Deirdre, who heretofore could not predict or envision her son's future, could at this moment speak so insightfully and perceptively of the baby's situation, one which echoes to some degree her own situation. For both are projections. It is not the baby who perceives what is or will not be happening. Deirdre, however, would appear to be making an unconscious parallel with her own condition here; she, herself, is unable to predict or envision her own future.

Patrick awoke at this point, murmuring sleepily and peering around the room. After a moment of eye contact with her son, Deirdre slumped backward and returned her focus to me. Her finger remained within Patrick's grasp, but it was as if her hand belonged to another person entirely. Patrick continued his fretting, until Deirdre settled him on her lap, located a bottle in her tote bag, and abruptly popped the nipple into Patrick's mouth. This time Patrick protested with hands and feet and began to cough. Deirdre adjusted her grip and more gently introduced the bottle to Patrick, who began to nurse contentedly. When he had finished feeding, he began to whine and fuss. Deirdre pulled on his head with one palm over each ear, put him on her shoulder, and began patting absently. Although Deirdre was more physically attuned to her son this week than I have ever seen, this gesture demonstrated that Deirdre has a long way to go in her understanding of adaptive and nurturing interactions.

## SESSION 7

Both Deirdre and her son had colds today. Patrick slept with his mouth open, his breathing loud during the occasional pauses in our conversation. When I entered the room, Deirdre sat slumped over, head down. She watched me cautiously, seemingly determined to participate only when necessary. Maybe as the psychotherapy unfolds, Deirdre resists interacting with Patrick in front of me. Last week I was cheered to see some evidence of improved interaction; this week, dyadic interaction appeared nonexistent. I asked Deirdre to relate any changes she might have observed in Patrick's development over the week. "Nothing happened," she responded dully.

After a brief silence I suggested, "Maybe there were some subtle changes; infants go through so many stages that it's hard to keep track of them all." I went on to outline briefly the difference between precursory behaviors and developmental milestones:

> For example, some months from now you may notice that Patrick is using his legs more, trying to hold himself up when you lift him. When he does this he will be coordinating his already attained skills so he can stand on his own. That's what we call a precursor to the actual milestone of standing—it's a hint or indication that a new skill is beginning to emerge. So when I ask you about changes, I'm asking about precursory behaviors as well as specific milestones.

I asked her to think about these "foundational skills" so that we might discuss them more at the next session. Given the apparent difficulty she has in predicting physical changes, I suspected it would be a while before Deirdre could consider mental and emotional growth or advances when discussing her son's development. For now, the failure of her ability to empathize or to recognize emergent growth patterns is still very evident.

Deirdre listened expressionlessly. "He's not doing anything different," she insisted. "He's eating the same and sleeping about the same."

"Have you recognized any pattern when he makes the 'Hi' sound?" I asked.

For a moment Deirdre looked blank. Then she nodded. "Yes, he's still doing it. Not very often," she qualified. She seemed detached and uninterested as her son slept. Despite continued encouragement, Deirdre insisted edgily that there had been no changes in Patrick over the week, finally saying "Patrick's been sick." In upcoming sessions, I planned to explore Deirdre's feelings about therapy and about me to understand better whether she viewed me as helper or critic of her caregiving efforts.

"Has it become difficult to take Patrick to the AA meetings?" I asked.

"Partly that, and partly I just need to be by myself sometimes. At AA it's hard because if Patrick starts crying, one of us has to take him out." Her strong feeling on this matter was obvious and her commitment to AA indicated that Deirdre was indeed capable of change.

Did she feel comfortable in leaving Patrick with his father? "Yes, Mike plays with Patrick a lot. He plays kind of rough with him, but Patrick likes it, I think." Deirdre's expression became wistful here, as if there were something special about the interaction between Patrick and his father. I asked if she could recognize any particular emotion when Mike and Patrick played together; Deirdre denied awareness of any special emotion, but the wistfulness in her expression remained.

After a moment's silence, Deirdre asked how much 9-week-old Patrick could understand of his parents' emotions. I said that rather than give her the standard answer for 9-week-old infants, we should address her perceptions regarding Patrick.

"I don't think he understands any of it," she replied, with her characteristic, deliberate sadness. "I wonder sometimes if the way I'm feeling makes him feel worse . . . I mean, if his restlessness rubs off on me and makes me feel bad, or if my anxiety rubs off on him and makes him feel bad." Asked how she had coped with Patrick's irritability, Deirdre was silent for a moment and looked at Patrick in the stroller. "I just kind of take a break. I put him down for 5 minutes and try to get calm." Withdrawal and remoteness, have been Deirdre's traditional responses to stressors. Her capacity to remove herself from personal interaction into a state of emotional isolation has until now provided her with an effective veil through which she could shield herself from the onslaughts of the outside world. With the challenge of her 9-week-old son, however, Deirdre's veil is no longer totally impregnable.

"When your mood changes does Patrick's mood also change?" I asked.

"I don't know. Sometimes I don't think I realize how stressed I am until he starts getting crazy, too." She said she realizes that Patrick is calming down when he stops whining and smiles. I am frequently startled by Deirdre's insight into her own behavior, and her sensitivity to Patrick's physical development and behavior. At the same time, her lackadaisical attitude in letting her 2-year-old niece pull Patrick around is distressing and certainly reflective of some latent hostility against the infant. Deirdre's reluctance to tune into Patrick's internal experience at this point definitely outweighs her occasional sophistication concerning Patrick's physical cues.

"When you're less overwhelmed, do you find it's easier to interact with Patrick?"

"Maybe. It takes him longer to calm down than me. And sometimes he needs to be changed or fed or something, which is part of what was making him upset," she said, returning to the issue to what for her remains the safer, less threatening physical realm.

The session was up. "Let's continue to discuss these issues at our next meeting," I said as we made our farewells.

## SESSION 8

Deirdre arrived neatly groomed, conveying the impression that she was happier and perhaps more emotionally accessible than she had been in several weeks. As I entered the room, Deirdre took Patrick from the stroller and seated him on her lap. Though his head lolled unsupported against her arm, he gave no sign of being uncomfortable; he watched his mother's fingers as she drummed them on her thigh—both sound and sight seemed to fascinate him. During the session, I noticed that each time she changed position, for the first time Deirdre would briefly look at Patrick; after that brief glimpse her focus would return to me.

The infant, now 10 weeks old, was demonstrating increasing alertness. Although he did not always respond to his mother's overtures, from his signals it was plain that he was aware of them. Patrick took advantage of his position on his mother's lap to observe his surroundings and examine them. When I commented on Patrick's alertness, Deirdre agreed. "Yes. He wants to be up more now. He really wants me to be around him more," she said, recognizing and acknowledging for the first time her son's need for interaction.

"It looks as if you and Patrick were playing a game with your fingers," I commented. She shrugged. "How do you feel when I bring up something I've observed, some interaction between you and Patrick?" I asked.

"Okay, I guess. If it's something like that, a game or something. If I was doing something wrong, I guess I wouldn't like it." She laughed nervously and went on. "He's got more control now and reaches for what he wants. Of course he can't get everything all the time." Once again, Deirdre's very simple language proves quite revealing. For as Patrick's physical control progresses, Deirdre's emotional control and her willingness to risk meaningful emotional contact with an "outsider" are also advancing—ever so hesitantly—but moving forward nonetheless.

"What do these new skills mean to you?" I asked. Deirdre looked blank, so I elaborated. "In the near future, how do you imagine you will feel when Patrick is able to reach anything he wants?" I asked.

Deirdre shrugged. "I guess I won't have to get things for him when he can take care of himself. That'll be nice. But I really haven't thought about it much," she stated flatly, as though, having inched forward and tested the reactive environment, she now would retreat to the safety of dull, unfeeling isolation.

"What about when he learns to crawl and starts exploring things around the house?" I asked.

Deirdre lapsed into silence; she now seemed plainly uninterested (or perhaps overwhelmed) in considering the impact of her son's development on her life. "I don't know. I guess when I need to, I will." Asked what other developmental milestones lay ahead, she replied like one deeply retreated into her protective shell of indifference, "I don't know. I guess he'll start walking and eating real food. I don't think about it much." Asked if she could imagine Patrick feeding himself, Deirdre shook her head, insisting, "I'm not good at imagining things like that." Here, Deirdre herself succinctly identifies the depth of her dysfunction—her abject, defensive refusal to preview both her own son's development and, indeed, any emotional responses to external events in her own life.

Taking a new tack, I asked Deirdre if she could think of any reason, other than general lack of imagination, why it was so hard for her to predict her son's future. "You're becoming more skilled at observing Patrick's current skills. It occurred to me that something might be stopping you from making projections about the future," I suggested. "Can you think of anything?"

Deirdre stared at her lap. "What's the point?" she announced at last, in an angry tone, revealing an underlying sense of despair. "He's going to do whatever he's going to do. My planning it in advance won't change anything." In her lap, Patrick waved one arm irritably, alternately clutching and rejecting Deirdre's finger. Deirdre looked down at the baby and stroked his hand gently. The tension and irritation evident a moment before seemed to have dissipated; now her expression was absorbed and somber.

Perhaps because of the presence of these adaptive behaviors, I was aware of a new dynamic between mother and infant: a physical exchange in which each action reciprocated proportionately the other person's action. This was the first evidence I had seen of such a "dialogue" between mother and son, but it was a dialogue that seemed vaguely like a contest, as if each participant were trying to assert dominance over the other.

After a moment of silence, I shifted the discussion to Deirdre's recent dreams. She related one dream in which she and Mike were in bed asleep. "While I was dreaming, I woke up terrified because in the dream the baby was in the bed with us and had suffocated under the sheets." Curiously, in her dreams, Deirdre is able to achieve what she dare not risk in a waking state—she can view herself as an observer from a yet deeper layer of consciousness from which she realizes a desire to "wake up," albeit "terrified," from the veil or "sheet" of emotional remoteness that is suffocating her psyche and not permitting her the breath of meaningful human interaction.

When asked to interpret her dream, Deirdre refused all but the most simplistic analysis, saying only that it must have something to do with how actively Patrick was "getting into stuff." Along those lines, I suggested an alternative interpretation, that the dream might indicate that Deirdre had some unconscious fear of hurting the baby. She shrugged and laughed. "Those fears aren't unconscious. I know they're there." Her admission provides therapeutic access. Before, in earlier sessions, she'd denied recognizing certain evident feelings or would simply refuse to relate (what we now see to be the explosive) material in her dreams. At this turning point, Deirdre finally relates the dream. And she risks saying some things that indicate she is far more alert to social dynamics than she led me to believe earlier. But although she is willing to relate her troubling dream, Deirdre is still not capable of any in-depth explorations. When asked to explain how she thought she might hurt her son, she resisted, shrugging again and retreated into "I don't know."

"Do you worry about someone else hurting the baby?" I asked.

Deirdre shook her head. "Not really. It was okay last week when my family was visiting and wanted to play with him. I felt left out; everyone crowds around and wants to play with the baby, and I'm just holding him, like I'm not really there." Increasingly, in her clumsy and vague responses, we sense the rudiments of emergent feelings and emotions in Deirdre. She hints at what frightens her so—"everyone crowds around"—that she is forced to defend with an almost flattened affect "like I'm not really there." Clearly, life has been so threatening for Deirdre that she has preferred to remain a shadow—able to vanish emotionally at the slightest threat of intimacy. Her feelings of insecurity are definitely beginning to surface. Yet as her parenting becomes more competent, she runs the risk (in her mind's eye) of being subsumed, lost at the picnic. As her healthy child becomes the major focus, she again becomes marginalized, in her estimation, as she had been before.

Deirdre looked down at her son and shifted his position, as if it suddenly occurred to her that he was not comfortable. Patrick continued to be restless, his glance traveling everywhere in the room except to his mother's face. Then, for a moment, when Deirdre shifted and glanced at him, Patrick was quiet, studying his mother's face. The moment her visual gaze was diverted, however, his fidgeting began again.

"He hasn't had his afternoon nap today," she added apologetically, as Patrick began to fret loudly. Deirdre shifted Patrick to one side and reached into her bag for a bottle. She demonstrated considerable improvement in feeding competence, holding the baby in a close embrace that was more supportive than any she had demonstrated in the past. Her physical interaction with Patrick was more attuned to his comfort and less like that of someone holding an inanimate object. Although the sense of warmth between the dyad was minimal, there was some feeling of connectedness, as if the two were united in a purposeful activity. For a few minutes Patrick appeared comfortable. Deirdre picked the baby up and draped him over her shoulder. Poised there, the infant seemed at ease, relaxing and closing his eyes. Within a few minutes, he fell asleep.

## SESSION 9

After the apparent progress the dyad had demonstrated in the last session, I was hoping to see further adaptive manifestations. At the start of the session, however, both mother and infant appeared quiet. This was explained in part by Deirdre's initial statement that her brother and his family had just returned to Ireland the day before. Deirdre said she was exhausted as a result of their stay.

Patrick, now 11 weeks old, was alert and curious, gazing around him. Physically he appeared strong. His psychomotor skills, including reaching and grasping, appeared to be well developed for his age. His personal-social skills, as reflected by his reactions to both his mother and to me, also appeared to be age appropriate—he smiled responsively and spontaneously, and his curiosity was easily aroused by sounds and visual stimuli. This might be a reflection of my interventions, the work of Patrick's father, and the contributions (however dubiously received) of Deirdre's mother. Otherwise, it would be rare to see such an emotionally deprived environment producing such age-appropriate development.

As the session started, Deirdre held Patrick against her chest. He sat there quietly, running his hand up and down the arm that held him in place. At one point she looked down as Patrick began to suck on his fist. "He's found his fist!" she said with a wry laugh. "He sucks on it all the time." Asked if he "likes it," Deirdre said he must, since he had been sucking on it "constantly." She described his happiness when he did it, saying it was like a game for him.

Whereas Deirdre now appears to be handling Patrick with more assurance and demonstrates some physical competence, including monitoring and eye contact, her interactions with her child are still devoid of emotion and warmth. "My 3-year-old niece really liked playing with the baby last week," Deirdre volunteered. I asked how they played together, hoping she wasn't still pulling Patrick around by his arms and legs.

"Oh, mostly Sheila would talk to him or make faces. I think he liked their accents." Deirdre said this last sentence in a perfect Irish brogue. At the sound, Patrick looked up, his eyes round in apparent surprise. Deirdre, seeing this, looked down at him and said in the same brogue, "Yes, we're talking about you, aren't we?" This was the first time during a session that Deirdre had, without my prompting, spoken directly to her son while gazing at him. After a few moments the conversation faded as she and Patrick studied each other. Then Deirdre sighed and gathered the baby to her chest with a cuddling gesture.

In the future I intend to encourage her increasing interaction with other parents as a strategy for enriching Deirdre's behavioral repertoire.

## SESSION 10

As is sometimes the case with very young children, Patrick seemed to have grown considerably since the previous week. He appeared larger, and his verbalizations had taken on a real eloquence. His physical and psychomotor development had improved significantly. Not only did he have no trouble sitting with support, but his motor control had progressed noticeably, as evidenced by the facility with which he turned to respond to sudden noises, by his increasing reaching and clutching, and by his general skill in controlling his body. In addition, I was impressed with how "related" Patrick was able to interact and to sustain interaction with me as well as with his mother.

By contrast, Deirdre looked rested and relaxed, although not free of the intangible aura of sadness that always seems to cling to her. She smiled when I entered, then ducked her head down, as if uncertain that smiling was appropriate. Asked to discuss her son's developmental gains in the last week, Deirdre—as was her pattern—drew a blank. "Nothing much has changed," she said at first, and then, hesitantly, "He's smiling." Remarkable in her statement is the fact that she can dispassionately discuss her sentiments of change or developmental milestones achieved, yet one never hears her say that she *loves* her son.

"Can you make him smile?" I asked.

Deirdre shrugged and said she could try. She leaned over and rubbed her nose against the side of Patrick's face. Her expression as she did this was serious and unsmiling, but her handling of Patrick seemed gentle. Patrick, feeling the tickling sensation of his mother's touch, turned his head to the touched side and raised his eyebrows. Both his hands clenched and un-clenched, but his posture remained relaxed, supported by his mother's hands. Deirdre leaned back to see the effect of her gentle playing on the baby. Although Patrick appeared to enjoy the contact, he did not smile.

"Usually he smiles if I do this," Deirdre said apprehensively.

"It's okay. He's in a different place, so his reactions may be a little differ-ent," I said. "Have you discovered other things that make him smile?"

"If I make strange noises sometimes. That gets him talking." Asked to ex-plain, she said, "He can't really talk yet. He's only a few months old." Her choppy, fractionated statements continue to reveal a lack of connection be-tween Deirdre and her baby. Certainly as her therapist, I, of all people, real-ize he's an infant. Deirdre's fragmented maternal conception and orchestrat-ing of events are a reflection of the paucity of the maternal communication operative here in general, and thus it is difficult for Patrick to overcome chal-lenges and master events. When she was reassured on this subject, Deirdre relaxed and explained: "He just makes sounds. He's a real talker. My brother's kids were talking to him all the time, and he started making noises at them. Sometimes it sounded like talking, sometimes it sounded like singing."

"Where do you think this verbalization will lead Patrick?" I asked.

"It doesn't lead anywhere—he's not saying anything yet," she said. Asked if she thought Patrick's sounds now could be precursors of speech, Deirdre agreed that this was possible. I asked her permission to make a noise directed to Patrick and leaned toward the infant. Patrick immediately fo-cused on me, clearly engaged and curious. When I repeated the noise, he smiled broadly, flapping his arms and vocalizing with a crowing sound. Deirdre watched the exchange between Patrick and me for a few minutes, smiling tentatively at the infant's apparent pleasure.

"How do you feel when Patrick 'talks' or 'sings'?" I asked at last.

Deirdre appeared flustered. "I don't know. I'm not a big talker," she said. I commented that Patrick was also sitting up much more strongly. Deirdre smiled, clearly viewing the comment as a compliment. When I asked whether his sitting up represented a developmental milestone for her, she shrugged and said nothing. When I asked Deirdre to predict Patrick's next maturational accomplishment, she replied impatiently, "I don't know. Going to college, maybe."

Her sarcasm here poorly masked a real fear. Deirdre's almost willful blindness to Patrick's newly emerging skills and her concomitant inability to nurture those behaviors as they move toward consolidation may be her strategy for slowing her son's maturation. I must now consider how much of Patrick's fussiness may be provoked by Deirdre as a way to rein in his devel-opment and thus delay the separation she fears. "I know you're kidding," I responded. "But it's interesting that Patrick's physical accomplishment suggests that he is slowly gaining independence and autonomy."

Deirdre said nothing. There was a pause, during which Deirdre's stiff posture and slumped shoulders gradually relaxed. For the next several minutes Deirdre held her right hand at Patrick's side, at such an angle that the infant could play with his mother's hand. As conversation resumed, this game continued, until Deirdre was playing with Patrick's hand. During this tactile exchange, Deirdre would casually glance at her son. It was certainly true that her interaction with the baby had considerably improved. She even appeared to take some physical pleasure during the interaction with Patrick.

"I notice that Patrick is much more involved in the session today," I commented.

With a sulking expression, Deirdre agreed. When I expressed some surprise, saying that I would have thought she would be pleased at her infant's progress, Deirdre shrugged. "Wasn't he involved last time?"

"What I said was meant as a compliment, but you heard it as a criticism— as if I were saying something is wrong. Why?" I asked.

Deirdre looked at me. "I guess it isn't as if something's wrong with Patrick, but as if something is wrong with me. If I was doing everything right he'd be more involved." For a moment a flash of distress and sadness crossed Deirdre's features. I am concerned again that Deirdre's fear that she is nurturing incorrectly will affect her nurturing skills. The wish to improve her parenting abilities is a positive one, but unless her apprehension is checked, she may begin to resent her baby. Still, we are working toward a decided improvement in Deirdre's parenting skills. Her expressed interest here to "do everything right" is leagues better than her neutral affect and expressed disinterest in our early sessions. As quickly as it had come, the expression of distress vanished, and Deirdre's expression once more became neutral. Squirming in her seat, Deirdre lowered her head and stated, "I wonder sometimes how much he picks up. I wonder if my sickness affects him and he knows about it." Her reality-based mention of her "sickness" here shows additional improvement in Deirdre's condition, especially considering her denial of any adverse influence of parental mood on her infant expressed in previous sessions.

I took this opportunity to explore the implications of Deirdre's illness for her child, asking how she thought she would explain her illness and whether she feared that her illness might make it difficult for her to cope with Patrick's needs. Deirdre acknowledged that she was afraid that her illness could make her "helpless" with the baby—particularly when he was being "a pest"—that is, fussy or demanding.

I noted that we had not had an opportunity to discuss any further her questions—how much could Patrick understand of her mood or the moods of others around him, and how much might he "pick up" of her emotional condition. Deirdre smiled apologetically and responded with apparent relief that it was almost time for the session to end. It is interesting to note that she is cleverer now at evading difficult challenges to her parenting competence by nonreactive measures. Now, rather than state directly that she won't relate a dream or engage in defensive dissimulation, she skips out at the end of a session as if "school's out!" and any challenge posed too close to "the bell" is not necessary to answer.

## SESSION 11

Today Patrick sat upright on his mother's lap, but with support, peering around curiously. Deirdre noted that he had refused to nap earlier and that "he [was] going to be a handful today." As she said these words, Patrick began a low, fretful murmuring, which continued almost throughout the session. "He doesn't want to lie around as much. He wants to sit up all the time now," Deirdre said firmly and as though she resented this new shift in emotional status her son's developmental prowess might herald. Control definitely promises to become a prominent issue in this relationship. When asked to remark on recent developmental changes, she also mentioned cautiously that he had been trying to sit up by himself. I remarked to Deirdre that her observance of precursory behaviors had improved. "Your helping him to sit up may be a form of previewing or rehearsing this behavior with him," I added.

I asked if Deirdre had had any recent thoughts about Patrick's development. Somewhat reluctantly, Deirdre said that she had actually been wondering if a baby could know what was going on in her head? "Can he tell if I'm upset, or if Mike and I have had a fight?"

"For a baby there is nothing in the world as important as his relationship with the person who takes care of him—for Patrick, that's you. Since that relationship is so important to him, he 'monitors' it intensely to make sure that things are all right with you," I said.

Deirdre shook her head. "Sometimes I think he takes that part too seriously. You should see the way he yells to get my attention." Asked if she felt he was too sensitive, she looked thoughtful. "I guess I wouldn't mind if he was a little less sensitive. Then maybe my illness wouldn't affect him too much. As it is, sometimes I feel like everything makes him yell." Asked if he always yelled for attention, Deirdre said sometimes he waved. "I guess when he's yelling he needs something. Even if it's just to go to sleep." Still we have some progress here in Deirdre's recognition of possible impact of her own emotional terrain on her child.

Patrick, who had been sitting quietly on Deirdre's lap, began to fuss again. After asking if it was all right, Deirdre brought several toys over and sat on the floor playing with Patrick. The infant immediately clutched the plastic rattle. While I watched Patrick's play, Deirdre stared absently. When I commented that she looked pensive, she said that she had been thinking it would be easy if she could deal with Mike the way she dealt with Patrick. "I can explain things to Mike that the baby doesn't understand, but sometimes I wish I could just set limits and not have Mike answer back."

"Can you explain what you mean by limits?" I asked.

"We used to be together a lot, and now that there's three of us, we aren't. I miss that. When Mike's around we're either at AA, or he's playing with the baby, or we're asleep." Deirdre's face softened as she spoke. "Mike had a motorcycle when we met, and we'd take long drives. We can't do that any-more," she said. "It's rough. We had known each other for about 4 months when we joined AA, and a month after that, I got pregnant. We didn't really have a chance to be a couple before we became a family, and neither of us had a lot of experience at being responsible. I wonder sometimes if he'd just rather chuck it all," she opined, possibly forecasting the resistance her desire to control Mike might soon begin to engender.

"Have you thought about it in terms of yourself?"

She shrugged. "Sometimes. I'm lucky that Mike's around. He's the one who evens things out when I'm crazy," she said perceptively—for the first time vocalizing the enormous pressure she has placed herself under in an at-tempt to maintain her state of emotional void. It occurs to me that, as easy as it would be to focus solely on the dysfunctional aspects of this case, it will be increasingly important to identify with Deirdre that many of the issues she faces are common to virtually all parents and not a function of her own emo-tional involution. In parting, she commented wistfully to me that she won-dered how much of her frustration was due to her "craziness."

## SESSION 12

Once we had settled in the treatment room and Patrick was comfortable in his mother's lap, I asked Deirdre about changes she had noticed in the past week. As usual, Deirdre was reluctant to commit herself, but she finally said she thought Patrick was beginning to reach and point to things. "He knows the bottle by now, because he reaches for it when he sees it coming." When I commented that she sounded a little sad at this development, she de-nied any sadness. "When he gets to the point where he doesn't need me to feed him, I'll have more time for myself," she countered defensively. On a seemingly unrelated note, she "casually" mentioned that Mike had been working long hours during the last 2 weeks, leaving Deirdre alone with the baby for extended periods.

"Have you felt lonely?" I asked.

Deirdre shrugged. "I don't mind being alone." Suddenly, in a surpris-ingly analytic mode for Deirdre, she noted, "I think Mike reads my signals better than he does Patrick's. Mike can always calm me down. We're lucky because we didn't get used to doing things one way before the baby came." Then breathlessly, "Mike is my best friend," she finished emphatically. Her lengthy (for Deirdre) exegesis here demonstrates her new willingness to share and her increasing promise as an analysand. Earlier sessions had failed to reveal the depth of feeling she harbored for Mike. Now, she is free with warm asides and open endorsement of the baby's father. The prognosis for this family unit now appears much improved.

The issue of loneliness is one Deirdre and I would address in the future. I suspected that, aside from the sheer amount of time Deirdre spent alone with her son, the greatest source of loneliness in Deirdre's life came from her fear of competition for Patrick's attention. This presents for her a distinct emotional dilemma. Does she feel that the interaction between her son and his father jeopardizes her own relationship with Patrick? Is she previewing (the very act of which represents an enormous step forward for her) abandonment resulting from Mike's interaction with her son? Although she acknowledges readily that she "reads Patrick's signals" better than Mike does, and that she's better with the baby, still, Deirdre the child-mother picks up on the vague possibility of anybody she loves abandoning her as her brother and father did so many years before.

Thus, my current aim is to focus on changing her expectations and making them more reality oriented. She must learn to realize that, because the past offered certain difficulties insofar as abandonment, this does not necessarily mean the past is a magical predictor of the future course of events. Future sessions will be directed at strengthening Deirdre's ability to reject such puerile cognitive fabrications based on fear and hopelessness (a hopelessness so profound as to have almost totally blunted her affect) and to foster an emergent egocentric-based reality.

Patrick began to fuss. He is exquisitely sensitive to his mother's emotions, and his behavior at times seems to be another voice for Deirdre's uneasiness, anger, or unhappiness. In that position, Patrick began to protest more loudly. For the next 5 minutes, Deirdre went through an almost robotic series of motions, offering Patrick the pacifier and removing it when he rejected it; shifting him from her shoulder to her lap, then back into the stroller. Throughout these efforts, her expression grew increasingly tight and her gestures more mechanical. At first each change of position soothed Patrick, but toward the end he cried constantly. By the time Deirdre returned Patrick to her arms, his entire body was tense and resistant, his face was congested with crying, and he kept avoiding Deirdre's gaze. I suddenly sensed the peculiar close enmeshment of this apparently distanced dyad. Deirdre picks up on many of her son's signals, interpreting them not as simple communications about his needs but as "accusations" or reproaches. In response to those "accusations" she may even try to thwart his desires as a way of demonstrating her own autonomy, effectively saying to him, "You can't boss me around!" or, more fundamentally, "You can't abandon me as long as I am in control!"

Eventually Patrick quieted down and clung to his mother. He's just an edgy kid, she volunteered, "You know: Get him comfortable, and 5 minutes later, he wants something different." Her own interpretation was clear: The infant was mirroring his mother's own demeanor, an attitude that was distinctly distant and "edgy." Therefore, her infant, too, became "edgy." Deirdre's strategy here represents a less sophisticated recognition of a common dyadic phenomenon.

The child's crying then might also represent *empathic distress:* His mother wanted to but could not express her own profound sadness and need to cry at the prospect of her abandonment so many years before, but the infant obligingly cues into this distress and begins to manifest the crying his mother cannot express. It is small wonder that Patrick refuses to be comforted!

## SESSION 13

When I arrived for today's session, I found Deirdre gazing out the window. Patrick lay in the stroller, apparently just waking, waving his arms, and occasionally kicking. I commented on his motor control, and Deirdre laughed quietly, "Yes, he's getting to be a real tough guy." Now 17 weeks old, Patrick's gross and fine motor skills are age appropriate or even slightly precocious. The infant's insistent striving to stand, to make himself physically independent from his mother, is—at 17 weeks—definitely in advance of the norm. His personal and social skills seem appropriate as well. In terms of prelanguage skills, he laughs and vocalizes in a manner that is age appropriate but to a lesser degree than many infants his age. He responds to voices, and particularly to someone calling his name, randomly. It is too early to say whether this is a deficit or merely a more slowly developing skill.

Today's session began with a discussion of developmental changes Deirdre had noticed in Patrick. Deirdre's attention focused on physical changes. "He's really getting coordinated; he has started clapping his hands." She noted, however, that he was not yet coordinated enough to bring whatever he was holding into his mouth. I asked how this inability affected Patrick. Deirdre responded that Patrick became frustrated when he couldn't get his hands "to do what he wants them to do." She looked sideways at Patrick, still lying in the stroller.

"He really wants to stand up," she noted at last. "He's always trying to push off with his legs like that," she added, nodding at Patrick's expression of intense concentration.

"What do you make of the fact that he is working so hard to stand up?" I asked.

Deirdre shrugged. "It's nice that he can sit up alone now," she said finally. Once again, Deirdre answers grudgingly and indirectly, as if she still feels that her son's progress is at her expense. This is a barometer I've been following since our first meeting. Thus, when presented with evidence that the child is making developmental headway, rather than acknowledge this milestone or the interpersonal sequelae of this change, she reluctantly admits only to a lesser achievement. (If Patrick can do less, there is less chance of her being left alone by another important figure in her life.) "I don't have to hold him any more," she said abruptly. Indeed, her casual grasp served more to keep Patrick from sliding off her lap than to support him. "I think Pat's development is good; I want him to be able to explore. When he starts getting around on his own, I guess we're really going to have to keep track of him."

She uses the nickname "Pat" for the first time, which would seem to indicate a progression toward accepting her infant into her day-to-day cosmogony and at the same time shows a casual affection not overly evident in most of our sessions. I hope to address Deirdre's sense of the speed at which developmental milestones are attained, so that she does not, for example, encourage Patrick to walk precociously. Despite Deirdre's uncertainty about the benefits of Patrick's ongoing physical development, this was one of the first times she had predicted anything about that development. The small improvement in Deirdre's predictive abilities, along with the impact these improvements have had on the overall functioning of the dyad, clearly leaves room for improvement and does not mean that all signs of improvement are straightforward. Her unconscious wish to control the pace of development, for instance, still shows her reluctance to face the child's eventual autonomy despite the fact she claims she "wants him to be able to explore." The distance that she was curtailing, again, by her evocative use of the nickname Pat also shows decided improvement in Deirdre's function. Her further improved ability to relate to Mike (and to me in sessions as well as outside of therapy) demonstrates a type of indirect functional achievement.

We will be carefully monitoring these and other barometers of achievement and progress in future sessions. For now, I decided to explore the subject of independence further.

"It's interesting to note that Patrick is developing on a lot of different levels now—the hand clapping is one milestone; the pushing with his feet is another precursory behavior; and sitting alone is yet another achievement. I'm also pleased at how much more open you are at previewing upcoming developmental skills and discussing Patrick's future accomplishments," I complimented Deirdre, who smiled shyly. "I'd like to spend some time talking about what you think the ultimate goal of all this development is and what it means for your relationship with Patrick," I continued. When Deirdre looked blank, I said, "Some mothers feel that when their infants start to walk, it means the beginning of separation between them."

Without pausing to consider the idea, Deirdre negated it. "I don't think anything will get any different," she said, apparently disquieted that issues related to separation were being related to distress. She returned instead to the idea that Patrick's multiplying physical abilities would mean he would be able to amuse himself for longer periods of time, saying that would be helpful because she and Mike were talking about a trip to Ireland. Her father in Ireland had never seen the baby. As she described their plans for the trip, Patrick began to fuss, starting with a low-pitched negative vocalization that quickly became a series of loud cries. Deirdre drew a bottle from her bag and began to feed him. Immediately the infant quieted, reaching up to touch his mother's hand. This exchange had a definite sense of communication to it, in contrast to the dyad's earlier feeding behavior. It is evident from their interaction that Patrick and his mother are forming a strong attachment, but with ambivalent overtones, characterized by some power struggles within the dyad.

"I'm very impressed with your improved feeding skills," I told her. "Are you aware that there has been a change?"

"What kind of change?" Deirdre asked.

"You seem more focused on Patrick, and you seem to be comfortable interpreting his signals."

Deirdre turned to look at her son seriously. "I think it's both of us, together," she said at last. "I think maybe it's because he's getting older and we communicate more."

"It's good," I confirmed, smiling.

Deirdre voluntarily returned to the topic of separation. "When we moved here from Ireland when I was a kid, I felt that was when I separated from my parents. I was really angry at the move, and I just broke away from my parents. When my Dad and mother got divorced, I guess that was another separation." After discussing this move, she finished, "I don't think separation is bad," revealing her continued resistance to tackling the significance of this topic for her. "I really don't think much about being separated from Patrick. I don't think he really misses me when I'm not around, anyway. I wouldn't want him to." Here Deirdre smiled inappropriately. As the attachment between them grows stronger, separation may no longer be an issue that can be so easily dismissed by Deirdre.

## SESSION 14

When Deirdre spoke today, there was a sense of excitement in her voice. It was not obvious whether the source of the excitement was pleasurable or negative. For the moment Patrick seemed unaware of his mother's mood: He lay on his back with one fist clenched close to his mouth. Deirdre began the session by saying that Patrick put everything in his mouth now. "I've started him on some solid food," she added. "So far, so good."

As if aware that he was being discussed, Patrick awakened and examined his fist. Both Deirdre and I watched Patrick for a moment or two. Then I asked if I could hold the infant. Deirdre agreed and picked him up to hand him to me. She seemed to find it easier to interact playfully with her son when someone else led the way. As she watched Patrick, she smiled. When I encouraged him to notice his mother, saying "Look, Patrick, where's your Mommy?" Deirdre smiled broadly and said "Hey, Pat, what's up?" At the sound of his mother's voice, the baby turned and his smile broadened. Deirdre lowered her eyes so that her face was effectively masked from her son's view by her hair. Then she slowly raised her face, smiling when she met Patrick's eyes. Patrick responded by imitating her action. There was no further reinforcement of this mimicking game—no applause or rewarding smile from Deirdre—but it appeared that both participants were pleased with each other. He continued to play as Deirdre sat back in her chair and said that she had an announcement to make: "I'm pregnant again."

Her expression to this statement was mixed. She was clearly watching to see my reaction, yet gave no clear signals concerning her own feelings. I asked how she had discovered that she was pregnant. Deirdre said that the pregnancy followed some confusion about her menstrual cycle, which had been irregular since Patrick's birth. "I started on the pill 6 weeks after Pat was born, and 2 weeks later I got my period and then again 3 weeks later. So I wasn't sure when I should be taking the pill." Her attitude was slightly defensive, as if she feared a reproach for not having been more careful. "So then I went to the doctor. When she said I was pregnant, it, it scared the hell out of me." I asked her to explain why she was so scared. "I wasn't expecting it. I've already got a child, and he keeps me going all the time. Imagine what I'd be like with two." She had thought about an abortion, she said, but Mike was strongly against it, and her own feeling was that she did not want to go through that experience again. "It's just that, with two kids, you really have to settle down. Money's already tight, and this won't make it any easier." She added that her mother had been strongly against this pregnancy, implying that she would not be willing to have Deirdre, Mike, Patrick, and a second child living in her house. "We've been hoping to find our own place, and we've been talking about maybe getting married. We just weren't planning on this."

Deirdre reported that she and Mike had then decided to visit her father in Ireland—"before it gets too difficult to travel." Had she informed her father about her new pregnancy? I asked. She had not, Deirdre said. She anticipated that he would have a hard time adjusting. Her father had been vehemently against Patrick's birth. Deirdre appeared very uncomfortable when talking about her father. She shifted uneasily in her chair. Her father thought she was still a crazy teenager. When she had become pregnant with Patrick, her father had volunteered to support her through her pregnancy until she could deliver her son and give him up for adoption.

"In a way, your decision not to give him up for adoption separates you even more from your father, doesn't it?" I asked. Deirdre agreed but shied away from further discussion of her father, returning to her own surprise at discovering the pregnancy. Deirdre denied that her shock at the news had had any particular impact on Patrick and was not ready to consider the idea that Patrick had picked up on the emotional turmoil the pregnancy had caused her. "I don't see anything changing between Pat and me. I get tired more easily, because of the pregnancy, that's all."

Asked what he did at such times, Deirdre responded that he "cries, or yells, or grabs me." Deirdre took the baby to sit in her lap and said, "What are you yelling about, huh?" Patrick stared up at his mother, as if he were attempting to maneuver himself up to a standing position. When Deirdre held him so that he was "standing" on her lap, the baby crowed with pleasure. Deirdre herself appeared to take pleasure in her son's enjoyment but made no communicative or imitative vocal overtures to him at this point. "He's showing a precursory behavior," Deirdre remarked.

"That's right. You're showing him what it will be like when he can stand on his own. You're also signaling to him that it's okay with you that he's making this progress in development. That kind of support is very important to him."

"I guess so. It's just a game to him, anyway," she said, negating the significant progress this represented for Patrick. Using the term "just" once again *under*estimates Patrick's development, the way Deirdre has in the past, so often, derogated or diminished her son's achievements. In so doing, she unconsciously minimizes his growth and autonomy, thereby maximizing his dependence on her and putting less distance between them (so she will feel less alone, less abandoned).

In the future, I will focus on other such usages as a barometer for Deirdre's progress in these issues of emotional autonomy and age-appropriate ego development.

Although I feel cautiously optimistic about Deirdre's gains, I am concerned about the effect of this unplanned pregnancy on the existing dyad. An issue to explore in upcoming sessions would be whether Deirdre conceived this child to safeguard herself against the impending separation of Patrick's burgeoning development. Moreover, this pregnancy—in the face of a shortage of funds and an inconstant relationship, a fear of enmeshing herself further in motherly responsibilities, and the disapproval of her relatives—is a strong suggestion, in fact, of how much she still fears abandonment.

In contrast to what it was in the past, Deirdre's demeanor now, despite difficulties, is one of far greater reality recognition. Whereas before she had been withholding in her sessions and unwilling even to consider various options, now she seemed to have achieved an intermediate and optimistic stage where she was both more forthright in her therapy exchanges with me and almost eager to consider options as they presented themselves.

## SESSION 15

Patrick was in a lively, playful mood today. His mother, by contrast, seemed listless, happier to watch her son's interaction with me than to initiate any interaction with him herself. With Patrick now close to 5 months old, he could look forward to having a younger sibling before he was a year old. When I mentioned this, Deirdre looked up at me and shook her head, saying she had not stopped to figure out the age difference. "I guess he'll have someone to play with," she added. I asked if Deirdre had had any further thoughts about her pregnancy. She stated that Mike's parents had flown in from Florida to take Deirdre and Mike out for a celebration. During that evening both parents had put considerable pressure on Mike and Deirdre to marry.

"How does Mike feel about that?" I asked.

Deirdre shrugged, saying that both she and Mike had been thinking about marriage and had decided that they would marry in the fall. "Right now we're worried about the new baby and finding a new apartment. It's really tough to think about planning a wedding in the middle of all that." Patrick made repeated efforts to stand up on his mother's lap. Deirdre was evidently prepared for this behavior; whereas she did not assist him in standing, as she had done the week before, she did not permit him to fall off her lap, retrieving him with an air of weary amusement each time the baby wobbled. It appears that, given overtly distinct physical cues, Deirdre is honing her predictive capacities. Absent such cues, however, she still cannot predict the more immediate developmental stages. Or she chooses, in some sense, to display a selective blindness not to do so.

I asked about changes she had noticed during the week. "He's really trying to stand up. And he can lie on his belly now and sort of swim around with his head up. He'll roll from side to side, though he can't make it all the way over onto his back yet. And he's learned how to slide out of his stroller. I knew that was coming, and then last Saturday I caught him at it, and he was halfway to the floor. Since then I strap him in."

Patrick, now seated on my lap, smiled up at me, then grabbed my tie, raising it to his mouth. As he played he became increasingly excited, occasionally squealing with pleasure. Finally the infant began to noisily suck on one of my fingers. "I know what that means," Deirdre said, settling her son back in her lap. She reached into her bag, brought out a bottle, and offered it to Patrick, who began to nurse eagerly. I commented that Deirdre had known exactly what her son wanted and asked if this was his regular feeding time. She said that because her own schedule was dictated so much by Mike's irregular hours and by their attendance at AA meetings, it was difficult to establish a real routine. "I think that's why Patrick has trouble with his own patterns." I suggested that Deirdre might want to set aside a few activities—play time, bath time, even time to massage her son—which would occur at the same time every day, to give Patrick a sense of predictable and controllable events in his life.

The pressure that others such as Mike's parents and her own mother were exerting appeared to be too much for Deirdre to handle. Even the adaptive behavior I observed at last week's session seemed to have vanished. I was concerned that much of the good work that Deirdre had accomplished over the last 3 months might be undone by a second pregnancy. At this point, feeling her to be at a crucial developmental stage of readiness, I had decided to become more directive in exploring Deirdre's predictive abilities; thus I asked her questions that might be viewed as more open-ended (and coercive of predictive responses) than in past sessions.

"How old will Patrick be when you don't have to take him everywhere with you?"

Deirdre shrugged. "When he starts school, I guess. When he's 7, maybe?" she replied unrealistically. She seemed unperturbed, as if the notion of a new baby was insulating her from her fears of separating from Patrick. I asked Deirdre several questions about Patrick's progress and particularly about the changes the pregnancy would create in their relationship. As in the past, Deirdre appeared to have difficulty assimilating Patrick's point of view. Each time I suggested something—that Patrick might regret the loss of her attention or that he was able to sense that she was thinking about something new—Deirdre agreed noncommittally. When I asked if she thought Patrick had come to associate her behavior immediately before a familiar routine— her reaching for the bottle immediately before he was fed, for example— Deirdre agreed with some alacrity.

"He recognizes the bottle, I think. And he knows when he's going to get a bath because I always put him on the bathroom counter beforehand, and he starts laughing."

I suggested that Deirdre might want to observe Patrick's behavior even before he saw the bottle or was placed on the bathroom counter. "You may be able to tell whether he expects you to understand his signals. How do you think he feels when you feed him or bathe him?"

"When he gets all excited? I think he likes that he's gotten me to do something he wants," she said, recognizing the potential for confrontation over the issue of control within the dyad. Deirdre noted that when he was not able to get something he wanted, Patrick would fuss unhappily. "He really makes a lot of noise. I bet he starts talking early, so he can tell me what to do." I see a new dynamic emerging in this dyad. Ironically, Patrick, the child, was beginning to predict and attempting to control their interactions. Previously I have sensed some reservation on Deirdre's part, a disinclination to cede any control to her infant, but at this moment—perhaps because she is distracted by her pregnancy—she finds Patrick's efforts at control and prediction not as threatening as in the past.

## SESSION 16

Deirdre was feeding Patrick when I arrived, but when I entered the room she removed the bottle from the baby's mouth and sat him on her knee. Patrick smiled broadly at me. Deirdre appeared to share my enjoyment of her son's behavior, but I observed that when she thought my focus was on Patrick, her smile disappeared, to be replaced by a gentle melancholy. I asked if I could hold Patrick. Deirdre surrendered her son without reluctance, watching as I settled the baby in my lap. Patrick smiled at me. At 20 weeks of age, he sat without support. After about 5 minutes, Patrick began to scramble furiously with his feet against my lap. The infant reached for any support he could find, until I assisted him to his feet. Patrick crowed with pleasure, making his triumph clear. I maintained a steady stream of praise and commentary on Patrick's accomplishments. I commented to Deirdre that because of his strength, Patrick could demonstrate his awareness of the milestone he was approaching, standing. "He's previewing standing for himself," I commented to Deirdre.

As I had earlier, I suggested that Deirdre and I try the exercise in which I would interact with Patrick, while Deirdre would "narrate" our activity. Deirdre agreed, and for the next few minutes, as I played with Patrick, she described our activity. Deirdre was very adept at saying what Patrick wanted. She noted several times that at home she had played the same game with her son. After a few minutes, Deirdre began to enter into the play, saying "Hi, Pat!" several times. Whereas most mothers have several kinds of exaggerated smiles with which they elicit responses from their infants, Deirdre appeared to have only serious expressions. At this point, Deirdre's face-making consisted merely of wide-eyed stares and grimaces. Although I am pleased to have witnessed more deliberately playful interaction between the dyad members, I wonder if it means that Deirdre is relaxed enough to show affectionate behavior toward her son in my presence? After a few minutes, I asked Deirdre if she had had any new thoughts about her current pregnancy. Her expression became sheepish. She was feeling a little happier, she said, but she was still not entirely certain that having the baby was the best thing to do.

"What are the drawbacks?" I asked.

Aside from the considerations she had already mentioned—primarily, Patrick's youth, the family's still undefined situation, and the financial burden of a second child—Deirdre mentioned a new consideration. "When the baby was conceived, I was taking psychiatric medication. I stopped now, and they tell me that it probably wouldn't affect the baby, but they can't be sure. It makes me nervous."

I then asked how Mike was feeling about the pregnancy. "He's still all for it," Deirdre replied, adding that she feared that terminating the pregnancy would cause problems. Mike did not object to abortion for religious or ethical reasons; but he's "just against abortion because it's his baby."

"How did you adjust to changes in your body when you were pregnant the last time?" I asked.

Deirdre shrugged. "The first 3 months, there weren't any changes. Then, in the last 6 months you just feel like you're fat and you can't wait for it to be over. I'm not looking forward to that part." When asked what aspects of the pregnancy she *was* looking forward to, or what she had enjoyed about her pregnancy with Patrick, Deirdre seemed perplexed: "I don't look back too much. I've liked it better as he [Patrick] got better at being a real person. The first couple of months I didn't feel much of anything for him." If at this stage Deirdre can say this ("I don't look back too much"), after so much intensive effort has gone into her situation, we must attribute her remark to aggressive resistance and simmering anger directed at both her therapist and the therapeutic process itself, by which he is trying to ameliorate her basically anhedonic condition. Deirdre has been obdurate for a longer time than many patients, and she has been notable in the tenacity of her stubborn refusal to acknowledge deficits or historical obstacles. Deirdre is plainly not as maladaptive as when she first entered treatment. However, this second pregnancy appears to have made it harder for her to consolidate her gains as a caregiver and to challenge her interactional resources in general.

"I found Pat turned around in the crib the other day," she said after several minutes. "He had moved himself around so he was lying in the other direction from where he'd started: It freaked me out! Pat was so pleased, and I was happy for him. You could tell he thought he was something special." Deirdre added that the more mobile Patrick became, the better she liked it.

Her choice of words here is crucial: My assessment is that the phrase "It freaked me out" is ominously negative; even though she follows this outburst with more positive feedback ("Pat was so pleased, and I was happy for him"), I sense that her response is not one of genuine pleasure but, rather, one of dismay. Similarly, when she says that the "more mobile Pat became, the better [she] liked it," I feel she is in active denial and again wishes him not to make such clear advances along the progress continuum. She seems in these exchanges to be trying to propitiate my "expectations" as a therapist, and since I would normally expect her to applaud Pat's advances, she cannot overtly express disappointment or distress over his developments.

I took this opportunity to initiate a discussion of how Patrick's accomplishment of developmental goals was related to his capacity for internal representation. Deirdre listened with apparent interest; when I used the term "sense of control," however, she seemed to have some difficulty discriminating between the infant's sense of control over himself and his attempts to control her. I also asked if the ability to predict Patrick's changes made a difference in the way she reacted when those changes actually occurred. Did she think that, because she had been aware of Patrick's efforts to stand on his own, it would be easier for her to adjust when he accomplished this milestone? Although Deirdre did not answer these questions, her body relaxed markedly. At those times when she refuses or neglects to answer, I suspect it is because she is in conflict with herself. She would wish Patrick not to be so strong and accomplished, but he is not asking her or depending on her for his achievement timetables. He is striving for his own success despite her efforts at control. I felt my question to her was straightforward, yet the only answer I received was a physical relaxation: In essence, this "relaxation" was another attempt at dissembling, this time played out on a somatic plane, since verbally I had "caught" Deirdre a number of times in the past sessions. Did she have any advice, I asked, that she would give a new mother to allow her to understand what was going on in her child's mind?

Deirdre smiled. "Yes. Try everything. If you don't know what he wants, try everything until he tells you that's the right thing." It strikes me that I have seen Deirdre do just that. This "try-everything" approach had an edge of frantic hysteria to it—as if there might be some penalty for failing to find a solution to Patrick's fussiness. With her increasing confidence, Deirdre's "try-everything" approach, now refined through her albeit clumsy efforts of previewing, is notably more successful.

## SESSION 17

My impression today was that Deirdre's fatigue was back in full force. She seemed melancholy today, displaying a palpably different emotion from the conflict that had enveloped her since her learning of the second pregnancy. She was able to summon some social reflexes, smiling briefly when I entered the room, falling easily into a conversation about Patrick's progress, even laughing in a subdued manner from time to time, but throughout, the sense of withdrawn affect was pervasive. Although I noted this sad and withdrawn affect, I preferred at this point to focus on the content of our sessions and to concentrate on key issues in the dyadic exchange.

Asked to describe the developmental progress of her son, Deirdre shrugged and said she thought he was going along "pretty much like always." She had not noticed any major changes; he was just becoming more insistent in practicing the skills he had learned. When I asked her to clarify these statements as in our last session, she expressed her emotions through negative verbiage. Deirdre gave as an example Patrick's efforts to stand. "He's always kicking me. He kicks my stomach. It's as if I were a hill and he's scrambling around trying to dig his heels in so that he can stand up," she noted resentfully. Again, we have here an instance of Deirdre's inability to recognize and applaud normative developmental milestones without internalizing these events as evidence of her baby's malice directed against her. To Patrick's display of normal maturation, Deirdre ascribes egocentric mischief. She added that maybe Patrick had been making some effort to crawl but that she was unsure. Asked to describe the cues that led her to believe Patrick was close to crawling, Deirdre said that the baby was often "on his belly. He just looks like he's going to start crawling soon," she said doggedly.

Then for several minutes Deirdre spoke of her upcoming trip to Ireland. I asked if she and Mike planned to take Patrick with them, and Deirdre nodded, saying that it was a good chance for her father to meet his grandson. After a brief silence, I asked Deirdre again if she had any thoughts about her pregnancy. She unexpectedly announced that she had decided to terminate the pregnancy. Her expression was a mixture of defiance and sadness, as if she had made a difficult decision and was prepared to defend it. "We decided not to have another baby just yet." I asked how she had arrived at this decision. "I was waiting for the air to clear so I could say something. I had to get over the shock of being pregnant. We decided there was too much uncertainty right now. And," she added fatalistically, "I just don't know how far I can hold up under stress. Mike is not sure whether he can cope with his new job. We weren't sure we could handle it." Asked how she and Mike now felt about the decision, Deirdre responded, "He says he wants to do whatever is right for me. When we stopped listening to his family and other people, it was a lot easier for Mike. I feel relieved and scared, not about the physical part, but about emotional side effects. I have girlfriends who've had abortions and have been depressed afterward. With my history, I get nervous thinking about what kind of effect it's going to have on me."

I commented that termination of the pregnancy would represent both a separation and a loss. Deirdre shook her head, yet again choosing to deny the emotional ramifications of a seminal event in her life. "I just want it to be over. I really need that right now," Deirdre said in a return to her earlier style of blunt declaration and resistance to exploration of any analytical component to her motivation. She explained that the procedure would be performed at a local Planned Parenthood center. She would make the appointment for the next day. "I want it done before I have a chance to get really upset," she said flatly. Here Deirdre did indicate she felt some reservations about her decision, but these were not moral ones. "I'd feel more guilty if I wasn't [sic] spending enough time with Pat, or if I was [sic] just miserable when I was with him. I just had this awful feeling I'd be unable to cope, and Mike would be left with me, Pat, and another baby, all three of us unable to take care of ourselves. He sees it's the right thing to do now."

With this discussion of "guilt" and misery and why her decision appeared correct in the eyes of others close to her, Deirdre has begun to mouth the clichés of child rearing. Though it would be unremarkable to hear these things from other women, perhaps, issuing from Deirdre's usually detached mood, such statements indicate substantial forward momentum in both cognitive awareness and emotional sequelae on her part.

"Are they going to provide counseling?" I asked.

"Yes, but it's, like, birth-control information."

"Who is going to take care of Patrick that day?" I asked. A sitter, Deirdre explained. "I'll be home for dinner." Because of the specific timing of this decision—as Deirdre and Mike are planning their trip to Ireland—I suspect that Deirdre might have been using the notion of abortion as a way of punishing herself for her first pregnancy, the one of which her father had disapproved so highly.

This notion of abortion as punishment was explored, but it yielded nothing new. What appeared to be at work with Deirdre was her fear that I would become (in loco parentis) moralistic and judgmental in view of the proposed abortion, that I would adopt a stern, Calvinist viewpoint. In a word, we had complete transference.

Patrick, who had been quietly playing with a set of small plastic boxes, apparently grew tired of the toy at last and became watchful. Then he went into a state of distress, evidenced by slowly intensified crying and unhappy postures. Deirdre bounced him gently several times until his crying stopped and then extracted a bottle and began to feed Patrick. The difference in the adaptiveness of her feeding style from the previous session and this one was marked. She continued talking, pausing to look down only long enough to dab at Patrick's face. Physically, her posture was rigid, providing little support for Patrick. The decline in Deirdre's adaptive responses was notable— and disheartening. When Patrick had finished feeding, Deirdre removed the bottle and sat him up again so that she could burp him. Then she settled her son back to lean against her; he appeared to doze for a time. I am concerned that Deirdre's disaffection during Patrick's feeding may be a way of acting out her ambivalence toward the fetus she is carrying. By making feeding such an act devoid of obvious nurturance, she is symbolically starving Patrick, who stands in place of the fetus.

Patrick gradually became more active, reaching up a hand to grab some of his mother's hair. Deirdre grimaced and smiled wanly at her son. But in repose, when her attention and mine were directed at Patrick, Deirdre's expression became one of deep sadness. If I had reservations about the advisability of Deirdre carrying this child to term, I am no less concerned about the repercussions of terminating the pregnancy. Whereas Patrick showed little sign of overt disturbance at his mother's behavior, of course knowing nothing of its cause, his aggressive attempts to manipulate Deirdre into interaction might have been in response to her mood and her new "condition." Unfortunately, Patrick's only tools in this struggle are negative behaviors that further add to the stress on Deirdre.

Deferring to Deirdre's discussions with her physician, I chose not to confront her further on the abortion issue. In this way I hoped not to engender resentment or further resistance. In trying to enhance the quality of the Patrick-Deirdre relationship, it would have muddied the original "contract" to bring in the emotionally fraught situation of an impending abortion. Effectively, Deirdre came to me with her decision to abort as a fait accompli. I did interpret the issue as one way of coping with Patrick's rapid development. Thus, my therapeutic decision was to stay within the limits of just interpreting the situation and not directly acting on or creating changes in the existing turbulent scenario.

## SESSION 18

I arrived for the day's session with some degree of curiosity, wondering how Deirdre had fared during the week. Deirdre stood wanly by the window, alternately looking out and turning to check on her son, who was playing on the floor. Patrick was cheerful, making playful vocalizations and rolling from side to side. I entered, said hello, and invited Deirdre to join me by bringing one of the chairs into range of our video camera, so we could start. Because of Deirdre's unusual reticence, I began by playing with Patrick, previewing crawling for the infant, who smiled and laughed in response to the activity. When I asked Deirdre if she had tried previewing rolling over for her son, she shrugged and said nothing. Since she showed no signs of initiating the subject herself, I finally asked Deirdre how she had fared with her appointment for the abortion.

"I didn't get a chance to think about it while it was happening—it goes real fast," Deirdre covered the entire situation in 17 brief words that tell worlds about her insistence on defensive denial and her refusal to delve into any of the emotional ramifications of her act. By this refusal, by having the procedure "go real fast," she has administered to herself a kind of psychic self-anesthesia. "And then things blew up at home," she said. She explained that, although her relationship with her mother was almost always tense, the fact that Deirdre had not discussed the abortion with her mother had been the cause of a major quarrel. Deirdre said it had not occurred to her to tell her mother about the abortion; she felt that the decision was a private one between herself and Mike. As she described the scene, Deirdre's voice shook: "I wasn't feeling great afterward—I had cramps for a couple of days, and it's like you're having your period, so it's easy to feel tense. I just told her that we weren't ready for a second child right now, and she went crazy. Wanted to know why I hadn't talked to her beforehand. She said it meant I hated her. But it wasn't her business! She said things like I came to visit you every day when you were hospitalized, and this is how you repay me. I was ready to kill her." "Hospitalization" here refers to the time Deirdre was psychologically dysfunctional. I was pleased to hear her strong affect at this point. She was more emotional and spontaneous than she had been just a few months before, an approach that betokens more intuitive reflection. This outbreak also shows the validity of my original hypothesis about the virulence and vigor of her suppressed anger. It didn't alarm me that she stated she wanted to "kill" her mother. I felt it was a belated effort to verbalize what she had long desired to say but could not previously permit herself to express and deal with.

"Did you try to explain your point of view to her?" I asked.

"No. Sooner or later she will have to realize that I'm not her little girl any more."

"So she was communicating that she felt the abortion was a way you were trying to separate from her? Do you think there is any validity in that statement?"

Deirdre shook her head. "I separated from her a long time ago. This was my business, mine and Mike's, not hers."

Deirdre began to speak again, once more negating an experience that usually engenders considerable emotional upheaval for women who abort. "The abortion wasn't much of anything—except there was a long wait beforehand. When I got home I sort of filed it all away emotionally. My mother thinks I hate her. I don't hate her, though I'm angry at her. She thinks I hate her for drinking, but I don't. I wish she wouldn't drink, but for her own sake." Sadly, this young mother has "sort of filed it all away emotionally" all her life—her parents' divorce, her own childhood abandonment, premature motherhood.

I brought Patrick back from the mirror. The infant resisted being given to his mother, who passed the bottle to me. Patrick, it seemed, was content to be fed by me. I asked Deirdre if Patrick had shown any signs of being affected by his mother's experience. Deirdre insisted that her attitude toward Patrick was the same and she could not see any sign that Patrick was worse because of her abortion. "He watches to see what's going on, whether there's going to be trouble or something. Then he forgets it all later."

Once more, Deirdre fell into silence, and the focus in the room shifted to Patrick, who was looking around again. I placed the baby on a table, where Patrick spent some minutes exploring its surface by tapping. Twice Patrick turned, caught sight of his mother, and smiled with recognition. However, when Deirdre attempted to catch Patrick's attention herself, he ignored her. This initiation of contact is a rarity for Deirdre. My hypothesis is that she is seeking Patrick out because she is uneasy and still upset about the abortion. Her rationale seems to be, "I've got only Patrick left; I'd better not mess up this existing relationship, too." Although Deirdre maintained that Patrick had been unaffected by her abortion, it was clear that her distress had been translated to her young son, who reacted with his own distress. If Deirdre bounced back from the emotional turmoil of this event, the effect on her relationship with Patrick, as well as on his development, might not be long term; I was hopeful that the considerable progress evidenced in the last 2 months would not be entirely undone.

## SESSION 19

Because of Deirdre's visit to her family in Ireland, 4 weeks passed before our next meeting. I was pleased to note that Deirdre's depression in the wake of her abortion had dissipated considerably. When she was not under direct observation, Deirdre's affect was still guarded and sober but far less depressed than during our last meeting. When I entered the room, Deirdre was seated, watching her son. Patrick sat next to her on the floor and looked up as I entered. He stood, but after a moment began to totter. Deirdre helped him to the ground and gave him several toys with which he occupied himself. I complimented her on easing his transition from standing to sitting. Embarrassed by the praise, Deirdre smiled and ducked her head. After a pause, she reported that Patrick had begun to stand while they were in Ireland, admitting "I think it was because everyone was playing with him; he got so much attention." Asked to relate other gains Patrick had made since the last session, Deirdre added that Patrick had less patience with being unable to attain a goal—"When he can't roll over to something he wants, he really hates it."

Asked how the trip had been, Deirdre smiled, "My Dad and Pat got along real well—Pop can have fun with the baby." When asked if she had discussed her abortion with him, Deirdre shrugged. "Yes. He was all for it. He didn't think we should have had Patrick, either, but now that he's here, Pop likes him fine." Her father, Deirdre added defensively, felt that she should not have had children until everything was perfect: "Money, a big house," and so on. Deirdre denied any lingering negative feelings about her abortion, saying that it was all in the past and that she wanted to concentrate on more immediate concerns, including finding a new apartment, being supportive of Mike in his new position at work, and raising Patrick. I was concerned about her complete denial of regret vis-à-vis the recent abortion. But I again chose not to be confrontational, so her defenses would not be activated, and progress in the chosen directions could continue uninterrupted. I asked Deirdre if she had any thoughts as to why she had become pregnant at this time. Deirdre replied that she had not thought about it. After I suggested that the pregnancy might have been a way of resisting her growing relationship with Patrick, Deirdre appeared incensed. Some minutes after this, she admitted that having the baby would have interfered with her relationship with Patrick. "I feel like now he's becoming a person, getting around on his own a little, and I could really have a relationship with him." "Of course I'll have another child at some point so that Patrick will have a brother or sister to play with," she added.

I leaned down and lifted Patrick so that he was standing in my lap. The baby waved his arms excitedly. I stood up, still holding Patrick, and began to preview walking for Patrick, pacing him across the floor. Patrick shrieked pleasurably, smiling and flapping his arms; for long moments he would carry his own weight before I moved him forward another "step." The baby evidenced his delight in this game several times. After 5 minutes or so, however, he showed evidence of tiring. I then took Patrick over to the mirror, where I pointed to the baby's reflection, saying "See the baby, Patrick?" At first Patrick referred back to his mother, peering anxiously at Deirdre until she looked up and smiled. Thereafter, Patrick would turn every 90 seconds or so to seek his mother's reassurance. This reflected a higher level of attunement in the dyad, but when I drew her attention to this form of referencing, Deirdre shook her head.

About halfway through the session, Deirdre began to preview walking for Patrick, leaning over in her chair and "walking" the baby a few steps. The baby rewarded his mother with an enormous smile, which Deirdre reciprocated briefly, almost embarrassed. Later, when Patrick was playing on the floor and reached for a toy slightly beyond his reach, Deirdre encouraged him, saying "You got it! You got it! Patrick!" Interestingly, although Deirdre appeared to be more verbal with her son, Patrick's vocalizations remained rare and largely noncommunicative. I congratulated her on her efforts to become more vocally active with her son.

## SESSION 20

Patrick, now 28 weeks old, was much steadier on his feet than he had been at our last session. He stood by his mother's chair and greeted me with his customary smile. Deirdre, legs crossed and hand casually touching Patrick's shoulder, looked relaxed but tired. As we began, I asked Deirdre if she could summarize the ways in which she believed the therapy sessions were helping her.

"It's helpful to know that I'm doing an adequate job with him," she said rather uncertainly. As she said this Deirdre's eyes were cast down and her hair hung around her face, effectively hiding her expression. I asked how she could tell she was doing an adequate job, at which point she looked concerned. "I mean, I am doing an okay job, aren't I? You seem to think Pat's okay, so I can't be doing anything too wrong."

"I agree with you, but have you learned anything during therapy that has helped you to know when you are doing something well?" Deirdre shrugged. "Let's look at that question another way. Have you learned anything in therapy that has reassured you about yourself as a mother? As I remember, when you started you had very little confidence in yourself as a mother and didn't trust your intuitions at all."

Deirdre drew a long breath as if to organize her thoughts. "Some of it is real practical," she said at length. "I've learned to catch myself when I'm being blank with him—not showing him any emotion at all. You showed me in that exercise a while back about how he needs a reaction from me." Asked how difficult reacting was for her, Deirdre responded:

> It's not the first thing I think of. It's hard for me to show him my emotions. I'm pretty good at getting angry, but the softer stuff is hard for me. That's why I was worried about how I'd be with the baby, aside from my sickness. Sometimes it's really tough to make myself react to Patrick when he smiles or makes noises, especially when I'm tired. When I'm not doing well I get very anxious, and if I don't think about it I can ignore him. Through therapy I've learned not to do it.

She reported that during her trip she had stopped taking her medication because it was "a pain" and she had "been doing so well since Pat was born." She had felt fine for a day or two, but then she began hearing voices that told her to hurt herself and Patrick. "I felt anxious and depressed. I really don't want to talk about it." As she spoke a mantle of depressed affect settled visibly over Deirdre; her shoulders slumped, her face was downcast, and despite Patrick's urgent signals, she kept her gaze on the floor. Now that she had resumed taking her medication, her auditory hallucinations had ceased.

"Patrick seems happier. I mean, when I was depressed he was whining all the time because I wasn't paying enough attention to him." Mike had recognized when her depression and anxiety were getting the better of her and had been the one to urge her to start taking her medication again. Indirectly this reveals how Mike stood with regard to these issues. It also showed me forcefully how substantial a support Mike could be with regard to the concerns with which we were grappling in our sessions.

Deirdre's motivation in having the abortion from this vantage point might well be seen as a cautionary act to prevent disturbing the growing bond between her and her son Patrick. Another aspect of Deirdre's evident connection with her son was that, subtly, having an abortion had reinforced her empathy for her live son, whom she was now feeding. She held him so that he was supported and permitted Patrick to grasp the bottle himself. When she judged that Patrick had had all the formula he wanted, Deirdre started to take the bottle away, only to have Patrick pull it back. Deirdre allowed him to do so, smiling. This interaction in particular was characterized by playful gestures.

I was heartened by the increasing playfulness in Patrick and Deirdre's interaction. The evidence is, however, that this increasingly open communication poses hazards for Deirdre. I have sensed that she experiences both admiration and resentment for Patrick's ability to get what he wants from her, and perhaps that resentment has to do with her feelings about her ability to satisfy her own needs. Patrick's ability to demand and to manipulate are markedly developed. I also feel that it is essential to continue investigating from where this controlling behavior emanates. One prime example that comes to mind was the so-called "mean face" that Patrick occasionally donned when interacting with his mother. The upper third of his facial expression indicated his intense upset and disapproval, and yet the lower third showed major evidence of propitiation for Deirdre's angry or ambivalent affect. Overall, his face reflected ambivalence from the dissonance of the two dissimilar segments.

Before the end of the session, Deirdre related a dream in which she had lost all her teeth. She could not remember whether they had fallen or been knocked out, "Just that I didn't have them and I was upset." When asked for her interpretation of the dream, Deirdre said it might have something to do with Patrick's teething. He had not begun to teethe yet, she admitted, "but it looks as though he will, very soon." The dream Deirdre described suggests that she feels vulnerable and defenseless and may have particular reference to the risks of her increasing openness with Patrick. The teeth she loses are somehow transferred to her son, and with them, might he not sever the attachment that binds them? Deirdre not only fears separation, but, clearly, she feels that Patrick's autonomy may only be achieved at the cost of some dramatic loss to herself.

## SESSION 21

About a month had passed since my last session with Deirdre and Patrick. Patrick was now 8 months old, husky for his age. His stance, still tentative a month ago, now showed his confidence. When I arrived, Patrick was sitting on the floor, banging two pots together and evidently enjoying the resulting commotion. Deirdre sat nearby, watching her son with distant amusement. I sat on the floor near Patrick, and, while engaging Deirdre in conversation, entered into Patrick's play, rolling a ball to the baby, who pushed the ball back in my direction.

Deirdre reported that, in addition to his growing skill at standing, Patrick had begun walking while using chairs and tables to support himself. It's noteworthy that Deirdre has noticed a change in Patrick that didn't have to be cajoled out of her by my questions, evidence of distinct progress in spontaneity on her part. "He's not very steady on his feet, but he's really happy when he's standing and trying to walk." She reported also that he was drinking from his bottle by himself. Deirdre went on to explain that during the hiatus between sessions she and Mike had found an apartment and had moved. "It was pretty brutal—by this weekend we weren't talking to each other at all. Pat weathered it pretty well, but the first night he was really cranky and wouldn't sleep." Her use of "brutal" to describe her current situation provides yet another example of this patient's repressed anger. It is more evidence to me that I have considerable distance to go in exploring the profound resentment that she still harbors. Patrick looked up at her, and she smiled. Much to the credit of Patrick, she has begun to smile at him, showing that he has been successful at engaging her at last. Deirdre repeated the week had been particularly difficult because she was so tired. "When I get tired, I get impatient and angry." Asked what she did when she felt angry, Deirdre shrugged. "I punch walls. That releases the anger. If I'm not that angry I go for long walks. Before I had Pat, I used to run. Now we go for long walks. He likes it because we get outside. During the last 2 weeks we took a lot of walks."

"Does the anger ever linger even after you've taken a walk?"

Deirdre looked uncomprehending. "No . . . if I can't walk it off or punch it off."

After several minutes of absorption in her son, and his reactions, Deirdre looked directly at me. "I'm happy to be out of my mother's house," she revealed. "I've been thinking about the way I grew up. I had no relationship with my parents, and I don't want things to be like that for Patrick. Mom is an alcoholic, and Dad is really rigid. I used to scream a lot when I was a kid. I'd have temper tantrums and get locked up in the closet or the garage. Nobody ever asked what I was angry about." Deirdre cocked her head to one side and said wryly, "I guess they thought locking me up was the same as saying 'Don't get so crazy.'" After 8 months we finally have the etiology of how her own poor family interaction persistently pushed her in the direction she now finds herself mired in. Her childhood angers were never explored (indeed even expression of them exacted terrible penalties), so no useful societally approved release was available for her. Deirdre has hit on one of the most frequently asked psychological parenting questions: How can I break with the cycle of undesirable parenting styles I experienced myself? The fact that she is aware of some of the unfortunate interactions she experienced—and their ramifications—gives her a direction to move toward.

"How would you interact with Patrick if he had a tantrum?" I asked.

She shook her head. "I'm just not very good at imagining stuff," she said.

When asked if there was something "dangerous" about imagining the future, Deirdre acknowledged that she couldn't rely on the future being safe, particularly with her illness, "So I don't like to think about it." When I asked if the future was "dangerous" for Patrick, Deirdre shrugged. In the wake of this conversation Deirdre appeared depleted and exhausted. She sat back in her chair and watched for a few minutes while I played with Patrick. During the silence I asked Deirdre if we could seat Patrick in a little "go-cart." Patrick enjoyed the toy itself, using his legs to move back and forth in jerky motions. After I showed him how to blow the horn by hitting the center of the steering wheel, Patrick appeared entranced by the noise: He sat very still, eyes wide, burst into a broad smile, then bounced up and down. Each time I blew the horn, Patrick exhibited similar signs of delight. Finally Patrick began to blow the horn himself, crowing with delight and triumph.

"Patrick is experimenting with contingency learning," I explained to Deirdre. "He's figured out that if he presses the center of the wheel something happens: He hears the noise. That's a very important developmental milestone. Can you imagine what the next milestone he develops will be?"

Deirdre smiled wanly and said, "Driving a car, the way he's going."

The use of this particular toy, I commented, required a great deal of coordination. Was there any developmental milestone to which she looked forward with reservations? Any stage that she felt now would be difficult for her to handle?

"When he starts school," Deirdre said without hesitation. "Once he leaves home, there's peer pressure and stuff; that's going to be tough. I'm afraid that he'll come home and start saying things to me that he's learned from other kids. My chance to influence him will have just gone out the window." This comment clearly raised the issue of separation. I am not clear, however, that previewing his attendance at school as the point at which her influence over him "will have gone out the window," is not a way of enabling her to live without the responsibilities of caring for her son.

## SESSION 22

When I entered the room, Patrick was seated on the floor playing with a collection of plastic toys. I said hello to him. He looked up briefly, then returned to his play. He appeared slightly more responsive to vocal cues, although he rarely imitates speech and Deirdre denies any "Dada" or "Mama" verbalizing at this stage. Deirdre, lounging back in a chair near her son, had been watching her son, smiling softly to herself; she appeared relaxed and comfortable. Deirdre began the session by volunteering comments on Patrick's development. She explained that recently she realized how much of Patrick's physical development—his standing and his attempts to walk alone—emerged from his desire to explore the world around him. "He's stubborn," she said. "When he sees something he wants he goes after it. He forgets about holding on when he's trying to walk, and he still doesn't really crawl." She had known for some time that her son was stubborn, she added; it was just more obvious now that Patrick was making efforts to achieve what he wanted.

"How do you feel when Patrick asserts his autonomy?" I asked.

Deirdre watched her son pensively, then smiled. "He's starting to get ticklish!" she said mischievously and demonstrated by running her fingers down Patrick's side. The infant squealed pleasurably and relaxed into his mother's hand, so that she found herself supporting his weight. Her moments of interaction with her son demonstrated a growing involvement with and attachment to him. Since Deirdre had not responded directly, I rephrased the question, asking her if any developmental milestones had caught her attention more than others. "Sitting up," Deirdre said thoughtfully. "And grabbing things he wants and playing with them. The standing and walking didn't surprise me because he was trying so hard to do it, I knew he was going to." Deirdre noted that in the last week she couldn't sit him down to play without his crying.

"How did you handle him?"

Deirdre shrugged. "I let him cry. It only went on for a minute or two each time." Asked why Patrick may have been reacting that way, she responded, "I think he's thinking differently about things from the way he used to. It used to be 'Out of sight, out of mind' for him—like he knew who I was when I was there but forgot me when I wasn't. Now, when I'm out of sight, he still remembers me. He doesn't have a name for me, but I'm not out of mind even when I am out of sight." Whereas such identification and behavior represent a distinct phase for young children and toddlers, Deirdre's fascination with separation and with the psychological umbilical cord uniting her with her son clearly reflects her own unresolved fears of standing alone (locked in a closet?) and being separate. However, Deirdre could speak of her son with a veiled gratification, as if she liked the idea that he was able to sustain an internal representation of her. I, in turn, am pleased with Deirdre's improving ability to describe her son's intellectual developmental changes, although her insight into her own psyche remains relatively rudimentary at this point.

Patrick turned and grimaced at his mother with the expression Deirdre had named "the mean face." Oddly, she commented that she knew he wanted to play when he wore that face. Asked why she calls his expression "the mean face," she responded, "I feel bossed around when he uses that face." I am concerned with the designation of the "mean face," particularly in light of Patrick's insistent intentions to engage his mother. Her terminology is an example of how Deirdre had begun to attribute negative controlling behaviors to her son. I am afraid that, when under pressure, Deirdre might hurt herself to signal that she, not Patrick, was in control. At present, however, she seemed to manage her feelings about this control because she is able to predict and explain it.

## SESSION 23

Unlike during our last session, Deirdre seemed to be in a somewhat withdrawn, laconic mood. Patrick, on the other hand, seemed curious today, although he easily became frustrated or upset. "Patrick's starting to get stubborn and angry when you take something away from him or stop him from going someplace," Deirdre commented. "Yesterday, I found him trying to open the cabinet under the kitchen sink with the cleaning stuff. I dragged him away and put him down in the kitchen to play, and he started kicking and screaming." She smiled wearily when I noted that she seemed somehow amused by this phase in Patrick's development. "It used to be he'd play with anything. Now he's only interested in some things. I think that's great."

"How do you feel with regard to Patrick's increasing autonomy?"

"I feel like I'm more independent. I keep an eye out for what he's getting into, but I don't feel like I'm the only thing that amuses him any more. I like this stage a lot better." Asked if he continues to display "the mean face," she replied, "Not so often." Then she added insightfully, "That was really a 'pay attention!' or 'play with me!' face."

At several points during the session, I observed that Patrick was becoming more responsive to verbal cues, particularly to his own name. On occasion, it appeared that while he heard his name, he chose to ignore it because of his deep involvement in play. He is reaching the phase of development where he is very attuned to his mother's verbal cues, but even with her it appeared that sometimes Patrick simply did not want to acknowledge that he was being called. There was little repetition of the enthusiastic babbling that he had demonstrated previously; frankly, despite the infant's excellent, almost precocious, psychomotor development, I am increasingly concerned that there may indeed be some sort of cognitive deficit, given his lack of verbal expression despite adequate verbal skills. However, this may still be due to Deirdre's generally nonverbal disposition. Although I sense that she has made efforts to improve, she is not integrating her physical interactions with language.

Patrick, who had been standing near Deirdre's chair, maintaining his balance with one hand, began to fuss. When asked what he wanted, Deirdre shook her head: "I don't think he knows." Whereas her tone was humorous, it seemed that her comment was an attempt to deny Patrick his capacity to choose—perhaps reflecting Deirdre's inability to control so many aspects of her own life. It also seemed to reflect her inability to deal with Patrick's growing maturity and eventual escape from her control. When Patrick continued to whine, Deirdre lifted him up and patted him, but nothing seemed to help. At last I asked if I could hold him. Patrick was soon all smiles as I walked across the room. Nevertheless, he glanced to his mother for reassurance. When Deirdre nodded and said "Okay, Pat," he seemed satisfied and allowed me to help him as he made his way back across the room.

Patrick's determination as he walked across the room was striking. When I commented on it, Deirdre agreed, likening her son to a steamroller. But when Patrick had returned to his starting point, he seemed quite content to play.

With no transition Deirdre suddenly raised a question she had discussed in her AA group concerning her son: Would Patrick "somehow acquire" her psychiatric disorder? She was curious as to how strong a genetic link to psychosis and alcoholism there was. "I mean, I know a lot of it is nurture, the environment I am creating for Patrick, but sometimes I wonder if Patrick's going to get into alcohol the way I did." She added that she had begun drinking when she was 11 and had drunk and abused drugs for almost 10 years; indeed, because of her mother's alcoholism, she had an example in the house. She had thought drinking had been a way to remain "a kid" and avoid responsibility. She smiled ruefully now and nodded toward her son. "I guess I've taken on some responsibility." She expressed her hope and intention that Patrick not grow up needing to escape from anything. This is, in effect, previewing her son as an adult, wrestling with problems she herself has agonized over and is still in the process of resolving. Deirdre has finally reached a milestone of her own! Is this a hopeful sign that the future—her own and Patrick's—is less threatening to her now?

## SESSION 24

Shortly before Deirdre and her son arrived, a thunderstorm began, and our session was punctuated by distant rolls of thunder. On arriving, I found Patrick sitting in the center of the room, playing intently with building blocks. Deirdre appeared depressed, slouched in her chair and fidgeting. From our earlier sessions it indeed seemed as if mother and son had changed roles. From time to time Patrick would look up, and he and Deirdre would exchange a somber glance; then, the infant would return to his play. Throughout the session Deirdre seemed to be fighting her depression. When she was actively engaged in conversation she appeared interested, almost animated, but as soon as the attention focused on Patrick, Deirdre returned to her pensiveness.

Asked about Patrick's developmental changes, Deirdre said ruefully that she couldn't hide anything from Patrick anymore. When she took something away, Patrick would search for it persistently. If he couldn't find it, he would display "the mean face," whine, and kick. Deirdre shifted in her chair. Patrick caught the motion and knew that something had changed (he seems exquisitely attuned to her mood shifts); he turned around to make sure that his mother was still there, obviously perturbed. Even when reassured that his mother was still within easy reach, Patrick was visibly upset and began to fret and whine. Deirdre offered him a variety of toys that he rejected. It seemed that Patrick did not want her to be distracted by anyone. In rejecting the proffered toys, Patrick was demonstrating how keen he was to keep his attention on his mother, and vice versa.

After a few minutes Deirdre mentioned that she needed to go to the bathroom. She rose and left the room. Patrick appeared disconcerted and made a noise of protest but was distracted by me. Deirdre's departure and return allowed us to stage an informal test of the attachment bond, as well as of Patrick's ability to represent his mother. I was particularly impressed with how persistent his image of his mother was while she was out of the room. Only by continuous interaction with him was I able to distract Patrick from looking for his mother. When Deirdre returned to the room, Patrick watched her, whining to be picked up. Deirdre leaned down, gave her son a brief hug and said, "Yeah, I'm fine," then settled him in her lap. His response upon her return suggests a secure attachment, and although Deirdre's response was casual, I had a sense, when her son's new calm helped to soothe her, that her attachment to her son is secure. Deirdre told me that when she was out shopping Patrick's usual reunion behavior was to laugh and smile, not to cry at her.

Deirdre placed the baby, standing, by her side. Occasionally, as he moved around her, bracing himself with one hand on a chair, Deirdre would lean over and pat him affectionately. These touches served to correct Patrick's stance, allowing him better balance and improving his ability to stand. The gestures seemed entirely unconscious on Deirdre's part—a spontaneously intuitive behavior. They represent a momentous development in Deirdre's interactive abilities from a few months before. When I complimented Deirdre, she smiled shyly and shrugged as if to say there was nothing special in what she had done.

As Patrick explored, he began commenting on his surroundings with a new sound: "Geggh!" Unlike the whining he had demonstrated before, this sound unmistakably communicated his intentions and was repeated with a powerful interpersonal flavor. In light of my concerns about Patrick's failure to rely on his language skills for communication, his use of one repeated word here was heartening. When his voice was pitched loudly enough to interrupt the conversation of the adults, Patrick would repeat his sound-word several times. As Patrick became more strident, Deirdre became more tense, handling him with less gentleness and a brusque touch. When Patrick continued to fret and Deirdre lifted him onto her lap, it was with a no-nonsense manner she had not used in some time. However, as Patrick drank his juice and quieted, Deirdre appeared to become less tense, as if Patrick's calmness, as well as his proximity as a loved object, were soothing to her. Does Deirdre's depression serve to keep Patrick enmeshed with her in some way? At times it appears as though she uses her mood to keep him dependent on her. With his mother's creating an atmosphere of emotional uncertainty, Patrick certainly has an insecure basis on which to establish autonomy. In a similar way, Deirdre's erratic striving for autonomy may serve to spark Patrick's own anger, creating a sense of independence in both members of the dyad. I would want to observe this dynamic carefully in coming sessions.

## SESSION 25

Deirdre's red hair was pulled back today in a severe ponytail, which added to her harried and depressed demeanor. Thirty-seven-week-old Patrick appeared gingerly aware of his mother's mood and played quietly. Asked about recent changes in Patrick's development, Deirdre commented that Patrick's sleeping patterns were changing. "The old tricks for putting him to sleep don't work anymore. He gets cranky and cries before he'll fall asleep." Asked if he is now making his intentions clearer to her, Deirdre shrugged and smiled. "I don't know that he's making his intentions clearer, but I understand his cues better. If he sees a bottle or a dish and he's hungry, he makes a sniffing face, like a rabbit: He tilts his head up and sniffs the air. Watch later when I give him a bottle, I bet he'll do it." Asked if he still uses "the mean face," Deirdre seemed slightly abashed at the term. "It just means he wants attention. And there are faces he makes when he's sleepy, or when he's uncomfortable. You know. It has become a lot easier to know what he wants."

"I think it must be an extraordinary thing to watch Patrick master a new skill and to see his progress," I said. Deirdre nodded but did not respond. I continued, "Of course, you are a very vital part of that mastery process. He really needs your support, your enthusiasm. What happens is that an infant outgrows some kinds of nurturing—holding him up as he tries to walk, for example—but he never outgrows the need for your support of his growth."

"He outgrows it when he's a grown-up," Deirdre protested. "I don't need anybody being a cheerleader for me," she remarked rather belligerently. Unresolved resistance again appears to rear its ugly head with Deirdre. No matter how I compliment her, she's ready to reject any supportive comment on her enhanced parenting skills.

I shook my head. "Doesn't it make it easier to follow through with something when you know you have Mike's support or the support of your friends?"

Deirdre listened intently. "Well, maybe." She sat back and said nothing further for several minutes. It is important that I reassure her that her own and Patrick's autonomy need not be exclusive. I think it possible, seeing the heightened referencing between mother and infant, to make Deirdre more open to this concept.

Deirdre commented, "I think Pat's more confident that he's going to be understood, so he's getting a little more patient. If he makes the 'hungry face,' he waits a little bit because he thinks I'll notice and do something about it." I was particularly impressed with Deirdre's observation. She seems to be describing the beginnings of mastery orientation, as Patrick learns of the effects of his actions. However, there is still a strong undercurrent of resistance to her son's manipulations.

"It tries your patience when Patrick is impatient?" I asked.

Deirdre seemed surprised. "Well, yes, of course. It feeds on itself, and he senses it, too. Sometimes when I'm really tense or angry, I think Pat senses it, because he pulls away; other times he puts up a fight. It's scary. Sometimes my anger is just overwhelming. I don't know what I'll do. When he starts crying and just goes on and on, I start biting my fist because I don't want to punch him or something. I go for a long walk with him or have Mike take care of him while I calm down by myself. But it's not a good time, and I wonder what he's remembering and if he's going to hate me for being so angry." I remarked that by being aware of these nuances she would be better able to understand her contribution to the relationship and perhaps improve her control over her own actions, yet the disproportional rage Patrick's cries bring out in her remains a matter of concern for me.

At the end of the session, Deirdre said self-effacingly that she had an announcement: She and Mike had decided to get married in 2 months. She was pleased, she reported, but still had mixed feelings. "I guess you don't get much more committed to someone than having a kid," she said. I am not surprised, given Deirdre's ongoing history, that she saved her important news for so late in the session but was pleased to note a certain shy pleasure expressed in her sharing of the news. She remains protective of herself, as if discussing her wedding plans in too much detail might influence her thoughts. I wonder how much of her sad affect is caused by the emotions this imminent change evokes in her.

## SESSION 26

I sensed a hidden excitement about Deirdre when she entered the room. Deirdre seemed significantly less overwrought than she had been the week before. As Patrick turned from his sitting position, Deirdre announced, "He's crawling!" This was evidently the source of her excitement. As we watched, Patrick crawled to his favorite toy, the telephone.

"Terrific!" I enthused. "When did you notice it?"

"Two days after our last meeting. I was just sitting, doing some paperwork, and I looked over and he was crawling to me." Asked how she had responded, Deirdre said, "I clapped. And Patrick had a big smile on his face. When he stopped and sat still for a minute, he was all excited, laughing and waving his arms. It was really quite a moment." As if in response to his mother's words, Patrick abandoned the telephone and crawled over to her chair, where he pulled himself to his feet. Deirdre had predicted her son's mastery of walking considerably in advance of her prediction that he would crawl. I now wondered how much of the validity of these predictions had sprung from her willingness to preview walking for her son rather than crawling. I asked what she predicted his next accomplishment would be. Deirdre smiled. "Running, I guess."

Once she made her disclosure and shared her pleasure at her son's new accomplishment, part of the excitement that had characterized Deirdre when she had entered the room seemed to leave her. She sat back and seemed content to focus on her son. I was troubled by the rapid shift in Deirdre's emotional tone—from pleasure in her son's new accomplishment to blank affect—as much as by her resistance to participating in any of Patrick's games. Where a more adaptive mother might have been less intrusive while her child was constructing a game, Deirdre's only response seems to be to remove her son from the game without negotiating this transition. One would understand if he were playing with a burning match, or sitting in a mound of jagged glass, that Deirdre would be compelled to remove him from the chance of danger. But absent any peril at all, to remove Patrick from a game without a word or any recognition of his subsequent pain shows considerable insensitivity and continued self-absorption. Her own defensive needs and her still somewhat fractionated and selective view of reality continue to govern much of her interactive behavior with her son.

"Do you feel tired?" I asked.

"I am. This wedding thing is getting me crazy—my mother's trying to run the whole thing. I just want to get it over with." She nodded in Patrick's direction. "Watching him with his new trick was the only good part of this week." Deirdre's comments about her wedding and her lack of control over it echo a larger theme in her life: that of responsibility. She plainly wants to be allowed to stage her wedding as she sees fit. When faced with the responsibilities that accompany self-management, however, she is less willing to be autonomous. This "do what I want—but don't expect anything in return" attitude resonates throughout her life, particularly in her relationship with her son.

For several minutes Patrick was absorbed in learning how to blow the horn on a little wagon. His pleasure on producing a clear sound was evident in his smiling face and proud laughter. Deirdre was not drawn to participate in the game, and after observing Patrick for a few minutes she abruptly reached down and picked her son up out of the wagon. When I pointed out the insensitivity of ignoring Patrick's little game of producing honk-honks, she seemed not to have been aware of it as a game. She was again demonstrating a blankness in receptivity that revealed the wisdom of her choosing not to have a second infant while she struggled so prodigally with the rigors of parenting this one child. She held him on her lap, then helped him to slide off her lap to his feet.

In his mother's lap, Patrick began fussing. With Deirdre's permission I distracted him by settling Patrick on the floor, taking three plastic cups and a small rubber ball, and playing a slow, simple version of the shell game by hiding the ball under one cup and waiting for Patrick to find the hidden ball. After three or four iterations, the child grasped the game and was able to find the ball most of the time. His enthusiasm for the game was notable and called to mind Deirdre's comments about the difficulty of keeping anything hidden from this infant; it also finally established that Patrick's grasp and intelligence is well developed for an infant of his age.

"He's doing very well at this," I confided to Deirdre. Patrick, who crowed with pleasure each time the ball was revealed, finally tired of the game and turned away. Asked how she felt when I played with Patrick, Deirdre shook her head as if to shake the question away. "Okay," she said at last. "He seems to like it. Sometimes . . . I feel a little left out, like when people fuss over Pat at AA."

"But you've said you don't want attention—is that true even during our sessions?"

Deirdre looked upset. What she evoked was a trapped little animal: She was caught in her own contradictory emotion. It's clear she *wants* attention but is driven to deny it. "I feel lonely . . . sometimes, not always," she added quickly.

Patrick pulled himself to his feet using the wagon, which was now behind him. This action indicated considerable strength in his arms and shoulders, as well as increasing upper-body coordination. Once standing, Patrick returned to the wall and began to explore. He babbled volubly. "What do you think he's trying to say?" I asked.

"He's not saying anything," Deirdre said. "He's just making noise. I don't think the noises mean anything." Her denial that Patrick's babblings were meaningful was vehement enough to concern me. Taciturn by nature, is Deirdre permitting some personal issue regarding talking or language to interfere with previewing language development in her son? Patrick overreached himself and fell forward. Although the infant was not injured, the misstep evidently frightened him, and he began to cry. Deirdre moved quickly, gathering her son to her and saying, "It's okay." Her grasp and her attitude were both gentle and affectionate. Deirdre looked at me over her son's shoulder, smiling as if to express her embarrassment. However, she actually said very little after her initial "It's okay" to soothe her son.

When Patrick's crying had diminished, Deirdre reached for a bottle and held it out to Patrick, who grasped it and began to drink thirstily. "He won't even let me hold it for him anymore," Deirdre said a little wistfully. With her son settled securely in her lap and holding his bottle himself, Deirdre seemed at loose ends, uncertain what to do to participate in Patrick's feeding. Finally she began to stroke one of his feet with an affectionate gesture. Patrick continued drinking. Despite Deirdre's statement last week that Patrick's new mobility and increasing self-reliance did not trouble her, I felt her distress at being "left behind" during Patrick's feeding. For Deirdre, self-feeding may be the emotional equivalent of weaning. I was pleased to note that she did come up with a gesture—stroking and playing with her son's foot—that enabled her to participate in the feeding process.

## SESSIONS 27 TO 29

During the next three sessions, Patrick's development continued to improve steadily, without any remarkable deviance. Psychotherapeutic intervention focused on exploring Deirdre's emotional responses to this growth. During this time her emotional status remained stable. Deirdre canceled two sessions, stating that she had car problems.

## SESSION 30

Patrick had made considerable developmental progress since our last session. At 11 months, he is large and handsome, no longer an infant but more appropriately characterized as a toddler. He uses a nimble combination of walking and crawling to get around. He was dressed in a colorful outfit that contributed to his air of maturity—indeed, announced him as the busy, explorative toddler he had become. Deirdre wore jeans and an oversized sweater. Her hair was combed forward so that it almost entirely obscured her face; after a moment I comprehended the reason for this camouflage. Deirdre had a fresh scar raking across her entire left cheek, almost 2 inches wide and 4 inches long. The lesion looked like a burn of some sort, and, although it appeared to be healing properly, this was by no means a minor injury. Turning to Patrick, I noted that he, too, had an injury: a bruise about the size of a quarter on his forehead. There was an eerie symmetry to these physical marks, and I determined to find out how each had been injured.

Deirdre responded readily to my inquiry about Patrick's bruise. "He . . . doesn't understand yet about tables—that they have tops as well as legs. He knocked his head the other day when we were at my mother's house."

I nodded, commenting that it must have been painful and startling for Patrick. When I then mentioned the scar on her face, Deirdre stiffened, then slumped down. After a chilling silence she volunteered, "I burned myself.

With some oven cleaner." Asked to describe the details of that event, for a long moment Deirdre said nothing. Then she said, "I did it on purpose. I got kind of sick for a little while, but it's under control now." Her tone made it clear that she did not want to continue. Although I am inclined to take her account of Patrick's bruise at face value, the self-destructiveness that led her to mar her face with oven cleaner is clearly still a frightening fact of Deirdre's life—and thus of Patrick's. In earlier sessions Deirdre indicated that she would hurt herself when in anger (by punching walls), as a way of dissipating some of her pain and rage. However, the cataclysmic explosion of anger that generated this disfiguring self-inflicted wound argues an equally large reservoir of pain and rage, unpredictably bubbling just below the surface of her consciousness—threatening to erupt with volcanic force and destroy mother and son in its wake.

Indeed, her propensity for self-mutilation of such extreme character at this late stage in her therapy clearly represents a very real and ongoing danger for Patrick. I can only opine that her desire to efface herself quite literally with a caustic chemical is a symbolic acting out of her psychological ploy of presenting with blunted, characterless affect. In light of this, her pathetically flat, little 19-word "explanation" ("I did it on purpose. I got kind of sick for a little while, but it's under control now") of the event is especially chilling. There is no elaboration here, no *real* explanation of the events or motivation that could precipitate such a drastic event—rather, in the weak assurance "it's under control now," a defiant avoidance. In sum, Deirdre's drastic act and her inappropriate matter-of-fact manner in its aftermath lead me to wonder—despite the progress she and Patrick have made in their dyadic interaction—how far Deirdre has actually progressed in abandoning her delusionary distortions. Today, her old defensive mask seems very much in place.

Sensing that Deirdre had closed herself off, I told her I would like to sit on the floor to play a game with Patrick. Eventually, I interested him in a toy lawnmower that made a loud ratchety sound. Patrick stood in one place, pushing the lawnmower back and forth and grinning broadly at the noise. Watching us, Deirdre nervously tossed a rubber ball back and forth from her right to her left hand. She seemed only vaguely interested in the interaction between me and her son. In particular, when Patrick had tired of the lawnmower and I had taken him over to the blackboard to draw, Deirdre observed the battle that took place when Patrick put a piece of chalk in his mouth and I took the chalk away. "He doesn't care much for 'No,'" she commented wryly. Patrick, reaching for the chalk, began to demonstrate his frustration by crying and wriggling, his face pinched in a frown. After my attempts to calm him, Deirdre reached out for Patrick and cuddled him. Patrick immediately stopped crying, but he remained fussy for some time. Once he stopped crying, Deirdre rose and walked to the window with her son. Quite unsubtly her gesture cut me out of the interaction entirely. The mother and child stood in silence for a little while.

This whole incident was quite revelatory. It manifested an acting out of the frequent usage of the word "boredom" in Deirdre's vocabulary as well as her desire to control. It was evident that Patrick had been enjoying himself immensely, yet without a thought Deirdre interrupted our (mine and Patrick's) interaction, her son's involvement, and the various currents in the interview room. Her reaction validates my original impression that "boredom" was generally a projection of Deirdre's mentation rather than an objectively verifiable state in her infant son.

"In contrast to when Patrick was younger, in what ways is taking care of him now different from taking care of him then?" I asked, attempting to break her wall of silence.

Deirdre returned to her seat and put Patrick down on the floor again. "We have a lot of fun. I feel good about Pat, really. He's the good part of things. But with the wedding 2 weeks away, almost everything else is more demanding than he is. When things get really crazy, I go and hang out with him."

Even when she verbalizes pleasure in her son's progress or childish developments, she expresses herself minimally, and the sense persists that she is saying so out of duty. Her affect still seems blunted and remote. She must be taken at her word, but it is clear Deirdre has some distance to go before her parenting pleasure has resurfaced enough to be internalized and genuine. As I have been monitoring her, this may still be interpreted as progress, since my interventions had been aimed at sharing and allowing her to express her suppressed (or to develop absent) feelings. This minimal pleasure she permits herself to verbalize was, I knew, merely one milestone in a lengthy continuum to fully realized and expressed pleasure.

"Do you see any connection between what you did to harm yourself and your interactions with Patrick?" I asked.

After a short silence, Deirdre shook her head emphatically. "No . . . not at all." Patrick had been experimenting, pushing a ball a short distance toward me and waiting to see if it was returned. Now he turned and looked at his mother. She met his eyes, smiled wanly, and said "That's great, Pat." Satisfied, the baby turned back to his game. Deirdre is slowly becoming more verbal with Patrick. She appears to be embarrassed to talk to her son in front of me, but her willingness to do so is increasing, perhaps because she believes he is closer to understanding her.

"I was wondering," Deirdre said several minutes later. "Should he be talking soon?"

"Most babies start to talk somewhere between 14 and 18 months. Patrick's already babbling. It's also important for you to talk to him and to preview a conversation with him as best you can. Baby talk has its uses. It familiarizes your baby with how people use sound to communicate. It also promotes mental representations of what he is trying to communicate." Deirdre did not respond and seemed somewhat uncomfortable with the topic. "Can you imagine the way that Patrick views the world—what his symbols are for the people and things around him? For example, if Patrick doesn't have a word for you yet, how do you think he represents you—imagines you—when you're not around him?"

Deirdre shrugged. "The one with the bottle." She grinned inappropriately. "The one who says 'No' all the time."

"How about the one who comforts me when I fall, or smiles at me to let me know that the game I'm playing is okay?"

Deirdre's smile became less tense. "Maybe that stuff, too."

"And how do you envision Patrick talking?"

"I don't know," Deirdre said flatly. She agreed that Patrick at 11 months was roughly the way she had imagined, but she could not say when she had begun to imagine him at this stage. She also claimed to be unable to recall any earlier predictions about talking or about her son at this age. And she said that she could not preview Patrick's future beyond his current stage. I wonder if this blockage and her seemingly complete inability specifically to predict or preview language acquisition in her son have its roots in some intensely painful past event from her own childhood or whether it is a maneuver to "hold the line" of Patrick's progress similar to those she has previously displayed.

After a few minutes of silence, I asked, "Have you had any wish to hurt yourself since you burned yourself?"

Deirdre replied that she had not but that she had been feeling angry and "tense" for some time. "I get that way and I feel like I'm not aware of what I'm doing." At this point, we must, unfortunately, substitute "potentially violent" for what Deirdre terms "tense." She immediately followed with an admission of an awareness of her frightening potential for explosive volatility. At least once, she reported, she had wanted to hit Patrick, but she had "convinced" herself that he didn't understand his crying was making her angry. After confiding this information, Deirdre looked uncomfortable and guilty.

"When you feel irritable, would you prefer to be away from Patrick?" I asked.

"Yes. That way it's easier to deal with my feelings. The trouble is that I don't know what's making me angry most of the time." At this point Deirdre became increasingly upset. "I don't find it particularly easy to talk about it with you." Here she is at least grappling with the effort to deal with her emotions, particularly her least manageable ones. She shifted in her seat with her typical avoidance, then rose and went to the window. Patrick looked at his mother and returned unenthusiastically to his play.

I asked Deirdre if she had consulted with any doctors, specifically a dermatologist or plastic surgeon about her injury. She replied that she had not spoken to anyone. Was Mike aware of her recent mood changes, I asked. "Not all that much," she replied. With her back turned, avoiding me entirely as she faced out the window, Deirdre spent the last minutes of the session describing a dream in which she and Patrick had been in the backyard of her mother's house. "There were these terrorists, and they had captured us. The next thing that happened was they were stabbing Pat. There was blood everywhere. I managed to get away, but suddenly I realized that Pat was still back there alone with those people. I woke up and looked over to see Patrick asleep in his crib." The savage imagery of the dream indicates that she still harbored enormous hostility for her son. The "terrorists" are her own unbridled emotions that indeed hold her enslaved and threaten to surface unpredictably, leaving violence in their wake. The fact that she does not solicit support, even from people as close to her as Mike, also remains an important issue. With her wedding only 2 weeks away, the dream had an added symbolism: It is as though the wedding itself were an act of terrorism that will somehow cut Deirdre off from her son. If she acknowledges her closeness with Mike through the marriage, Patrick will pay the price. Deirdre clearly feels that she has to surrender to the "terrorists" in her life—including Mike.

When she had finished relating her dream, the session was over. Beyond her superficial insights of the dream, a large component of it, I felt, also referred to the feelings she had squelched at the time of her recent abortion. In short, she still carried considerable guilt for having let herself abort ("left") her infant "back there." In this manner, her dream served as a path to externalize carefully tamped-down and latent feelings. Deirdre put Patrick into his stroller and prepared to leave without making any further comment. I remarked that there were a few issues that I was not clear about in the dream and said I hoped we could review her dream during our next session.

## SESSION 31

I met Deirdre and Patrick in the waiting area before our session today. The scar on Deirdre's cheek has not yet disappeared, and it is a potent reminder that many of the issues in Deirdre's life have not yet been completely resolved. Once in the room, Deirdre placed her son on the floor. For the first few minutes of the session, Patrick played with some of the toys gathered there. "He's getting good at doing small stuff—his coordination with his fingers is getting really good." For example, Deirdre continued, Patrick had been eating cornflakes one at a time. "He won't even use the spoon—he wants to have contact with what he's eating. Gets pretty messy."

"That's a sharp observation," I commented. "Pretty much a textbook example of fine motor coordination."

Deirdre thought for a few minutes and added, "He's curious. He wants to know how things work; he's getting persistent about poking at something until he understands it." She nodded toward Patrick, who had found a toy from which a foam ball popped out. Having found the right spot once, Patrick was busily trying to find the spot again. When he pressed a button and another ball popped up, he crowed in triumph. Deirdre smiled depre- catingly, as if she found it embarrassing to exhibit the feelings she shared with her son. I applauded Patrick, praising his success.

"That's mastery motivation," I explained. "It's really terrific that Patrick follows through until he realizes how things work. He's very determined to interact with the external world, as though it represents a challenge to be re- solved. And of course, your support really helps him." It is interesting to note here that her son's involvement and desire to interact with the external world both surpass and are in direct conflict with his mother's interactional mode. As Deirdre and I watched Patrick play, I turned back to the mother and commented that she looked rested. "How are things coming along with your wedding plans?" I asked.

Deirdre smiled and shook her head, tossing the hair out of her eyes. "Most of the arrangements for the wedding are made. We're not making a big deal out of it. And," she paused and laughed sheepishly, "I'm pregnant again." Deirdre had just discovered this a few days ago, and this time she planned to have the baby. "I don't want to go through an abortion again—it made me feel miserable." She believed Mike felt good about the pregnancy, but, for now, their attention was occupied by the wedding. Their avoidance, I felt, presaged an inflammation of latent conflict in the future. The wedding might be one contributor to Deirdre's refusal to confront the issue, but I was certain the (for her) rapid-fire growth of Patrick in both size and indepen- dence was also implicated in her unexpected near self-immolation. Her pregnancy was also a signal for the world at large to notice how unsettled she was about the status of events around her. Deirdre's pregnancy con- cerned me for an additional reason: It meant she would undoubtedly go off the neuroleptic medication she had been using to control auditory hallucina- tions.

Patrick stood up and marched to his mother, attempting to pull himself up on her lap. Deirdre picked her son up, then reached for a bottle, which she offered to her son. Patrick grasped the bottle and began to drink thirstily. Deirdre played with her son's free hand as he nursed. The small gestures be- tween them were marked with tenderness and quiet pleasure. "Life in the fast lane, that's Patrick. He sleeps less, eats less, wants to spend all his time poking into things. The only thing that slows him up is if I yell at him," re- vealing that violence (albeit verbal) still plays a part in Patrick's develop- mental activities. She reported that yelling didn't always work, so she then would tell him she was going to leave him alone. Asked if she has ever left him alone, Deirdre nodded, "Yes. Not too many times, though." I roughly outlined stranger anxiety and separation behaviors, both of which she might normally observe in Patrick at this age. After this explanation, I asked Deirdre if she had noticed any of these behaviors in Patrick. She stated emphatically that they did not leave Patrick that often and that she had not had enough opportunities to observe such behaviors.

Deirdre was operating on several levels of denial here that all indicate the degree of her resistance. On one tier, she was denying her culpability: She here uses the term "they" in "they did not leave Patrick often." But earlier, she'd employed the term "she." Thus, the effect is to spread any blame rather than shoulder it herself. On another level, she's self-deluding if she truly expects an analyst to put credulity aside and simply accept what she says at face value. In 8 or 9 months she certainly has had ample opportunities to note a wide spectrum of separation behaviors in her infant. As in the past, degree of her denial serves as a barometer for Deirdre's refusal to confront reality. It presages other denials.

I now asked Deirdre if she wanted to comment on the dream she had described last week. Deirdre shook her head. "No. Not at all," thus pursuing the course of total denial she had already established in the session.

Patrick grabbed Deirdre's shirt, pulling on it. His face took on a rapt expression, as if he were sniffing something. Deirdre observed that this was Patrick's "hungry face." Yet to an objective observer, Patrick's face was more an expression of healthy active interest, rather than a quintessential "hungry face," whatever that may engender in the listener's mind. By virtue of these "masks" that she attributes to her son, Deirdre is almost psychically sculpting into the baby what he "should" be feeling. Actually, it is Deirdre herself who presents a featureless, delusionary masklike face to the world. I handled this by veering toward a probe of her interpretations to try to make her reveal why she saw her Patrick's face in archetypal terms. My effort was to help to lead her to interpret her actions and statements rather than merely to react. As if regressing to the comfort of the nipple herself when presented with "threatening" thoughts, she took out the bottle again, pulled Patrick up on her lap, and put it in his mouth. "I like it when he comes back to me after he's been playing," she said simply.

## SESSION 32

As of this morning, I had been involved with this case for over a year. Patrick would soon be 1 year old. At today's session, Deirdre looked tired but reasonably cheerful. Patrick was full of energy, immediately climbing down from his mother's arms to tramp determinedly around the room, investigating. Last week Deirdre and her son could not make our session because it was the day of Deirdre's wedding, so my first question today was about the occasion and how everything had gone. "Pretty well," she told me with her characteristic lack of enthusiasm. "I'm glad it's over, though." She and Mike would wait for their honeymoon for a couple of years. "Right now we need new tires for the car, and there's other stuff we have to spend money for. We'll wait a while and then go away," was her flat, depressing reaction as the family embarks on its future together.

Patrick now walked so steadily and with such assurance that he was able to cross the room carrying something in each hand. "That's very impressive!" I remarked. "Not just his skill at walking, but the fact that he feels so confident." Leaning down, I tried to engage Patrick by talking to him. Initially Patrick showed no particular interest in my comments. I showed him a little doll, and when Patrick tried to reach for it, I moved it just a little away from him. Patrick began to scream loudly, waving his fists. His ability to make his needs understood without crying is appropriate for his 49 weeks.

"That's his new thing," Deirdre confided. "If I yell at him—he screams. If I take something away from him—he screams. Sometimes he just screams, and I can't tell what's going on. It's awful." She thought the screaming might be a response to the wedding. "The wedding was disruptive—my father came from Ireland, and that was really hectic. Both of my parents bickered the whole time. It's exhausting to be around. Pat and Mike and I are all bushed."

The depressing circumstances of what should have been a happy occasion aside, the order she uses here is interesting: Despite what she feels like, Deirdre is taking the wishes and comfort of her son first, when months earlier she was routinely placing her needs, or those of herself and Mike, first. Therefore, hard as it is to place the dyadic relationship in a progressive context, she is making slow but constant advances.

Patrick slipped from his mother's lap and began examining various toys within his reach. One of the objects he found was a small sponge ball. Fearing that Patrick would try to put the ball in his mouth, I asked Deirdre what would be the best way to interact with him in order to take it away. Deirdre responded, "There's a way to take things away from him. You have to take the object slowly, and talk to him while you're doing it. Distract him, sort of." Thus, she had not only developed some strategies for dealing with Patrick's behavior, but she was able to describe those strategies in an attempt to help me interact more effectively with her son. I complemented her on this strategy, found a safer toy and, following Deirdre's suggestion, took the ball away from Patrick, offering the new toy in its stead. The infant continued to play.

"Have you noticed any relation between his mood swings and your mood swings?" I asked.

Deirdre looked startled. "Are you saying that I'm causing him to get upset that way?"

"No, I don't mean that there is a correlation. But you have mentioned how hard it is for you to control your impulses when you feel angry or unhappy. I wonder if you saw any parallel to Patrick's outbursts."

"Yes. I don't know. Maybe." Deirdre looked distressed, almost frightened at the idea. "He's growing so fast—this year has gone by so fast. He keeps changing so much that it's hard to know what he's responding to. It's funny and aggravating at the same time."

Patrick again approached his mother, trying to climb into her lap. Deirdre leaned down to pick her son up; there was a moment of direct eye contact that seemed particularly intense. However, the moment Deirdre's attention turned to me, Patrick became upset. He seemed unwilling to share his mother with another person.

"Have you noticed any of these reactions when you interact with other people?"

"Yes," Deirdre replied. "Especially when I'm with Mike." Deirdre held her son on her lap and spoke to him repeatedly, asking "What do you want?" At last she loosed her hold on him and put him on the floor. Then she followed him to a pile of toys and games. While Patrick examined one toy, Deirdre would put the last one back in the toy box. After 5 minutes the game changed, so that Patrick was helping his mother put the toys in the box himself. Mother and son were briefly united in a common project. Overall, their communication is immensely improved. I believe this progress is greatly assisted by Patrick's development and Deirdre's increasing intent to support that development.

## SESSION 33

It had been raining steadily this week, and the general dreariness seems to have affected people's moods. Both Deirdre and Patrick seemed out of sorts today. Patrick, freshly awakened from a nap, began the session sitting on the floor, poking listlessly at a toy that on other occasions had delighted him. There were dark circles under Deirdre's eyes, and her mouth seemed sunk in unhappy lines.

I asked Deirdre for permission to take Patrick on an "adventure," a trip out of the room. Doing so served to set up a "separation episode," during and after which I could gauge the attachment and representational abilities of both mother and son. Deirdre approved and watched without protest, but her expression was blank, as if this "abandonment" raised feelings in her with which she did not have the energy to cope. Although Patrick made no commotion as he was taken out of the room, when we returned he was protesting strenuously. This increased to full-blown crying when he saw his mother. Patrick reached for his mother, crying loudly. I asked Deirdre if this reaction seemed familiar. Deirdre reached up to embrace the baby. Once in his mother's grasp Patrick calmed down. She did not offer him a bottle as once she might have done. Instead, she held him closely, with a slight bouncing and rocking motion. "He hasn't had enough sleep. It's getting tough, because he doesn't want to take a nap; he just wants to explore. So he is hard to deal with."

Pronouncing Patrick's name, I endeavored to woo the infant's attention. "I don't think you're going to win him over today," Deirdre said flatly. "He's not in the mood for sweet talk." With a flash of humor, she admitted, "Neither of us is." Asked why, she responded, "Pat won't go to sleep. When he doesn't go to sleep, I don't go to sleep. My pregnancy is making me crazy. I feel irritable, especially at night. Morning's not too bad. Now it's all I can do to stay up through our AA meetings. I'm really exhausted." Patrick appeared to resent the fact that he did not have his mother's attention. He began to struggle, wriggling in his mother's arms. Deirdre tried physically to contain her son's protest. Her expression grew strained as Patrick refused to be soothed.

"Would you be amenable to trying something?" I asked. "Let's try talking while you hold Patrick. He may find it soothing to hear you talking without any distress. Many babies are reassured when their caregivers reassure them intentionally." It was clear from Deirdre's expression that she did not expect this strategy to work. I asked her a question about her predictions of Patrick's future development, which Deirdre tried, at first, to answer. However, as Patrick's whining intensified, Deirdre was increasingly distracted. She could not finish her sentence. Her expression became tighter until she appeared barely in control of her temper. Patrick's crying was the last straw for his mother.

"That's it; this isn't going to work," she said emphatically. Despite my encouragement, she refused to continue the session. It was notable that, despite her obvious frustration, Deirdre's handling of her son was both competent and careful; she did not physically act out her anger as she prepared Patrick to leave. Deirdre's barely controlled anger seemed directed at me, as if I had provoked her. Indeed, in retaliation for my habitual provoking of unwanted subjects and my exploration of unresolved conflictual material, Deirdre "took charge" of the session and responded by controlling me with its termination. In retrospect, it may be that her hostility stemmed from the staged "separation" incident. Deirdre's apparent exhausted passivity seems to have been masking deeper feelings of anger. She is not yet ready to separate from her son.

There was something of a pattern here—one that I noted months ago: After two relatively productive sessions at which Deirdre's developing skills were evident, there was now a difficult session. I telephoned Deirdre later that afternoon and offered her the opportunity for an extra session. She replied that she would set up an appointment if she felt that things were getting out of control. Deirdre canceled the following two appointments. During the second week I suggested a home visit by one of our clinic social workers; the visit took place without event.

## SESSION 34

Patrick had immediately located his favorite toy, the lawn mower, and was stomping purposefully around the room. At 53 weeks, his gait is steady, and his fine motor coordination increasingly developed. Patrick's attention is also optimal. He seems single-minded in his play. At the same time, even though he is attracted to loud noises such as those made by the toy lawn mower, Patrick responds only infrequently to his own name. He makes his needs known by a variety of nonvocal means, and at times the communication between Patrick and Deirdre has an almost balletic quality. Still, he tends not to rely on his language skills.

I asked Deirdre if she had observed any new changes in Patrick. "He's got four new teeth. He uses them, too," she added ruefully. "He hasn't figured out that it hurts the person getting bit." I mentioned her dream of several months ago about losing all her teeth. Deirdre said she had been "looking ahead. Previewing, right?" Asked how she responded when Patrick bit her, Deirdre twisted in her seat. "I try not to get mad. He doesn't know what he's doing." Her manner as she said this was suspiciously casual, so I asked her if it was hard for her not to get angry when her son caused her pain. She responded thoughtfully: "Sometimes it is very hard. I don't want to get out of control with him, you know?" After a pause she added, "It's hard even to talk about it."

"Do you feel that you may gain increased control if you come to understand the issues involved?"

"I suppose. But I don't feel like talking about it now," she responded with one of her characteristic dismissals.

Sensing that to press further was inadvisable, I inquired about her pregnancy. "How is it progressing?"

"Okay. I had ultrasound, and they think I'm almost 4 months. I thought I was about 2 months." If this is indeed so, Deirdre became pregnant again immediately following her abortion. Deirdre wrinkled her nose as if to indicate that the surprise of learning how advanced her pregnancy was had been a mixed blessing. I asked her if Patrick had noticed any of the changes she was experiencing. "That's impossible," she said. I asked if she felt aware of her moods. "I don't feel like getting into it right now," she responded sullenly. Deirdre leaned forward in her chair and watched Patrick intently. He had played with the lawn mower for some time after the session began but had abandoned that toy in order to play a new game. A dismantled playhouse was stacked against the wall, and Patrick discovered that by shaking the playhouse wall he could produce loud noises and vibrations. He continued with this game for almost 10 minutes. When he had apparently exhausted it, Patrick began moving chairs from one place to another in the room. His entire body was bent purposefully to this task, and his facial expressions were intense and deliberate. I was interested that Patrick's interest in the toys had evolved to a greater exploration of understanding them cognitively than had been displayed in the past, almost as if Patrick, grasping the notion of contingency, wanted to understand all the situations he encountered. "What is your sense of how different Patrick is now from the way he was when he was younger?" I asked.

"He cooperates more," she said. "He sits still when I'm dressing him or changing his diapers. In the past, changing a diaper was an unbelievable production!"

"Do you have a sense of how much he understands he is cooperating with you?" I asked.

"I think he's aware that if I get angry, it's not good for him." She laughed softly, observing Patrick passing with another chair. He stepped away from the chair, went to his mother and touched her knee briefly, then returned to the chair. "Just checking in," Deirdre noted.

Finally he returned to Deirdre, agitating to be picked up by burying his face in his mother's sweatshirt. Deirdre picked her son up and smoothed the hair away from his face, but Patrick refused to be quieted and struggled to be let down again. I sensed a new adaptability in Deirdre. She did not seem unduly flustered by Patrick's repeated interruptions and could find a solution to distract him. I suggested to Deirdre that she might join a playgroup for mothers and babies. Deirdre took this recommendation well. I then asked her if she could describe aloud what she observed as Patrick played; hesitantly she did so. Her observations were interesting in that she bypassed any description of Patrick's affects; she could tell me that Patrick was exploring the texture of a rubber toy, but she did not delve into details of his pleasure in his discoveries. After receiving some guidance in this, however, Deirdre began cautiously to describe her son's emotional and motivational inclinations. Deirdre's inability to represent affective and psychological changes mirrors her own inability to focus on the emotional issues in her own life. As he played Patrick babbled, occasionally glancing at his mother before returning to his play. I pointed out to Deirdre that Patrick seemed very aware of her verbalizations and attention.

"Screaming is his thing these days," Deirdre noted. "He's throwing tantrums." As if to demonstrate, Patrick approached his mother and whined piercingly, demanding her attention. Deirdre picked the infant up and held him for a moment, which did not pacify him; then she put him down on her lap and began to joggle him; this apparently soothed him, and he began to giggle.

## SESSION 35

Deirdre and Patrick arrived promptly today, despite inclement weather. Both mother and child appeared to be in good spirits as we began, although Deirdre seemed slightly edgy. After a brief silence, I asked Deirdre if she had noticed any new developments in her son. Interestingly, she had noted, "None, really . . . except his temper!" She didn't believe he understood the concept of "No" when she tried to set limits. "He just wants his own way, especially when he wants to do something dangerous, like standing up in his high chair. When I stop him from doing something like that, he screams!" Deirdre still seemed to have little realization that Patrick takes his cues from her. Laughing, she went on to say, "I wanted this kid to have some strength of mind, but I didn't realize he was going to be this strong!" Asked if she observed similarities between Patrick's temperament and her own, Deirdre suddenly confided she had often feared that Patrick's temper might be an early version of her own disorder. She felt sad and angry about this: "Sad because it is my fault that he may become vulnerable, like me. Angry because I feel as if he defies me. I end up feeling like showing him who is in charge."

"How would you feel if you realized that by showing his temper Patrick is not trying to evoke sadness or anger but just trying to catch your attention?" Deirdre seemed interested in this idea. I continued, "It could also be that Patrick has learned to make you angry with his behavior. He can validate his predictions about your moods—particularly about anger, to which you feel vulnerable. How do you feel when you see Patrick getting around on his own so well?"

Deirdre thought for a moment. "Mostly good. I mean, he can amuse himself, and I don't have to be constantly moving him around. But sometimes he sneaks up on me and scares me." She admitted that Patrick's sudden appearances only scared or worried her when she had been hearing voices prior to his arrival. This is her first admission of a recurrence of her auditory hallucinations since she had omitted medication on her trip to Ireland. The voices were abusive and cruel, insulting Deirdre because she was a "bad" person.

"Do you think that the voices come from Patrick?" I asked.

She hung her head, obviously unhappy. "Sometimes."

Her revelation might signal a point at which she would be able to discuss such issues with less resistance and therefore be more amenable to therapeutic guidance. Despite her obvious deep discomfort, Deirdre continued to talk and did not retreat into silence or abruptly leave, as she had done in the past. I feel strongly that she is far better equipped to deal with the current pressures in her life than she would have been 6 months ago. There was a pause of a few minutes, and then I commented, "Why would Patrick say unkind things to you?"

"I don't know." After a pause she continued, "I know he isn't saying those things. I'm just imagining the voices are coming from him. It's my sickness. But I hear them!"

"I think that voice is summing up your fears about yourself, and you're projecting that voice into Patrick," I replied. "By voicing those feelings you are telling him to see if he is feeling the way you think he is feeling. It allows you to voice your doubts about yourself." Deirdre looked intently at her son and did not answer. "Do you think that Patrick needs more attention than other children?"

"I don't think about it."

"You're attuned to Patrick's wants and needs, Deirdre. If you feel you're doing the right things with Patrick, why are the voices you hear so critical?"

Deirdre sighed, "I don't know."

I have wondered before if there was a specific cause for Deirdre's apparent inability to preview language. Now it is only the hallucinatory voices that accuse and berate her; what if her son gains his voice only to join the chorus of criticism? Deirdre's sense of self is still, we see, so unpredictable and fragile that she conceives of her child to be joining in a chorus of criticism against her. It is not surprising, then, that Deirdre's response to these voices is so varied—an anger that molds Patrick into an extension of herself. The danger is that in an extremely distraught state, perhaps induced by an auditory hallucination, Deirdre might attempt to hurt herself or her son as she did with her face-burning incident some time ago.

"Are you concerned about sometimes being angry at Patrick?"

Deirdre shook her head. "I do get angry at him. I love Patrick, but sometimes I'm scared to death to be with him. I'm afraid Pat will have a tantrum and I'll just lose it. Once, when Pat sneaked up on me in the kitchen—I'd been hearing a voice, and suddenly there he was—I smacked him." Deirdre stared at me in a challenging way.

"Deirdre, many parents, no matter what their psychiatric history, can have the urges you describe for me. It's very hard for you, because in your case these urges take the form of voices. But you may want to consider the possibility that your fatigue and your fears are natural emotions."

Deirdre recapitulated my comments. Her tone was less angry, as if she wanted to believe what I had said but could not.

Patrick had learned to wave "bye-bye." At the close of the session he waved to me, grinning broadly. This represents the attainment of another milestone—a representation of separation, with appropriate social acknowledgment.

SESSION 36

When I arrived for today's session Patrick was playing with the toy lawn mower, marching intently around the room. He stopped when I entered and smiled at me. I commented on this to Deirdre, telling her I felt honored to receive such a greeting. She smiled, although faintly. Now that she is in her fourth month of pregnancy, her condition is beginning to show. Her affect today was agreeable but nervous; she showed signs of edginess, twisting and turning in her chair, tapping absently on the arm of her chair.

Deirdre said that she had joined a mother-infant playgroup and felt it was a good decision. As she spoke, Patrick brought the lawn mower to his mother and repeatedly pushed the toy up to her foot, then stood back looking at her. Deirdre did not allow herself to be engaged in his play, but she waved her hand at him in a curious gesture that might have been an approximation of a pat on the head. I attempted to catch his attention by calling his name. As usual, Patrick ignored his name, going about his own business. For several minutes we watched Patrick as he investigated a child-size playhouse that had been set up near one corner of the room. I asked Deirdre if she had observed any new changes in Patrick's development.

"He's not eating. He won't eat anything when he's fed. He wants to hold everything by himself. Most of the time he's too busy to stop for meals and starts screaming if I try to sit him down and give him lunch or dinner. He's a real 'fast-food' baby, all right." This change, Deirdre admitted on consideration, had been going on for some time, approximately since Patrick first began to walk. "He'd rather explore than eat," she said.

"Do you enjoy feeding him?" I asked.

"Sometimes. Other times I wish I could have more time during the day."

"Do you think that some of Patrick's impatience may be a reflection of your own impatience?"

"Maybe." After a few moments of silence, Deirdre stated, "I had another dream. I'm in a junkyard. There's garbage all over the place, mountains of junk. I'm running, trying to get away. I look down and realize that I'm running on a soft mattress, and I can't get away." She said its interpretation was "obvious." "I think it's the whole thing of feeling tired all the time." When she's confronted by events that she perceives as uncontrollable, she manifests, almost immediately, her own considerable vulnerabilities. Deirdre feels totally engulfed, almost smothered by the events of her life. In this instance, I worked toward making her confront and best her conflicts. That she is beginning to share her dreams so readily demonstrates how far along she has come.

In the future, we will be working toward her relaxing her vigilant over-determinism and motivation. When I asked what made her feel so tired and

overwhelmed, Deirdre responded that taking care of Patrick, being pregnant, maintaining her relationship with Mike, and tending to their home all
contributed to her fatigue.

"So each one of those factors is 'a mattress,'" I said, half-jokingly. "And
you have to divide your time among them."

Deirdre nodded. "Yes. And I feel like I could get swallowed up by any
one of them." This dream is certainly positive when contrasted with dreams
she reported previously. Clearly, Deirdre feels overwhelmed by her responsibilities. But despite the fact that she is trying to run away from the "junk"
in her life, there is no evidence of overt violence or reference to hurting her
child or herself. The fact that a more traditional symbolism is at work is, in
itself, a sign of improvement.

Patrick began to make a loud noise. I mentioned to Deirdre that I was
going to join him and for some minutes the two of us played peek-a-boo, to
Patrick's evident delight. Each time I appeared, I made a broad face of surprise, and gave an exclamation such as "Oh, my! It's Patrick!" Patrick responded with giggles and immediately hid behind the partition. At one
point in the game Patrick stopped, hid behind the partition, and craned his
head until he had made eye contact with his mother. Then he made a loud
noise. Deirdre smiled and laughed. She did not join in the game, but she did
encourage her son when he referred back to her by nodding and smiling. I
pointed out that Patrick's ability and delight in the game of peek-a-boo was
evidence of his strong representational ability. Although she gave no evidence of pleasure at this comment, she was curious enough to ask me to
elaborate. When I had explained, Deirdre nodded as if she could now take
my comment as a compliment.

"Can you imagine what it will be like when Patrick talks?" I asked
Deirdre.

She shrugged. "I don't know. I guess he'll sound just like he sounds now,
except with words." She joked that his first word would probably be "No,"
but added more seriously, "I guess it will probably be 'Daddy.'" Asked if he
might say "Mommy" first, Deirdre responded, "Patrick's really glad to see
Mike when he gets home, so he'll probably remember 'Daddy' better."
Despite the fact that her suggestions were voiced ambivalently, this was a
marked improvement from the Deirdre who a week before had been unable
to imagine her son saying anything but on another occasion had "heard"
him hurling sophisticated verbal insults at her.

Exploring why Patrick did not respond to his name, I took a toy telephone
and, making it ring, "answered" a pretend call for Patrick. "Who? You want
to speak with Patrick? Just one moment, please!" I gave the handset to
Patrick, who approached and held the earpiece to his head. This game
seemed to fascinate the infant, but he was clearly interested in listening for
sounds at the other end of the phone and in making the bell on the phone

ring. I felt encouraged after I observed Patrick's reactions and I shared my observations with Deirdre. I did, however, mention to her that she and Mike should continue to stimulate Patrick's expressive language abilities. I explained to her that the exercise could be done easily by showing Patrick the names of his body parts: "This is your nose," and so on.

At session's end, I asked Deirdre about the emotional expectations she had of an upcoming trip to Canada she and Mike were planning. Deirdre felt that everything was under control and said she looked forward to the visit.

## SESSION 37

Because of Deirdre and Patrick's visit to Mike's family in Toronto, 5 weeks had elapsed between sessions. Carrying a mental image of the dyad as they had appeared at Christmas time, I was somewhat startled at the changes in both. Deirdre's pregnancy, now in its 24th week, was evident; in addition, she had cut her hair in a short style that framed her face becomingly. I noted this change, and she smiled, averting her eyes as if embarrassed. As for Patrick, now 60 weeks of age, his face had gained a more mature expression and shape. Although his expression often fluctuated between seriousness and somberness, an occasional smile lightened his face. Patrick soon woke from his nap and began to investigate the room thoroughly.

I commented to Deirdre that I assumed everything had gone well during her trip, since I had not heard from them. Deirdre confirmed this impression. I then asked about developmental changes in Patrick since our last session. Deirdre reported that her son now knew his tongue, eyes, and nose by name and location. They had a game they played together in which Deirdre would ask him "Where's your nose," pause, then touch his nose gently, saying "There's your nose!" Deirdre explained that if Patrick learned how to talk he would be able to begin earlier at nursery school. Whereas I am pleased with Deirdre's increasing willingness to stimulate Patrick's language skills, she was effectively using her projection of Patrick's speech acquisition to push the infant away. I suspect, given the preponderance of adaptive cues this mother has been demonstrating, that this is not yet a serious problem; however, it is something I must be aware of.

"What about your ability to understand his motivations and feelings?"

She smiled. "I've been talking to him more, or trying to. It feels weird, talking to someone who doesn't answer back." Talking to the baby, it was apparent, was too much like talking to herself—a supposed sign of mental illness that made Deirdre uncomfortable. She changed the subject, talking about the courses she was planning to take at her local community college. Her mother was going to take care of Patrick while Deirdre was in school. "Mom complains about it. I don't think she'd be happy if she couldn't complain about something. I hope it will work out okay. Pat does okay with her. It's not like she's not good with him."

"How do you think Patrick feels about your moods now?" I asked next.

Deirdre shrugged. "I think he feels pretty good. Of course, if I'm in a bad mood he gets cranky. You were right in what you pointed out to me." Although she reported using adaptive strategies for dealing with her anger—taking walks or having Mike take care of Patrick, she also reported that a few times she had been so angry that she locked herself in the bathroom to get away from Patrick. She said that during these times Patrick had fallen asleep.

I suggested that Deirdre teach him to understand her cues that signal she doesn't feel like interacting: "Even saying so to him may help him to understand." Again Deirdre said that she thought Patrick was too young to understand. I continued, "With a second baby coming, one of the things you should think about is how to structure some time for yourself. Do you remember how demanding it was to have a newborn?"

"It doesn't seem to be that way now," she responded. "Now I feel like I'm constantly needed. Until about 6 or 7 months, Patrick napped more, he didn't run around so much. I thought I'd be freer when he could walk." She sniffed. "I had no idea."

"Do you think of Patrick as someone with whom you have a relationship?" I asked.

It became evident that Deirdre had not thought in these terms before. She paused before saying, "He's a baby, so you don't expect the same things you do from an adult. I realize he does have different relationships with different people. With me he smiles and guides his attention. He checks with me to make sure what he's doing is okay. He needs to sit on my lap sometimes. Just checking in, I guess."

As we walked together to the elevator, I complimented Deirdre on how proficient she had become at reading Patrick's cues and how much I felt she had tried to understand her son. "It's something that I am becoming aware of as time goes by," she said. She added that since about the time of Patrick's first birthday she had been increasingly aware of her ability to anticipate and predict Patrick's needs. Deirdre appeared slightly embarrassed when I complimented her, so I did not persist.

## SESSION 38

Two previous sessions had been canceled because Patrick had caught a cold. When I said "Hello" to Patrick today, he broke away from his mother and toddled over to the toy telephone on the floor near my chair. Patrick is now 63 weeks old; his physical development continues to be age appropriate or better, as does his ability to manage complex chores such as climbing onto a chair to reach the contents of a box of toys. As Deirdre removed her own cold-weather clothing, Patrick and I played "telephone." Deirdre settled herself in her chair and watched blankly as her son played. There was a sense of exhaustion about her movements today. I commented empathically that Deirdre looked tired. Had she had a bad week? She shook her head, saying that it was no worse than any other week. "But I'm back on my medication again," she added. "I'm just too up-and-down. I just feel like I have to be more even. Mike's not happy about it, but I told him it was necessary."

"What persuaded you to start your medication again?" I asked.

"Patrick was sick over the last 2 weeks. And it was very hard keeping my cool. I can't afford to feel like that with two kids." I nodded, and asked again if there was a specific incident that had troubled her. "I slapped Patrick once," Deirdre said at last. "I was in the kitchen making his lunch, and I burned my hand. While I was running cold water on it Patrick started bugging me. I kind of lost it." After a long silence, Deirdre said, "I hit him. He stopped in his tracks. Then he began to cry." Deirdre shrugged. "I don't know how I feel about what happened. Maybe I should feel guilty about hitting Pat, but right now I don't feel much of anything." I commented that Deirdre had made the right decision about resuming her medication.

At that moment Patrick ran up to his mother and stamped his foot once very decisively. Deirdre, appearing startled, looked down at her son and said "Hi." Although the intentionality of the gesture was pleasing, his concomitant refusal to use verbal cues with his mother concerned me. I have observed that in interaction with me Patrick was more likely to verbalize. Patrick immediately turned away and began to investigate a box full of small toys that sat on a low table. In order to examine the contents of the box more easily, he climbed nimbly onto a chair next to the table and sat for several minutes picking toys out of the box and putting them on the table.

I commented on Patrick's agility, and Deirdre agreed, "He went down the slide at his playgroup today all by himself." Deirdre also commented that she had begun talking to other women who shared some of their concerns. "He's starting to imitate the older kids—he applauds himself when he's pleased. He's learning the rules of the playgroup. This morning he put his toy down before he got on the slide!" With increasing animation, Deirdre reported that Patrick was walking backward—"all on his own, too"—and that it was now possible to put him to bed without a fuss. "Even when he's not tired, he seems to understand that bed is for sleeping in. It's great."

"Could you describe Patrick's ability to tolerate frustration and limit setting in more detail?"

Deirdre nodded. "His tolerance for frustration is much higher than it used to be. He was always pretty persistent, but now he doesn't get as upset by failures as he used to. It's like he's beginning to get the idea that 'No' on one thing doesn't mean 'No' on everything. He doesn't scream the way he used to." Interestingly, at little more than one year of age, Patrick's ability to integrate environmental stresses is superior to his mother's. Patrick climbed down from the chair and went to his mother, tugging urgently at her sweater. Deirdre leaned down and picked her son up on her lap, holding him in an affectionate embrace. He sat there for a few minutes, then signaled to be let down again by wriggling. "I keep doing the speech exercises you told me about," Deirdre noted. "But I don't see any difference." When I suggested that Patrick might be quite receptive to language, Deirdre replied, "Maybe so, but he sure isn't receptive to *using* language." Patrick returned to her again. Deirdre fished a package of animal crackers out of her tote bag and held one up. "Say 'Yes,' Pat. Yes? Yes?" The toddler stared at the cookie; then he turned away and returned to the telephone toy.

I remarked that in the future she might want to verbalize what she intended to do, instead of just deciding what to do quietly; then I asked if she thought Patrick was uncooperative on purpose. Deirdre thought his behavior was intentional, but she denied that it was purposefully uncooperative. "It's not like he wants to be bad. It's a little strange, because I have to balance my feeling that he's doing or not doing something on purpose with the understanding of what he can and can't do."

At times, my questions about Patrick's behavior elicited a demonstration of Deirdre's ability to effectively, even vehemently, deny her own perceptions. By denying her perceptions of Patrick's behavior, she effectively denies Patrick's impulses. Thus, she is able to feel she retains control. If Deirdre's impulse is to become angry, she denies Patrick's impulses, frustrating him and causing him to become angry. Patrick's anger, in turn, permits her own impulses free rein.

For Deirdre, the transformation of Patrick into a miniature version of her own internal chaotic cosmos represents her way of telling Patrick, "You want me to nurture you? Then you must become a victim like me. You must manifest tantrums in order to deprive yourself of control, and if you deprive yourself of control, your need for aggression will increase. If you satisfy your aggression with tantrums, you'll be nurturing yourself and won't need me." Thus, Deirdre was teaching her infant how to survive on his own. She was shaping a relationship in which there was no commitment or responsibility on her part. And in the process she was denying her own responsibility for her impulses.

Deirdre added that she had discovered that in both her family and Mike's there was a history of learning disabilities. "That makes me feel that there may be some reason for what we're going through. Pat's not a stupid kid." Asked if she thought Patrick might be learning disabled, Deirdre shook her head. "I don't know. I know he's not stupid, but it's good to know there's a history of this stuff in the families, so that," she paused. "It'd be rough for all of us if he was the only one in the family with a learning disability."

It sounded as if she felt that if Patrick was stupid, it would be her fault. Her discovery of the history of learning disabilities in both families appeared to have permitted her to evade that issue and to focus on working with Patrick. Whereas this approach was certainly better geared to Patrick's needs than self-recrimination was, I was concerned about the underlying attitude shaping her fears.

## SESSION 39

Patrick presented as an extremely nice-looking toddler for this meeting; the darkness of his clothes accentuated his fair skin and the deep red of his hair. Deirdre wore a denim maternity dress with a lace collar. Despite traces of fatigue, she had an expression of serenity today, and she now moved with slow grace. She was in her 7th month of pregnancy; Patrick is nearly 16 months old. Patrick greeted me with a smile, offering a toy truck he held in his hand; I took the truck, examined it with exclamations of interest, then returned it to the toddler, who began to walk the perimeter of the circle in which the adults sat. He stopped by his mother's chair and offered the truck for her inspection. I commented to Deirdre that it was pleasing to note Patrick's ability to integrate both of us in his pleasure. Deirdre nodded and called her son "the little diplomat." When he found another toy that interested him, Patrick sat down and began to play with the new toy, a puzzle. In the next few minutes both Deirdre and I tried to get Patrick's attention by calling his name, but the child did not respond. Deirdre finally commented that Patrick preferred his toys to her.

"Do you feel that's the choice? Toys or you?"

Deirdre shrugged and nodded. "I have such mixed feelings about him. I love him, but sometimes I hate him. Sometimes it's harder to keep things on an even keel." When I encouraged her to give an example, Deirdre commented that last weekend she had had some trouble with Patrick. "We were at the playground, and I realized that we were late—I had to get back home to start dinner, because a friend was coming over. Patrick became very stubborn, and when I tried to pick him up he gave one of those screams. I became really angry and crazy. Finally I grabbed him by one hand. Pat was following me, but I went too fast, and he fell and bumped his head. It didn't even leave a bruise. But he was crying and carrying on, and I felt lousy. I felt like I could have prevented it by just being a little more in control. He's only a baby."

Although Deirdre looks and appears almost serene, it is evident that she still feels emotionally vulnerable to sudden, dangerous mood swings. Her feelings about her own anger are bound up in her feelings toward Patrick ("I love him, but sometimes I hate him"), with whom she now has a very close relationship. It is clear how justifiably frightened she feels when she senses she is losing control. Because of this, she is capable of considerable self-condemnation. For Deirdre to feel her frustration is appropriate; however, acting out the anger on her child remains inappropriate. Despite her considerable defenses, sometimes Deirdre completely failed to protect Patrick and herself from the results of her rage. The most immediate goal would be to help Deirdre to work out strategies to deal with her anger more effectively. One strategy would be to help her to imagine scenarios of how her feelings are triggered, and then handled, by virtue of verbalizing such perceptions.

"In retrospect, do you think that you, or we, could have done something to help you deal with those emotionally overwhelming moments more effectively?"

"It's hard to say. Nothing much comes to mind," said Deirdre. I asked about her feelings toward her unborn child.

"I feel it's going to be a girl," she said. Although Deirdre had resolutely expressed no preference when I had asked this question previously, today she affirmed her preference, as if she had suddenly decided that she was entitled to distinct feelings in the matter. "Mike wants a girl, too," she added. "I don't have time to think about it much," she said. Right now, she added, she just wanted to get through everything. "It's hard to get out of bed in the morning, and all I think about is going to bed at night—I'm just so tired. But there's the baby, and my schoolwork, and the house, and Mike. That's enough to deal with in a day."

Patrick had discovered a box filled with Lego blocks. He put one of the blocks in his mouth, but when his mother and I both remonstrated with him, saying "Patrick, no!" he allowed it to fall out. He reached for another, put it in his mouth, then opened his mouth to let the block fall out next to the first one. This time Patrick smiled, looking up at his mother, who smiled but raised her eyebrows, as if to convey both her interest and her concern. Patrick continued this game through several more rounds, babbling to himself between blocks. His verbalizations were more distinct and imitative than they had been previously.

"Do you think he verbalizes deliberately?" I asked.

"Yes. He does most things deliberately. It's just that what he means by it isn't necessarily what an adult thinks." She reported that, although Patrick knew the meanings of many words such as "no," he didn't use them. "I've been meaning to tell you," she said after a silence. "Mike's got a job offer up in Toronto, where his parents live." She went on to explain that while he was considering the job, they had not made a commitment yet. "We'd have to get an apartment. But if we do go I'll be quitting here."

"How do you feel about that?" I asked.

Deirdre smiled. "It's like thinking about the new baby—right now I have too much in the present to worry about the future." Asked how this might have an impact on her therapy, Deirdre said, "I figure there must be thera-pists up in Canada—maybe you know someone up there?"

## SESSION 40

Before the session began, Deirdre announced that she and Mike had de-cided to make the move to Toronto, probably within the next few months. Deirdre explained that she wanted to have the move over before the baby came, noting that things would be confused enough after the baby arrived. Today Deirdre seemed more animated than in the past few sessions, as if the prospect of action cheered her. This more than most developmental changes manifested by Deirdre showed her progress with me. Rather than just wait until the last moment of our session she opened with this momentous news. She thus shows trust, faith, and an increasing grip over uncontrollable events.

"Anything new to report about Patrick's development?" I asked.

"He's climbing a lot. I've had to hide everything away, which is okay be-cause we're packing again, but I keep thinking 'What's going to happen if he gets into one of those boxes?'" She turned playfully to address Patrick. "That right, Pat? You fall into a box and we'll just tape it up and mail you to Toronto." Asked if she had noticed any other changes, she replied, "He's hiding things. It drives me crazy. He hid my wallet the other day. I found it behind some records. I thought that cabinet was child-proofed, but he got in. I guess that's resourceful, but it could drive you nuts." Asked why he hides things, Deirdre shrugged and grinned. "He probably just had the wallet with him when he was exploring, and dropped it there. He isn't aware of the importance of driver's licenses, and bank cards, and things."

Patrick approached his mother, reaching to tug her blouse. His expression was intent, and he watched her face as he tugged. Deirdre, looking down at her son, briefly touched one of his hands, then turned to reach for a con-tainer in her tote bag. Patrick evidently recognized the container and its con-tents, bite-sized cereal pieces. He gurgled and reached to intercept his mother's hand. "Want some Chex, Pat?" Deirdre held out a few pieces of ce-real. Patrick took one and popped it into his mouth. As Patrick ate his snack, Deirdre turned to me and explained, "I've been talking to him as much as I could—asking questions, singing songs. I still feel stupid talking about everything." Despite Deirdre's stated feelings, it was obvious that her will-ingness to verbalize to her son had increased. Her conversation with Patrick was more fluent and relaxed than at any earlier time.

She now spoke of the move ahead. She was concerned about the demands it would make on her, particularly now when her pregnancy and her rela-tionship with Patrick seemingly took all the energy she had. "But we have to do it now. Aside from Mike's new job, I couldn't face trying to move after the baby was born."

This was the first time Deirdre had volunteered a prediction about the effect of a second child on her life. I asked her to elaborate. "I don't mean bad, you know. It makes sense it's going to be tough coping with two kids in a new place. I don't know."

"You may be able to predict the likely outcome if you consider where you've come from. You now have experienced the infancy of one child. Your experience with the new baby will be different in many ways, but that does give you a solid basis to start from. Can you picture anything more of what it will be like when the baby is born?"

Deirdre shook her head. "Like with Pat, I guess, except busier. I guess the baby will sleep a lot, so I can spend some time with Pat, too."

"It's also very important to make sure there's some time for yourself. It's vital if you have two small children to make some time that is your own. That way you're much less likely to be distressed in stressful times."

Deirdre nodded, but her attention appeared to be with Patrick, who had gone to the window. After a moment she rose and went to her son, lifting him up to stand on the sill. She did not speak with Patrick as she did this, nor did she comment on any of the things going on outside—a man on a tractor cutting the grass, several people walking down a path. There was an aura about mother and child that marked this interaction as being particularly close; however, no verbalization was exchanged.

"I wonder what Patrick is observing?" I said.

Deirdre smiled. "That's my line, I guess. See anything good?" The infant twisted around to smile at his mother, then returned to gazing out the window. Her generalized question reveals her continued inability to direct appropriately specific questions to her son. Deirdre said that she just wasn't much of a talker. "Sometimes it's easier to keep my temper than to talk about something with him. But I'm trying real hard." Again, we must note the leitmotiv of anger lurking ever near the surface of Deirdre's temperament.

"Is it a choice between one or the other—talking or keeping your temper? What would happen if you kept talking?"

After thinking carefully, Deirdre said that she was afraid if she talked too much she would blow up, spill over with anger. The anger, I gathered, was directed toward herself in the same way that her auditory hallucinations were self-critical and had commanded her to mutilate her face in the past. I suggested that Patrick may have picked up on her ambivalence about verbal communication and that might be one cause for Patrick's slow language acquisition. Deirdre nodded slowly. "I can see that. But if I can't change fast enough myself, I still have to help him. That's the hard part." I went on to assure her that her verbal interaction with Patrick had improved enormously, even in the last two or three sessions. Upon my recommendation, Deirdre and Patrick will be working with a speech therapist during the next 3 months.

My feelings, of course, are mixed at seeing this therapy end. Given her psychiatric history, I feel that Deirdre will be at risk for some time to come; since intuitive behaviors are not her forte, many of the strategies she brings to bear as Patrick's mother, and as the mother of the child she carries now, will have to be carefully structured. I am also concerned about the potential for acting out the violence that her occasional hallucinations and deeply rooted low self-esteem instigate. However, in the 18 months since Patrick's birth, I have watched Deirdre's struggle to master her feelings of anger and self-destruction. I believe that with appropriate medication and medical supervision she will master the struggle. I am also somewhat concerned about the quality of the attachment that is emerging between Deirdre and her son and what effect Patrick's inevitable autonomy will have on his mother, for whom separation has been a powerful issue.

Although I am confident that Deirdre's ability to cope with a new child is far greater than it would have been a year ago during the pregnancy that was terminated, I am of course concerned about the stress that caring for two children will exert on her reserves. How will she balance the needs of her firstborn against those of the child she carries now? There are many questions at the end of this process. I firmly believe, though, that in the last year Deirdre has learned many skills and exercises that will help her both to maintain her relationship with Patrick and to nurture a relationship with her new baby.

## Addendum

Deirdre's circumstance, even after 2 years, was left unresolved in the end. Through these last sessions, I was aware of evidence that her mourning (for her aborted fetus) was not by any means over. The dream material Deirdre presented was quite clear about the nature and depth of her anxieties. But despite her far greater willingness to share these dreams and insights, she was still not completely forthcoming. I felt, however, that she was at the threshold of making appropriate predictions for her son Patrick's growth and change; and her personal liaison with her new husband Mike seemed to be on a fairly firm basis.

Several days ago I received a postcard from Deirdre. She and her family had rented a small house in a suburb of Toronto, about half an hour's drive from Mike's parents. Patrick now has a sister, Kathleen, and things have been, in Deirdre's words, "pretty okay." Deirdre has located a playgroup near their home, and in a few months she hopes to start taking courses at a local college and to finish her degree there. Deirdre also assured me that all the pertinent materials had been received by the local practitioners I referred her to and that she remembered that she could call on me whenever she needed to do so.

Reflection offers a final interpretation on her recent move. This move quite possibly represents an escape to a fresh start—one way of dealing with her difficulties and past conflicts, a quick and convenient way to "handle" the threat of processes that were clearly going to continue to be present in her life.

It had been a turbulent 2 years for Deirdre. She was, in that relatively brief time, a girlfriend, a pregnant woman, an unprepared, somewhat dysfunctional mother, the carrier of an unwanted second child, an abortive mother, a new bride, a second-time mother, and a prospective homemaker. Yet she had made vast strides in self-realization and self-actualization, in establishing healthier and more normative dyadic relationships with both her son and her spouse and in recognizing and controlling the parameters of her illness. All in the space of 2 short years.

# References

Ainsworth, M. D. S., & Bell, S. M. (1979). Attachment, exploration, and separation: Illustrated by the behavior of one-year-olds in a strange situation. *Child Development, 41*, 49–67.

Ainsworth, M. D. S., & Wittig, B. (1969). Attachment and exploratory behavior of one-year-olds in a strange situation. In B. M. Foss (Ed.), *Determinants of infant behavior, IV*. London: Methuen.

Akiskal, H. S. (1981). Subaffective disorders: Dysthymic, cyclothymic, and bipolar II disorders in the "borderline" realm. *Psychiatric Clinics of North America, 4*, 25–46.

Akiskal, H. S. (1983). Dysthymic disorder; psychopathology of proposed chronic depressive subtypes. *American Journal of Psychiatry, 140*, 11–20.

Alexander, F., & French, T. M. (1946). *Psychoanalytic therapy*. New York: Ronald Press.

Ambady, N., & Rosenthal, R. (1992). Thin slices of expressive behavior as predictors of interpersonal consequences: A meta-analysis. *Psychological Bulletin, 111*, 256–274.

Ammaniti, M., Baumgartner, E., Candelori, C., Perucchini, P. M., Tambelli, R., & Zampino, F. (1992). Representations and narratives during pregnancy. *Infant Mental Health Journal, 13*, 167–182.

Arend, R., Gove, F. L., & Sroufe, L. A. (1979). Continuity of individual adaptation from individual adaptation from infancy to kindergarten: A predictive study of ego-resilience and curiosity in preschoolers. *Child Development, 50*(4), 950–959.

Argyle, M., Alkema, F., & Gilmour, R. (1971). The communication of friendly and hostile attitudes by verbal and non-verbal signals. *European Journal of Social Psychology, 1*, 385–402.

Atkinson, A. K., & Rickel, A. U. (1984). Postpartum depression in primiparous parents. *Journal of Abnormal Psychology, 93*, 115–119.

Babad, E., Bernieri, F., & Rosenthal, R. (1987). Nonverbal and verbal behavior of preschool, remedial, and elementary school teachers. *American Educational Research Journal, 24*, 405–415.

Babad, E., Bernieri, F., & Rosenthal, R. (1991). Students as judges of teachers' verbal and nonverbal behavior. *American Educational Research Journal, 28,* 211–234.

Bardwick, J. M. (1971). *Psychology of women: A study of bio-cultural conflicts.* New York: Harper & Row.

Bargh, J. A. (1988). Automatic information processing: Implications for communication and affect. In L. Donohew & H. E. Sypher (Eds.), *Communication, social cognition and affect* (pp. 9–32). Hillsdale, NJ: Erlbaum.

Barr, R. G. (1990). The "colic" enigma: Prolonged episodes of a normal predisposition to cry. *Infant Mental Health Journal, 11,* 340–348.

Becker, E. (1987). Prosocial skills for handicapped preschoolers: A study of parents' and professionals' values. *Dissertation Abstracts International, 47*(7-A), 15–31.

Bellak, L., & Rosenberg, S. (1966). Effects of anti-depressant drugs on psychodynamics. *Psychosomatics, 7,* 106–114.

Belsky, J., Goode, M. K., & Most, R. K. (1980). Maternal stimulation and infant exploratory competence: Cross-sectional, correlational, and experimental analyses. *Child Development, 51,* 1163–1178.

Benedek, T. (1959a). Parenthood as a developmental phase. A contribution to the libido theory. *Journal of the American Psychoanalytic Association, 7,* 1–4.

Benedek, T. (1959b). Sexual functions in women and their disturbance. In S. Arieti (Ed.), *American handbook of psychiatry* (Vol. 1, pp. 727–748). New York: Basic Books.

Benoit, D., Zeanah, C., & Barton, M. (1989). Maternal attachment disturbances in failure to thrive. *Infant Mental Health Journal, 10,* 185–202.

Bentovim, A., & Kinston, W. (1978) Brief focal family therapy when the child is the referred patient: I. Clinical. *Journal of Child Psychology & Psychiatry & Allied Disciplines, 19,* 1–12.

Beres, D., & Joseph, E. D. (1970). The concept of mental representation in psychoanalysis. *International Journal of Psycho-Analysis, 51,* 1–9.

Berlin, L. J., & Cassidy, J. (1990). Infant-mother attachment and the ability to be alone in early childhood. In C. Rovee-Collier (Ed.), *Abstracts of papers presented at the Seventh International Conference on Infant Studies, Montreal* (p. 274). Norwood, NJ: Ablex.

Bittman, S., & Zalk, S. (1978). *Expectant fathers.* New York: Hawthorn Books.

Blanck, R., & Blanck, G. (1986). *Beyond ego psychology: Developmental object relations theory.* New York: Columbia University Press.

Blos, P. (1980). Modifications in the traditional psychoanalytic theory of female adolescent development. *Adolescent Psychiatry, 8,* 8–24.

Bonime, W. (1982). Psychotherapy of the depressed patient. *Contemporary Psychoanalysis, 18*(2), 173–189.

Bornstein, M. H. (1985). How infant and mother jointly contribute to developing cognitive competence in the child. *Proceedings of the National Academy of Sciences, 82,* 7470–7473.

Bowlby, J. (1969). *Attachment and loss: Vol. 1. Attachment.* New York: Basic Books.

Bowlby, J. (1982). *Attachment and loss: Vol. 1. Attachment* (2nd ed.). New York: Basic Books.

Boyd, J. H., & Weissman, M. M. (1981). Epidemiology of affective disorders. *Archives of General Psychiatry, 38,* 1039–1046.

Brazelton, T. B., Koslowski, B., & Main, M. (1974). The origins of reciprocity: The early mother-infant interaction. In M. Lewis & L. A. Rosenblum (Eds.), *The effect of the infant on its caregiver* (pp. 49–76). New York: Wiley.

Bretherton, I. (1987). New perspective on attachment relations: Security, communication and internal working models. In J. Osofsky (Ed.), *Handbook of infant development* (pp. 1061–1100). New York: Wiley.

Buckley, P., Hope, C. B., Conte, R., Plutchik, R., Wild, K. V., & Karasu, T. B. (1984). Psychodynamic variables as predictors of psychotherapy outcome. *American Journal of Psychiatry, 141*(6), 742–748.

Budman, S. H., Demby, A., Redondo, J. P., Hannan, M., Feldstein, M., Ring, J., & Springer, T. (1988). Comparative outcome in time-limited individual and group psychotherapy. *International Journal of Group Psychotherapy, 38,* 63–86.

Buesching, D. P., Glasser, M. L., & Frate, D. A. (1986). Progression of depression in the prenatal postpartum periods. *Women & Health, 11,* 61–78.

Buist, A., Norman, T. R., & Dennerstein, L. (1990). Breastfeeding and the use of psychotropic medication: A review. *Journal of Affective Disorders, 19,* 197–206.

Butcher, J. N., & Koss, M. P. (1978). Research on brief and crisis-oriented therapies. In S. Garfield & A. E. Bergin (Eds.), *Handbook of psychotherapy and behavior change* (2nd ed., pp. 725–768.) New York: Wiley.

Caplan, G. (1979). Social support, person-environment fit, and coping. In L. A. Ferman & J. P. Gordus (Eds.), *Mental health and the economy* (pp. 89–138). Kalamazoo, MI: Upjohn Institute for Employment Research.

Cappell, C., & Heiner, R. B. (1990). The intergenerational transmission of family aggression. *Journal of Family Violence, 5,* 135–152.

Chaikin, A. L., Sigler, E., & Derlega, V. J. (1974). Nonverbal mediation of teacher expectancy effects. *Journal of Personality and Social Psychology, 30,* 144–149.

Chatoor, I. (1989). Infantile anorexia nervosa: A developmental disorder of separation and individuation. *Journal of the American Academy of Psychoanalysis, 17,* 43–64.

Chehrazi, S. (1986). Female psychology: A review. *Journal of the American Psychoanalytic Association, 34,* 141–162.

Chessick, R. D. (1988). Thirty unresolved psychodynamic questions pertaining to feminine psychology. *American Journal of Psychotherapy, 62,* 87–95.

Christensen, D., & Rosenthal, R. (1982). Gender and nonverbal decoding skills as determinants of interpersonal expectancy effects. *Journal of Personality and Social Psychology, 42,* 75–87.

Clinton, J. F. (1987). Physical and emotional responses of expectant fathers throughout pregnancy and the early postpartum period. *International Journal of Nursing Studies, 24,* 59–68.

Cohn, J. F., & Tronick, E. Z. (1983). Three-month-old infants' reaction to simulated maternal depression. *Child Development, 54,* 185–193.

Cohn, J. F., Matias, R., Tronick, E. Z., Connell, D., & Lyons-Ruth, K. (1986). Face-to-face interactions of depressed mothers and their infants. In E. Z. Tronick

& T. Field (Eds.), *Maternal depression and infant disturbance* (pp. 31–45). San Francisco: Jossey-Bass.

Condon, J. T. (1987). The battered fetus syndrome. *Journal of Nervous and Mental Disorders, 175,* 722–725.

Cramer, B., Robert-Tissot, C., Stern, D. N., Serpa-Rusconi, S., De Muralt, M., Besson, G., Palacio-Espasa, F., Bachmann, J., Knauer, D., Berney, C., D'Arcis, U. (1990). Outcome evaluation in brief mother-infant psychotherapy: A preliminary report. *Infant Mental Health Journal, 11,* 278–300.

Cramer, B., & Stern, D. (1988). Evaluation of changes in mother-infant brief psychotherapy: A single case study. *Infant Mental Health Journal, 9*(1), 20–45.

Crits-Christoph, P. (1992). The efficacy of brief dynamic psychotherapy: A meta-analysis. *American Journal of Psychiatry, 149,* 151–158.

Crits-Christoph, P., Beebe, K. L., & Connolly, M. B. (1990). Therapist effects in the treatment of drug dependence: Implications for conducting comparative treatment studies. *NIDA Research Monograph, 104,* 39–49.

Crittenden, P. M. (1985a). Maltreated infants: Vulnerability and resilience. *Journal of Child Psychiatry, 26,* 85–96.

Crittenden, P. M. (1985b). Relationships at risk. In J. Belsky & T. Nezworski (Eds.), *Clinical implications of attachment.* Hillsdale, NJ: Erlbaum.

Cutrona, C. E., & Troutman, B. R. (1986). Social support, infant temperament, and parenting self-efficacy: A mediational model of postpartum depression. *Child Development, 57,* 1507–1518.

Davanloo, H. (Ed.) (1978). *Basic principles and techniques in short-term dynamic psychotherapy.* New York: SP Medical & Scientific Books.

Davanloo, H. (1980). A method of short-term dynamic psychotherapy. In H. Davanloo (Ed.), *Short-term dynamic psychotherapy* (pp. 43–71). New York: Jason Aronson.

Davanloo, H. (1984). Intensive short-term dynamic psychotherapy. In H. Kaplan & B. Sadock (Eds.), *Comprehensive textbook of psychiatry* (4th ed.) (chap. 29). Baltimore, MD: Williams & Wilkins.

Davanloo, H. (1986). Intensive short-term psychotherapy with highly resistant patients. *International Journal of Short-Term Psychotherapy, 1*(4), 107–133.

Davanloo, H. (1989). The central dynamic sequence in the unlocking of the unconscious and comprehensive trial therapy. Part I. Major unlocking. *International Journal of Short-Term Psychotherapy, 4*(1), 1033.

Davidson, E. S., & Liebert R. M. (1972). Effects of prior commitment on children's evaluation and imitation of a peer model's perceptual judgments. *Perceptual and Motor Skills, 35*(3), 825–826.

DeCasper, A. J., & Carstens, A. A. (1981). Contingencies of stimulation: Effects on learning and emotion in neonates. *Infant Behavior and Development, 4,* 19–35.

Dodd, B. (1979). Lip reading in infants: Attention to speech presented in- and out-of-synchrony. *Cognitive Psychology, 11,* 478–484.

Dolgoff, R., & Feldstein, D. (1984). *Understanding social welfare.* Green, NY: Longman.

Edelson, J. L., Eisikovits, Z. C., Guttmann, E., & Sela, A. M. (1991). Cognitive and interpersonal factors in woman abuse. *Journal of Family Violence, 6*(2), 167–182.

Eich, E. (1984). Memory for unattended events: Remembering with and without awareness. *Memory & Cognition, 12,* 105–111.

Emde, R. N. (1983). The prerepresentational self and its affective core. *Psychoanalytic Study of the Child, 38,* 165–192.

Erikson, M. (1966/1980). The interspersal hypnotic technique for symptom correction and pain control. In E. Rossi (Ed.), *The collected papers of Milton H. Erickson on hypnosis: Vol. IV. Innovative hypnotherapy* (pp. 229–232). New York: Irvington.

Estes, S. G. (1938). Judging personality from expressive behavior. *Journal of Abnormal and Social Psychology, 33,* 217–236.

Fagen, J. W., & Ohr, P. S. (1985). Temperament and crying in response to the violation of a learned expectancy in early infancy. *Infant Behavior and Development, 8,* 157–166.

Fairbairn, W. R. D. (1954). Schizoid factors in the personality. In *An object-relations theory of the personality.* New York: Basic Books.

Field, T. M., Woodson, R., Greenberg, R., & Cohen, D. (1982). Discrimination and imitation of facial expressions by neonates. *Science, 218,* 179–182.

Fiese, B. H., & Sameroff, A. J. (1989). Family context in pediatric psychology: A transactional perspective. *Journal of Pediatric Psychology, 14,* 293–314.

Fincham, F. D., Beach, S. R., & Bradbury, T. N. (1989). Marital distress, depression, and attributions: Is the marital distress-attribution association an artifact of depression? *Journal of Consulting and Clinical Psychology, 57,* 768–771.

Fleming, A. S., Ruble, D. N., Flett, G. L., & Van Wagner, V. (1990). Adjustment in first-time mothers: Changes in mood and mood content during the early postpartum months. *Developmental Psychology, 26,* 137–143.

Fogel, A., Diamond, G. R., Langhorst, B. H., & Demos, V. (1982). Affective and cognitive aspects of the two-month-old's participation in face-to-face interaction with its mother in social interchange. In E. Tronick (Ed.), *Infancy, affect, cognition, and communications* (pp. 37–57). Baltimore, MD: University Park Press.

Fraiberg, S. (Ed.) (1980). *Clinical studies in infant mental health: The first year of life.* New York: Basic Books.

Fraiberg, S. (1982a). The adolescent mother and her infant. *Adolescent Psychiatry, 10,* 7–23.

Fraiberg, S. (1982b). Pathological defenses in infancy. *Psychoanalytic Quarterly, 51*(4), 612–635.

Framo, J. L. (1981). The integration of marital therapy with sessions with family of origin. In A. S. Gurman & D. P. Kniskern (Eds.), *Handbook of family therapy.* New York: Brunner/Mazel.

Frank, E., Kupfer, D. J., Jacob, M., Blumenthal, S. J., & Jarrett D. B. (1987). Pregnancy-related affective episodes among women with recurrent depression. *American Journal of Psychiatry, 144*(3), 288–293.

Frank, J. D., Gliedman, L. H., Imber, S. D., Nash, E. H., Jr., & Stone, A. R. (1957). Why patients leave psychotherapy. *Archives of Neurology and Psychiatry, 77,* 283–299.

Freeman, D. S. (1992). *Multigenerational family therapy.* New York: Haworth Press.

Freud, S. (1910). Five lectures on psycho-analysis. In J. Strachey (Ed. and Trans.), *The standard edition of the complete psychological works of Sigmund Freud,* Vol. 11 (pp. 7–55). London: Hogarth Press.

Freud, S. (1926). Inhibitions, symptoms and anxiety. In J. Strachey (Ed. and Trans.), *The standard edition of the complete psychological works of Sigmund Freud,* Vol. 20 (pp. 75–175). London: Hogarth Press.

Freud, S. (1931). Female sexuality. In J. Strachey (Ed. and Trans.), *The standard edition of the complete psychological works of Sigmund Freud,* Vol. 21 (pp. 223–240). London: Hogarth Press.

Freud, S. (1937). Analysis terminable and interminable. In J. Strachey (Ed. and Trans.), *The standard edition of the complete psychological works of Sigmund Freud,* Vol. 23 (pp. 209–253). London: Hogarth Press.

Gaensbauer, T. J., Harmon, R. J., Cytryn, L., & McKnew, D. H. (1984). Social and affective development in infants with a manic-depressive parent. *American Journal of Psychiatry, 141*(2), 223–229.

Garfield, S. L. (1986). Research on client variables in psychotherapy. In S. L. Garfield & A. E. Bergin (Eds.), *Handbook of psychotherapy and behavior change: An empirical analysis* (pp. 213–256). New York: Wiley.

George, C., & Solomon, J. (1989). Internal working models of caregiving and security of attachment at age six. *Infant Mental Health Journal, 10,* 222–237.

Gilbert, D. T., & Krull, D. S. (1988). Seeing less and knowing more: The benefits of perceptual ignorance. *Journal of Personality and Social Psychology, 54,* 193–202.

Goldsmith, H. H., & Campos, J. J. (1982). Toward a theory of infant temperament. In R. N. Emde & R. J. Harmon (Eds.), *The development of attachment and affiliative systems* (pp. 161–193). New York: Plenum.

Gomes-Schwartz, B. (1978). Effective ingredients in psychotherapy: Prediction of outcome from process variables. *Journal of Consulting and Clinical Psychology, 46,* 1023–1035.

Grigoroiu-Serbanescu, M., Christodorescu, D., Magureanu, S., Jipescu, I., Totoescu, A., Marinescu, E., Ardelean, V., & Popa, S. (1991). Adolescent offspring of endogenous unipolar depressive parents and of normal parents. *Journal of Affective Disorders, 21,* 185–198.

Gunnar, M. R. (1990). Emotion regulation in infancy: Relations between regulatory behavior, affect and physiological responses to stressful events. In C. Rovee-Collier (Ed.), *Abstracts of papers presented at the Seventh International Conference on Infant Studies, Montreal* (p. 107). Norwood, NJ: Ablex.

Guntrip, H. (1961). *Personality structure and human interaction: The developing synthesis of psychodynamic theory.* New York: International Universities Press.

Gustafson, J. P., & Dichter, H. (1983). Winnicott and Sullivan in the brief psychotherapy clinic, Parts I and II. *Contemporary Psychoanalysis, 19*(4), 624–651.

Haccoun, D. M., & Lavigueur, H. (1979). Effects of clinical experience and client emotion on therapists' responses. *Journal of Consulting and Clinical Psychology, 47,* 416–418.

Harper, J. (1991). Children's play: The differential effects of intrafamilial physical and sexual abuse. *Child Abuse and Neglect, 15,* 89–98.

Harris, M. J., & Rosenthal, R. (1985). Mediation of interpersonal expectancy effects: 31 meta-analyses. *Psychological Bulletin, 97,* 363–386.

Hartlaub, G. H., Martin, G. C., & Rhine, M. W. (1986). Recontact with the analyst following termination: A survey of seventy-one cases. *Journal of the American Psychoanalytic Association, 34,* 895–910.

Hartmann, H. (1950). Comments on the psychoanalytic theory of the ego. *Psychoanalytic Study of the Child, 5,* 74–96.

Hayne, H., Rovee-Collier, C., & Perris, E. E. (1987). Categorization and memory retrieval by three-month-olds. *Child Development, 58,* 750–767.

Healy, J. M., Malley, J. E., & Stewart, A. J. (1990). Children and their fathers after parental separation. *American Journal of Orthopsychiatry, 60,* 531–543.

Heckhausen, J. (1987). Balancing for weaknesses and challenging developmental potential: A longitudinal study of mother-infant dyads. *Developmental Psychology, 23,* 762–770.

Heinicke, C. M. (1990). Patterns of husband-wife adaptation. In C. Rovee-Collier (Ed.), *Abstracts of papers presented at the Seventh International Conference on Infant Studies, Montreal* (p. 414). Norwood, NJ: Ablex.

Henderson, N. D. (1982). Human behavior genetics. *Annual Review of Psychology, 33,* 403–440.

Higgins, E. T., & King, G. (1981). Accessibility of social constructs: Information-processing consequences of individual and contextual variability. In N. Cantor & J. F. Kohlstrom (Eds.), *Personality, cognition, and social interaction.* Hillsdale, NJ: Erlbaum.

Hoffman, M. L. (1982a). Development of prosocial motivation: Empathy and guilt. In N. Eisenberg (Ed.), *The development of prosocial behavior* (pp. 281–313). New York: Academic Press.

Hoffman, M. L. (1982b). The measurement of empathy. In C. E. Izard (Ed.), *Measuring emotions in infants and children* (pp. 279–296). Cambridge, England: Cambridge University Press.

Hopkins, J., Campbell, S. B., & Marcus, M. (1987). Role of infant-related stressors in postpartum depression. *Journal of Abnormal Psychology, 96,* 237–241.

Hopkins, B., & Westra, T. (1990). Motor development, maternal expectations and the role of handling. *Infant Behavior and Development, 13,* 117–122.

Horowitz, M. J., Marmar, C. R., Weiss, D. S., Kaltreider, N. B., & Wilner, N. R. (1986). Comprehensive analysis of change after brief dynamic psychotherapy. *American Journal of Psychiatry, 143,* 582–589.

Howard, G. S., Nance, D. W, & Myers, P. (1987). *Adaptive counseling and therapy.* San Francisco: Jossey-Bass.

Izard, C. E. (1978). On the ontogenesis of emotions and emotion-cognition relationship in infancy. In M. Lewis & L. A. Rosenblum (Eds.), *The development of affect* (pp. 103–131). New York: Plenum.

Jacoby-Miller, E. S. (1985). Successful treatment of the mother-infant relationship in a mother suffering from severe postpartum depression. *Infant Mental Health Journal, 6,* 210–213.

Jenkins, J. M., & Smith, M. A. (1991). Marital disharmony and children's behaviour problems: Aspects of a poor marriage that affect children adversely.

*Journal of Child Psychology and Psychiatry and Allied Disciplines, 32,* 793–810.

Jones, L. C., & Thomas, S. A. (1989). New fathers' blood pressure and heart rate: Relationships to interaction with their newborn infants. *Nursing Research, 38,* 237–241.

Jouriles, E. N., Murphy, C. M., & O'Leary, K. D. (1989). Effects of maternal mood on mother-son interaction patterns. *Journal of Abnormal Child Psychology, 17,* 513–525.

Kalin, N. H., & Carnes, M. (1984). Biological correlates of attachment bond disruption in human and nonhuman primates. *Progress in Neuropsychopharmacology and Biological Psychiatry, 8,* 459–469.

Kaye, K. (1982). Construction of the person. In K. Kaye (Ed.), *The mental and social life of babies: How parents create persons.* Chicago: University of Chicago Press.

Kennerley, H., & Gath, D. (1985). Maternity blues reassessed. *Psychiatric Developments, 1,* 1–17.

Kernberg, O. F., Burstein, E. D., Coyne, L., Applebaum, A., Horwitz, L., & Voth, H. (1972). Psychotherapy and psychoanalysis: Final report of the Menninger Foundation's Psychotherapy Research Project. *Bulletin of the Menninger Clinic, 36,* 1–176.

Kestenbaum, R., & Nelson, C. A. (1990). The recognition and categorization of upright and inverted emotional expressions by 7-month-old infants. *Infant Behavior and Development, 13,* 497–511.

Kinston, W., & Bentovim, A. (1990). A framework for family description. Special Issue: I. First World Conference of Family Therapy. *Contemporary Family Therapy: An International Journal, 12,* 279–297.

Klaus, M. H., & Kennel, J. H. (1976). *Mother-infant bonding.* St. Louis, MO: Mosby.

Kochanska, G., Kuczynski, L., & Maguire, M. (1989). Impact of diagnosed depression and self-reported mood on mother's control strategies: A longitudinal study. *Journal of Abnormal Child Psychology, 17,* 493–511.

Koester, L. S., Papousek, H., & Papousek, M. (1989). Patterns of rhythmic stimulation by mothers with three-month-olds: A cross-modal comparison. *International Journal of Behavioral Development, 12,* 143–154.

Kohler, F. W., Strain, P. S., Maretsky, S., & DeCesare, L. (1990). Promoting positive and supportive interactions between preschoolers: An analysis of group-oriented contingencies. *Journal of Early Intervention, 14,* 327–341.

Kohut, H. (1978). The search for the self. In P. Ornstein (Ed.), *Selected writings of Heinz Kohut: 1950–1978* (Vols. 1–2). New York: International Universities Press.

Kopp, C. B. (1990). Language, toddlers and emotion regulation. In C. Rovee-Collier (Ed.), *Abstracts of papers presented at the Seventh International Conference on Infant Studies, Montreal* (p. 105). Norwood, NJ: Ablex.

Landry, S. H., & Chapieski, M. L. (1989). Joint attention and infant toy exploration: Effects of Down syndrome and prematurity. *Child Development, 60,* 103–118.

Landy, S., Montgomery, J., & Walsh, S. (1989). Postpartum depression: A clinical view. *Maternal-Child Nursing Journal, 18,* 1–29.

Lanktree, C., Briere, J., & Zaidi, L. (1991). Incidence and impact of sexual abuse in a child outpatient sample: The role of direct inquiry. *Child Abuse and Neglect, 15*, 447–453.

Lask, B. (1982). The child within the family. In J. Apley & C. Ounsted (Eds.), *One child* (pp. 166–174). Philadelphia: Lippincott.

Lee, R. A. (1983). Flextime and conjugal roles. *Journal of Occupational Behaviour, 4*(4), 297–315.

Lester, E. P., & Notman, M. T. (1988). Pregnancy and object relations: Clinical considerations. *Psychoanalytic Inquiries, 8*, 196–221.

Lin, N. (1986). Conceptualizing social support. In N. Lin, A. Dean, & W. Ensel (Eds.), *Social support, life events, and depression* (pp. 17–30). Orlando, FL: Academic.

Long, P. J., & Jackson, J. L. (1991). Children sexually abused by multiple perpetrators: Familial risk factors and abuse characteristics. *Journal of Interpersonal Violence, 6*(2), 147–159.

Luborsky, L. (1984). *Principles of psychoanalytic psychotherapy: A manual for supportive-expressive treatment.* New York: Basic Books.

Luborsky, L., Auerbach, A. H., Chandler, M., Cohen, J., & Bachrach, H. M. (1971). Factors influencing the outcome of psychotherapy: A review of quantitative research. *Psychological Bulletin, 75*, 145–185.

Luborsky, L., Barber, J., & Crits-Christoph, P. (1990). Theory-based research for understanding the process of dynamic psychotherapy. *Journal of Consulting and Clinical Psychology, 58*(3), 281–287.

Lyons-Ruth, K., Zoll, D., Connell, D., & Grunebaum, H. U. (1986). The depressed mother and her one-year-old infant: Environment, interaction, attachment, and infant development. In E. Z. Tronick & T. Field (Eds.), *Maternal depression and infant disturbance* (pp. 61–82). San Francisco: Jossey-Bass.

MacKenzie, K. R. (1988). Recent developments in brief psychotherapy. *Hospital and Community Psychiatry, 39*, 742–752.

Madanes, C. (1981). *Strategic family therapy.* San Francisco: Jossey-Bass.

Maheler, M. S., Pine, F., & Bergman, A. (1975). *The psychological birth of the human infant: Symbiosis and individuation.* New York: Basic Books.

Main, M., Kaplan, K., & Cassidy, J. (1985). Security in infancy, childhood and adulthood. A move to the level of representation. In I. Bretherton & E. Waters (Eds.), Growing points of attachment and research. *Monographs of the Society for Research in Child Development, 50*(1–2, Serial No. 209), 66–104.

Malan, D. H. (1975). *A study of brief psychotherapy.* New York: Plenum.

Malan, D. H. (1976). *The frontier of brief psychotherapy: An example of the convergence of research and clinical practice.* New York: Plenum.

Malan, D. H. (1979). *Individual psychotherapy and the science of psychodynamics.* London: Butterworth.

Malan, D. H. (1980). *Toward the validation of dynamic psychotherapy.* New York: Plenum.

Malan, D. H. (1986). Beyond interpretation, initial evaluation and technique. *International Journal of Short-Term Psychotherapy, 1*(2), 59–106.

Mann, J. (1973). *Time-limited psychotherapy.* Cambridge, MA: Harvard University Press.

Mann, J. (1986). Review of *A casebook in time-limited psychotherapy* by James Mann and Robert Godlman. *International Journal of Short-Term Psychotherapy*, 1(3), 217–218.

Mann, J., & Godlman, R. (1982). *A casebook on time-limited psychotherapy*. New York: McGraw-Hill.

Marzialli, E. A. (1987). People in your life. Development of a social support measure for predicting psychotherapy outcome. *Journal of Nervous and Mental Disease*, 175, 327–338.

Maxim, P. E., & Hunt, D. D. (1990). Appraisal and coping in the process of patient change during short-term psychotherapy. *Journal of Nervous and Mental Disease*, 178, 235–241.

McCall, R. B. (1979). The development of intellectual functioning in infancy and the prediction of later I.Q. In J. D. Osofsky (Ed.), *Handbook of infant development* (2nd ed.). New York: Wiley.

McCall, R. B., & McGee, P. E. (1977). The discrepancy hypothesis of attention and affect in infants. In I. C. Uzgiris & F. Weizmann (Eds.), *The structuring of experience* (pp. 179–210). New York: Plenum.

McConnell, S. R., Sisson, L. A., Cort, C. A., & Strain, P. S. (1991). Effects of social skills training and contingency management on reciprocal interaction of preschool children with behavioral handicaps. *Journal of Special Education*, 24, 473–495.

McGoldrick, M., & Carter, E. A. (1982). The family life cycle. In F. Walsh (Ed.), *Normal family processes* (pp. 167–195). New York: Guilford.

McNeil, W. J. (1986). Equilibration and the identification of issues in personality and social development. *Dissertation Abstracts International*, 46(10-B), 3618–3619.

Medin, D. L. (1983). Structural principles in categorization. In B. Shepp & T. Tighe (Eds.), *Interaction: Perception, development and cognition* (pp. 203–230). Hillsdale, NJ: Erlbaum.

Mehrabian, A. (1972). *Nonverbal communication*. Chicago: Aldine-Atherton.

Meltzoff, A. N. (1981). Imitation, intermodal coordination, and representation in early infancy. In G. Butterworth (Ed.), *Infancy and epistemology* (pp. 85–114). London: Harvester Press.

Meltzoff, A. N. (1988). Infant imitation after 1-week delay: Long-term memory for novel acts and multiple stimuli. *Developmental Psychology*, 24, 470–476.

Meltzoff, A. N., & Moore, M. K. (1977). Imitation of facial and manual gestures by human neonates. *Science*, 24, 75–78.

Miller, W. S. (1990). Span of integration for delayed-reward contingency learning in 6- to 8-month old infants. *Annals of the New York Academy of Sciences*, 608, 239–266.

Murray, L. (1991). Intersubjectivity, object relations theory, and empirical evidence from mother-infant interactions. *Infant Mental Health Journal*, 12, 219–232.

Nelson, K., & Gruendel, J. (1981). Generalized event representations: Basic building blocks of cognitive development. In M. E. Lamb & A. Brown (Eds.)., *Advances in developmental psychology* (Vol. 1). Hillsdale, NJ: Erlbaum.

Nicolson, P. (1990). A brief report of women's expectations of men's behaviour in the transition to parenthood: Contradictions and conflicts for counselling psychology practice. *Counselling Psychology Quarterly, 3,* 353–361.

Nisbett, R. E., & Wilson, T. (1977). Telling more than we can know: Verbal reports on mental processes. *Psychological Review, 84*(3), 231–259.

O'Hara, M. W. (1986). Social support, life events, and depression during pregnancy and the puerperium. *Archives of General Psychiatry, 43,* 569–573.

Orlinsky, D. E., & Howard, K. I. (1986). The psychological interior of psychotherapy: Explorations with the therapy session reports. In L. S. Greenberg & W. M. Pinsof (Eds.), *The psychotherapeutic process: A research handbook.* New York: Guilford Press.

Ottinger, D. R., & Simmons, J. E. (1963). Maternal anxiety during gestation and neonate behavior. *Recent Advances in Biological Psychiatry, 5,* 7–12.

Paffenbarger, R. S., Jr., Steinmetz, C. H., Pooler, B. G., & Hyde, R. T. (1961). The picture puzzle of the postpartum psychoses. *Journal of Chronic Diseases, 13,* 161–173.

Palacio-Espasa, F., & Cramer, B. (1989). Psychothérapie de la relation mère-enfant. *Revue de Médicine Psychosomatique, 19,* 59–70.

Papousek, H., & Papousek, M. (1987). Intuitive parenting: A dialectic counterpart to the infant's integrative competence. In J. D. Osofsky (Ed.), *Handbook of infant development* (2nd ed.). New York: Wiley.

Papousek, M., Papousek, H., & Haekel, M. (1987). Didactic adjustments in fathers' and mothers' speech to their 3-month-old infants. *Journal of Psycholinguistic Research, 16,* 491–516.

Paris, J., & Guzder, J. (1989). The poisoned nest: Dynamic aspects of exogamous marriage. *Journal of the American Academy of Psychoanalysis, 17,* 493–500.

Pines, D. (1972). Pregnancy and motherhood: Interaction between fantasy and reality. *British Journal of Medical Psychology, 45,* 333–343.

Pines, D. (1982). The relevance of early psychological development of pregnancy and abortion. *International Journal of Psychoanalysis, 63,* 311–319.

Piper, W. E., Azim, H. F. A., Joyce, A. S., & McCallum, M. (1991). Transference interpretations, therapeutic alliance, and outcome in short-term individual psychotherapy. *Archives of General Psychiatry, 48,* 946–953.

Piper, W. E., Azim, H. F. A., Joyce, A. S., McCallum, M., Nixon, G. W. H., & Segal, P. S. (1991). Quality of object relations versus interpersonal functioning as predictors of therapeutic alliance and psychotherapy outcome. *Journal of Nervous and Mental Disease, 179,* 432–438.

Piper, W. E., Azim, H. F. A., McCallum, M., & Joyce, A. S. (1990). Patient suitability and outcome in short-term individual psychotherapy. *Journal of Consulting and Clinical Psychology, 58,* 475–481.

Polan, H. J., Kaplan, M. D., Kessler, D. B., Shindledecker, R., Newmark, M., Stern, D. N., & Ward, M. J. (1991). Psychopathology in mothers of children with failure to thrive. *Infant Mental Health Journal, 12,* 55–64.

Polster, E. (1990). Tight therapeutic sequences. In J. K. Zeig & S. G. Gilligan (Eds.), *Brief therapy: Myths, methods, and metaphors* (pp. 378–389). New York: Brunner/Mazel.

Proskauer, S. (1971). Focused time-limited psychotherapy with children. *Journal of the American Academy of Child Psychiatry, 10,* 619–639.

Radke-Yarrow, M., Cummings, E. M., Kuczynski, L., & Chapman, M. (1985). Patterns of attachment in two- and three-year-olds in normal families and families with parental depression. *Child Development, 56,* 884–893.

Raphael-Leff, J. (1986). Facilitators and regulators: Conscious and unconscious processes in pregnancy and early motherhood. *British Journal of Medical Psychology, 59,* 43–55.

Ratcliff, R., & McKoon, G. (1978). Priming in item recognition: Evidence for the prepositional structure of sentences. *Journal of Verbal Learning and Verbal Behavior, 17,* 403–417.

Ratcliff, R., & McKoon, G. (1981). Automatic and strategic priming in recognition. *Journal of Verbal Learning and Verbal Behavior, 20,* 204–215.

Reid, W. J. (1990). An integrative model for short-term treatment. In R. A. Wells & V. J. Giannetti (Eds.), *Handbook of the brief psychotherapies* (pp. 55–77). New York: Plenum.

Resnick, J. S., & Kagan, J. (1983). Category detection in infancy. In L. P. Lipsitt (Ed.), *Advances in infancy research* (Vol. 2, pp. 79–111). Norwood, NJ: Ablex.

Richardson-Klavehn, A., & Bjork, R. A. (1988). Measures of memory. *Annual Reviews of Psychology, 39,* 475–543.

Robin, A. (1962). Psychological changes of normal parturition. *Psychiatric Quarterly, 36,* 129–150.

Rogers, C. (1957). The necessary and sufficient conditions of therapeutic personality change. *Journal of Consulting Psychology, 21*(2), 95–103.

Rosenberg, P. E. (1988). Transference in psychoanalysis and intensive short-term dynamic psychotherapy. *International Journal of Short-Term Psychotherapy, 3,* 47–76.

Rosenberg, S., & Jones, R. A. (1972). A method for investigating a person's implicit theory of personality: Theodore Dreiser's view of people. *Journal of Personality and Social Psychology, 22,* 372–386.

Rosenthal, R., Hall, J. A., DiMatteo, M. R., Rogers, P. L., & Archer, D. (1979). *Sensitivity to nonverbal communication: The PONS Test.* Baltimore, MD: Johns Hopkins University Press.

Saks, B. R., Frank, J. B., Lowe, T. L., Berman, W., Naftolin, F., & Cohen, D. J. (1985). Depressed mood during pregnancy and the puerperium: Clinical recognition and implications for clinical practice. *American Journal of Psychiatry, 142,* 728–731.

Sameroff, A. J., Seifer, R., & Zax, M. (1982). Early development of children at risk for emotional disorder. *Monographs of the Society for Research in Child Development* No. 199 [entire issue], *47*(7).

Sander, L. W. (1983). Polarity, paradox and the organizing process in development. In J. D. Call, E. Galenson, & R. L. Tyson (Eds.), *Frontiers of infant psychiatry* (pp. 334–346). New York: Basic Books.

Sargeant, J. K., Bruce, M. L., Florio, L. P., & Weissman, M. M. (1990). Factors associated with 1-year outcome of major depression in the community. *Archives of General Psychiatry, 47,* 519–526.

Schank, R. C., & Abelson, R. (1977). *Scripts, plans, goals and understanding.* Hillsdale, NJ: Erlbaum.

Schneider, D. J., Hastorf, A. H., & Ellsworth, P. C. (1979). *Person perception* (2nd ed.). Reading, MA: Addison-Wesley.

Searle, A. (1987). The effects of postnatal depression on mother-infant interaction. *Australian Journal of Sex, Marriage and Family, 8,* 79–88.

Seligman, M. E. P. (1972). Learned helplessness. *Annual Review of Medicine, 23,* 407–412.

Shapiro, D., & Shapiro, D. (1982). Meta-analysis of comparative therapy outcome studies: A replication and refinement. *Psychology Bulletin, 92,* 582.

Sharpley, C. F., & Webber, R. P. (1989). Coparenting: An alternative to consider in separation counselling. *Australian Journal of Sex, Marriage and Family, 10,* 111–117.

Sherwen, L. (1981). Fantasies during the third trimester of pregnancy. *American Journal of Maternal Child Nursing, 6,* 398–401.

Shoda, Y., Mischel, W., & Peake, P. K. (1990). Predicting adolescent cognitive and self-regulatory competencies from preschool delay of gratification: Identifying diagnostic conditions. *Developmental Psychology, 26,* 978–986.

Sifneos, P. E. (1972). *Short-term psychotherapy and emotional crisis.* Cambridge, MA: Harvard University Press.

Smith, M. L., Glass, G. V., & Miller, T. I. (1980). *The benefits of psychotherapy.* Baltimore, MD: Johns Hopkins University Press.

Spitz, R. A., & Wolf, K. M. (1946). Anaclitic depression: An inquiry into the genesis of psychiatric conditions on early conditions, II. *Psychoanalytic Study of the Child, 2,* 313–342.

Steinmetz, J. L., Lewinsohn, P. M., & Antonuccio, D. O. (1983). Prediction of individual outcome in a group intervention for depression. *Journal of Consulting and Clinical Psychology, 51,* 331–337.

Stern, D. N. (1985). *The interpersonal world of the infant.* New York: Basic Books.

Stern, D. N. (1989). The representation of relational patterns: Developmental considerations. In A. J. Sameroff & R. N. Emde (Eds.), *Relationship disturbances in early childhood.* New York: Basic Books.

Stern, M., & Karraker, K. H. (1989). Modifying the prematurity stereotype: The effects of information on negative perceptions of infants. *Journal of Social and Clinical Psychology, 8,* 1–13.

Stern, M., & Karraker, K. H. (1990). The prematurity stereotype: Empirical evidence and implications for practice. *Infant Mental Health Journal, 11,* 3–11.

Streissguth, A. P., Sampson, P. D., & Barr, H. M. (1989). Neurobehavioral dose-response effects of prenatal alcohol exposure in humans from infancy to adulthood. *Annals of the New York Academy of Sciences, 562,* 145–158.

Strupp, H., Hadley, S., & Gomes-Schwartz, B. (1977). *Psychotherapy for better or worse: The problem of negative effects.* New York: Jason Aronson.

Sturm, L., & Drotar, D. (1991). Maternal attributions of etiology in nonorganic failure to thrive. *Family Systems Medicine, 9,* 53–63.

Sullivan, H. S. (1940). *Conceptions of modern psychiatry.* New York: Norton.

Sullivan, H. S. (1953). *The interpersonal theory of psychiatry.* New York: Norton.

Sullivan, H. S. (1964). *The fusion of psychiatry and social science.* New York: Norton.

Sullivan, M. W., & Lewis, M. (1990). Contingency intervention: A program portrait. *Journal of Early Intervention, 14,* 367–375.

Tamis-Lemonda, C., & Bornstein, M. H. (1990). Language, play, and attention at one year. *Infant Behavior and Development, 13,* 85–98.

Thomas, A., & Chess, S. (1984). Genesis and evolution of behavior disorders: From infancy to early adult life. *American Journal of Psychiatry, 141,* 1–9.

Thomas, A., Chess, S., & Birch, H. G. (1968). *Temperament and behavior disorders in children.* New York: New York University Press.

Thomas, A., Chess, S., & Birch, H. G. (1970). The origin of personality. *Scientific American, 223,* 102–109.

Trad, P. V. (1986). *Infant depression, paradigms and paradoxes.* New York: Springer-Verlag.

Trad, P. V. (1987). *Infant and childhood depression: Developmental factors.* New York: Wiley.

Trad, P. V. (1989). *The preschool child: Assessment, diagnosis, and treatment.* New York: Wiley.

Trad, P. V. (1990). *Previewing: Predicting and sharing interpersonal outcome.* New York: Springer-Verlag.

Trad, P. V. (1991). The application of development strategies to short-term psychotherapy. *International Journal of Short-Term Psychotherapy, 6,* 219–235.

Trad, P. V. (1992a). *Interventions with infants and parents: The theory and practice of previewing.* New York: Wiley.

Trad, P. V. (1992b). Mastering developmental transition through prospective techniques. *International Journal of Short-Term Psychotherapy, 7,* 59–72.

Trevarthen, C. (1980). The foundations of intersubjectivity: Development of interpersonal and cooperative understanding in infants. In D. R. Olson (Ed.), *The social foundations of language and thought: Essays in honor of Jerome S. Bruner* (pp. 316–342). New York: Norton.

Trevarthen, C. (1985). Facial expressions of emotion in mother-infant interaction. *Human Neurobiology, 4,* 21–32.

Tschann, J. M., Johnston, J. R., Kline, M., & Wallerstein, J. S. (1990). Conflict, loss, change and parent-child relationships: Predicting children's adjustment during divorce. *Journal of Divorce, 13,* 1–22.

Ursano, R. J., & Hales, R. E. (1986). A review of brief individual psychotherapies. *American Journal of Psychiatry, 143,* 1507–1517.

Vygotsky, L. S. (1978). *Mind in society: The development of higher psychological processes.* Cambridge, MA: Harvard University Press.

Walker, A. S. (1982). Intermodal perception of expressive behaviors by human infants. *Journal of Experimental Child Psychology, 33,* 514–535.

Ward, M. J., Brinckerhoff, C. B., Lent, L. A., Gruber, S. K., Carlson, L. S., & Kessler, D. B. (1990). Adolescent mother-infant attachment: Continuity in adaptation from 12 to 14 months. In C. Rovee-Collier (Ed.), *Abstracts of papers presented at the Seventh International Conference on Infant Studies, Montreal* (p. 662). Norwood, NJ: Ablex.

Ward, M. M., Carlson, E. A., Altman, S. C., Levine, L., Greenburg, R. H., & Kessler, D. B. (1990). Predicting infant-mother attachment from adolescents' prenatal working models of relationships. In C. Rovee-Collier (Ed.), *Abstracts of papers presented at the Seventh International Conference on Infant Studies, Montreal* (p. 661). Norwood, NJ: Ablex.

Watson, J. S. (1972). Smiling, cooing and "the game." *Merrill Palmer Quarterly, 18,* 323–339.

Watson, J. S. (1977). Perception of contingency as a determinant of social responsiveness. In E. B. Thomas (Ed.), *Origins of the infant's social responsiveness* (pp. 33–63). Hillsdale, NJ: Erlbaum.

Watzlawick, P., Beavin, J., & Jackson, D. (1967). *Pragmatics of human communication.* New York: Norton.

Werner, H. (1948). *The comparative psychology of mental development.* New York: International Universities Press.

Winnicott, D. W. (1960). The theory of the parent-infant relationship. In D. W. Winnicott (Ed.), *The maturational process and the facilitating environment* (pp. 37–55). New York: International Universities Press.

Wolberg, L. R., Aronson, M. L., & Wolberg, A. R. (1976). *Group therapy: An overview.* New York: Stratton.

Wood, D., Bruner, J. S., & Ross, G. (1976). The role of tutoring in problem solving. *Journal of Child Psychology and Psychiatry and Allied Disciplines, 17*(2), 89–100.

Worchel, J. (1990). Short-term dynamic psychotherapy. In R. A. Well & V. J. Gianetti (Eds.), *Handbook of brief psychotherapies* (pp. 193–216). New York: Plenum.

Wyer, R. S., & Srull, T. K. (1981). Category accessibility: Some theoretical and empirical issues concerning the processing of social stimulus information. In E. T. Higgins, C. P. Herman, & M. P. Zanna (Eds.), *Social cognition: The Ontario Symposium* (Vol. 1). Hillsdale, NJ: Erlbaum.

Wyman, H. W., & Rittenberg, S. M. (Eds.). (1992). The use of medication with patients in analysis: Panel of the New York Psychoanalytic Society, March 26, 1991. *Journal of Clinical Psychoanalysis, 1*(1), 1–133.

Yalom, I., Lunde, D., Moos, R., & Hamburg D. (1968). "Postpartum blues syndrome": A description and related variables. *Archives of General Psychiatry, 18,* 16–27.

Yarrow, L. J., Morgan, G. A., Jennings, K. D., Harmon, R. J., & Gaiter, J. L. (1982). Infants' persistence at tasks: Relationships to cognitive functioning in early experience. *Infant Behavior and Development, 5,* 131–141.

Zahn-Waxler, C., & Radke-Yarrow, M. (1990). The origins of empathic concern. *Motivation and Emotion, 14,* 107–130.

Zazlow, M. J., Pederson, F. A., Cain, R. L., Suwalsky, J. T. D., & Kramer, E. L. (1985). Depressed mood in new fathers: Associations with parent-infant interaction. *Genetic, Social, and General Psychology Monographs, 111,* 133–150.

Zeanah, C. H., Benoit, D., & Barton, M. L. (1986). *Working model of the child interview.* Unpublished manuscript, Brown University.

# Index

Abelson, R., 33

Abuse: effect on dyadic rapport, 37–38, 128, 163; effect on maternal perception of childhood, 202, 212–14; potential for child, 214

Adaptive caregivers: descriptions of infant's development, 186; mothers' responses as, 163

Adaptive interaction: effect of parental, 14; of father with infant, 133; hindrances to, 46; of mother threatened by infant autonomy, 173–74, 176–77; of mother with postpartum depression, 140; reassertion for depressed mother, 134; reinstating or beginning, 134; using previewing, 243

Adaptive patterns: ensuring, 129; previewing contributing to infant's, 10–11

Adaptive previewing: encouraged by therapist, 46; inability to engage in, 42

Ainsworth, M. D., 31

Akiskal, H. S., 242

Alexander, F., 52

Alienation, 249

Alkema, F., 59

Ambady, N., 58

Ambivalent behavior, 249, 251

Ammaniti, M., 6

Amodal perception, 14–15, 16, 43

Anaclitic depression, 4

Antonuccio, D. O., 56

Anxiety attacks, 145–48

Apathy: of mother with postpartum depression, 137–38, 139–40, 142; of mother with psychiatric disorder, 250–51, 252–53

Apprenticeship, 10

Archer, D., 58

Arend, R., 31

Argyle, M., 59

Aronson, M. L., 50

Assessment. *See* Evaluation

Atkinson, A. K., 127

Attachment relationship, 31–32; bond in, 294; evaluation of capability for, 242–43

Attunement: affect, 9; to moods in marital conflict case, 236; in mother-infant dyad, 286, 292, 293–94; observed in previewing, 61; previewing enabling, 47

Auerbach, A. H., 56

Autonomy: balance between intimacy and, 37, 45, 163; conditions hindering development of, 163; defined, 162; development of infant's, 35–37, 45; effect of maternal possessiveness on, 179–80; excuses to prevent infant's, 223–24; mother's response to infant's increased, 292; role of previewing in developing infant, 58; self-esteem necessary for, 45; walking as signal of, 36–37, 44–45, 63. *See also* Independence; Separation

Awareness: contingency, 14; discrepancy, 5, 14; expectancy, 14; in pre-